ADOBE PHOTOSHOP™ 5

An Introduction to Digital Images

PRENTICE HALL
Upper Saddle River, NJ 07458

Library of Congress Cataloging-in-Publication Data

Adobe Photoshop 5.0: an introduction to digital images/Against The Clock.
p. cm. -- (Against the clock series)
ISBN 0-13-021323-3
1.Computer graphics. 2. Adobe Photoshop. I. Against The Clock (Firm)
II. Title: Adobe Photoshop five. III. Series.
T385.A3583 1999
006.6' 869 -- dc21

98-53292
CIP

Acquisitions Editor: *Elizabeth Sugg*
Developmental Editor: *Judy Casillo*
Supervising Manager: *Mary Carnis*
Production Editor: *Denise Brown*
Director of Manufacturing & Production: *Bruce Johnson*
Manufacturing Buyer: *Ed O'Dougherty*
Editorial Assistant: *Brian Hyland*

Formatting/page make-up: *Against The Clock, Inc.*
Printer/Binder: *Banta*
Cover Design: *Joe Sengotta*
Icon Design: *James Braun*
Creative Director: *Marianne Frasco*
Marketing Manager: *Shannon Simonsen*
Sales Director: *Ryan DeGrote*
Director of Marketing: *Debbie Yarnell*

Printed in the United States of America

10 9 8 7 6

ISBN 0-13-021323-3

Prentice Hall International (UK) Limited, London
Prentice Hall of Australia Pty. Limited, Sydney
Prentice Hall Canada Inc., Toronto
Prentice Hall Hispanoamericana, S.A., Mexico
Prentice Hall of India Private Limited, New Delhi
Prentice Hall of Japan, Inc., Tokyo
Pearson Education Asia Pte. Ltd., Singapore
Editora Prentice Hall do Brasil, Ltda., Rio de Janeiro

Contents

Preface

Purpose

The Against The Clock series has been developed specifically for those involved in the field of graphic arts.

Welcome to the world of electronic design and prepress. Many of our readers are already involved in the industry — in advertising and design companies, in prepress and imaging firms, and in the world of commercial printing and reproduction. Others are just now preparing themselves for a career somewhere in the profession.

This series of courses will provide you with the skills necessary to work in this fast-paced, exciting, and rapidly expanding business. Many people feel that they can simply purchase a computer, the appropriate software, a laser printer, and a ream of paper, and begin designing and producing high-quality printed materials. While this might suffice for a barbecue announcement or a flyer advertising a local hair salon, the real world of four-color printing and professional communications requires a far more serious commitment.

The Series

The applications presented in the Against The Clock series stand out as the programs of choice in professional graphic arts environments.

We've used a modular design for the Against The Clock series, allowing you to mix and match the drawing, imaging, and page layout applications that exactly suit your specific needs.

Titles available in the Against The Clock series include:

Macintosh: Basic Operations
Windows: Basic Operations
Adobe Illustrator: An Introduction to Digital Illustration
Adobe Illustrator: Advanced Digital Illustration
Freehand: An Introduction to Digital Illustration
Freehand: Advanced Digital Illustration
Adobe PageMaker: An Introduction to Electronic Mechanicals
Adobe PageMaker: Advanced Electronic Mechanicals
QuarkXPress: An Introduction to Electronic Mechanicals
QuarkXPress: Advanced Electronic Mechanicals
Adobe Photoshop: An Introduction to Digital Images
Adobe Photoshop: Advanced Digital Images
File Preparation: The Responsible Electronic Page
Preflight: An Introduction to File Analysis and Repair
TrapWise: Digital Trapping
PressWise: Digital Imposition

How to Use This Workbook

We've designed our courses to be "cross-platform." While many sites use Macintosh computers, there is an increasing number of graphic arts service providers using Intel-based systems running Windows (or Windows NT). The books in this series are applicable to either of these systems.

All of the applications that we cover in the Against The Clock series are similar in operation and appearance whether you're working on a Macintosh or a Windows system. When a particular function does differ from machine to machine, we present both.

Icons and Visuals

Pencil icon indicates a comment from an experienced operator. Whenever you see the pencil icon, you'll find corresponding sidebar text that augments or builds upon the subject being discussed at the time.

Bomb icon indicates a potential problem or difficulty. For instance, a certain technique might lead to pages that prove difficult to output. In other cases, there might be something that a program cannot easily accomplish, so we might present a workaround.

Pointing Finger indicates a hands-on activity — whether a short exercise or a complete project. This will be the icon you'll see the most throughout the course.

Key icon is used to point out that there is a keyboard equivalent to a menu or dialog-box option. Key commands are often faster than using the mouse to select a menu option. Experienced operators often mix the use of keyboard equivalents and menu/dialog box selections to arrive at their optimum speed.

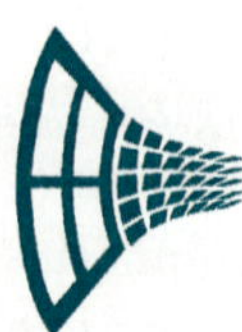

If you are a Windows user, be sure to refer to the corresponding text or images whenever you see this **Windows** icon. Although there isn't a great deal of difference between using these applications on a Macintosh and using them on a Windows-based PC, there are certain instances where there's enough of a difference for us to comment.

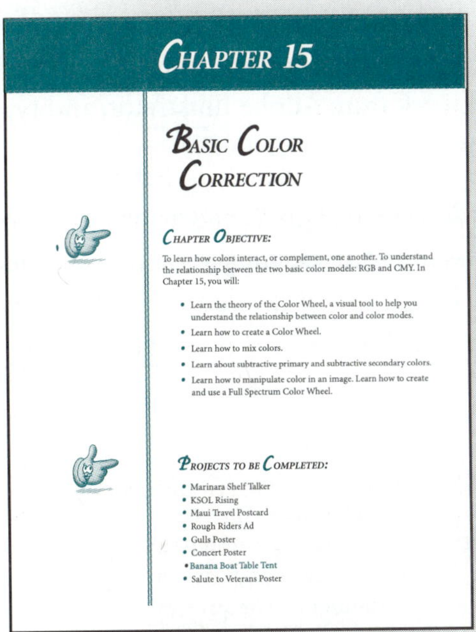

CHAPTER 15

BASIC COLOR CORRECTION

CHAPTER OBJECTIVE:

To learn how colors interact, or complement, one another. To understand the relationship between the two basic color models: RGB and CMY. In Chapter 15, you will:

- Learn the theory of the Color Wheel, a visual tool to help you understand the relationship between color and color modes.
- Learn how to create a Color Wheel.
- Learn how to mix colors.
- Learn about subtractive primary and subtractive secondary colors.
- Learn how to manipulate color in an image. Learn how to create and use a Full Spectrum Color Wheel.

PROJECTS TO BE COMPLETED:

- Marinara Shelf Talker
- KSOL Rising
- Maui Travel Postcard
- Rough Riders Ad
- Gulls Poster
- Concert Poster
- Banana Boat Table Tent
- Salute to Veterans Poster

***CHAPTER OPENINGS** provide the reader with specific objectives.*

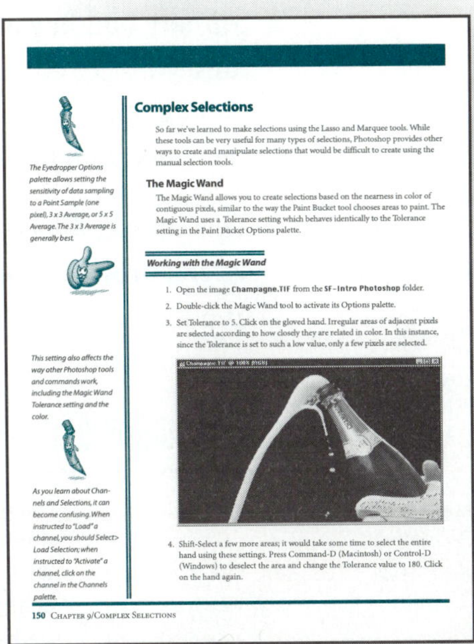

Complex Selections

So far we've learned to make selections using the Lasso and Marquee tools. While these tools can be very useful for many types of selections, Photoshop provides other ways to create and manipulate selections that would be difficult to create using the manual selection tools.

The Magic Wand

The Magic Wand allows you to create selections based on the nearness in color of contiguous pixels, similar to the way the Paint Bucket tool chooses areas to paint. The Magic Wand uses a Tolerance setting which behaves identically to the Tolerance setting in the Paint Bucket Options palette.

The Eyedropper Options palette allows setting the sensitivity of data sampling to a Point Sample (one pixel), 3 x 3 Average, or 5 x 5 Average. The 3 x 3 Average is generally best.

Working with the Magic Wand

1. Open the image **Champagne.TIF** from the **SF-Intro Photoshop** folder.
2. Double-click the Magic Wand tool to activate its Options palette.
3. Set Tolerance to 5. Click on the gloved hand. Irregular areas of adjacent pixels are selected according to how closely they are related in color. In this instance, since the Tolerance is set to such a low value, only a few pixels are selected.
4. Shift-Select a few more areas; it would take some time to select the entire hand using these settings. Press Command-D (Macintosh) or Control-D (Windows) to deselect the area and change the Tolerance value to 180. Click on the hand again.

This setting also affects the way other Photoshop tools and commands work, including the Magic Wand Tolerance setting and the color.

As you learn about Channels and Selections, it can become confusing. When instructed to "Load" a channel, you should Select>Load Selection; when instructed to "Activate" a channel, click on the channel in the Channels palette.

150 CHAPTER 9/COMPLEX SELECTIONS

***SIDEBARS and HANDS-ON ACTIVITIES** supplement concepts presented in the material.*

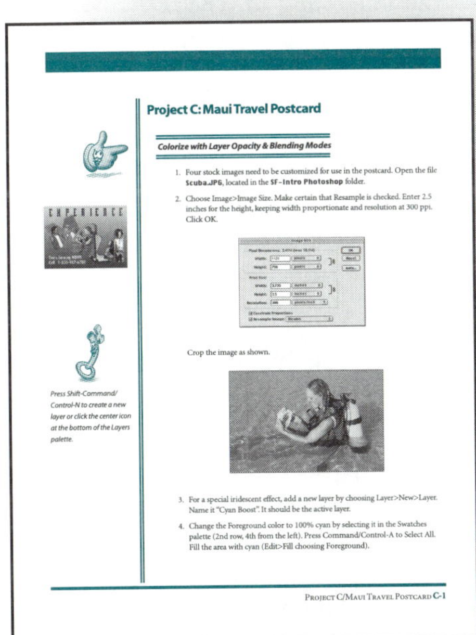

Project C: Maui Travel Postcard

Colorize with Layer Opacity & Blending Modes

1. Four stock images need to be customized for use in the postcard. Open the file **Scuba.JPG**, located in the **SF-Intro Photoshop** folder.
2. Choose Image>Image Size. Make certain that Resample is checked. Enter 2.5 inches for the height, keeping width proportionate and resolution at 300 ppi. Click OK.

Crop the image as shown.

3. For a special iridescent effect, add a new layer by choosing Layer>New>Layer. Name it "Cyan Boost". It should be the active layer.
4. Change the Foreground color to 100% cyan by selecting it in the Swatches palette (2nd row, 4th from the left). Press Command/Control-A to Select All. Fill the area with cyan (Edit>Fill choosing Foreground).

Press Shift-Command/Control-N to create a new layer or click the center icon at the bottom of the Layers palette.

PROJECT C/MAUI TRAVEL POSTCARD C-1

***SUPPLEMENTAL PROJECTS** offer practice opportunities in addition to the exercises.*

***PROJECT ASSIGNMENTS** will result in finished artwork — with an emphasis on proper file construction methods.*

The Projects You Will Work On

The Against The Clock course materials have been constructed with two primary building blocks: exercises and projects. Projects always result in a finished piece of work — digital imagery built from the ground up, utilizing photographic-quality images, vector artwork from Adobe Illustrator, and type elements from the library supplied on your student CD-ROM.

This course, *Adobe Photoshop 5.0: Introduction to Digital Images*, makes use of several projects that you will work on during your learning sessions. You will find the projects that you will complete by the end of the course displayed on the inside front and back cover of the book. Here's a brief overview of each.

Project A: Marinara Shelf Talker

The *Marinara Shelf Talker* project requires a certain amount of retouching to properly arrange the vegetables in the original image. From there, the student must use the selection techniques they learn early in the book to isolate and darken the background, creating their first silhouette. The project requires (as do all the projects in the course) the use of type.

Project B: KSOL Rising

When preparing ads, the more striking they are the more memorable and effective they become. KSOL Rising incorporates the use of opacity, color adjustment, and the merging of multiple images to create an interesting ad. The resulting display ad could be used in a magazine or other publication, or as a flyer.

Project C: Maui Travel Postcard

A simple postcard can have many relatively complex elements. The Maui Travel Postcard incorporates four images to which the student applies a variety of effects. Colorizing, using layer opacity, a variety of selection techniques and channel effects are employed. Although the project is is designed to be a postcard, it could also be used effectively as a web page graphic.

Project D: Rough Riders Ad

The *Tropical Suites Ad* is a prime example of how Photoshop can be used to create type-intensive visuals. Normally thought of solely as an image editing program, its ability to apply subtle pastel coloring, along with extremely fine shadows, allow it to be used to create very striking type effects. Both layers and channels are employed to build the image and drop shadows.

Project E: Gulls Poster

Sometimes art is produced just for the art of it, and this is the case with the Gulls Poster. Manipulation of the image includes cutting and pasting from an image, then blending images together to create an interesting effect. Texture and accent are added to the image, utilizing a variety of the student's skills.

Project F: Concert Poster

The *Concert Poster* requires that the student make use of all the skills they've developed during the course. Using layers, type elements, blending modes, adjustments to highlight and shadow regions, color correction and modification, and sophisticated selection techniques, the Poster is another example of Photoshop's ability to meet very demanding project requirements. While we've chosen to keep this image at a manageable size to facilitate its creation, in real life a file for a full-sized poster could easily reach 100 megabytes or more.

Project G: Banana Boat Table Tent

In the *Banana Boat Table Tent,* the student works with images they're already familiar with from hands-on exercises they completed during the course. Using a retouched image of people in a cafe, they import and create type elements, and utilize a logo supplied on the CD-ROM that came with the course. The finished display ad could be used in a color publication, or for flyers and other marketing materials.

Project H: Salute to Veterans Poster

Producing the Salute to Veterans Poster takes into consideration the requirements of the printing press, and calls upon students to use a variety of skills in preparing images that are imported into the base document. Layer effects, opacity, image adjustment, and colorization are all employed to create this multi-purpose poster.

Support Materials

For the Student

On the CD-ROM, you will find a complete set of Against The Clock (ATC) fonts, as well as a collection of data files used to construct the various exercises and projects.

The ATC fonts are solely for use while you are working with the Against The Clock materials. These fonts will be used throughout both the exercises and projects and are provided in both Macintosh and Windows format.

A variety of student files have been included. These files, necessary to complete both the exercises and projects, are also provided in both Macintosh and Windows formats.

For the Instructor

The Instructor Kit consists of an Instructor's manual and an Instructor's CD-ROM. It includes various testing and presentation materials in addition to the files that come standard with the student books.

- **Overhead Presentation Materials** are provided and follow along with the course. These presentations are prepared using Microsoft PowerPoint and are provided in both "native" PowerPoint format as well as Acrobat Portable Document Format (PDF).
- **Extra Projects** are provided along with the data files required for completion. These projects may be used to extend the course, or may be used to test the student.
- **A Test Bank of Questions** is included within the instructor kit. These questions may be modified, reorganized, and administered throughout the delivery of the course.
- Halfway through the course is a **Review** of material covered to that point, with a **Final Review** at the end.

Acknowledgments

I would like to give thanks to the writers, illustrators, editors, and others who have worked long and hard to complete the Against The Clock series. Foremost among them are Bob Cusano, Gary Paul Howland, Ric Withers, David Broudy, Lisa Bochatey, Win Woloff, Merilynne Johnson, Michael Barnett, Gavin Nagatomo, and Jim Wheaton, whom I thank for their long nights, early mornings, and seemingly endless patience.

Thanks to the dedicated teaching professionals whose comments and expertise contributed to the success of this book, including Ed Mineck and Patricia Russotti of Rochesteer Institute of Technology, Doris Anton of Wichita Area Technical College, Ron Bertolina of The Graphic Arts Technical Foundation, and Dr. Mitchell Henke of Bemidji State University.

A big thanks to Judy Casillo, Developmental Editor, and Denise Brown, Production Editor, for their guidance, patience, and attention to detail.

A special thanks to my husband for his unswerving support and for living in a publishing studio.

Ellenn Behoriam, December 1998

About Against The Clock

Against The Clock was founded in 1990 as a part of Lanman Systems Group, one of the nation's leading systems integration and training firms. The company specialized in developing custom training materials for such clients as L.L. Bean, *The New England Journal of Medicine, Smithsonian Magazine,* National Education Association, *Air & Space Magazine,* National Wildlife Society, and many others.

The success of Systems Group can be attributed to the thousands of pages of course materials developed at the company's demanding client sites. Throughout the rapid growth of Systems Group, founder Ellenn Behoriam developed the necessary expertise to manage technical experts, writers, editors, illustrators, designers, layout artists, proofreaders, and the rest of the chain of professionals required to develop structured and highly effective training materials.

In 1990 Ellenn embarked on a project to redevelop a library of training materials designed specifically for the professional graphic artist. The result of this effort is the ATC training library.

Ellenn lives in Tampa, Florida with her husband and her dogs Boda and Chase.

About the Authors

Rob McAllister has been speaking and writing about creating effective pages since before desktop publishing was invented. In the process of teaching others, he has written various "how to" guides and training manuals. Rob is a contributing editor for Hayden Books' FreeHand Graphics Studio Skills, and is the author of a series of eight books for Delmar Publishers on a variety of desktop publishing topics.

Rob is a technical editor for Electronic Publishing and contributing editor for Printing News in addition to Project Manager for Against The Clock.

Ed Mineck is an associate professor in Digital Imaging & Publishing Technology at the Rochester Institute of Technology. He is also a trainer for professionals and a regular presenter at national and international conferences. Ed creates and delivers state of the art skill building curricula that enables future independent learning on a wide range of imaging topics. He has been training and presenting on Photoshop since the first version of the application.

Gary Paul Howland, PhD, is a well-known and respected systems integrator, consultant, and trainer to the graphic arts industry, was one of the earliest adopters of desktop prepress, and has been designing and creating course materials, educational programs, and support systems for over twelve years. His expertise includes Macintosh and Windows platforms. Gary lives in Nokomis, Florida, with his son, Noah, and their friends, Lucky Dog and Gwen the (alpha) cat.

Bob Cusano has seen the graphic arts evolve from the days of hot metal through creating art and pages on personal computers to migrating those pages to the internet. He lives in Hamden Connecticut, and is lead instructor for Desktop Publishing for the Graphic Arts courses at Gateway Community Technical College in North Haven, Connecticut.

Ric Withers has worked in conventional and electronic prepress and digital printing. Originally from Richmond, VA, Ric now lives in Rochester, NY where he is pursuing a Masters of Science degree in Printing Technology from RIT.

David Broudy is an experienced prepress professional. David lives in Rochester and is a graduate student in the College of Imaging Arts and Sciences at RIT. He is currently writing a book on variable-data printing, and working on a thesis project in rotogravure cost reduction.

Lisa Bochatey has been involved with graphics and computers for over twenty years. She spends her time training and consulting for Newspapers, publishers, designers, and general business clients in the midwest. Lisa has Masters degrees in both Print Technology and Management, as well as in Instructional Design from Rochester Institute of Technology.

Bill Morse has been involved in computer graphics since the late 1970s, pioneering a computer-driven special-effects camera system that produced high-resolution transparencies which predated the era of Photoshop — photocompositing with rendered art, glows, textures, motion graphics, and natural media simulation. He was dragged, kicking and screaming, into the Digital Age, and now does his artwork primarily in Adobe Illustrator, Adobe Photoshop, and MetaCreations Painter.

GETTING STARTED

Platform

The Against The Clock series is specifically designed to apply to both Macintosh and Windows systems — the courses will work for you no matter what environment you find yourself in. There are some slight differences in the two, but when you're working in an actual application, these differences are limited to certain types of functions and actions.

Naming Conventions

In the old days of MS-DOS systems, file names on the PC were limited to something referred to as "8.3," which meant that you were limited in the number of characters you could use to an eight-character name (the "8") and a three-character suffix (the "3"). Text files, for example, might be called *myfile.txt*, while a document file from a word processor might be called *myfile.doc* (for document). On today's Windows-based systems, these limitations have been somewhat overcome. Although you can use longer file names, suffixes still exist. Whether or not you see them is another story.

When your system is first configured, the Views are normally set to a default that hides these extensions. This means that you might have a dozen different files named *myfile*, all of which may have been generated by different applications and be completely different types of files.

On a Windows system, you can change this view by clicking on *My Computer* (the icon is on your desktop) with the right button, and choosing View>Options. From this dialog box you may choose whether or not to display these older, MS-DOS file extensions. In some cases, it's easier to know what you're looking at if they're visible. This is a personal choice.

To ensure that the supplied student files are fully compatible with both operating systems, we've named all the files using the three-character suffix — even those on the Macintosh.

Key Commands

Key commands are fairly consistent between the Macintosh and the Windows versions of Adobe Photoshop. The major difference lies in the names of special function keys. The Macintosh has a key marked with an Apple and an icon that looks like a clover leaf. This is called the Command key. Whenever you see this icon, you will need to hold this key down. The Command key is a *modifier* key; that is, it doesn't do anything by itself, but changes the function of a key pressed while it's being held down. A good example is holding Command while pressing the "S" key: this Saves your work. The same thing applies to the "P" key; hold down Command and press it to Print your work.

On Windows-based systems, the Control key is almost always the equivalent of the Command key on the Macintosh. (This is sometimes confusing to new users, since the Macintosh also has a Control key, although, on the Macintosh, it's hardly ever used in popular applications.)

Another special function key on the Macintosh is the Option key. It's also a modifier key, and you'll need to hold it down along with whatever other key is required for a specific function. The equivalent modifier key on a Windows system is called the ALT key (for alternative). Besides these two nomenclature issues, there isn't really a lot of difference between using a Windows system and a Macintosh system (particularly when you're within a particular application).

The CD-ROM and Initial Setup Considerations

Before you begin using your Against The Clock course book, you will have to set up your system so that you have access to the various files and tools that you'll need to complete your lessons.

Student Files

This course comes with a complete collection of student files. These files are an integral part of the learning experience, as they're used throughout the course to help you construct increasingly complex elements. Having these building blocks available to you throughout your practice and study sessions will ensure that you will be able to experience the exercises and complete the project assignments smoothly and with a minimum of time spent looking for the various required components.

In building the Student Files folders, we've created sets of data for both Macintosh and Windows users. Locate the appropriate version of the "**SF-Intro Photoshop**" folder for your platform of choice and simply drag the icon onto your hard disk drive. If you have limited disk space, you may want to copy only the files for one or two lessons at a time.

Creating a Project Folder

We strongly recommend that you work from your hard disk. However, in some cases you might not have enough room on your system for all of the files that we've supplied. If this is the case, you can work directly from the CD-ROM.

Throughout the exercises and projects, you'll be required to save your work. Since the CD-ROM is "read-only," you cannot write information to it. Create a Project folder on your hard disk and use it to store your work-in-progress. Create your project folder while you're at the desktop level. This will create the folder at the highest level of your system, where it will be easy to find. Name this folder "Work in Progress".

Fonts

Whatever platform you're working on — Macintosh or Windows — you will have to install the ATC font library to ensure that your lessons and exercises will work as described in the course book. These fonts are provided on the student CD-ROM. Separate versions for Windows and Macintosh are provided.

Instructions for installing fonts are provided in the documentation that came with your computer. If you're using a font utility such as Suitcase or Font Juggler, then be certain to refer to the instructions that came with the font management application for installing your ATC fonts onto your system.

Preferences

We recommend that you throw away your Preferences file before you begin the lessons in this course. The "Adobe Photoshop 5 Preferences" file may be found inside your Adobe Photoshop 5.0>Adobe Photoshop Settings folder.

Prerequisites

This book assumes that you have a basic understanding of how to use your system. Whether you're working on a Macintosh or a Windows workstation, the skill sets are basically the same.

You should know how to use your mouse to point and click, and how to drag items around the screen. You should know how to resize a window, and how to arrange windows on your desktop to maximize the space you have available. You should know how to access pull-down menus and how checkboxes and radio buttons work. Lastly, you should know how to create, open, and save files.

If you're familiar with these fundamental skills, then you know all that's necessary to utilize the Against The Clock courseware library.

Notes:

INTRODUCTION

This course has been designed to familiarize you with the fundamentals of Photoshop, which is really several programs in one. Photoshop produces *rasterized* images. The working files of normal-sized documents for print may be huge — 50 megabytes or even more.

First and foremost, Photoshop is an *image editing* program. Image editing refers to the process of making changes to existing images. These are usually scans taken from original transparencies or prints. They might be in color or in black-and-white. Image editing is sometimes referred to as *retouching*. You can combine images to create a *composite image*, or *montage*, to which you may add special effects.

Secondly, Photoshop is a *painting* program. By using the program's paint brushes, color palettes, and specialized tools, you can create original artwork from scratch. In addition, you can combine painting, airbrush, and other Photoshop techniques with art created in other programs, or combine Photoshop images with type created in other programs, such as Adobe Illustrator or Macromedia FreeHand.

Third, Photoshop is a *color correction* program, capable of making very fine adjustments to specific colors or *tones* in an image. The color corrections can be as minute as altering a color shift on the overall image or as extreme as colorizing a black-and-white photo. It provides *calibration* tools to synchronize your scanner, monitor, proofing printer and even external devices, such as a printing press, to obtain consistent, predictable results throughout the printing process.

Lastly, Photoshop provides many tools specific to the *prepress* function. These include controlling halftone creation, generating color separations, controlling ink densities, traps, and performing many other production-specific functions. These last two issues, color correction and prepress, are normally performed by professionals with skill and experience in producing high-quality digital images.

In addition to the functionality built into Photoshop for the printing process, the program is invaluable for producing graphics for the Web. They may range from simply using compressed file formats, such as GIF and JPEG to creating animated files to spice up a Web site. In addition, Photoshop files may be saved in Adobe's PDF format for distribution in either print or electronic form.

Photoshop has an *extensible* format. Third party developers may write programs that actually work within Photoshop to extend its capabilities, or to make achieving complex effects much easier. These extensions, called *Plug-ins*, may be designed to remove the tedium from tasks that are not difficult of themselves, or they may combine a series of actions to achieve special effects that require a deeper understanding of the program than many are willing to embark upon. Relying too heavily on Plug-ins often means that the user doesn't learn to use the program effectively, and can be lost when new versions are introduced.

The focus of this course is to introduce you to Photoshop as an image editing and painting *tool set*, to demonstrate methods for adjusting tonal range in photographic images, to learn techniques of managing the elements of complex images, and to teach you some basic special effects suitable for both offset printed pieces and multimedia applications.

CHAPTER 1

WHERE IMAGES COME FROM

CHAPTER OBJECTIVE:

To build an understanding of the many different sources from which images can originate, and how to deal with these images in a graphics environment. In Chapter 1, you will:

- Learn that all analog images must be converted to a digital format before they can be worked on in Photoshop.
- Become familiar with the various devices used to capture and convert images for use in your layout.
- Begin to learn the different file formats that you will be working with in Photoshop.
- Learn that there are a number of variables that affect the quality of images.
- Begin to understand resolution, and its effect on images.
- Become familiar with Calibration and Color Models, and their relevance to your image.

Where Images Come From

The images brought into Photoshop come from two primary sources: they originate as either digital images or as analog images. A digital image is one that exists in digital form. It can be a CD image; a program that has its origins in a paint or draw program, such as Illustrator, FreeHand, CorelDraw!, Painter, or Canvas; or it may come from a digital camera. An analog image is a photograph, illustration, or painting that must be converted to digital format by scanning it or by taking a picture of it using a digital camera. Ultimately, all images are digital images.

Analog Images

There is a lot of technical information presented in the next few chapters. We recommend you don't try to memorize the facts contained here; instead, refer back to these sections as needed. For now, we simply want you to be familiar with the topics and how they may affect your work.

Photographs are probably the most common types of images used in desktop published documents. The color, contrast, density, and sharpness of each photo will vary due to the type of film, camera, lighting, or the ability of the photographer. Although they are scanned less often, paintings, pastelles, charcoal, and pencil drawings are also used in the publishing process. All these images are called "continuous tone" images because the colors or shades blend smoothly from one to another. Images such as black-and-white photos and pencil drawings are also called "grayscale" images. Photoshop excels at manipulating continuous tone images, producing excellent results when printed.

Line drawings, usually produced with pen and ink, are another type of analog image. When they are scanned, they have only two shades — black-and-white. They are called "bitmapped" images.

An additional variable that occurs with analog images involves the scanner. Although this is less obvious with grayscale images, the scanner's capabilities and the color cast it can introduce affects the end product as much as the type of film; the experience of the scanner operator can be nearly as important to the production quality of the image as the capabilities of the artist or photographer.

In theory, technology permits a poor quality snapshot to be scanned and enhanced electronically. This capability is no substitute for good original image quality. Those unfamiliar with electronic processes may base color judgments on low-resolution, uncalibrated screen images, without a clue as to how they will reproduce in print.

Digital Images

In addition to analog images that are converted to digital form, many images are readily available as digital data. Photo CD images are available for downloading from online sources, or they may be purchased from photo stock houses. Digital cameras produce images ranging in quality comparable to those from professional large-format cameras to quality approximating that of an inexpensive consumer camera. Video capture capability produces a similar range of capability.

As in the analog world, photographs comprise the majority of digital images brought into Photoshop for manipulation. Digital original images created in drawing and painting programs are also manipulated from time-to-time. Although it is often easier to make adjustments to these images in their originating program, images from dissimilar sources are often merged in Photoshop to create a composite image.

Photo CD

The amount of information available on CD-ROM disks is expanding rapidly. It is very common for a prepress shop to have CDs of fonts, stock photography, and software with tutorials that incorporate Quicktime movies. The CD-ROM now provides a compatibility with Kodak Photo CD services. Combined with the availability of the services of Kodak Scanning Centers, the Photo CD is a popular storage device for digital images. These images are scanned from original color negatives or slides, and offer better quality than a flatbed scanner can produce from a color print.

The YCC color model is a variation of the CIE model. It provides a broader color range than either RGB or CMYK models. Photoshop includes the Kodak Color Management Software (CMS), which you may use to adjust colors, set resolution, and define the color mode to be used.

The Pro Photo CD offers an additional size — 4,096 × 6,144 pixels (72 MB). This format accommodates 70mm and 4 × 5 film size and resolutions. The capacity of a Pro Photo CD is only 25 image sets per disk compared to 100 images for standard Photo CD.

The cost of scanning an image onto a CD-ROM can be less than a dollar per image. "Pro" Photo CD scans cost about $9. Compared to the price per scan charged by service providers using high-end scanning equipment, the Kodak CD-ROM is likely to be used by photographers to digitize their work. Photo stock agencies have adopted the Photo CD for both catalog purposes and as a means of delivering a usable high-resolution image to the client.

Photoshop can open Kodak's YCC format. The Photo CD stores five resolutions of each image, ranging in size from 128 × 192 pixels (74K) to 2048 × 3072 pixels (18 MB). The Kodak high-resolution professional formats can be used for direct input to the project.

Digital Cameras

Eventually, digital cameras may replace conventional film cameras in commercial applications where resolution and dynamic range of the image are adequate for the printing conditions. Digital cameras can produce scans ranging from beautiful to truly horrible, depending on the device.

Generally speaking, "low-end" digital cameras will produce photographs that are fine for use on a web page at a size of approximately 6″ × 9″. They will print well at a size of 1.5″ × 2.25″. While that is clearly inadequate for almost all print applications, the "next level" of digital cameras will allow good reproduction of a 5″ × 7″ photograph — quite adequate for many applications.

Many professional studios are using digital camera backs with their professional systems. Even these prices have fallen below the $10,000 range — and the quality is pretty much what should be expected from a high-end camera system.

Digital Art

Continuous tone images are also derived from other computer applications or original artwork created entirely in Photoshop. Photoshop may also import and incorporate a wide variety of file formats. Within the Adobe family of graphic applications, Adobe's Illustrator, Dimensions, and Premiere can provide a variety of image effects requiring four-color output.

Scanners and Digitizers

Once original source photographic film is processed (making the image visible and permanent), the image can be "scanned"— that is, digitized and recorded on magnetic media and manipulated on a computer.

There are many types of scanners. They differ in their methods of collecting the image data, the type of media they can scan, how accurately they reproduce the image in digital form, and whether or not they can record color.

All scanners share the same principle of operation: they convert images into a pattern of squares called "pixels" (for Picture Elements). A pixel is the smallest distinct unit of an image that can be recorded or displayed by a digital device at any given resolution.

Scanning devices include the following:

- **Hand-held** — This is usually a T-shaped device that is about four inches wide. The scanner is dragged over the surface of the image. A roller mechanism synchronizes the recording of the image with the page position. This is a manual operation and requires a steady hand, capable of moving at a consistent speed. Since the recording surface is only four inches wide, recording a standard 8 x 10 print requires splicing two or more parallel passes together. The output of these scanners is usually black-and-white (monochrome or grayscale), and generally lacks the quality required for professional work.
- **Sheet-fed** — The user inserts a page into the scanner and it moves through the device. The drawbacks to this method are similar to those of a fax machine. The original may be mutilated, or it may slip, stretch, tilt, or jam. Resin-coated or glossy photographs are more likely to slip than uncoated paper stocks. Sheet-fed scanners are usually reserved for optical character recognition (OCR) conversion of typed or printed information into text that can be edited in a word processing program.
- **Flatbed** — These scanners are similar in operation to office copy machines. The page or book is placed face down on a clear glass sheet and the cover is lowered. The movable sensing device glides back and forth beneath the glass, recording the image. Because the original is immobile and the recording process is automatic, this method is capable of producing excellent results from reflective copy. Some very good, high-quality color scanners now use flatbed design.

Early scanners (manufactured around 1984) not only cost a lot of money, but they were relatively crude compared to today's devices.

You can still spend over a million dollars on scanning equipment, but many devices capable of perfectly good scans can be had for less than $50,000. Even inexpensive desktop scanners have their place in certain projects.

- **Slide or transparency scanners** — These devices accept 35mm mounted slides, projecting light through the transparency or negative and scanning the transmitted light of the image. These units are generally capable of producing good quality images.

- **Drum scanners** — These devices range from desktop models to massive units that cost a quarter of a million dollars or more. Either transparencies (removed from their mountings) or reflective originals (prints) can be attached to the surface of the drum. Although these scanners generally have very high-resolution, the quality of the scans produced results from the higher-quality Photomultiplier Tube (PMT) sensors. PMTs have a much better dynamic range of sensitivity than do the Charge Coupled Device (CCD) sensors used in less expensive flatbed scanners and digital cameras.

Other factors in scanning include color capabilities and image resolution. These factors will be discussed later in the course.

Lithographic reproduction refers to printing press reproduction methods as opposed to photographic methods. The former requires color separations to be made to produce a composite color image.

Digitizers and Framegrabbers

Video capture is another means of digitizing images. The source of the image may be a VCR, video camera, or a laser disc player. The computer must be equipped with a "video board" to accept the video input and convert it to digital format. Such a card can capture a single frame from a movie and load it into a window in Photoshop.

Image file formats

Drawing programs are often used to create original art. Some, such as Apple's original MacPaint, MetaCeations Painter, and Photoshop, produce bitmapped images; others, such as Illustrator and FreeHand, produce PostScript vector objects. The variety of image sources is compounded by the number of image formats available.

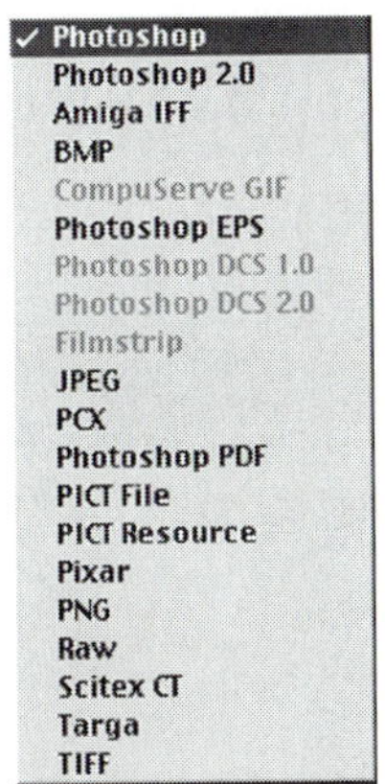

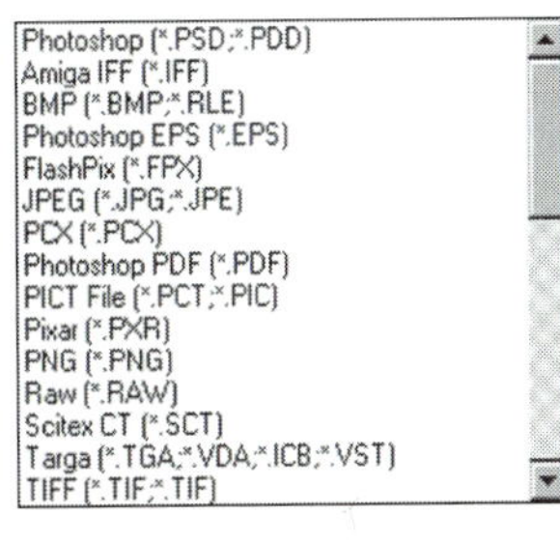

The list of files that you can "Save As" changes depending on the type of image.

Photoshop can open many file formats; however, not all image formats are suited to lithographic reproduction methods. One format important to color printing is the Encapsulated PostScript (EPS) format. Photoshop can open EPS formatted files saved in the Illustrator EPS format, as well as 72 ppi EPS previews from other applications such as QuarkXPress. Photoshop can also rasterize EPS graphics from a variety of sources.

Scanned images are defined by the software and hardware used when the image is scanned. They are also affected by the hardware and software used to print the file. If the scanner and printer are not synchronized, there may be unpredictable results.

Scanners collect color data in RGB format, wherein each color in the image is defined as a mixture of Red, Green, and Blue. Lower-end desktop scanners pass this RGB file to Photoshop for color correction and conversion to CMYK (Cyan, Magenta, Yellow, and Key [Black]) separations for process color printing. High-end desktop scanners are designed with built-in color computers that convert the RGB data into a separated CMYK format. Photoshop can perform the color conversion from RGB to CMYK, but at a loss in productivity — it can take more time than it saves, and may require additional color adjustments. This is less important for a publisher, who may have fewer scans to produce than a trade shop.

If the photograph is to be color-corrected in Photoshop, it should be scanned in RGB and converted to CMYK after color adjustment. The RGB colorspace is much larger than the CMYK colorspace, allowing more accurate color adjustment before the final conversion to CMYK.

The table that follows explains many of the file formats that are available in Photoshop.

You can refer back to this table once you go home. You will usually be dealing with Photoshop, TIFF, EPS, and JPEG formats for print. Production for web pages will include JPEG, GIF, and PNG formats.

Do you use presentation programs to generate high-resolution slides? PICT format is important to certain presentation programs. Mention this to your teacher.

Photoshop's File Formats

Photoshop	Default format for newly-created images; supports all available image modes, guides, channels, and layers.
Photoshop 2.0	(Macintosh only.) Used for applications supporting only Photoshop 2 format. Flattens the file and discards layer information.
Amiga IFF	Commodore's Amiga is popular among Video users. The IFF (Interchange File Format) graphics format functions like the PICT format on a Macintosh.
BMP	Windows Paint's BMP (Windows Bitmap), the native format of Microsoft Paint, is the standard image format for DOS and Windows-compatible computers. Supports RGB, indexed, grayscale, and bitmap modes.
CompuServe GIF	GIF (Graphics Interchange Format) is used for images for the World Wide Web. Its 8-bit images may be grayscale or indexed color. 8-bit images can produce 256 colors or shades of gray. GIF89 is an Export command that allows GIF graphics to be interlaced and include background transparency.
Photoshop EPS	Encapsulated PostScript allows combining both vector and raster (bitmap) graphics in the same file. It supports all color modes, and is the preferred format for producing images with clipping paths. The preview option may be Macintosh or TIFF. Macintosh preview includes a PICT file, and can only be viewed on a Macintosh; a TIFF preview can be viewed on Macintosh or Windows.
Photoshop DCS	Desktop Color Separations are a subset of the EPS format. DCS 1.0 supports CMYK, and does not support alpha channels. It preseparates the files into a preview, plus four plates. DCS 2.0 supports multichannel files, and CMYK with a single alpha channel, and multiple spot channels. It does not preseparate the file.
Filmstrip	Used for RGB animation within Adobe's Premiere Quick-Time movie application.
JPEG	This lossy compression format was created by the Joint Photographic Experts Group. It is commonly used on the World Wide Web. It sacrifices some image quality to achieve higher levels of file compression.
PCX	PC Paintbrush's native format is commonly used on PC-compatible computers. It uses a standard VCA palette.
Photoshop PDF	Portable Document Format can represent both vector and raster graphics and can contain electronic document search and navigation features. It supports all color models, but does not support alpha channels.
PICT File	Macintosh system software's native graphic format. It supports RGB, indexed, grayscale, and bitmap color modes.
PICT Resource	(Macintosh only.) Used for storing splash screens and Scrapbook contents. It supports RGB, indexed, grayscale, and bitmap images.
Pixar	Pixar workstations produce high-quality animation. This format supports RGB and grayscale images.
PNG	Portable Network Graphics is a lossless compression format that supports RGB images and produces background transparency.
Raw	This binary format supports all color modes.
Scitex CT	Scitex Continuous Tone format supports RGB, CMYK, and grayscale color modes. Scitex is a high-end color scanning system.
Targa	Targa (TGA) is used in many video and modeling applications. It supports RGB, indexed, and grayscale color modes.
TIFF	Tagged Image File Format is the most common raster file format. It is cross-platform compatible.

Where Images Go

It's clear that people don't cart their computers around for everyone to see the documents they've created. However, the documents don't magically transfer from the computer to the medium on which they're ultimately going to be displayed. Additionally, each medium is different, providing new challenges and opportunities. It is as important to know where images come from as it is to understand where they go. As with incoming images, files are either converted to analog images as printed documents or they are left in digital form for distribution on the World Wide Web, on CD-ROM, to be shown directly from the monitor in presentations, or retained in a file as electronic documents.

Printed Documents (CMYK)

Most of what will be discussed in this book assumes the documents will be printed — usually on a traditional printing press — but they could also be printed on a digital press, photocopied, or printed as limited run posters from a wide format printer. How files are prepared for each of these devices is important to the final appearance of the document. A file should never be prepared until its final disposition is known. This may necessitate preparing a document for muliple imaging solutions.

The lithographic printing process is based on the principle that oil and water don't mix. A printing plate is chemically treated to attract an oil-based ink, and reject water. The ink prints at full intensity, so the image is either black (or another ink color) or not black (no color at all). This is why grayscale images must be simulated by halftones, which we discuss later in this section.

Each color of an image is printed from a separate printing plate. A two-color job will usually have a black plate and one plate of another color. A process-color job will have a black plate, plus a plate for each of the process colors: cyan, magenta, and yellow. Colors must be defined as "spot," or as "process" (CMYK) to print correctly.

When different colors abut one another, it is necessary for the colors to overlap slightly (called trapping) to allow for the imperfections in the printing process, including paper stretch and some mechanical variations. On rasterized images, such as photographs, the colors are allowed to blend with one another to accomplish this effect. The process is called "Anti-Aliasing."

There are a number of other variables that affect the quality of images. The porosity of the paper affects the spread of the ink, which is referred to as "dot gain." When printing dots become larger, they make the image darker. When a photo is printed, dot gain must be taken into consideration. Cooperation between the imaging service bureau and printer is necessary to achieve desired results.

UnderColor Removal (UCR) and Gray Component Removal (GCR) are closely related to dot gain. They keep ink coverage to a minimum, so the sheet will dry more quickly, and to avoid a scummy ink buildup on the page. As a general rule, total ink coverage in any area of a page should be less than 270% when all ink percentages are added together. To accomplish this, percentages of black are substituted for CMY percentages in neutral color areas.

RGB-savvy Printers

Innovations in the printing industry include printing small quantities with inkjet and toner printers. These printers have a wider gamut of color than traditional lithographic presses, and often use RGB files, then convert them to their proprietary CMYK range. In addition, since all four colors are introduced to the page simultaneously, or at least on a straight paper path, there's no need for trapping.

Electronic Documents

Today, documents are prepared for the World Wide Web and for distribution on CD and through corporate intranets. These documents need to use the widest range of color available, so they're prepared using the RGB color gamut. A primary drawback of electronically distributed documents is that their display depends on how the recipient's monitor is set up. Chances are, colors will not be "true"; they will use each monitor's display gamut.

PPI, DPI, and LPI are often confused. PPI represents the number of coordinate points per inch at the scanned resolution; it will display differently on monitors of different resolutions. DPI is a measurable quantity, but the resolution is high enough so that we can't see it unless it is magnified many times. LPI refers to the viewable "dots" visible in a halftone or tint.

Photographs prepared for electronic distribution need only have enough resolution to accommodate the monitor. As a result, files are much smaller. Compressed formats, such as GIF and JPEG, are used for electronic distribution, because the object must display quickly to keep the viewer's interest. Web designers employ a number of techniques to obtain fast display of graphics on the internet.

Because the medium doesn't wiggle or stretch as paper does, there is no need to employ trapping. Since monitors are capable of displaying grayscale and continuous tone color images, the problems associated with printing dots no longer exist; dot gain, UCR, and GCR don't come into play.

Compression technology is important when creating CDs in order to present the image well, and to fit enough data on the medium. Images must also display in a reasonable amount of time.

When publishing to the internet and to intranets, the same compression issues arise, but the difficulties are even greater. People won't wait even a minute for an image to display; they'll simply go away. This creates a variety of compression issues, including the compressing of the color gamut, which occurs when creating GIF images. In addition, different computers support different colorspace — and most designers want color displayed accurately. The potential problems are monumental.

Understanding Resolution

Resolution is the measure of accuracy of a device, file, or process. The acronyms DPI, LPI, and PPI all represent resolutions of different aspects of the desktop publishing process.

DPI, or dots per inch, is a measurement of the resolution of an output device — usually a laser printer or imagesetter. A "dot" in this instance is the smallest printable element a device can produce. For example, on a 300 dpi laser printer, the smallest element would be a square pixel that is 1/300 of an inch in size. DPI is sometimes also referred to as SPI, or spots per inch; a spot is the technical term for an imaging device's dot.

LPI, or lines per inch, is a measurement of the screen frequency in a halftone screen; that is, the number of lines per inch used to convert the image to black-and-white for printing. If a 60-line round halftone screen is specified, the largest dot (100% black) is 1/60 inch. The halftone dot simulates shades of gray by varying the dot size; a smaller dot is used for lighter shades of gray and a larger dot for darker shades of gray.

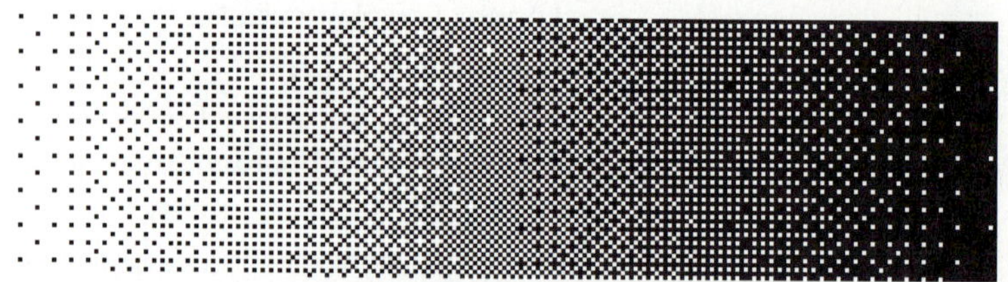

PPI, or pixels per inch, denotes the resolution of a scan. Each pixel is a coordinate for a point in an image, with color information attached. Data in scanned images such as TIFF files includes height and width in pixels, and the number of pixels per inch. Photoshop software uses these numbers to determine the height and width in inches with which to display the image.

DPI and LPI

When printing color and grayscale images, gradients, or blends to a laser printer, print quality is dependent on the relationship between LPI and DPI. The printer's DPI designation represents the smallest it can print. The LPI value determines the largest dot used when printing the document. This means that the entire tonal range in the image must be represented by dots which fall between these two sizes.

A smaller *halftone* dot (and a higher LPI specification) maintains detail in images. It's also easier for the human eye to blend these smaller dots, perceiving a shade of gray rather than a series of black spots. Remember, however, that the smallest print element available is determined by the printer's DPI. If you use a high screen frequency, the number of shades of gray the printer can produce is reduced, because the range of dot sizes it can print (between the smallest and largest dots) is compressed.

You'll need to experiment with your printer and different screen frequencies to achieve the best results for your documents. To determine the number of gray levels PostScript will produce at a given frequency (LPI) and resolution (DPI) use either of these formulae:

$$\left(\frac{\text{resolution}}{\text{frequency}}\right)^2 + 1 = \text{max gray levels}$$

This can also be expressed as

$$\frac{\text{Imagesetter Resolution} \times .0625}{\text{Max Screen Ruling}}$$

For example, using a common default of 53 lpi for a 300 dpi printer will generate 32 levels of gray. This will cause minor banding in gradients, but will maintain adequate gray shades and detail for photographs.

This may cause gradients to "band" and images to "posterize," which makes them look like artwork rather than photographs. A gradient spanning 0 to 100% on a 600 dpi printer at 100 lpi would break into 18 distinct bands, and a 25 to 75% gradient would contain a mere 9 shades of gray. The only remedies are to output the file to a higher-resolution device, such as an imagesetter (for a smaller minimum dot), or to use a lower LPI value (for a larger maximum dot).

Printing the document theorized above with a 37 lpi screen will yield 256 levels of gray. This is the maximum 256 shades of gray that PostScript Level 1 devices can produce. Gradients and blends are smooth, but a 37-line screen produces a chunky dot. It's distracting in photographs and lacks adequate detail. When printing shaded text in smaller sizes, a low screen frequency may render it unreadable.

PPI should be based on the size at which the image is to be printed. If you print a 5″ × 7″ photograph at 2.5″ × 3.5″ by scaling it within a page layout application, you've essentially changed the resolution of the file in our example from 90 ppi to 180 ppi, giving a laser printer more information than it needs. If you plan to reduce or enlarge an image, make certain that you adjust your PPI value accordingly.

LPI and PPI

When scanning an image for output, it is a common misconception that "bigger is better." The assumption is that the higher the PPI, the clearer the output. While this is true for scans of black-and-white images such as line art, the output quality of photographic scans is determined by the LPI and PPI values together.

A 5″ × 7″ photograph scanned at 300 ppi to match the resolution of a laser printer produces a 3.2 megabyte file if it's a grayscale image, or around 9.5 megabytes for an RGB color scan — 12.8 megabytes when converted to CMYK. When printing with a 60-line screen to a 300 dpi laser printer, more than 90% of the image data is unused by the printer, though it still has be to processed, sent to a printer, and stored. In this example, a black-and-white laser printer will print just one halftone dot for every 25 pixels' worth of information.

In reality, a 90 ppi image is adequate for printing on a low-resolution laser printer. This file clocks in at 285K for a grayscale image, 850K for an RGB file, or 1.14 megabytes when converted to CMYK. For film output on a high-resolution imagesetter, the PPI should be proportionately higher. Choosing a scan resolution is discussed in Chapter 4.

Calibration and Color Models

System calibration, or adjusting the monitor, software, and printer so that what is seen on the screen will more closely match what can be printed, is a very complex topic and beyond the scope of a beginner's course. However, it is important to understand what to expect when producing images using Photoshop.

Color Space and Gamma

A color space, or color model, is a mathematical representation of a set of colors that can be produced using a particular process or device. The range of colors which can be produced within a given model is known as the "gamut." The visible spectrum consists of all colors normally perceived by the human eye. Within this spectrum, the two *types* of color models we'll concentrate on for use in Photoshop are additive models and subtractive models.

If you have ever seen a color key, you'll have a better understanding of how CMYK works. With a color key, each color channel is printed on its own piece of film, but instead of the film being black, it is the color of the CMYK primary. When laid on top of each other, the image is formed, much as though it were printed on a press.

Color keys are less popular for proofing these days because the film substrate skews the color slightly. Proofs of film today are usually laminate proofs — very thin layers of film laminated together, and onto a substrate that closely simulates the actual paper on which the job will be printed.

An additive color model contains colors created by adding together different wavelengths of light. A good example of an additive color device is a computer monitor. All of the colors that the monitor shows are created by light emitted from three guns: red, green, and blue, at varying intensities.

Subtractive color models encompass colors that are created when light strikes an object or image, and certain wavelengths are absorbed or subtracted. The light which is reflected back is perceived as a particular color. Subtractive color models include all color in printed materials: i.e., CMYK or PMS. They are comprised of dyes and pigments.

These models overlap, but do not coincide exactly. For example, there are man-made pigments available that do not appear in nature, and there are many colors in nature which can't be emulated on a monitor or printing press. More important, for the purpose of our discussion, there are many colors that do not coincide between the large additive model (the monitor) and the much smaller subtractive model (the printed page).

RGB Color

Colors in the RGB color model are created by combining red, green, and blue light. As mentioned above, this additive color model is used to describe the colors produced by the monitor. Other examples of devices which use the RGB color model are spotlights with colored gels, and film recorders, such as those used to create slides and transparencies.

Scanned RGB images are also known as 24-bit or True Color images. Each pixel contains 8 bits of information for each color channel (eight each for red, green, and blue). In the RGB model, 100% each of red, green, and blue light combine to make white; 0% of each define the absence of color, or black.

CMYK Color

The CMYK color model is defined as the range of colors that can be created using the process printing colors cyan, magenta, yellow, and black. Each set of CMYK inks has a different color gamut. This color model is also referred to as *four-color process*, and is used in commercial printing and for most color desktop printers.

CMYK is a subtractive color model. Zero percent (0%) each of cyan, magenta, yellow and black — that is, no pigment on a page — produce white in the CMYK model. CMY is the mathematical opposite of the RGB model. Theoretically speaking, just as 100% each of RGB combine to make white, 100% each of CMY *should* combine to make black. In reality, printing pigments are impure. For example, most magenta absorbs some cyan and a little yellow, as well as the magenta component of light. The result of mixing 100% of these colors is usually a muddy, purplish brown. Consequently, black is added to produce a true black, add depth to shadows, and reduce the total amount of ink on the printed page.

An image in the CMYK color space will yield a file 33% larger than an RGB file — it uses 8 bits for information per color channel, just as an RGB file does, but it has four channels worth of information (C, M, Y, and K).

L*a*b Colorspace

To bring these different colorspaces together, a larger colorspace incorporating both CMYK and RGB models is needed. This was seen in the late 1920s, as color printing became more prevalent. It became obvious that a standard for color description was needed. If two colors appear the same, they should be described in the same manner. For example, we might define"pure red" as R-255, G-0, B-0 using RGB colorspace, or C-0, M-100, Y-100, K-0 using CMYK space. Of course, someone else might call it simply "bright red."

Because different programs and monitors will describe color differently, and printing devices will create it differently, there will be widely divergent definitions for the same color. This is particularly so if we describe it in one space (RGB) and create it in another (CMYK).

In 1931, CIE developed the first widely used independent colorspace, known as CIE XYZ, named for the three axes used to describe the location of the colors. The values in this colorspace are derived from the relative amounts of RGB present in the color, and expressed as a percentage of luminance, together with 256 levels (ranging from 128 to +128) across two axes. In 1976, CIE XYZ was redefined and renamed CIE L*a*b.

Does this mean that you can now see colors on your monitor that you couldn't see before, since a small portion of CMYK space extends outside of the RGB space? No. It means that you can describe that space so that it's printable. It also means that you can, by creating a profile of input and output devices, reduce the colorspace of your monitor to match the imageable colors of your printing device

Gamma

Gamma represents the contrast in the midtones of an image. The monitor's gamma is linear: when viewing a white-to-black gradient on a non-gamma-corrected monitor, the eye will perceive the darker shades as encroaching far into the lighter shades. The human eye perceives gamma in a logarithmic fashion, with the darker shades compressed.

Calibration

The differences in color models mean that it is impossible to get an exact match between the printed page and a monitor. For example, true cyan cannot be reproduced on the monitor, and many CMYK greens are very difficult to reproduce; the monitor can produce a wide array of blues, while the CMYK model is strongly lacking in these hues.

To compensate for the lack of a one-to-one relationship between colors in each model, Photoshop has several methods to control the way it converts between RGB and CMYK and for adjusting monitor gamma. If a monitor is not gamma corrected, colors can appear much lighter or darker than they will actually print.

Photoshop includes options to adjust the monitor display and to match ink sets used by different color printers or offset presses. For the purposes of this course, the default Photoshop values are fine, but be aware that what what is displayed on the screen isn't necessarily what will print to the printer!

Finally, it's important to realize that the purpose of color calibration is *not* to attempt to rectify all differences between monitors and the printed page; due to the physics of color, it's impossible to create an absolute match. Instead, calibration is used to create a stable system from which to gain enough experience to allow you to *predict* how graphics will appear on a printed page.

Chapter 2

A Photoshop Document

Chapter Objective:

To understand Photoshop's working environment, how to control this environment, and the basics of creating and saving your work. In Chapter 2, you will:

- Become familiar with the Toolbox palette, and its different variables for graphic modifications.
- Learn what the different palettes allow, and the controls they bring to you.
- Learn the importance of Photoshop's preferences, and how to adjust and save them for your work.
- Learn the many different formats in which you can save your document.

A Photoshop Document

Starting Photoshop can be done several ways: by double-clicking on either the application icon or its alias icon (Macintosh) or shortcut (Windows); double-clicking on a Photoshop document icon; or single-clicking on any one of these icons to select it, then selecting Open in the File menu (Macintosh), or by clicking Start>Run, then entering the application path and name to execute (Windows).

The Working Environment

Once started, the program briefly displays the title or splash screen and then the familiar menu bar and the selections: File, Edit, Image, Layer, Select, Filter, View, Window, and Help. To the left of the screen is the Toolbox palette.

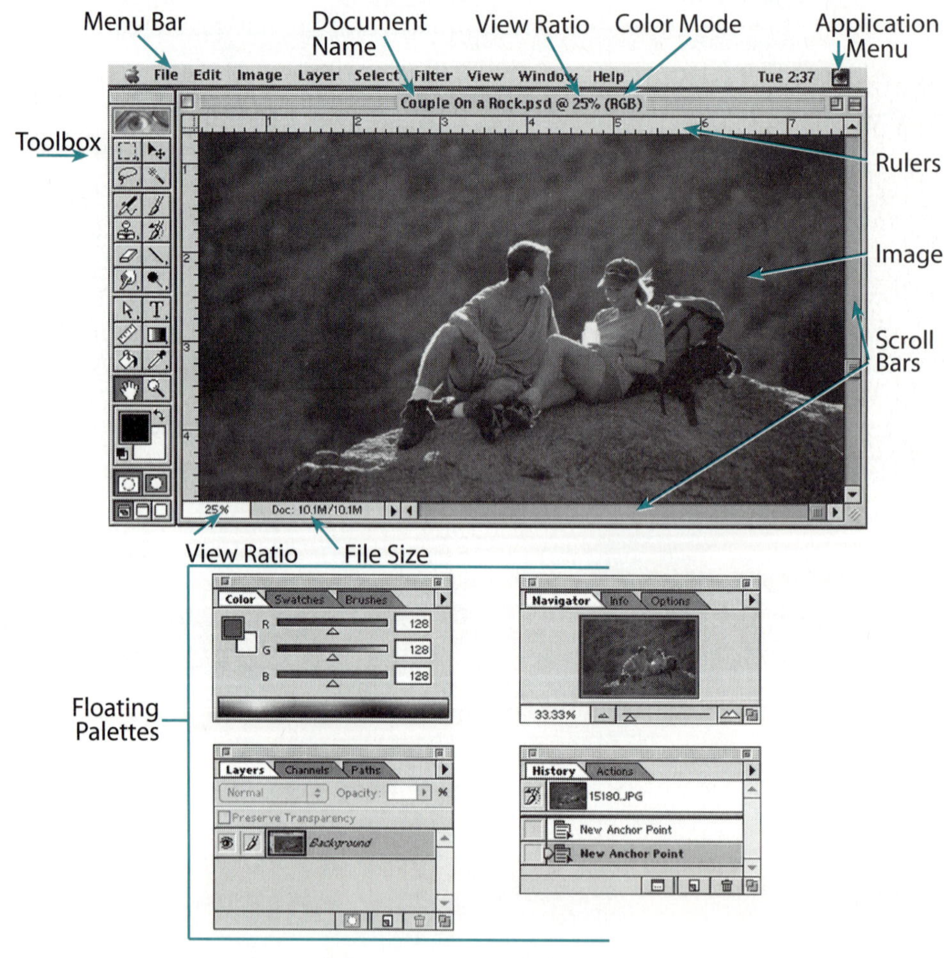

The keyboard shortcut for Open is Command-O (Macintosh) or Control-O (Windows). For New, use Command-N (Macintosh) or Control-N (Windows).

Setting Painting Cursors to Brush Size from Preferences>Display>Cursors shows brushes at their actual size when you're painting. If they're set to Standard, they look like the tool and are very inaccurate and difficult to see. Precise makes any brush show as a crosshair. This option is popular with many artists. At first, though, seeing the size of the brush as you paint will help. You can still toggle the Precise tools on and off by pressing the Caps Lock key.

- Menu Bar shows the names of the menus to choose from.
- Toolbox shows the tools to use for graphic modifications.
- Document Name shows the name of the document in use.
- Color Mode shows the document's current color model.
- The Application Menu icon shows the icon of the application that is currently in use.
- Rulers are toggled with Show/Hide Rulers in the View menu.
- Scroll Bars let you scroll the screen up/down/sideways to view the different parts of the image.
- The Color palette allows you to select colors from a variety of color models, and from several color bars.
- The Swatches palette provides a pre-loaded set of colors from which to select; it will vary according to the properties of the image.
- The Brushes palette allows you to select and adjust brushes.
- The Layers palette controls the stacking order of images within a document.
- The Channels palette contains controls for viewing individual color components of the image (i.e., the red, green, or blue data), and controls for masking different parts of the image.
- The Paths palette allows creation and adjustment of paths within an image.
- The Navigator palette allows you to move easily to different areas of an image when zoomed in.
- The Info palette provides RGB and CMYK color information, X/Y coordinates of the cursor, and the width and height of a selection within an image.
- The Options palette allows you to adjust settings for different Photoshop tools.
- The Actions palette performs repetitive tasks with the click of a mouse.
- The History palette allows "undo" to a given state of editing the image.

Controlling the Photoshop Environment

1. Before you begin working with Photoshop, let's make certain that all of our screens will look the same. Select File>Preferences>Display & Cursors. The Preferences dialog box will appear:

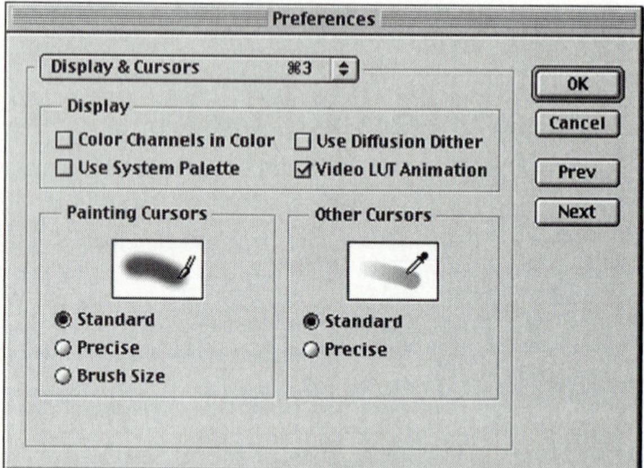

Two items are of primary importance: Painting Cursors, which should be set to Brush Size, and Other Cursors, which should (at this point) be set to Standard. Change these settings if necessary, and click OK.

2. Palettes may be moved on screen by clicking the gray bar at the top of the palette and dragging. Click and hold the bar at the top of the Layers/Channels/Paths palette, and drag the mouse.

   You will find the palettes to be sort of "magnetic," and stick to each other when close enough. They will also stick to the edges of your monitor. This facilitates putting them around the edges of your working area, or organizing them in the best manner for a particular function.

3. Click and hold the Window menu. All the available palettes are displayed.

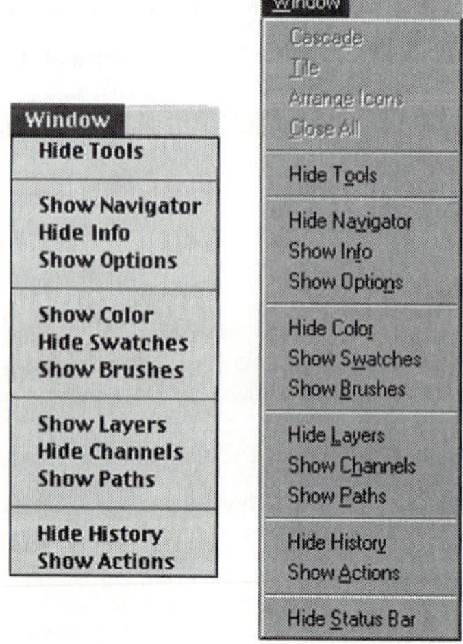

4. If they are not already visible, choose Show Brushes from the Window menu. (If this palette is already visible on screen, the submenu will read Hide Brushes instead.) If the palette group is visible, the tab that activates that palette will be automatically selected; if the palette group is not visible, the entire palette group will appear on screen again, with the chosen tab activated.

5. Choose Window>Hide Brushes. The entire palette group disappears.

6. Palettes may be moved between palette groups by clicking and dragging a tab from one group to another. Click a tab on any palette, and drag it to another palette group.

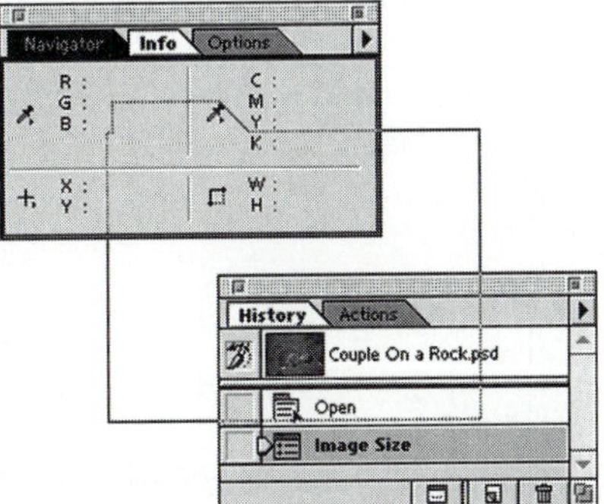

7. To make certain that the palettes on all of our monitors look the same, we'll reset them to Photoshop's defaults. Select File>Preferences>General and click the Reset Palette Locations to Default button. Click OK.

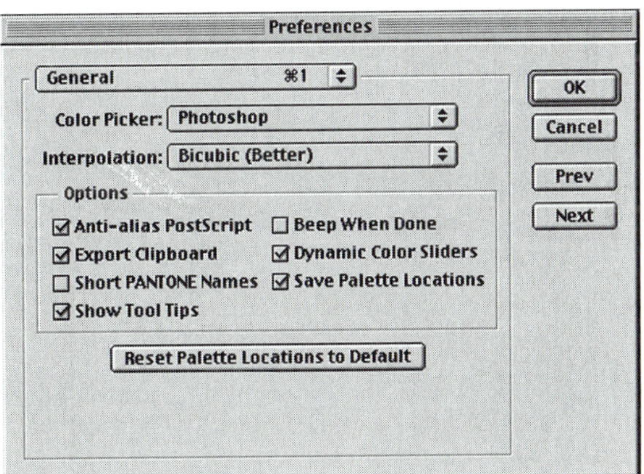

Creating a New Document

1. Select File>New. The New dialog box appears:

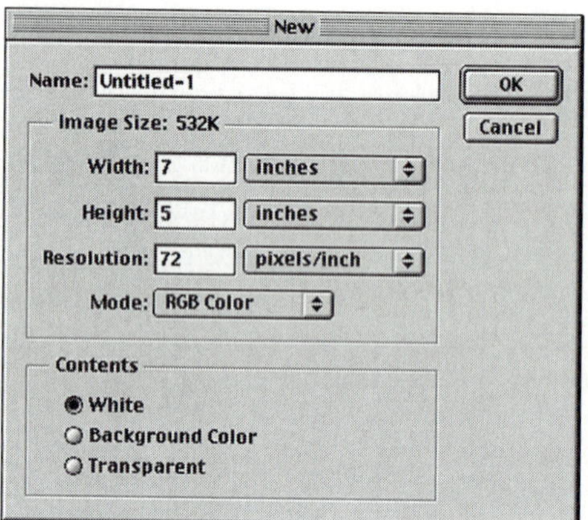

2. The New dialog box has three sections. Name allows you to enter a name for your document. In the Name box type "First Image".

3. Image Size controls the dimensions, image resolution, and the color mode. The Width and Height of the image can be set in units of pixels, inches, centimeters, points, picas, or columns by clicking on the pull-down list to the right of each dimension.

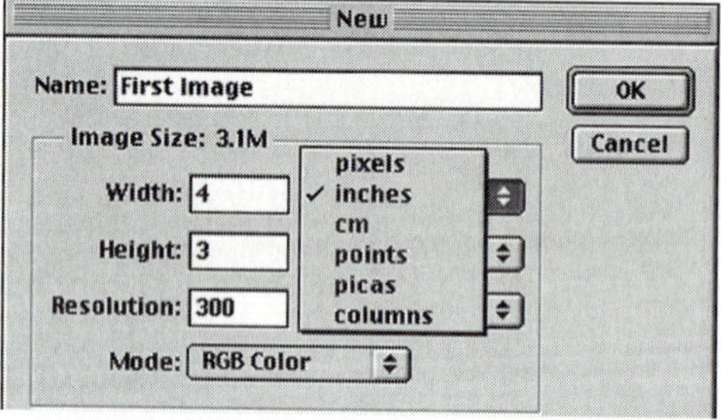

Set the measuring units for inches.

4. Enter "4" for Width and "3" for Height. Press the Tab key after entering each value to change fields.

5. Click on the pull-down list next to the Width setting. Select the picas setting. Notice that the 4 changed to 24; there are 6 picas to an inch, and Photoshop automatically makes this calculation for you.

6. Change the units back to inches; the units change again. Generally speaking, files you will create during this course will be in units of inches or pixels. For our first image, we'll set both dimensions, Width and Height, to inches.

7. If the dimension units are set to anything except pixels, the Resolution setting will also change the file size. Type "300" in the Resolution box; then type "50" in the Resolution box. Notice that the file size gets larger or smaller, depending on the resolution you entered.

8. The units pull-down list beside the Resolution setting allows the resolution to be interpreted as either pixels/inch or pixels/cm.

Changing units will not affect file size; it merely changes the default size at which certain applications such as PageMaker will initially display the image when it is imported.

For this image, set Resolution to 72 and units to pixels/inch.

9. The last Image Size section is Mode. Though Photoshop can work in eight different color modes (which we'll discuss later in the course), only five of them are available when creating a new document. For now, set this to RGB Color.

10. The final section in the New dialog box is Contents.

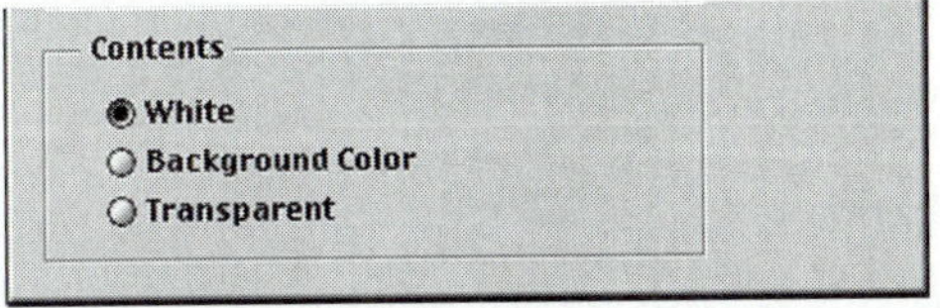

This option sets the initial background of your file. The choices here are White, Background Color, and Transparent. Make certain that the White radio button is selected, and click OK.

11. You've just created your first Photoshop document! Keep this document open for the next exercise.

Before we actually save the document, let's take a detour back to the Preferences menu. It's a good idea to always save files with the appropriate extension. If you're working under Windows, it is necessary, but even on a Macintosh it's a good idea, so you know what you're working with.

Setting the Saving Files Preferences

1. Select Preferences>Saving Files… from the File menu.
2. From the Append File Extension: dialog, select Always (Macintosh).

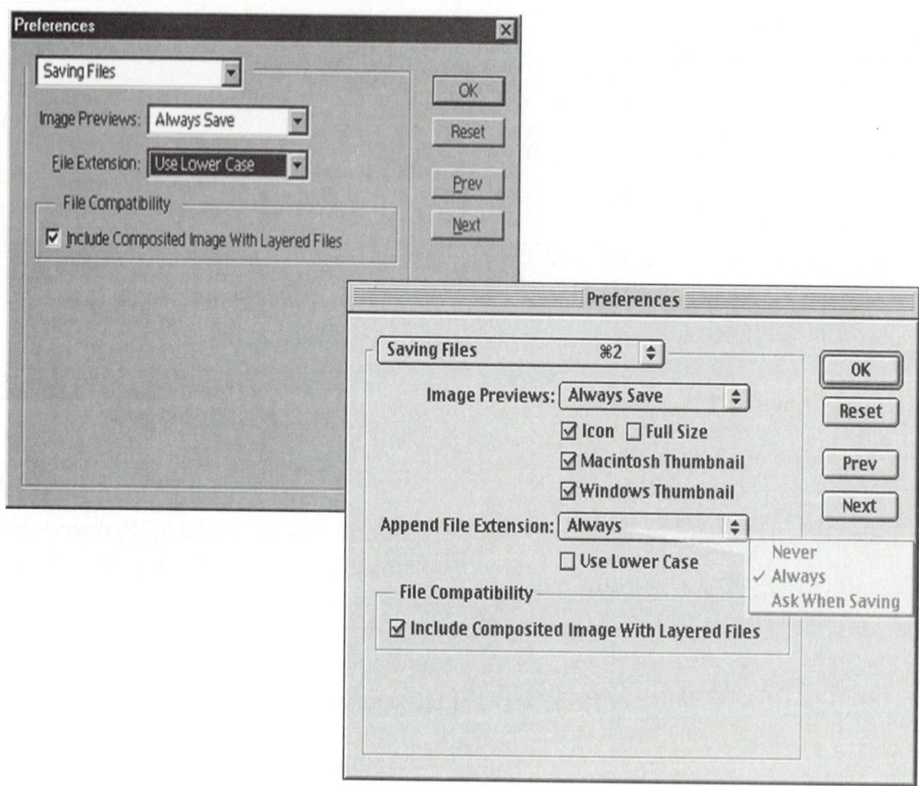

3. Click OK.

This is just a little thing, but it means that Photoshop will always select the correct file extension for you — it's one less thing to worry about.

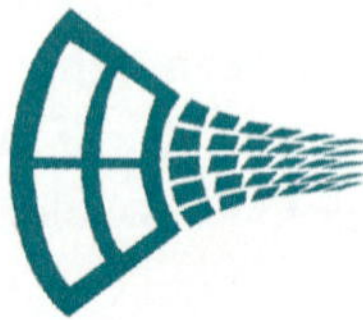

Windows must use the naming convention for extensions. When files are moved between Macintosh and Windows platforms, files are truncated to the old DOS 8.3 standard, so it's best to use that file naming convention whenever possible.

This will occur automatically on Windows-based machines, though the extensions may not display. It is best to set your computer to display the file extensions.

Saving the Document

1. Select Save As from the File menu.
2. Click-hold on the Format (Macintosh) or Save As (Windows) box to see the list of formats to choose from. Scroll down to the bottom and highlight TIFF (Tagged Image File Format).

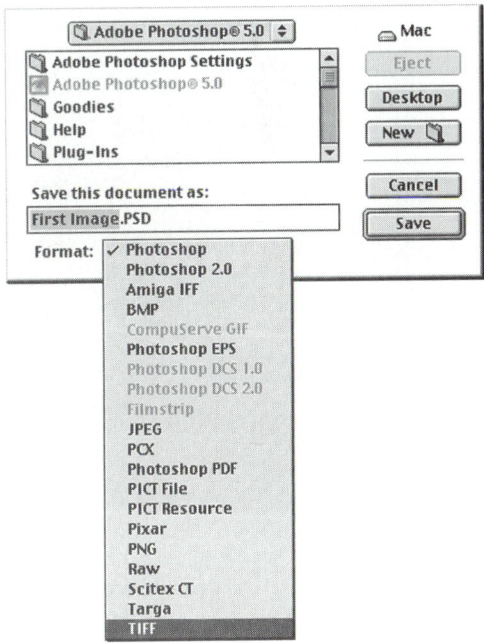

3. Click Desktop in this window to save it to the Desktop. Save the image as "First Image". Click Save. Notice that Photoshop automatically assigned the ".TIF" file extension.
4. Because the document is being saved as a TIFF, an extra dialog box appears. The LZW Compression option will make the file size considerably smaller. (Note, however, that not all programs will import an LZW compressed TIFF.) For our purposes, click this option.

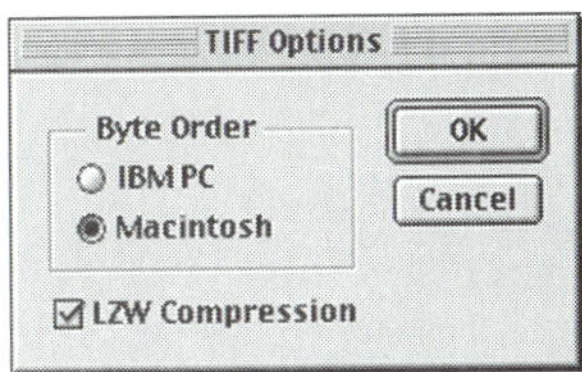

5. You can save in either IBM PC or Macintosh format (though most applications will read either). Select the option according to the platform you are using.
6. Click OK. Your saved file will be on the Desktop. Close the file. Drag the file to the Trash or Recycle Bin.

Notes:

CHAPTER 3

GETTING AROUND

CHAPTER OBJECTIVE:

To learn how to navigate in Photoshop; to learn the three areas of navigational control, and how to use them to their utmost efficiency. In Chapter 3, you will:

- Learn about Photoshop palettes and the functions they perform.
- Learn about pop-up sliders, and when to use them.
- Learn about Help Wizards, and how they relate to a variety of Photoshop functions.
- Study the Selection tools, and learn their functions.
- Understand the basics of the Actions and History palettes.
- Learn to adjust Image View.
- Study and learn the functions of the Painting and Drawing tools.
- Study and learn the functions of the Photo Effects tools.
- Gain a basic understanding of the Type and Type Mask tools.
- Become familiar with the Photoshop menu bar.
- Learn how to use keyboard navigation to increase your efficiency.

Getting Around

Photoshop is a feature-rich application. To make navigation a little easier, controls are divided into three areas: menus, palettes, and the Toolbox. In addition, many commands are also available using the keyboard.

Photoshop Palettes

Palettes are usually grouped together according to the functions they perform. For example, the Navigator, Info, and Options palettes all give feedback about different aspects of Photoshop, and generally appear in the same group. Other groups include the Layers, Channels, and Paths palettes, the Color, Swatches, and Brushes palettes, and the History and Actions palettes.

All the palettes and groups have certain features in common:

- Palette groups have tabs which can be clicked to activate a palette within a group. Clicking on the Brushes tab in the Color/Swatches/Brushes palette group displays a selection of brushes; clicking on the Swatches tab displays color swatches in the same palette group.

- Palettes have a Close button in the upper left corner (Macintosh) or upper right corner (Windows).

- Any palette can be shrunk to its smallest possible size by clicking in the "zoom" (minimize/maximize) box in the upper right corner of each palette. Click it again, and the palette will expand back to its original size.

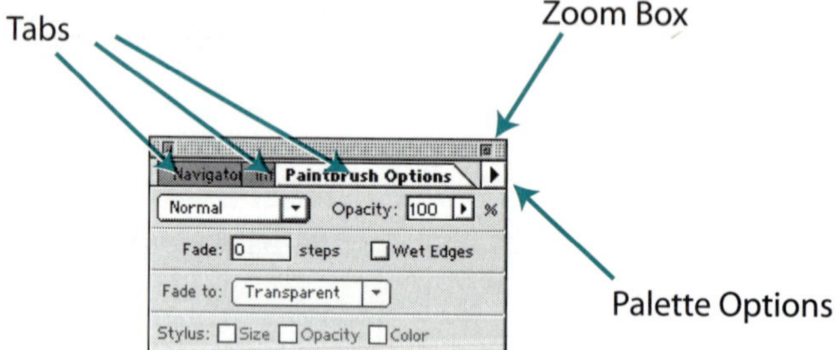

- All palettes have a Palette Option pull-down list, which is activated by clicking the black triangle in the upper right corner of the palette.

Using Pop-up Sliders

The Layers palette and many of the Options palettes for various painting tools use a pop-up slider. These sliders are used to control the opacity or angle of a layer, tool, or effect. To use this feature, click on the arrow next to the value to open the pop-up slider, then drag the slider control triangle to change the value. Clicking outside the slider (Windows) or releasing the mouse button (Macintosh) closes the pop-up slider box. Of course, the value can be changed directly by typing a new number into the appropriate box.

Help Wizards

Interactive assistance is available via the help menu for two tasks in Photoshop 5.0. Choosing Help>Export Transparent Image... opens a series of dialog boxes designed to assist the user in creating transparent GIF graphic files for use on the World Wide Web. Choosing Help>Resize Image... opens a series of dialog boxes to assist in properly resizing images for a variety of print or multimedia conditions. To use these features, be certain that a document is open, select the appropriate option, and then carefully follow the instructions that Photoshop presents. Resizing and exporting images will be covered in depth later in this course.

The Layers, Channels, and Paths Palettes

The Layers palette, located in the Layers/Channels/Paths palette group, controls the order and processing of layers within a Photoshop document. Layers allow the user to place images or parts of images over one another for compositing and special effects. Many Photoshop commands generate layers automatically, including the Paste command and type created with the Type tool. Type or a pasted object can be freely moved around within an image without permanently affecting the image beneath it.

The word Normal in the upper left corner of the palette indicates how the layer is to be blended with the one below it. The pop-up slider labeled Opacity either allows the layer to be completely opaque, or makes it partly transparent. The order of the layers may be changed by dragging one layer name above or below another. Layers may be turned on and off by clicking on the Eye icon next to the layer name. The layer you are actually working on, called the active layer, is indicated by a paint brush in the second column, next to the layer name. The page icon at the bottom of the palette is used to create or duplicate a layer. The trash can is used to delete layers. The Background layer, shown in italic, is a special type of layer — one that cannot contain transparent areas or be moved above other layers.

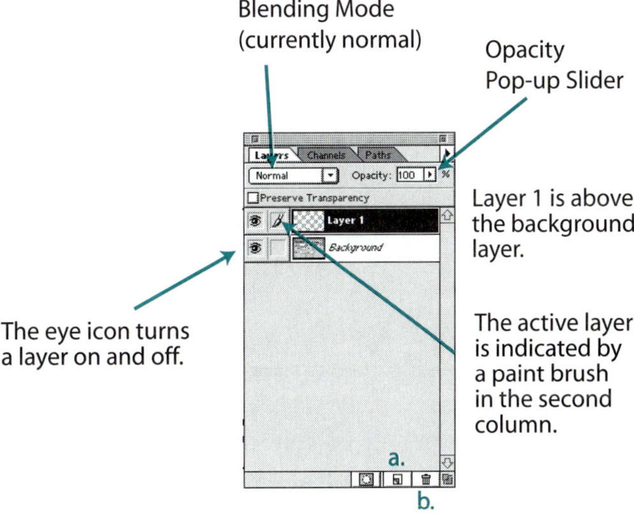

The page icon (a.) is used to create new layers.
The trash can (b.) is used to delete layers.

The Channels palette, also located in the Layers/Channels/Paths palette group, allows access to separated color information for an image; for example, the red information, the green information, and the blue information for an RGB image. The Channels palette may also contain special types of channels. An alpha channel acts as a sort of digital stencil. A spot color channel allows you to define areas where special pre-mixed inks can be used.

In the bottom right of the palette are four icons. The left-most icon activates a channel for use as a selection, or stencil. The second icon saves information currently selected as a channel. The page icon is for creating and duplicating channels. The trash can is used to delete channels from a document.

The eye icon can be toggled on and off. If the eye is visible then the channel is being viewed.

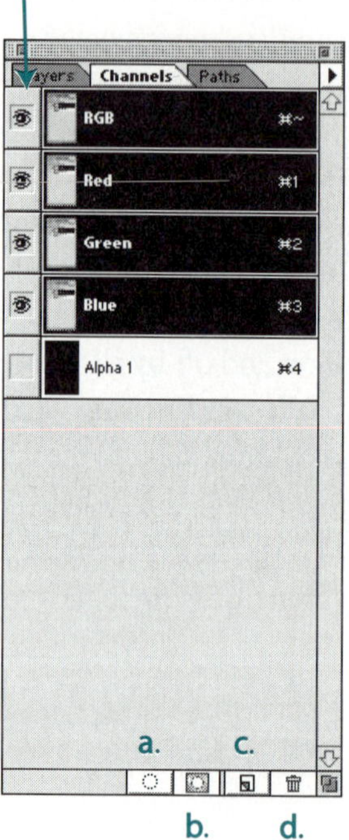

The RGB composite channel is active.

Channel #4 is an alpha channel

There are four icons at the bottom of the palette, the load selection icon (a.), the save selection icon (b.), the page icon (c.), and the trash can icon (d.).

The third palette in this group is the Paths palette. The Paths palette is used to draw vector-based lines and curves, similar to those used in Adobe Illustrator and MacroMedia FreeHand. Paths are activated by clicking once within the box containing the name of the path. Paths are highlighted in the paths palette once they are selected.

The icons on the bottom of the Paths palette are tools for manipulating paths, which are drawn and edited with the pen tools. The first two icons on the lower left of the palette control path filling and stroking; the next two icons create selections, or stencils, from a path, or vice versa. The last two icons are for creating, copying, and deleting paths.

The Paths palette, below, shows a path that was created by clicking the new button (Path 1) and a path created by clicking the Pen tool, then drawing a path on the canvas (Work Path).

Click the Fill Path icon to apply a fill to the path (a.). You can also stroke the path by clicking the Stroke Path icon (b.). To make a selection from a path, click the third icon (c.).

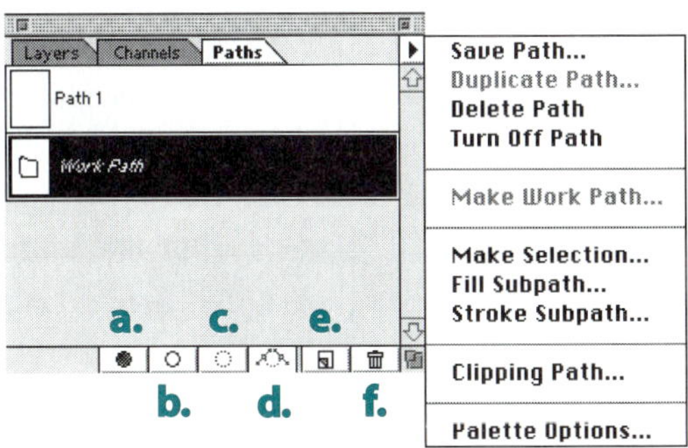

If needed, you can make a path from a selection by clicking the fourth icon (d.). The Create New Path icon makes a new path (e.). The Delete Path icon will remove any path (f.).

The Color, Swatches, and Brushes Palettes

The Color and Swatches palettes allow the selection of foreground and background colors for painting.

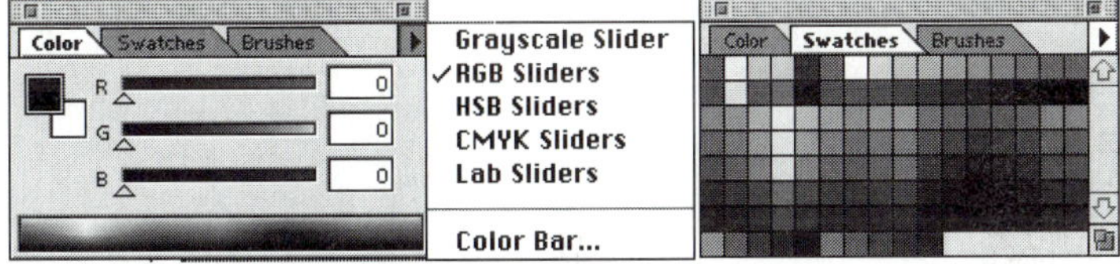

The Color palette specifies colors using a color picker, which allows you to mix the components of the color using sliders. The color model used in the picker, RGB or CMYK, for example, is selectable from the Palette Options triangle.

The Swatches palette contains small squares of color from which to set foreground and background colors. You may also create a custom swatch set, or load a computer-generated simulation of a commercial color set, such as the Pantone (PMS) Color Formula Guide.

The Brushes palette is used to select brush sizes and types for painting tools.

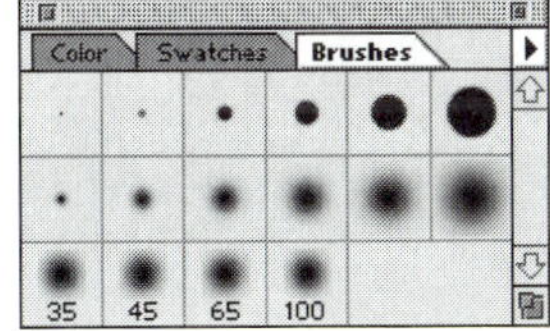

The default brushes in the palette are either hard-edged, like the brushes at the top of the palette, or soft-edged, like the second and third row of brushes. The brushes with numbers at the bottom of the palette mean a brush is too large to be displayed within the box. The number indicates the size of the brush in pixels.

The Navigator, Info, and Options Palettes

The Navigator allows you to move easily around an image when viewing a part of the image close up; you can also change the current zoom percentage.

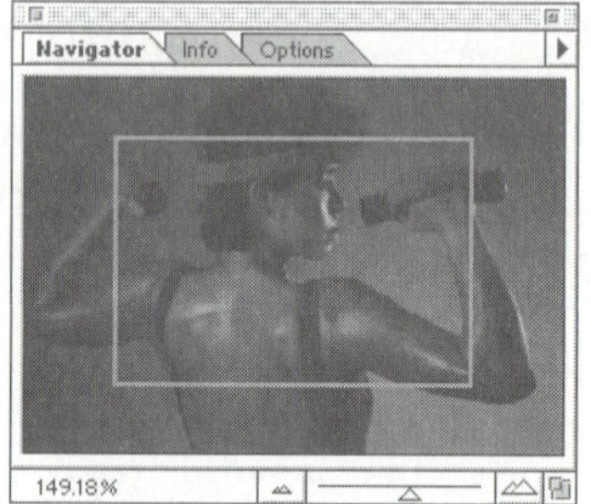

The Info palette displays information about the active image or tool, including color and color sampler information, cursor location, and drawing angles when using certain tools.

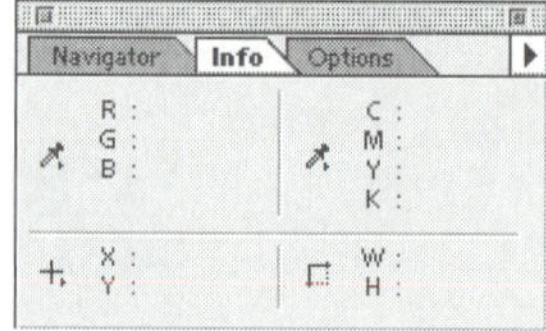

Most tools (though not all) have an Options palette associated with them. The Options palette specifies settings which give more control over the way each tool works, such as determining how paint from a painting tool will interact with the color beneath it.

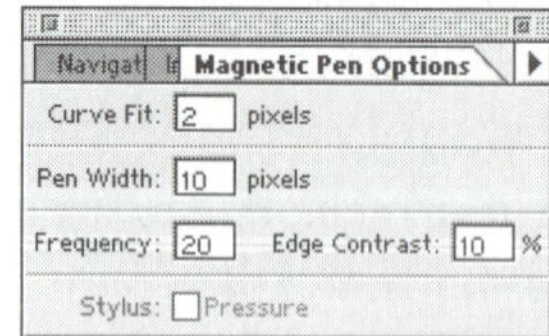

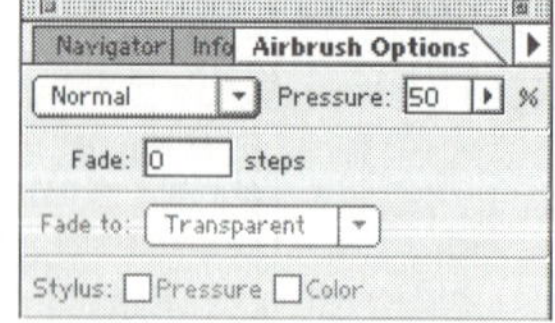

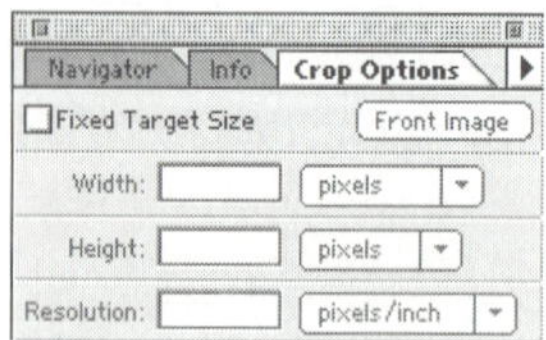

The information in the Options palette changes with the tool that is selected.

The Actions and History Palettes

The Actions palette contains scripts which allow you to automate Photoshop tasks. It comes with a few scripts, or you can create your own. An action can include tools, effects, paths, layers, history, or even a call to another action. They can also be grouped into sets, just like organizing files within folders. Actions can be performed on a single file or on all files within a specified folder.

The Actions palette controls scripts that automate Photoshop functions. Individual or grouped sets are turned on and off with the far left check boxes.

When the dialog box is checked it tells Photoshop to prompt for user input when that script is initiated.

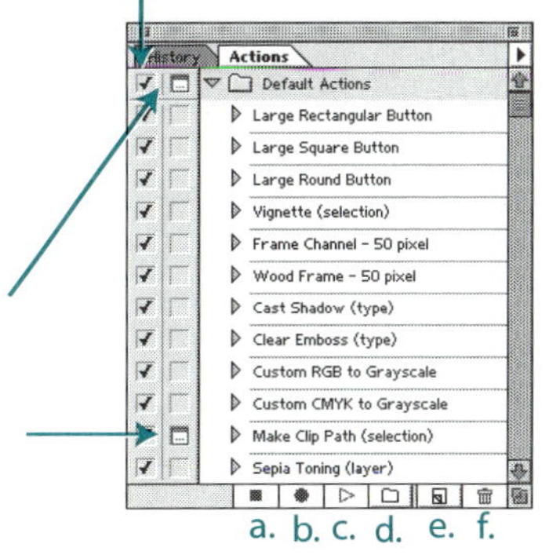

Actions can exist individually or be grouped into sets.

The controls at the bottom of the palette are similar to VCR controls. The first three buttons are used to stop playing or recording an action (a.), begin recording a new action (b.), or begin playing an action(c.). The folder icon (d.) groups actions into a new set. The last two icons create a new set (e.) or delete an action (f.).

The buttons at the bottom of the palette are similar to VCR buttons. The first button stops recording or playing an action, the second begins recording a series of commands for inclusion in an action, and the third allows you to play back an action into Photoshop. To perform an action on a group of files select File>Automate>Batch. It's a great way, for example, to do basic color correction of a series of images automatically.

The History palette allows you to move through various states where an image has been since it was opened. Each edit that alters the condition of an image is recorded and labeled in the History palette and can be recalled by clicking within the appropriate box in the palette. For example, if you crop, sharpen and then paint an image, each of these states is recorded. You can then use the History palette to revert back to any previous state of the image. The maximum number of states is set from within the palette options, but is also limited by the size of the image and the amount of memory available to Photoshop.

The History palette is organized into two sections. The top of the palette contains snapshots; the bottom contains individual image states.

The far left checkbox activates a state as the current source for the History brush.

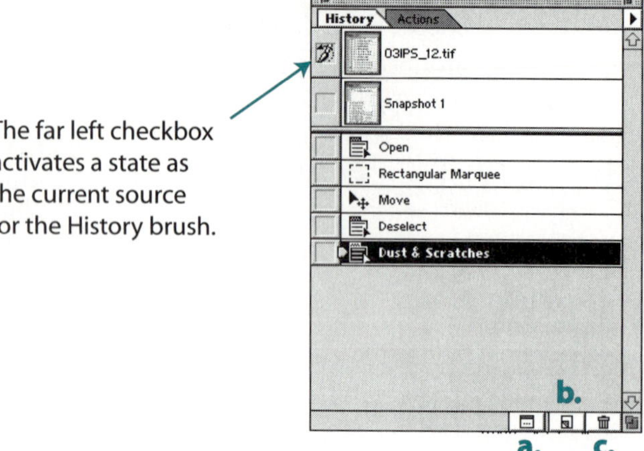

The boxes at the bottom of the palette are used to create a new document from the selected state (a.), create a new snapshot (b.), or delete a snapshot or state (c.).

The inclusion of the snapshot feature allows a number of different work options with the History palette. Taking a snapshot creates a permanent state that appears in the top of the History palette. Judicious use of this feature makes it possible to experiment with several editing techniques at the same time. When a state is deleted by default, all subsequent states are deleted. This option can be turned off by checking the Allow Non-Linear History button in the History Options menu, but makes the interpretation of the palette display more difficult.

History Palette Exercise

1. Open the file **Exercise.TIF** from the **SF-Intro Photoshop** folder. If the History palette is not already open, select it by choosing Window>Show History.
2. From the Toolbox, select the Magic Wand tool and click once on the blue background in the upper left quadrant of the image. The Magic Wand tool selects contiguous pixels similar in value to the area you selected. Notice that this state has been added to the History palette.

3. Expand the selection by choosing Select>Similar. This gives Photoshop the command to select all pixels in the image similar in value to the original one chosen. Later in this course you will learn to adjust this tool to select either a large or small variance in pixel value, called tolerance, but here you are only using the Photoshop default. Note that a new state has been added to the History palette.

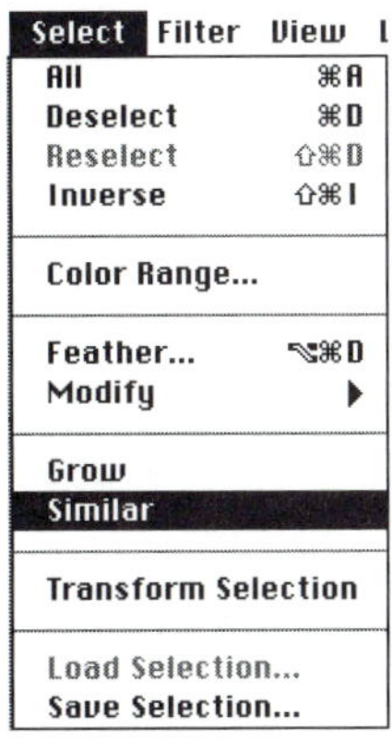

4. Now deselect everything by choosing Select>Deselect from the menu bar. There are now four items in the History palette representing each of the states you created since opening the image. Click on each state and notice how this feature allows you to backtrack through each edit.

5. Click on the Magic Wand state and delete it. In this mode when you delete a state you also delete all subsequent states. Select Edit>Undo Delete States to restore the states.

6. From the Palette menu select History Options, check the box next to Allow Non-Linear History, and click OK. Now delete the Magic Wand state again. In this palette mode you can delete any state from the list while leaving the other states intact. Delete the rest of the states from the palette.

7. Close the image without saving.

The Photoshop Toolbox

Many features in Photoshop are accessible through the Toolbox. Activate the Options palette by clicking on its tab and click on each tool as it is discussed to see what options are available for the tool. If the palette is not visible, go to Windows>Show Options.

All of the Toolbox tools have keyboard shortcuts. Pressing Shift–(shortcut) toggles through the Tool flyout menu.

Marquee – M

Crop – C

Move – V

Lasso – L

Magic Wand – W

Airbrush – J

Paintbrush – B

Eraser – E

History Brush – Y

Rubber/Pattern Stamp – S

Smudge/Sharpen/Blur – R

Dodge/Burn/Sponge – O

Pen – P

Type/Type Mask – T

Pencil/Line – N

Measure – U

Gradient – G

Paint Bucket – K

Eyedropper/Sampler – I

Hand – H

Zoom – Z

Swap Foreground/Background Colors – X

Default Colors(B&W) – D

Quick Mask/Standard – Q

Toggle View Modes – F

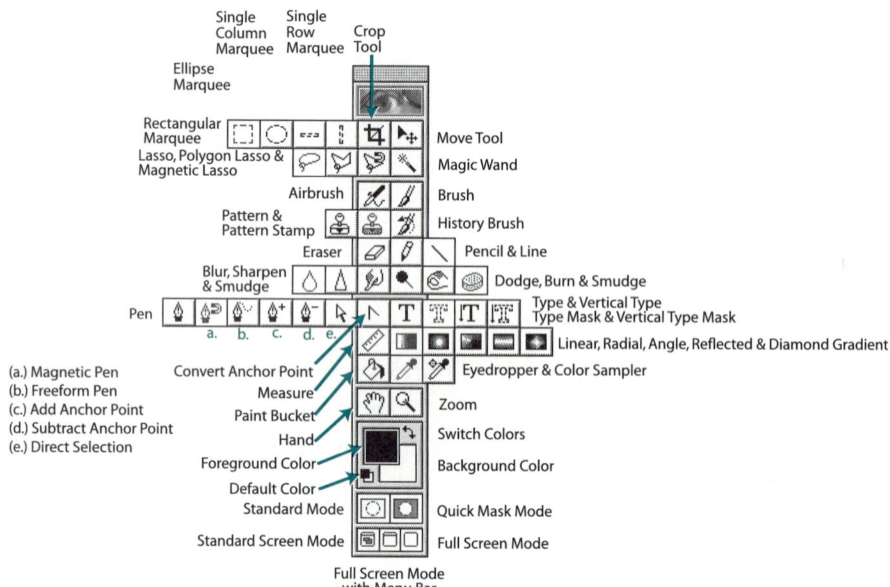

Notice that some of the tool buttons pull out to reveal several similar tools under one button. The extra tools are accessed by clicking and holding the mouse button until the selection of tools appears, then dragging over to the selected tool. You can also cycle through certain groups of similar tools using the keyboard command for that tool group. For example, pressing the Shift-O key combination repeatedly will toggle through the Dodge, Burn, and Sponge tools, which are all on the same tool pull-out.

Selection Tools

The first four tools in the Toolbox, and the Type Mask and Vertical Type Mask tools (with an outlined capital "T") are used for isolating and repositioning specific areas of an image without affecting the rest of the picture.

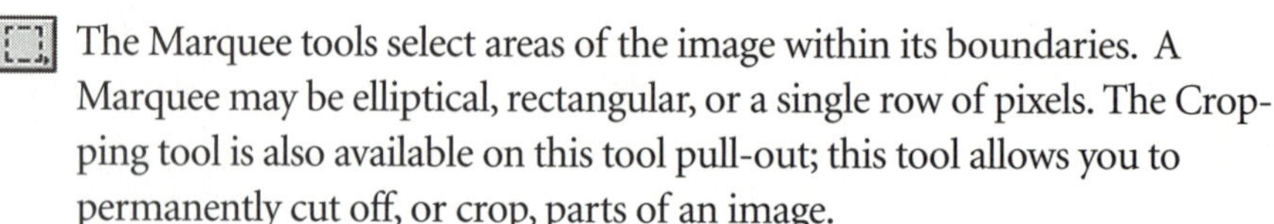

The Marquee tools select areas of the image within its boundaries. A Marquee may be elliptical, rectangular, or a single row of pixels. The Cropping tool is also available on this tool pull-out; this tool allows you to permanently cut off, or crop, parts of an image.

The Lasso, Polygon Lasso, and Magnetic Lasso tools draw a freehand marquee, capturing the image area within its boundary. The Lasso encircles parts of the image freehand; the Polygon Lasso uses straight lines created by point-to-point clicking; the Magnetic Lasso traces an edge on the basis of the color of the pixels and the tolerances you have set for the tool.

The Magic Wand captures contiguous pixels that are similar to the initial pixel clicked upon. The range of pixels selected is determined by the Tolerance setting on the Magic Wand Options palette.

The Move tool moves a selection or layer within the boundaries of the document window.

The Type Mask and Vertical Type Mask create an empty selection border in the shape of the characters typed into it. They may be filled, stroked, or used to mask parts of an image, just like any other selection. Type masks appear on the active layer; they are not editable as type. Standard type masks place type horizontally from left to right; vertical type masks place type from top to bottom.

Using the Toolbox

1. Navigate to the **SF/Intro Photoshop** folder. Double-click the document **Archery Target.TIF.**
2. Select the Rectangular Marquee tool by double-clicking on it. This will also bring up the Options palette for the tool.
3. Make certain that the Rectangular marquee is chosen.

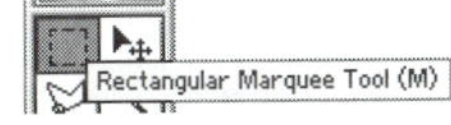

If it isn't, press the Shift-M keys repeatedly until the Rectangular Marquee tool is displayed in the Toolbox.

4. Begin dragging in the upper left corner above the target. Drag toward the lower right corner of the target and release the mouse. This will add a marquee around the round target. The moving border, commonly called "marching ants," is your selection.

5. Select the Move tool.

6. Click on your selection and move it toward the upper left corner. Observe how the selected area moves with the mouse. Also, note that the area the selection was moved from is filled with the background color.

7. Press Command-Z (Macintosh) or Control-Z (Windows) to undo, and move the selection back to its original location.
8. Press Command-D (Macintosh) or Control-D (Windows) to turn off the selection marquee and deselect the image.
9. Keep the file open for the next exercise.

Tools That Affect Image View

 The Hand tool moves the image around within the document window.

 The Zoom tool is represented by an icon that looks like a magnifying glass. This tool enlarges the area of the screen that you click on, allowing you to check fine details within the image. By clicking and dragging, you can draw a marquee box that will isolate and magnify a specific area of your page. To reduce the image, you can press the Option key (Macintosh) or Alt key (Windows) while using the tool.

Adjusting Image View

1. Select the Zoom tool by clicking on the white magnifying glass near the bottom of the Toolbox.
2. Click the tool on the image several times. The view will enlarge on the screen. If you zoom in more closely, you can see the individual pixels on the screen.

3. Notice the percentage listed in the lower left corner of the image window. This is the current image view percentage, in pixels. 100% means that there is one pixel displayed on screen for each pixel in the image, 200% means that each image pixel is displayed by 4 screen pixels (2 × 2), etc. Click in this box, enter the value "400", and press the Return or Enter key. The image view will change to reflect the new scale percentage.

4. Hold down the Option key (Macintosh) or Alt key (Windows); the plus sign inside the magnifying glass will turn into a minus sign. Now click the image with the Zoom tool and notice how the view zooms out, making the image smaller. Double-click the Zoom tool (not the image) and the image returns from the current percentage to 100%.

5. Now double-click on the Hand tool in the toolbox. The image will display as large as possible on screen.

6. Click and drag the magnifying glass to zoom in closely on an area in the image.

7. Click on the Navigator tab to activate the palette. Notice that the palette displays the entire image; the red box indicates the area currently viewable on screen. Click somewhere on the image inside the palette. Notice that the image view changes.

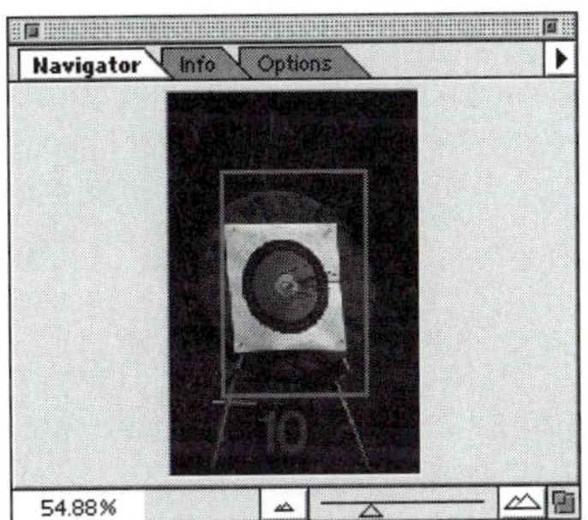

8. Move the slider at the bottom of the palette to the left or right. Notice that the zoom percentage changes again.

9. Close the document without saving.

Painting and Drawing Tools

The Paint Bucket tool fills areas of similar color with the foreground color or a pattern. By adjusting the Tolerance, you can determine how close the color of the image pixels needs to be in order to be affected by the tool.

The Gradient tool creates linear, radial, angular, and reflected gradients — smooth blends between shades of a color, between two colors or as a mixture of several colors and transparent areas. The Linear tool creates a smooth gradient in a straight line. The reflected gradient produces a mirror-image linear gradient, with each side of the image half the width. Radial and diamond gradients begin at center point and radiate in concentric circles or diamonds from one color to another. The angular gradient creates shades in a counterclockwise sweep around the beginning point of your blended area. Photoshop comes with a default set of gradients, although you can create and save custom sets.

The keyboard shortcut for Undo is Command-Z (Macintosh) or Control-Z (Windows).

The Eyedropper tool and Color Sampler tools are used to select and monitor color for adjusting an image. The Eyedropper tool allows you to select foreground and background colors, either from one of the color palettes, or directly from an image. You can sample the color of a single pixel, or average the color of an area 3 pixels by 3 pixels or 5 pixels by 5 pixels. Simply clicking on the image will change the foreground color used for painting. Holding down the Option key (Macintosh) or Alt key (Windows) while clicking will change the background color. The Color Sampler tool allows you to place up to four sample markers which can then be monitored from the Info palette. Delete a sample by holding down the Option key (Macintosh) or Alt key (Windows) while clicking on the color sample.

The Eraser tool allows you to paint with any of the other painting tools by selecting a brush size and erasing to the background color if you're working on the Background layer of the image, or to transparent if you're working on another layer. This tool can also erase to a point on the History palette.

The Pencil tool creates hard-edged lines. Generally, this tool is useful only in bitmapped images, which are hard-edged by nature.

The Line tool will draw straight lines in an image, with or without arrowheads. It can also be used as a measuring device.

The Airbrush tool behaves in a manner very similar to an actual airbrush; the color grows more opaque and the spread widens (to the maximum width of the brush selected) the longer you hold the brush in a given area. When painting with the Airbrush, the edges are much softer than with other painting tools.

The Paintbrush tool applies color to an image. The width of the stroke is determined by the brush selected from the Brushes palette. The edges created by this tool are softer than those from the Pencil tool, but harder than those from the Airbrush.

The History Brush tool will repaint parts of an image to any selected state in the History palette. The desired state is selected by turning on the history brush source at the far left of each listed state or snapshot.

The Rubber Stamp tool, and the Pattern Stamp tool will overprint part of an image to another area within the same image or into another image. The Rubber Stamp clones one part of the image to the other from a reference point on the image; each stroke paints more of the image. The Pattern Stamp uses the rectangular selection marquee to select part of the image as a pattern. A command then defines the pattern. It will paint over designated parts of the image with that repetitive pattern.

The Type tool and Vertical Type tool create type filled with the foreground color (by default) or any other color you select. Type is created on a special type layer, labeled on the Layers palette with a "T." This is "live" type and may be edited at any time.

The Pen tool pull-out contains seven tools used for selecting, creating, and editing paths. Paths may be created directly in Photoshop or pasted from the clipboard from Adobe Illustrator. The standard Pen tool creates paths using Bézier curves. The Magnetic Pen and Freeform Pen allow you to draw a path as if you were drawing the path on paper; while you draw completely "freehand" with the Freeform tool, the Magnetic Pen adheres the path to an image. Add-and Delete-anchor point tools are self-explanatory. The Convert-anchor point tool first compresses the Bézier handles to allow you to redraw the point from scratch. The Direct-selection tool allows you to select and move or alter any point or segment in the path.

Photo Effects Tools

The last two tools in the second section of the Toolbox are used to apply effects to specific areas of an image.

The Smudge tool and Focus tool allow you to alter the immediate relationship between parts of an image. The Smudge tool mixes the colors in an image, creating an effect similar to that of dragging your finger through wet paint. The Focus tools include the Blur tool to soften hard edges in specific areas of an image and the Sharpen tool for increasing the contrast on softer edges.

The Dodge/Burn/Sponge tools are used to Dodge (lighten), Burn (darken), or adjust the saturation of the image using a Sponge. Dodge and Burn are terms used for lightening and darkening in traditional photography. Decreasing the saturation removes color from an area in an image, bringing it closer to gray. Saturating an image makes the colors more "pure."

Using the Eyedropper

1. Choose File>Open, and navigate to the **SF-Intro Photoshop** folder. Select the file **Sailboat Beach.TIF.**

2. Select the Eyedropper tool in the Toolbox.

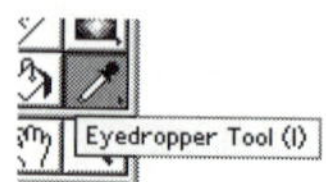

3. Click-hold and drag the Eyedropper across the image. Observe how the foreground color swatch near the bottom of the Toolbox changes as you move through the different colors in the image.
4. Release the mouse button when you see a color you like on the foreground color swatch. The foreground color will be changed.
5. Change the background color swatch by holding down the Option key (Macintosh) or Alt key (Windows) as you drag again. Stop when you find a color for the background.
6. Use the Marquee tool to select a portion of the photo. Press Delete. The deleted portion is filled with background color. Press Command-Z (Macintosh) or Control-Z (Windows) to undo this deletion. Press Command-D (Macintosh) or Control-D (Windows) to deselect all.
7. Select the Eraser tool in the Toolbox. Drag the Eraser across the photo several times. Observe how, in its path, the Eraser has painted the background color.
8. Leave the file open for the next exercise.

Using Painting Tools

1. Activate the Swatches palette. Click on a swatch color in the palette to select a new foreground color.

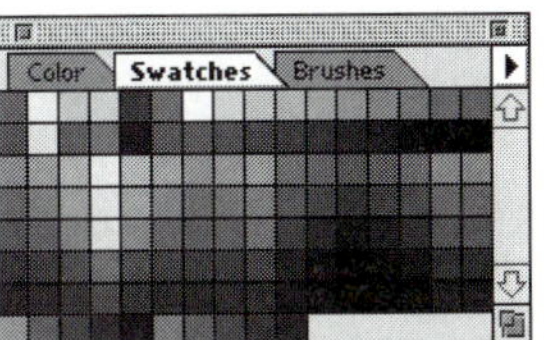

2. Hold down the Option key (Macintosh) or Alt key (Windows) to set the background to white by clicking on the white swatch in the Swatches palette.

3. Select the Paintbrush tool and activate the Brushes palette by clicking on its tab. Select a medium brush with a soft edge.

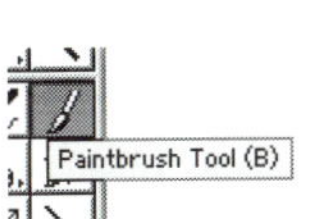

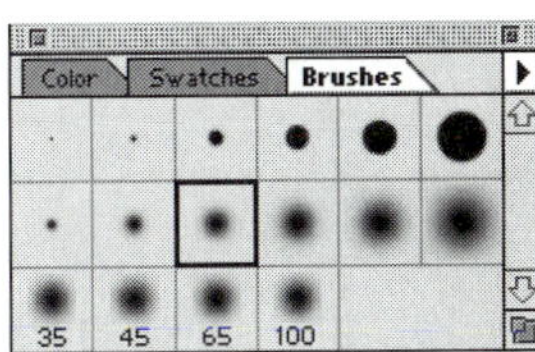

4. Paint a few strokes on your image. In the Brushes palette, select a smaller diameter stroke width and paint a few more brushstrokes. Delete all the states in the History palette to remove these changes.

5. The transparency of the Paintbrush may be set in the Options palette. Select a new foreground color from the Swatches palette and activate the Options palette. The Opacity pop-up slider, activated by clicking on the arrow next to the opacity value, adjusts the amount of paint you wish to apply to the image. Move the slider to about 50%.

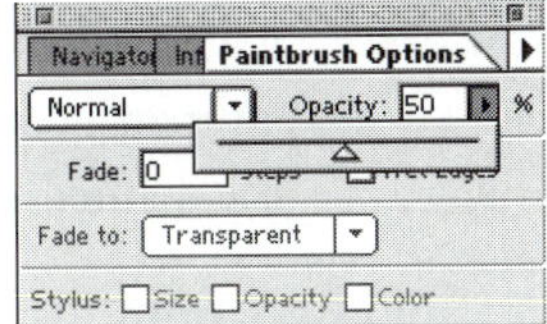

6. Paint with your new color opacity. Fifty percent of the image shows through the paint. Note that successive applications (after each release of the mouse button) of a color will increase the opacity of the painted image.

7. In the File menu, choose Revert. This will revert the file to its last saved version. Using the Revert command returns the file to the last version saved to disk. It has the same effect as deleting all the states in the History palette.
8. Close the file without saving.

Using the Pattern Stamp

1. Open the file **Pumpkins.TIF** in the **SF-Intro Photoshop** folder.
2. Activate the Rectangular Marquee tool in the toolbox.
3. Click and drag to create a selection around one of the pumpkins.

To Cancel (deselect) a selection, type Command/Control-D.

4. From the menu bar select Edit>Define Pattern. The area within the selection will now be the source for the Pattern Stamp tool. Note that only the rectangular marquee can be used to define an area as the pattern stamp source. Deselect the defined area — otherwise it will be the only area you will be able to paint in.
5. Activate the Pattern Stamp tool in the Toolbox, and make certain that the aligned box is checked in the Options palette. Using a medium sized brush, begin painting anywhere in the image. Notice how the area you defined earlier

in the exercise is repeatedly tiled wherever you paint. Painting over an already tiled area causes no change in the image. This is because the aligned option creates contiguous tiles from the tool source even if you stop and begin painting in some other area of the image.

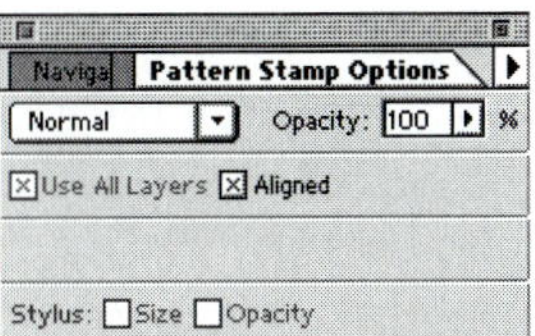

6. In the History palette, delete all the states marked Pattern Stamp to return the image to an unedited condition. Now go to the Pattern Stamp Options palette and deselect the box next to aligned. Paint over the image again with the Pattern Stamp tool, making certain to stop and go over areas again that have already been painted. This time Photoshop allows you to create new tiles on top of tiles. With the aligned option disabled, the program starts painting from the center of the tool source each time you start to paint with the tool.

7. Select File>Revert to remove changes and leave the file open for the next exercise.

Using the Type and Type Mask Tool

1. Select the Type tool and click anywhere inside the image. Select any bold typeface, set the font size to 48 points and type the word "Autumn". Click OK.

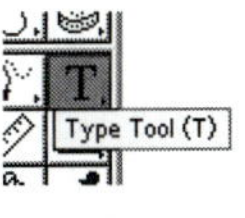

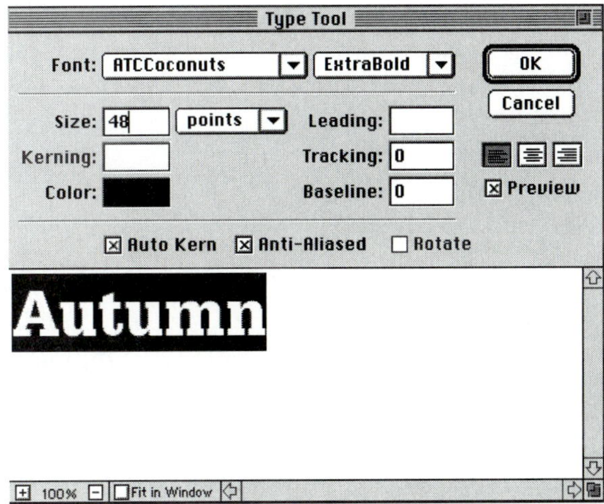

2. Open the Layers palette. There is now a new layer named Autumn with a capital "T" at the right. The Type tool places type on a new layer so you can move it around without affecting the image below it. Select the Move tool and click and drag on the image to move the type.

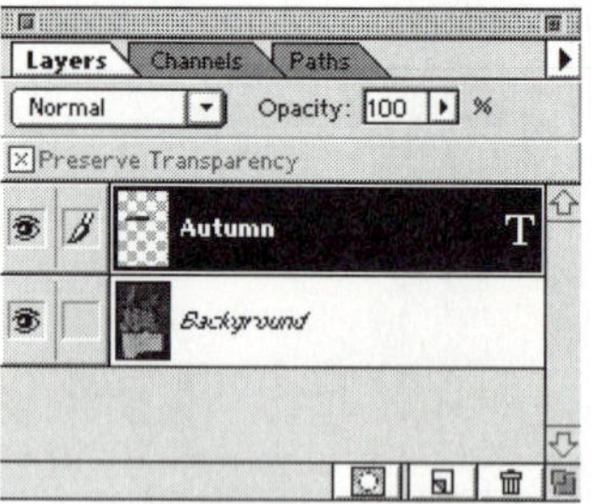

3. Type on a type layer can be edited at any time. Double-click on the "T" in the Layers palette to open the specifications dialog, highlight the text and change the point size to 72. If you check the preview box you can view your changes before clicking OK.

4. Select File>Revert. Now click and hold on the Type tool until the flyout appears, then drag across and select the Type Mask tool.

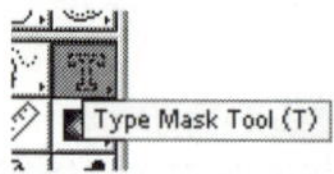

5. Recreate the type as you did above. This time an outline of the type displays on the image. The Type Mask tool creates a selection of the type over the image.

6. With the Type Mask tool still selected, reposition the type mask within the image. Using the Move tool, click within the type and move the selection to a different part of the image. Now the selected image moves, and the "hole" left behind is filled with the background color. Unlike the Type tool, the Type Mask tool creates a selection on the same layer as the image. Once created, the selection cannot be edited as type.

7. Close the file without saving.

Other Toolbox Controls

The bottom of the Toolbox palette holds a few more controls. The color swatches, which you have already used, display the current foreground and background colors.

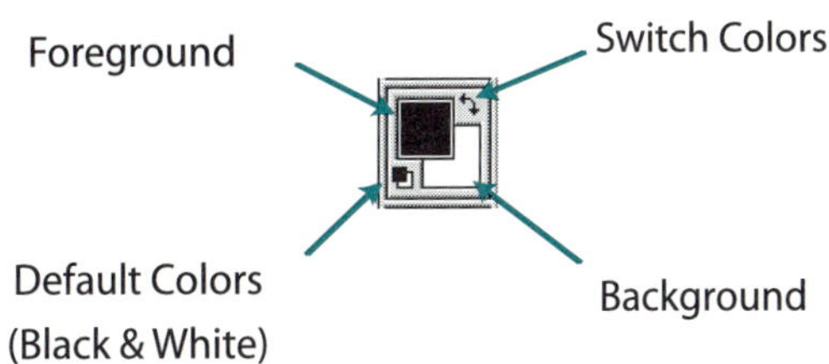

Clicking on the foreground or background swatch will activate Photoshop's Color Picker, which allows you to enter color information directly according to one of several color models.

Clicking on the tiny black-and-white swatches in the lower left corner of the palette resets the foreground and background colors to their default — black-and-white. The small curve with arrows on both ends to the upper right of the swatches is the Switch Colors icon. Click on this icon to swap foreground and background colors.

The two rectangles inscribed with circles set the painting mode.

Regular mode, the icon on the left, is the default for painting. The icon on the right, Quick Mask, allows you to create a marquee selection using painting tools rather than the marquee tools.

The last three buttons at the bottom of the Toolbox are window controls.

They change the way Photoshop displays the image on your monitor. The left icon can display multiple images, each in its own window; this is Photoshop's default mode. The middle icon displays a full-screen image. The last icon also displays a full-screen image, but on a black background without menus visible.

Using the Window Controls

1. Open the image **Archery Target.TIF** from the **SF-Intro Photoshop** folder.
2. Click the left button of the window controls. This mode permits viewing several images at a time; the menu bar and title bars are visible. The rulers, if turned on, abut the image.

3. Click the center button; the Full Screen Mode with Menus Bar, and the image window will enlarge to fill the screen. This view allows display of only a single image at a time. The menu bar is still available while in this mode. The rulers are at the edges of the screen.

4. Press the button on the right; the Full Screen Mode button changes the view to full screen with no menu bar, though the status line and rulers, if on, are still visible. The screen turns black.

Photoshop's rulers may be made visible at the top and sides on most image windows by selecting View> Show Rulers (Command/ Control-R). They allow for more accurate positioning of elements within an image.

Snap-to guides may be dragged from the rulers by clicking on the ruler and dragging the cursor to the position in the image where you want the guide. This is useful for a quick alignment of elements.

Show Guides, Hide Guides, and Clear Guides (when you want to get rid of them permanently) are available from the View menu.

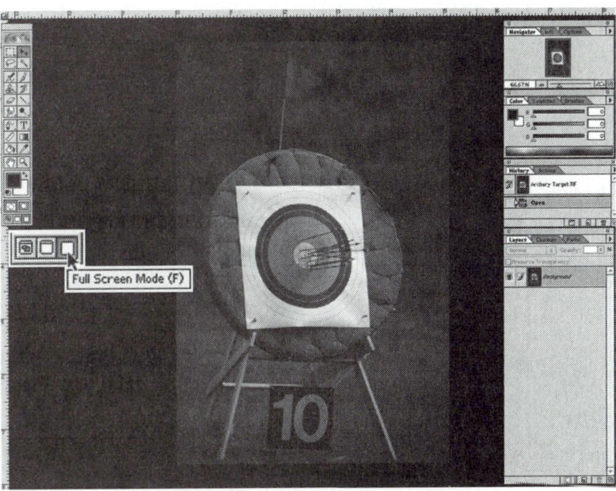

5. Press the Tab key while displaying an image to temporarily toggle off the palettes, allowing you to examine your image with less distractions. Press the Tab key again to restore the palettes, then click on the left (standard screen mode) icon to restore the window to its default mode.

6. Press the "F" key three times to toggle through the various view modes.

7. Close the file without saving.

The Photoshop Menu Bar

The final and most extensive set of commands is available in Photoshop's menu bar. You'll learn many of these commands during this course, but for now we'll just touch briefly on the types of commands listed under each menu.

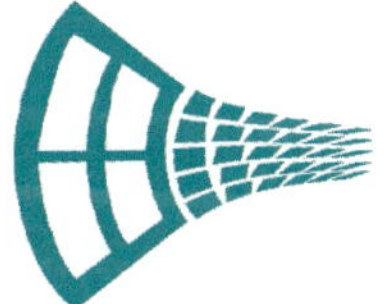

Windows users: If you have more than one document open, and are having difficulty locating the one you want, choose Window>Tile. All open documents will be arranged on the screen and you can easily select the one you want.

File

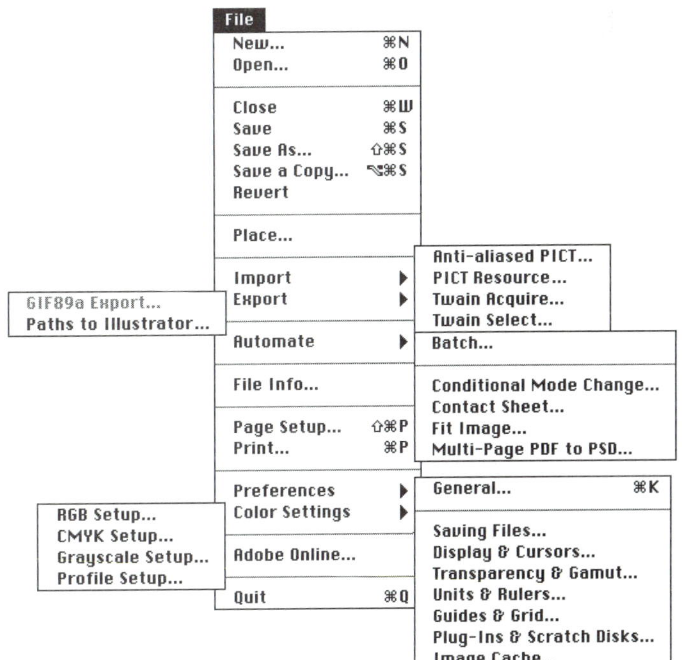

Conditional Mode Changes are valuable when a variety of color modes are being worked with. For example, if images originate as RGB or Grayscale, and the RGB images should be converted to CMYK, that condition can be set.

ICC is the international Color Consortium. They have created a system, supported by Apple, Microsoft, and much of the graphics community, that allows synchronizing the appearance of color from a variety of devices through creation and application of "profiles" of any ICC-compliant device.

Some of the elements under the File menu are probably familiar to you or have already been addressed in this course. A few commands of particular interest:

- **Save a Copy** is used when a file is in a state that will not allow it to be saved in the format into which you wish it to be saved. For example, you may have live type layers and wish to save the file as a TIFF or EPS. Since those file formats don't support layers, the Save a Copy command is used and the layers are flattened.
- **Revert** reloads the image from the point of your last save.
- **Import** contains options for scanning, and other ways of bringing information into Photoshop.
- **Export** to export information such as paths, which cannot be individually saved using the Save command.
- There are five Automate commands.
    - **Batch** allows you to specify a number of actions to occur sequentially.
    - **Conditional Mode Change** changes the color mode of a document from predefined original color mode to a specified target mode.
    - **Contact Sheet** creates a thumbnail preview of all images in a specified folder to a user-defined number of images per page and resolution.
    - **Fit Image** resamples the current image to fit within a specified height and width without changing its aspect ratio.
    - **Multi-page PDF to PSD** will convert each page of a PDF file into a separate Photoshop file.
- The **File Info** area allows you to include information in the Photoshop file that will be useful when using a digital asset management tool.
- **Color Settings** includes advanced features for color management, providing you with the ability to create ICC profiles of devices on your system, including devices used by your GASP.

Creating a Contact Sheet

1. Select File>Automate>Contact Sheet.

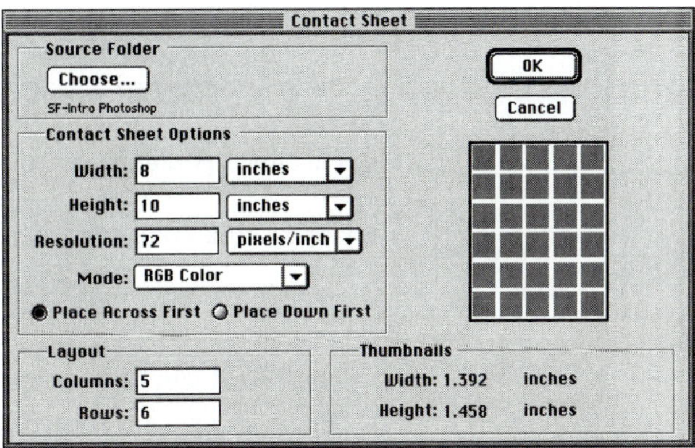

2. Click on Choose, and select the **SF-Intro Photoshop** folder. Note the options in the dialog box to select number, size, resolution, and color mode, but leave them at their default settings. The preview box on the right shows you how the images will fit into the new file.

3. Click OK and enjoy some hands-off Photoshop. The Contact Sheet command initiates a script, just like the Actions palette, that automatically opens, resizes, and places all of the images from the selected folder into a new composite image.

4. Close the file without saving.

Edit

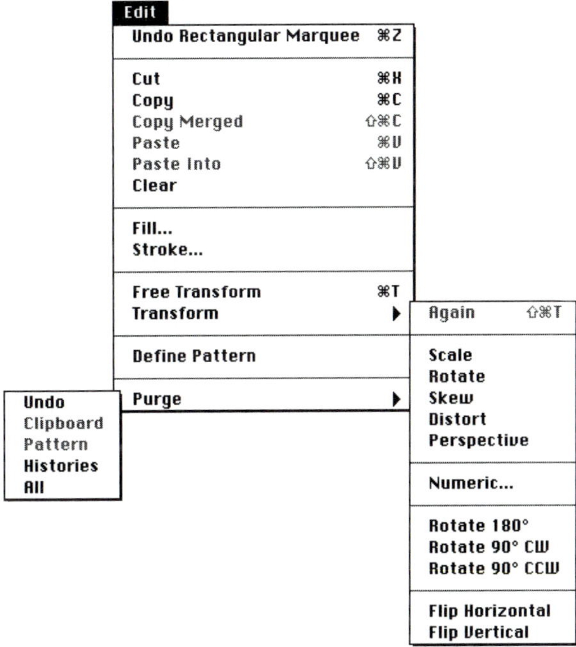

Much of the Edit menu will be familiar to you, such as Cut, Paste, and Copy. The Photoshop Edit menu goes much further offering extra options to allow for special treatment of objects.

- **Copy Merged** creates a composite copy of a selection from all visible layers.
- **Paste Into** lets you import the contents of the clipboard within a selected area.
- **Fill** allows you to insert color or patterns into a selection.
- **Stroke** adds color of assigned thickness to the selection line.
- **Free Transform** allows you to arbitrarily rotate, resize, or skew a selection.
- The **Transform Flyout** menu contains controls for individually performing the actions in Free Transform. The Transform menu also contains some other extremely useful functions:
    - **Numeric** allows any transform function to be precisely controlled by entering specific values into a dialog box.
    - **Rotate** 180, Rotate 90 CW, and Rotate 90 CCW rotate the selection by the specified amount.
    - **Flip Horizontal and Flip Vertical** create a mirror image of the selection in the respective direction.
- **Define Pattern** creates a repeating pattern from the selection for use by the Pattern Stamp tool, which is temporarily stored in a special pattern buffer.
- The **Purge** command clears the History palette states, or any other information stored in one of Photoshop's memory buffers.

Image

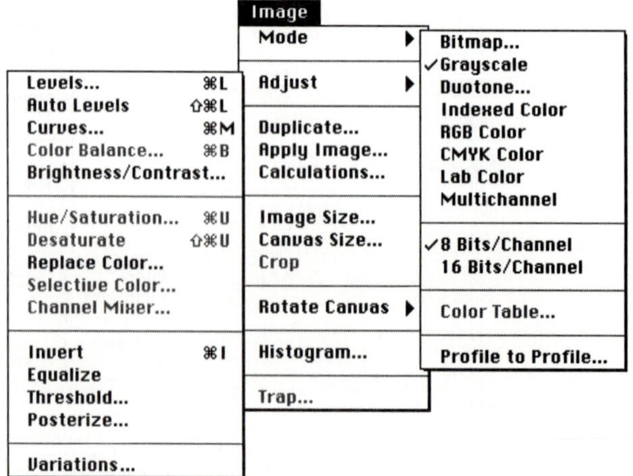

The Image menu contains commands for color and tone correction, tools for changing the size or canvas of your image, and commands for converting between color modes (i.e., convert a scanned RGB image to a CMYK image for printing). This menu also contains options for using selections to create special effects under the Calculations menu item.

Layer

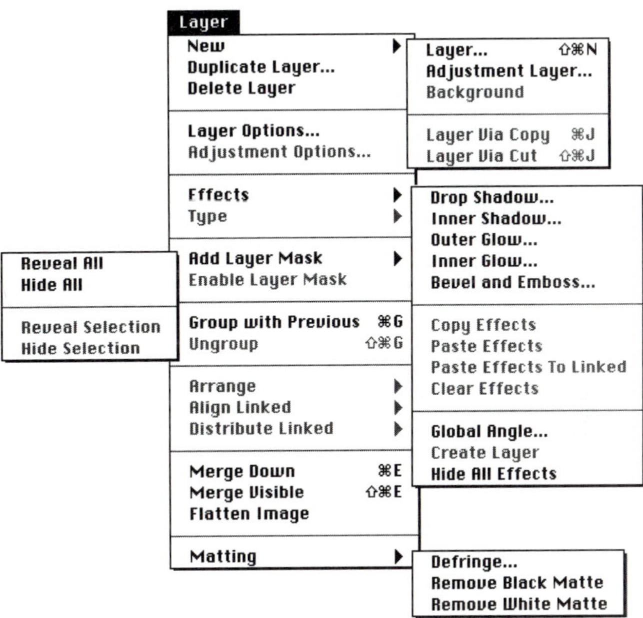

The Layer menu has commands for manipulating and adjusting layers, including Flip, Rotate, and Scale, and commands for combining multiple layers together into a single layer. A number of effects can also be accessed from this menu and applied to an entire layer (rather than just a single selection).

Select

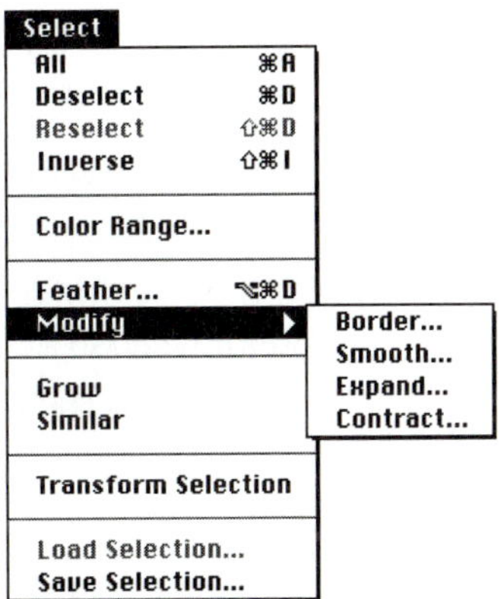

The Select menu is used to manipulate selections. From this menu you can perform tasks such as make a selection a little larger or a little smaller; turning on and off saved selections, called "channels;" or expanding selections based on pixel brightness values.

Filter

The Filter menu contains preprogrammed effects called filters, which can be used to enhance an image or apply special effects. Photoshop comes with a wide array of filters. Filters added to Photoshop, called Plug-Ins, will also be listed in this menu.

View

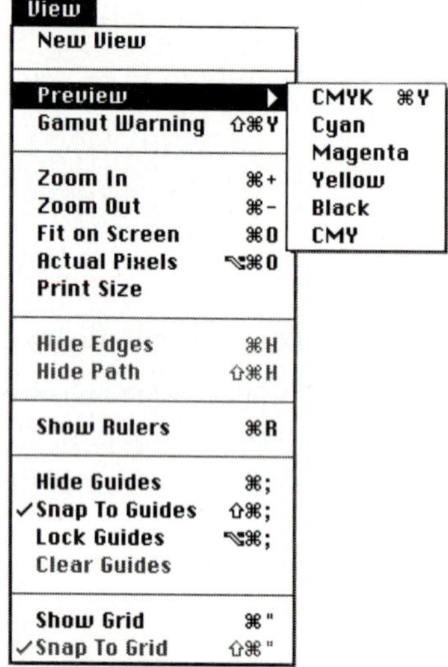

The View menu contains commands that change the on screen appearance of Photoshop. From this menu you can turn on and off grids, guides, rulers and selection borders, change the view percentage, change the way color is displayed on your monitor when working in different color modes, and define how Photoshop will interact with certain on screen elements, such as grids, guides, and rulers.

Window

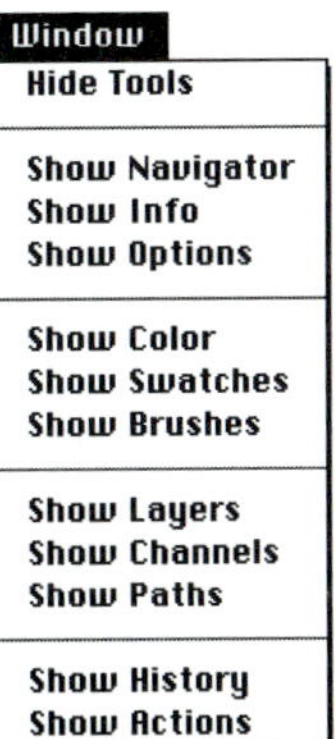

The Window menu allows you to individually turn palettes on and off.

Help

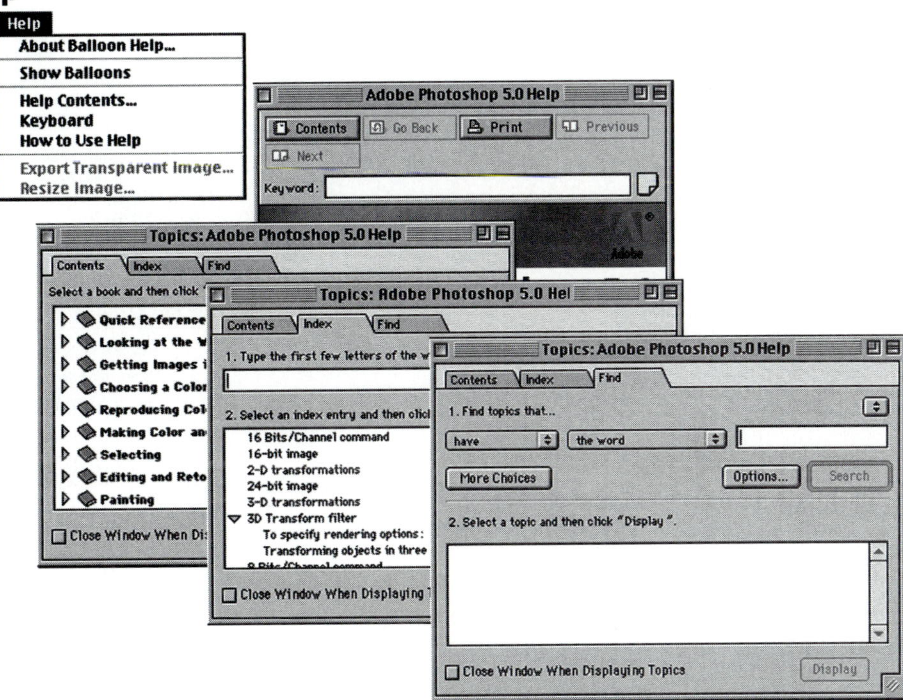

Macintosh Help Menus

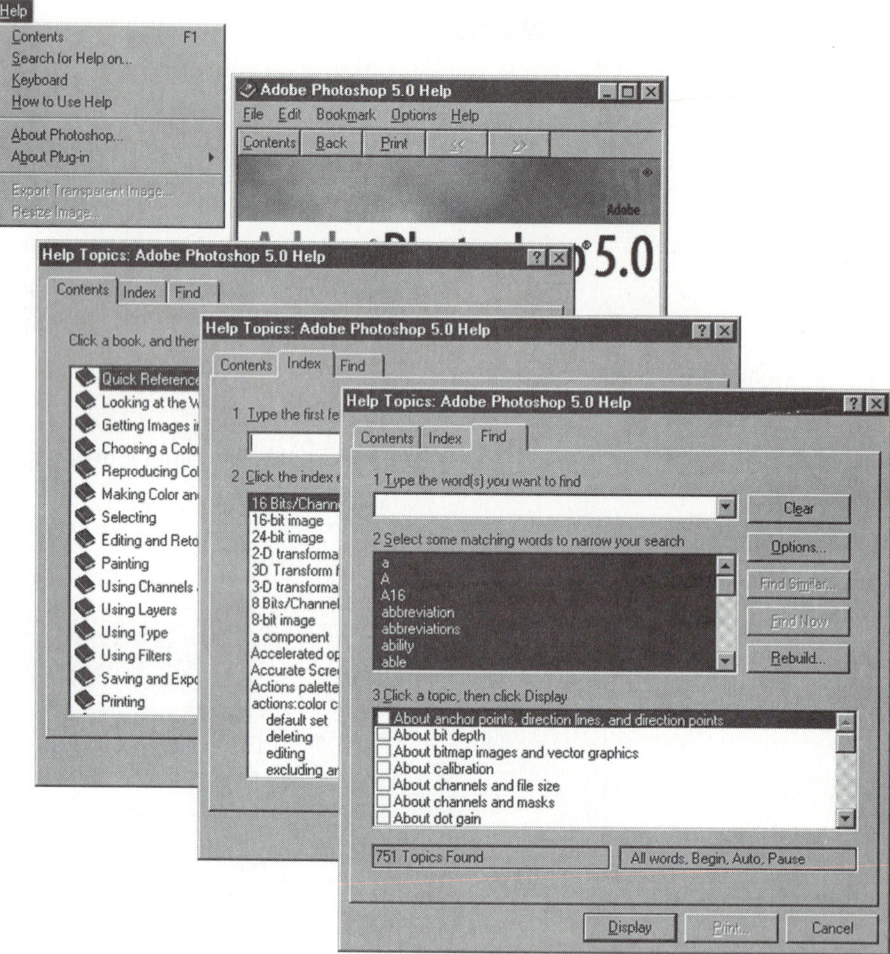

Windows Help Menus

The Help menu includes online, searchable information about Photoshop and Photoshop commands. There are slight differences between Windows and Macintosh platforms.

Navigating Photoshop

The Photoshop window offers feedback about your image:

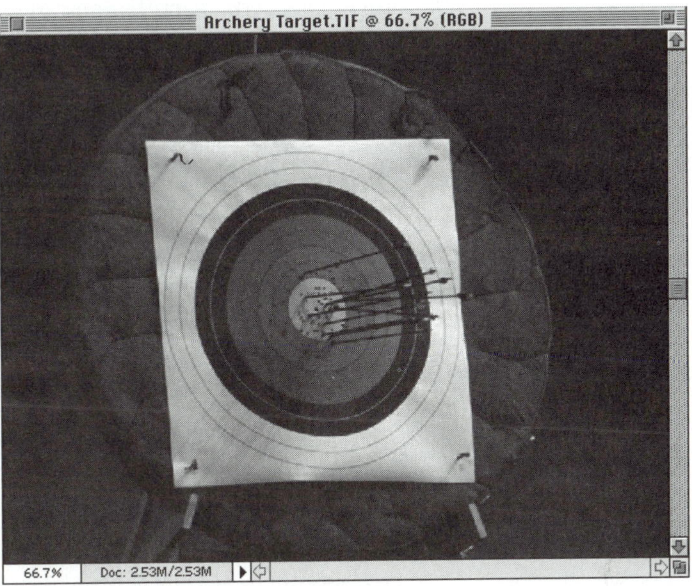

The reversed bar at the top of the document window contains the name of the image, and in parentheses, the color mode (i.e., RGB) and Zoom percentage for the current image. If there are layers in the document, the active layer is shown. You can move a window by clicking on the title bar and dragging.

When attempting to paint or create selections near the edge of an image, it is often easier if you either resize the image first, by dragging the lower right corner of the window, or press the "F" key to toggle through the Window View modes. Precise selections along edges are much easier if the image is moved slightly away from the window frame.

The status bar, which is located in the lower left corner of the window on the Macintosh, or the lower left corner of the application window for Windows machines, contains information on the amount of memory necessary to work on an image, the amount of memory currently available in the system, and the scale percentage. Clicking the arrow to the right of the status bar allows you to switch the display to show system efficiency, speed, buffer memory, or the current tool.

If you click and hold the file size on the status bar, a print preview box will appear which shows you where on the page your image will print at the current print settings. Command-clicking (Macintosh) or Control-clicking (Windows) the file size info shows you print tiling info; Option-clicking (Macintosh) or Alt-clicking (Windows) displays information about the size, resolution, and color depth of the image.

Keyboard Navigation

As you learn Photoshop, you'll find that there are many different ways to perform similar tasks. For example, you can select the Zoom tool either by clicking on it in the Toolbox or by typing "Z". In addition, you can zoom by:

- Selecting Zoom In or Zoom Out from the View menu.
- Pressing Command+ or Command- (Macintosh) or Control+ or Control- (Windows).
- Pressing Command-Spacebar or Option-Spacebar (Macintosh) or Control-Spacebar or Alt-Spacebar (Windows) to temporarily toggle the Zoom tool.
- Changing the View Percentage in the lower left corner of the window.
- Changing the scale factor on the Navigator palette.

Any of these options will work, but when starting out in Photoshop, it is easiest to concentrate on a few shortcuts that work for most purposes. You will gradually learn the rest of them as you become more familiar with the program.

In the above example, the two best choices are Command or Control, along with the Spacebar, and the Navigator palette.Why? Because when dialog boxes are open, the items in the toolbox are not available and the character sequence Command or Control, along with the Spacebar will activate the Zoom tool temporarily from nearly any dialog box, as well as when working on the document with another tool. The Navigator palette combines the functionality of both the Zoom and Hand tools in a visual format; it's just quicker and easier to get where you need to go.

We've already listed several keyboard commands in the material covered so far. Here are a few more useful keyboard combinations available in Photoshop:

- The Option key (Macintosh) or Alt key (Windows), when used with any painting tool, will temporarily toggle the Eyedropper tool.
- The Spacebar, when pressed, activates the Hand tool.
- The Shift key, when used while dragging any painting or effects tool, constricts tool movement to straight horizontal and vertical lines.
- The "D" key returns the swatch colors to their default, black-and-white.
- The "X" key swaps the foreground and background colors.
- Option-Delete (Macintosh) or Alt-Delete (Windows) fills a selection with the current foreground color.

- Pressing the Option key (Macintosh) or Alt key (Windows) while in a dialog box changes the Cancel button to Reset, allowing you to reset the dialog box to its default values without starting over.

Remember, nearly every tool in Photoshop has some keyboard equivalent. If you're not certain what the shortcut is for a particular tool, move the cursor over the appropriate tool in the Toolbox and hold it there for a few seconds. A help box will usually appear giving the name of the tool and its shortcut in parenthesis.

Notes:

CHAPTER 4

IMAGES: SIZES & RESOLUTION

CHAPTER OBJECTIVE:

To learn factors affecting the size of a Photoshop image, and the relationship to the image's complexity and output. In Chapter 4, you will:

- Learn the relationship between PPI and line screens, and understand that the quality of optical illusion depends on the line screen frequency.
- Learn how to resize an image with the Cropping tool and the Canvas Size command.
- Understand tones in relation to image quality, and how bit depth affects that quality.
- Learn the difference between Bit depth and Video Bit depth.

Images: Sizes and Resolutions

A "pixel" is the smallest element of an electronic image.

A silver grain is the smallest element of a conventional photographic image.

Adobe recommends that the amount of RAM and hard disk space be at least twice the size of your image. For some operations, Photoshop requires RAM equal to 3 to 5 times the size of your image. Surveys show that over 75% of all separations are smaller than 10 megabytes though, so don't design your systems for the absolute largest image you might ever work on. You can always farm out a few jobs to high-end vendors.

How big is a digital image?

There are several factors affecting the size of a Photoshop image:

- The physical dimensions of the image, usually measured in pixels, inches, or picas.
- The resolution of the image. The monitor can only display 72 pixels (or dots) per inch. A digital image that will be output on an imagesetter is normally between 266 and 350 pixels per inch. This is usually referred to as PPI (or less preferably, as DPI).
- Size in Bytes. This is the amount of disk space the image occupies on your hard drive. Some file formats can compress images on disk; as a result, these images may require less actual hard drive space to save them than RAM needed to edit them.
- The complexity of the image. At the time an image is going to be output, the only factors affecting the size are resolution, color depth, physical dimensions, and file format. While an image is being constructed, layers, which allow you to combine multiple images, and alpha channels, which allow you to mask portions of an image, can increase the amount of disk space required to store the image and the amount of RAM required to edit the image. However, the complexity of the image is more inclusive than file size alone. Masks and clipping paths may add substantially to the image's complexity and the time it takes to print.

The Relationship Between PPI and Line Screens

Many of you may already understand the concept of a line screen, or line ruling. This refers to the number (also called frequency) of halftone elements (usually dots) per inch used to create a halftone.

Since the offset process cannot print shades of ink (only solid areas of ink), a method was developed to represent the continuous gradation of tones in a photographic image. This is halftone screening, which represents areas of lighter tone by a field of small dots, and areas of darker tones by fields of larger dots. These variations in dot size create an optical illusion that fools the human eye into seeing a continuous tone image.

The large and small dots are generated on a constant spacing, called line screen frequency or line ruling. Common line rulings range from around 85 lines per inch (lpi) for newspapers and other very "porous" stock being run on high-speed web presses, all the way to 175 lpi (and higher) on glossy stock being run on slow, highly accurate sheet-fed presses. The finer the line screen frequency, the better the optical illusion.

Although this course doesn't delve too deeply into the science and art of image reproduction (and it is both science and art), there is one very important factor that must be discussed early on in your training: the relationship between the resolution of the image and the line ruling at which the image will be output.

It's easy to tell when a scan is at too low a resolution — you can often see the pixels when printing. Knowing when the resolution is too high can be a bit trickier. If you have an adequately powered system and your images are taking a very long time to load, save, or print, check the resolution of your file. You may need to reduce the resolution to work efficiently.

For every halftone dot you require, you must start out with somewhere from 1.5 to 3.5 pixels of image information. This is the quality factor (QF). Although certain output conditions might produce a totally acceptable halftone using only 1.5 pixels for each halftone dot, you should generally use a factor of two. The drawback to this approach is that each image is larger than it would be if you reduced the factor, and therefore it occupies more disk space and slows down the machine. The selection of quality factor depends in part upon the composition of the image. An image with sharp diagonal lines (like shingles or fabric) or subtle skin tones requires a higher QF, perhaps from 2.5 to 3.5; while a landscape or softened image may reproduce well with a QF of about 1.5.

Here are some of the common line screen rulings and the resolution at which an image should be scanned or created to produce a quality halftone:

Line Ruling	QF=1.5	QF=2	QF=3.5
85 (newsprint)	128 ppi	170 ppi	298 ppi
100	150 ppi	200 ppi	350 ppi
133 (common sheet-fed)	200 ppi	266 ppi	466 ppi
150 (the most common line screen)	225 ppi	300 ppi	525 ppi
175 (high-quality on gloss stock, sheet-fed)	263 ppi	350 ppi	613 ppi

These QF values assume that the image will not be significantly resized before the final output. If resizing is expected, an additional Sizing Factor (SF) must be applied to calculate the proper scanning resolution.

Resizing an Image

1. Navigate to the **SF-Intro Photoshop** folder and Open the file named **Oranges.TIF**. Choose Image>Image Size.

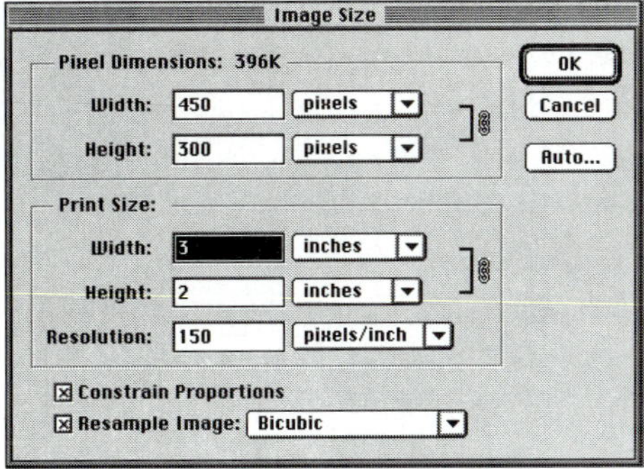

2. If necessary, change the print size units to inches. You can see in Print Size that the image is 150 ppi, and 3″ wide by 2″ high. This refers to the size that the image will default to when printed or imported into another application.
3. At the current Print Size, the image size on disk is 396 KB; the dimensions in pixels are calculated according to the print size. Notice the Pixel Dimensions section. In this area you can change the size of the image by specifying either pixel dimensions or a percentage.
4. Make certain that the Constrain Proportions box is checked. This way you only have to change one setting, for width or height; the other dimension will change proportionally.
5. Make certain that Resample Image is selected.
6. Change the Resolution to 300 and notice the size next to the Pixel Dimensions section. It jumps to 1.55 MB.
7. Click on Resample Image to deselect it. Notice that the Resolution stays at 300, but the dimensions are reduced to 1.5″ × 1″. The size of the file is reset to its original size, 396 KB.
8. Change the Resolution to 150. Observe the Width and Height dimension boxes. Type "200" in the Resolution box. Note how the dimensions change as you type different numbers into the Resolution box, but the New Size stays the same. Change the Resolution to 72; the dimensions change again.
9. Click the Resample Image checkbox to select it.
10. Resize the image to fit 8″ wide at 150 pixels per inch. Click OK.
11. Double-click the Zoom tool icon to make certain that you are viewing the image at 100%. Look closely at the detail in the oranges. You can see a noticeable degradation in image quality and sharpness:

Assuming that Resample Image is unchecked, if you reduce an image you increase its resolution; if you enlarge an image you decrease its resolution — not a good thing to do. Always scan (or create) your images at the size they will appear in the final printed piece. If design changes call for a major resizing, you must rescan — or worse, recreate the artwork. The best way to approach this problem is to scan or create the artwork at the maximum size at which it will be reproduced. Reducing an image is far less damaging than enlarging an image.

12. Select Filter>Sharpen>Sharpen More. Some of the detail comes back, but not all of it. Press Command-Z (Macintosh) or Control-Z (Windows) a few times to Undo and Redo the sharpening so that you can see the difference. If you do have to increase the size of an image to this degree (and you really can't re-scan), then be certain to check the details closely, and sharpen if necessary. Don't oversharpen the image, though — this causes color loss.

13. Leave the file open for the next exercise.

Sizing with the Cropping Tool

1. The Cropping tool allows you to size an entire image (or just a portion) and determine the resolution of the crop at the same time. Press "C" To change the Marquee to the Cropping tool, then double-click the Cropping tool in the Toolbox to bring up the Options palette. Make certain that the Fixed Target Size checkbox is checked.

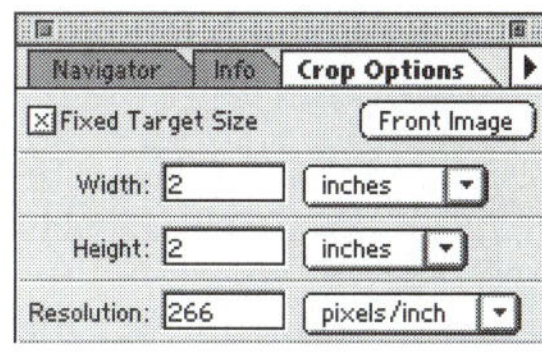

2. Set the Resolution to 266 ppi and Height and Width to 2 inches. Drag the Cropping tool across the image while depressing the mouse button. Whatever portion of the image you select will be automatically resized to the new size and resolution you selected in the Cropping tool Options palette.

3. You can adjust the size of your Cropping box by repositioning the handles at the corners of the box.

4. Move the marquee box to a new location by clicking inside of the box and dragging.

When you sharpen an image you're enhancing the edges, which makes the image appear more detailed. Don't get carried away with sharpening though — too much will create distracting halos and artifacts in the image. Use sharpening judiciously until you develop a feel for how it affects the final printed image.

5. Rotate the cropped area by clicking the mouse just outside the cropping box handles and dragging; the cursor will turn into a curved, double-headed arrow.

6. To finish the crop, press the Return or Enter key.
7. Go to Image>Image Size to check the size of the image you have cropped. It should now be 2″ Width/Height at 266 ppi. Click Cancel, then press Command-Z (Macintosh) or Control-Z (Windows) to Undo the cropping.
8. Though in our example we used the Cropping tool to resize the image, most of the time you will wish to crop without resizing or changing the resolution. Deselect the Fixed Target Size checkbox on the Cropping tool Options palette. This will allow you to choose an area to be cropped, but won't "rez" (change the resolution of) the file.
9. Select a new area and press Return or Enter.
10. Close the file without saving.

The Canvas Size Command

Another way to change the physical size of your image without changing the resolution is the Canvas Size command. Canvas Size adds a specified amount of blank image area around your document. The resulting empty space is set to the background color if you are working on the Background layer, or to transparent when working on any other layer. This is useful for framing an image, or when you need more room to build a composite of several images.

Using Canvas Size

1. Create a New document. Make it an RGB image, 2 inches square, at 75 ppi, with Contents set to White. Click OK.

2. Press "D" to reset the color swatches to default colors, then press "X" to swap (eXchange) the foreground and background colors so that the background color is black.

3. Select Image>Canvas Size. The Canvas Size command allows you to enlarge the available image area without resizing the existing image data. The size of the area can be set in the Width and Height boxes. The Placement grid specifies the position of the existing image data in relationship to the final document size.

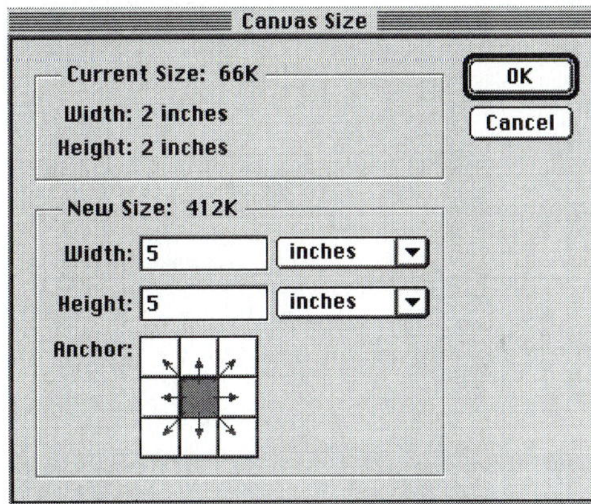

For example, if you click on the center of the grid (the default), the canvas is added equally all around the image; if you select the upper left square, the extra canvas is added to the right and bottom of the image.

4. Set the Width and Height for 5 inches. Click on the upper left square in the Placement grid. Click OK. Notice where the image was placed with the new canvas size. Press Command-Z (Macintosh) or Control-Z (Windows) to Undo.

When you order a scan from an outside vendor, specify the enlargement or reduction as well as the final resolution of the image. The formula is very simple:

Image Resolution = LPI x Quality Factor

When using the Canvas Size command, pay attention to the units you use. If you're working on a 300 ppi image there's a big difference between 15 inches and 15 pixels!

5. Go to Image>Canvas Size again. Set the Width and Height to 5 inches. Click on the right-center square in the Placement grid. Click OK. Notice where the image was placed. Press Command-Z (Macintosh) or Control-Z (Windows) to Undo.

6. Select Image>Canvas Size once more. Set the Width and Height to 5 inches. Let the Placement grid default to the center square. Click OK.

The image is surrounded by a black (background color) border which is equal on all sides. Be aware that if you add different amounts to the existing Height and Width, the top/bottom and the left/right borders will vary accordingly.

7. Close the file without saving.

You can use Canvas Size to crop an image exactly the same amount on all sides, leaving it perfectly centered. Simply enter values in the Canvas Size dialog box smaller than the current image size and click OK. When Photoshop warns you that you're about to clip the image, click OK again.

Understanding Tones

The more shades of gray or color an image can display, the more "photo-realistic" it will appear. The eye cannot distinguish between adjacent tone levels if the steps or gradations are fine enough. How fine do they have to be to fool the eye?

An image that contains 1 bit of tone data per pixel can only display black or white. Adding bit depth increases the number of tones that can be displayed by an image. While 8-bit images appear to be continuous in tone with 256 levels (2^8), a 7-bit image may look banded with only 128 tones.

1 bit per pixel

8 bit, 256 gray levels

Bit Depth

Bit depth refers to the number of information units, or bits, holding image information for a single pixel, representing the pixel's color and brightness values.

Image Bit Depth

1-bit (Bitmap Mode) — Only 1 bit per pixel: only black-and-white is possible, because the bit is either ON (white) or OFF (black).

4-bit (16-value Grayscale) — 16 variations (2^4) of gray.

8-bit (Grayscale/Indexed Color Mode) — One-byte bit depth allows 256 (2^8) grays, or 256 colors in a palette, typically either generated from the image or duplicated from the computer's system palette.

24-bit (RGB Color) — 8 bits each are used for the red, green, and blue channels. More than 16 million (2^{24}) colors are possible.

32-bit (CMYK Color) — 8 bits each may be stored for the cyan, magenta, yellow, and black channels, for a total of more than 4 billion (2^{32}) colors. In Photoshop, however, the CMYK primaries are specified in percentages from 0 to 100%, yielding approximately 100 million colors.

PHOTOSHOP FILE FORMATS AND COLOR MODES

	BITMAP	GRAYSCALE	DUOTONE	INDEXED	RGB	CMYK	LAB	MULTICHANNEL
BMP	yes	yes	no	yes	yes	no	no	no
EPS	yes	yes	yes	yes	yes	yes	yes	no
FILMSTRIP	no	no	no	no	no	no	no	no
GIF	yes	yes	no	yes	no	no	no	no
IFF	yes	yes	no	yes	yes	no	no	no
JPEG	no	yes	no	no	yes	yes	no	no
PCX	yes	yes	no	yes	yes	no	no	no
PICT	yes	yes	no	yes	yes	no	no	no
PICT RSC	yes	yes	no	yes	yes	no	no	no
PIXAR	no	yes	no	no	yes	no	no	no
PNG	yes	yes	no	yes	yes	no	no	no
RAW	no	yes	yes	yes	yes	yes	yes	yes
SCITEX CT	no	yes	no	no	yes	yes	no	no
TARGA	no	yes	no	yes	yes	no	no	no
TIFF	yes	yes	no	yes	yes	yes	yes	no

Video Bit Depth

Video bit depth is often discussed using the same language as image bit depth. Bit depth, in these instances, refers to something quite different. It represents the number of colors your video card can display on your monitor at one time.

8-bit — Allows a total of 256 colors or grays. This mode can accurately represent a grayscale image on the screen, but will show noticeable dithering and banding in RGB or CMYK images.

16-bit — The color information is divided into three channels. There are 32,768 colors (2^{15}), with one bit left over for a color overlay. This mode does a reasonable job of reproducing color on your monitor, but still does not display all of the information in the file.

24-bit — 24-bit or True Color video cards display both RGB and CMYK images with a great degree of accuracy. Eight bits each are used for the red, green, and blue channels.

32-bit — This bit depth is similar to a 24-bit card, but an extra byte is included for an Alpha channel. This extra channel is used for titles and special effects in video.

Chapter 5

Basic Selection Techniques

Chapter Objective:

To build an understanding and learn how to make accurate selections of target pixels, one of the most important skills you can develop. In Chapter 5, you will:

- Become familiar with the basic selection tools: the marquee tools, lasso tools, Freehand lasso tool, Polygon lasso tool, Magnetic Lasso tool, and other selection commands.
- Learn how to use the Rectangular Marquee.
- Learn how to move and manipulate selections.
- Learn how to flip and rotate selections.
- Learn how to copy and paste selections.
- Learn how to fill and stroke selection areas.
- Learn about Mirrored Tiles and how to create them.
- Learn about the Elliptical Marquee.
- Learn the importance of Adding or Removing portions of a selection.
- Learn how to create a Type Mask.
- Be introduced to Layers.

In general, Photoshop functions can be applied globally to the entire image, or locally to a selected portion of the image.

The terms "select" or "selection" are also used when discussing which button options in dialog boxes and menu options to choose. In the present context, selection refers to any technique that will allow subsequent modification of parts of an image while protecting the rest of the image from any change.

Basic Selection Techniques

Photoshop has many tools that can be used to modify the entire image at once. A blur filter can be applied to the whole picture; or the intensity of a yellow cast can be reduced globally using the curves control. (We will learn more about these functions in another chapter.) But in many cases the edit or modification must be applied to a selected portion of the image pixels. These target pixels must be selected first.

If you wish to change a model's sweater from red to blue, you would first make a careful selection of the pixels making up the sweater portion of the image; and then change the hue (color) of those selected pixels only. In another example, your photograph of the model home was taken on an overcast day. No problem: Just select the pixels making up the sky and Paste Into with a bright, blue, sunny sky image.

Frequently, you will create a *silhouette* of an object that appears against a background. By selecting the background pixels, they can be deleted to some uniform shade, often white.

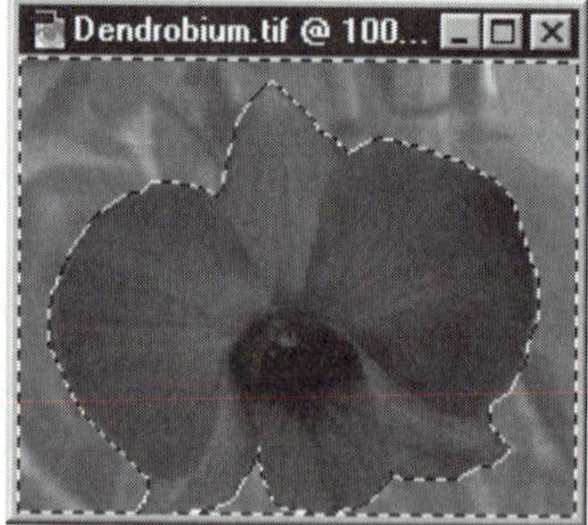

Without a doubt, one of the most important Photoshop skills you can develop is the ability to make accurate selections. If you understand selections and how they work, you will be on your way to mastering the application of many Photoshop functions.

The airbrush artist uses a masking material called "frisket" to cover those areas of the artwork that are not to be painted. Photoshop uses electronic friskets. For an area of the page to be painted or affected in any way, it must first be "selected." The electronic frisket is the unselected area of the image; these pixels are temporarily protected from change.

Visually, the selected area is highlighted by a blinking marquee, sometimes called "marching ants." When you apply paint tools, filters, or other controls, they'll change only the selected area. If we use Photoshop's airbrush tool, electronic "paint" is sprayed only into the selection.

With Photoshop's Zoom tool, you can enlarge the display of the image to inspect and select areas as small as a single pixel. Pixels, or picture elements, are the smallest unit of selection in a digital image.

The images we use in this course are not high resolution because we have no way of knowing how powerful your system might be; and sometimes this can make it difficult to create an accurate selection. In the real world you will use higher resolution images, making it much easier to build a precise selection.

Anti-aliasing allows edge pixels to assume intermediate values between the object and background tone levels. Otherwise, the selection may display a hard edge revealing the jagged, stair-stepped pixels in any painted diagonal edges. Except when working on a black-and-white bitmap image, anti-aliasing should always be used with painting and selection tools.

Selections can be accomplished using selection tools or by selectively activating layers that contain individual components of the image in Photoshop. There are many different ways to use the selection tools on specific pixels in an image; they fall into two categories: manual selection methods, and automated selection methods. First, we'll explore several manual methods.

Basic Selection Tools

Photoshop provides a variety of selection tools. Each selects portions of an image, but each is best suited to a different selection situation.

For all of Photoshop's selection tools:

- Each selection tool's Options palette has a checkbox for anti-aliasing (though it is unselectable when using the Rectangular Marquee, as this tool needs no anti-aliasing). This should usually be checked.

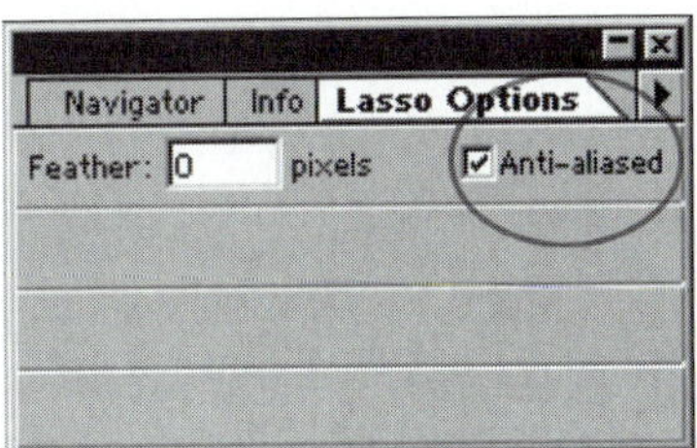

- When a selection exists, pressing Shift *before* making another selection will *add* the new selection to the current selection. If the selections overlap, they will merge into a single selection. Note that multiple selections can be discontinuous.
- Pressing the Option key (Macintosh) or Alt key (Windows) *before* beginning a selection will *subtract from* an existing selection.

The Marquee Tools

There are four Marquee Selection tools, available by clicking and dragging from the first tool in the upper left corner of the Toolbox. (The last tool in the flyout is the Cropping tool.)

The Rectangular Marquee tool is suited for selecting horizontally- or vertically-oriented areas with 90-degree corners; the Elliptical Marquee tool is ideal for selecting elliptical areas. A selection is applied by clicking and dragging the cursor from the upper left corner of the area to be selected to the lower right corner. When the mouse button is released, a marquee outline of "marching ants" remains.

Selections can be constrained to eqilateral shapes (squares, circles) by holding the Shift key while dragging the Selection tool. However, if you press Shift before you drag, you will add this selection to any active selection.

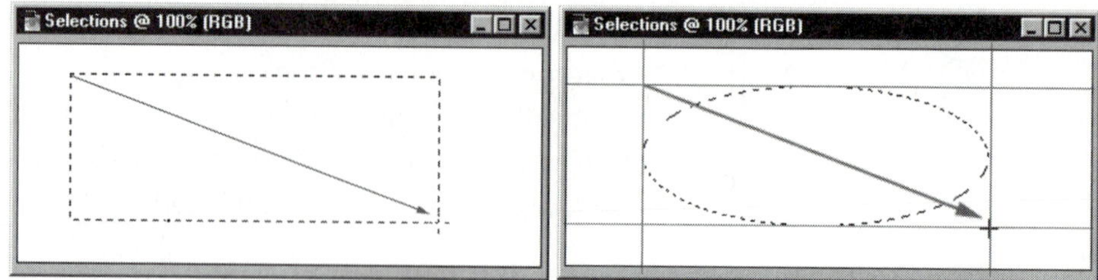

By pressing the Shift key after you start to drag the cursor diagonally, the shape of the selection is constrained to a square when using the Rectangular Marquee, or to a circle if using the Elliptical Marquee.

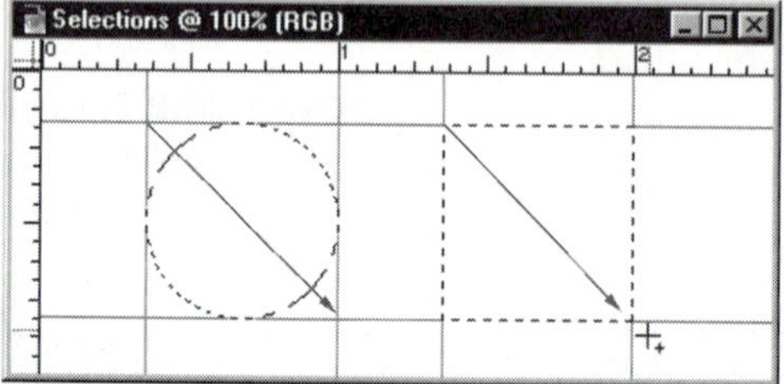

The two other Marquee tools allow you to select a single row or column of pixels. These tools are especially useful for cleaning up the edges of a rectangular image, such as a dialog box screen shot.

The Lasso Tools

The Lasso tool can be used to create a "U" shaped selection so that when the mouse button is released, the selection marquee closes between the ends of the "U." If an irregular selection is drawn, the marquee could cut through the desired selection instead of around it unless the end is drawn close to the beginning of the selection drawing.

Not all selections are rectangular or elliptical. To handle other shapes the three Lasso tools can be used. Rather than a restricted rectangular or elliptical shape, the Lasso tools offer a free-form, "follow-the-cursor-anywhere" mode. When you release the mouse button, the selection joins the last point to the first point enclosing the selection.

Freehand Lasso tool

If you select the Lasso tool and drag the cursor across the page, the freehand line will trail the cursor in any direction you move (below, left). When the mouse button is released, the line becomes a selection marquee (below, right).

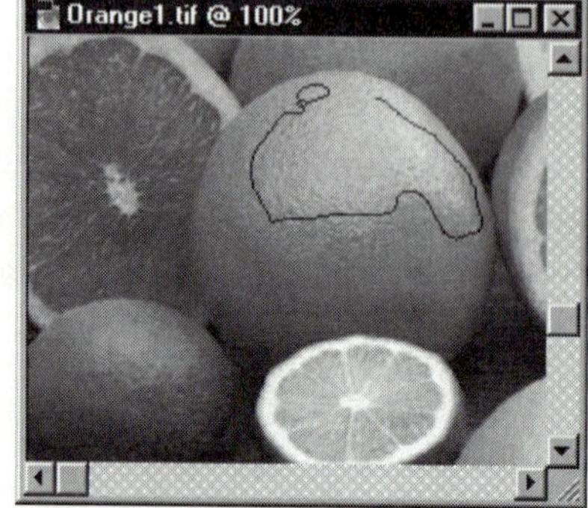

Looking closely at this (or any) selection shows how it follows pixel boundaries.

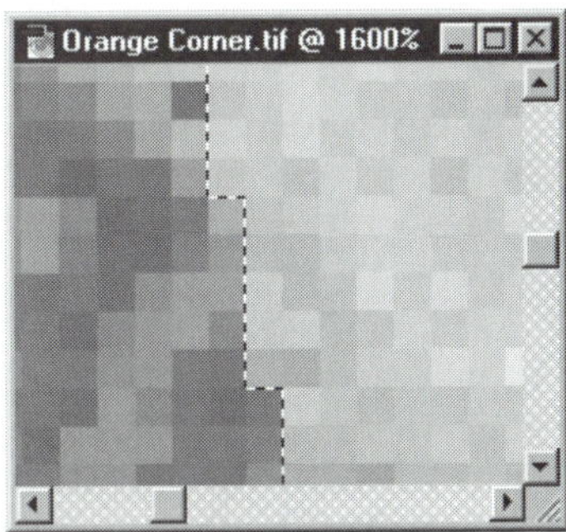

By holding down the Option Key (Macintosh) or Alt key (Windows) after starting a selection with either lasso tool, you can access freehand lines with the Polygon Lasso, or straight lines with the Lasso tool.

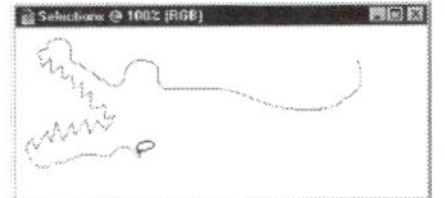

Polygon Lasso Tool

The Polygon Lasso allows you to click from point to point in a series of straight line segments. The dashed line will stretch like a rubber band, allowing straight-edged selections. To close the polygon, either double-click or click on the starting point of the selection.

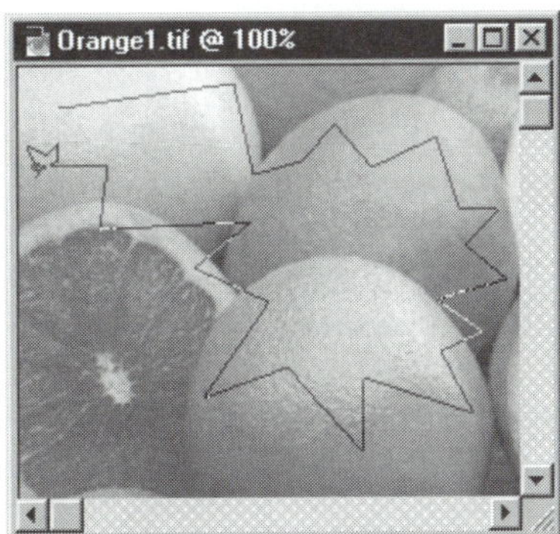

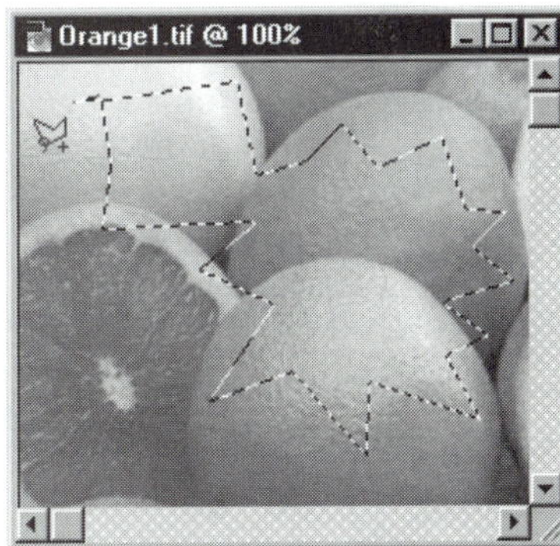

Magnetic Lasso Tool

Trying to accurately outline a selection with the Lasso tool can be a tedious process, especially if you are using a mouse instead of a graphic tablet and stylus. It's sort of like drawing with a bar of soap. The Magnetic Lasso tool's built-in intelligence may be at least a partial solution to reducing your selection stress.

Tool sensitivity can be adjusted to individual image conditions. The Lasso Width specifies the tool's sensitivity to color change. To make a precise edge between two relatively subtle shades, increase Width to the maximum of 40.

The Lasso Frequency determines the number of anchor points placed along the selection edge. Higher numbers increase the complexity of the selection.

From the View Menu, selecting Hide Edges/Show Edges (Command/Control-H) removes the "marching ants" from the monitor without deselecting them. This is useful for more clearly viewing the effect the changes made.

Other Selection Commands

The Select Menu contains commands for working with selections. Here are just a few of the commands available:

- Select All (Macintosh: Command-A or Windows: Control-A) — The Select>All command encloses the entire image in a selection marquee.

- Deselect (Command-D or Control-D) — The Select>None or Deselect command should only be used once you have finished your manipulations on the selection. It releases the current selection.
- Inverse — Select>Inverse (Command-Shift-I or Control-Shift-I) switches the selection area from what is selected to what is not selected; in other words, what *was* selected is now *deselected*. This tool allows you to work on foreground features without affecting the background.

Note that in Photoshop, the Select All command is in the Select menu; not in the Edit menu as found in many other applications.

Using the Rectangular Marquee

1. Open the file **Oranges.TIF** from the **SF-Intro Photoshop** folder.

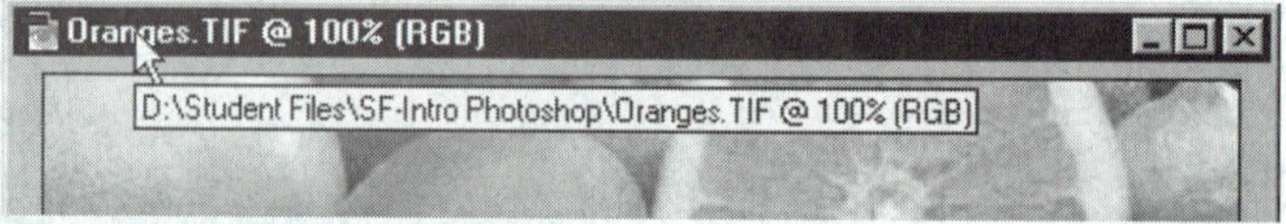

2. Press the "F" key once. The image (which opened into its own window) will center in the screen with a gray background.
3. Click the Rectangular Marquee tool on the Toolbox flyout or press "M" for *marquee*. If pressing "M" produces an Elliptical Marquee tool, either change it with the mouse on the tool flyout or press Shift-M.
4. Drag the tool diagonally over the image to form a rectangle; release the mouse button. A selection rectangle of "marching ants" appears.

The "F" key rotates through 3 versions of viewing the current image windows: as overlapping windows, as a single active image with neutral gray surround (good for color correcting), or with the active image on a black surround.

5. Sometimes you'll need a square rather than a rectangle. Press Command-D (Macintosh) or Control-D (Windows) to deselect. Draw another rectangular selection, but this time, hold down the Shift key while making the selection. The shape is constrained to a square. Remember not to start holding the Shift key before making the selection, because that command is used to add to a selection.
6. Keep the image open and the selection intact for the next exercise.

Moving and Manipulating Selections

1. With the Rectangular Marquee tool still selected, hold the mouse pointer inside the selected area. The pointer turns into a hollow arrow with a tiny marquee next to it; this is the Selection pointer. Click and drag to move the selection border without moving the selection contents.

2. Press the Command key (Macintosh) or Control key (Windows) and hold the pointer over the selection. The pointer turns into a solid arrow with a pair of scissors. This is the Move Selection pointer. Move the selection around the image by positioning the mouse pointer inside of the selection and clicking and dragging. Notice that when you release the mouse button, the area where the selection used to be is filled with the current background color.

The History palette can be used to restore the image to an earlier state.

3. Press Command-Z (Macintosh) or Control-Z (Windows) to Undo the move and return the selection to its original location.

4. Press Command/Control-J to create a New Layer via Copy. A copy of the selected area is added to the Layers palette and the selection border disappears.

Press the Command or Control key and click-drag the mouse where the selection border used to be. This time the image area underneath is untouched.

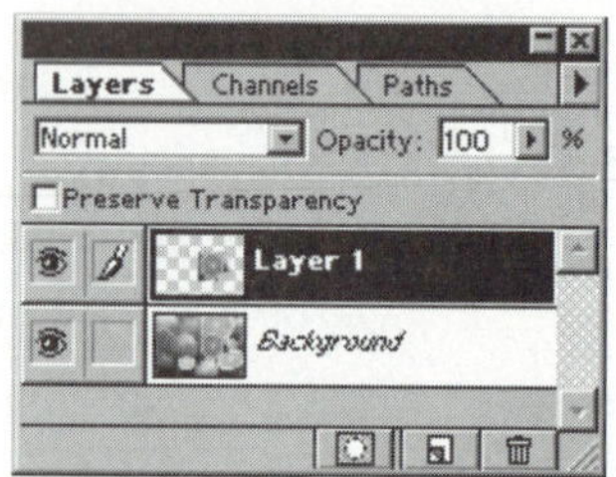

5. Press Command-E (Macintosh) or Control-E (Windows) to merge Layer 1 back into the *Background* layer. Note that the area of the image that was copied to Layer 1 has now replaced the corresponding area in the Background layer.

6. Make a new selection, then hold down the Shift key and make another selection. Instead of constraining your selection to a square, a *second* rectangle is activated in addition to the first selection. The Shift key *adds to* a selection when another selection already exists within the image.

7. Begin another selection, but this time press the Shift key *after* you begin your selection. The first selection disappears and another square is drawn.

8. Suppose you want to *add* a square to an existing selection? Press the Shift key, then start a new selection; release and press the Shift key again while drawing the selection. The first Shift *adds to* the selection; the second *constrains* the selection.

9. Add another rectangle to the current selection (by pressing Shift before beginning the selection); this time, make certain that your new selection overlaps part of the existing marquee border. The two selections are merged into one.

10. Now press the Option key (Macintosh) or Alt key (Windows), and draw a selection which overlaps one corner of your existing selection. When you release the mouse button, the part of the selection is "deselected" — the Option or Alt key *subtracts from* an existing selection.

11. Leave the image open for the next exercise.

Flipping and Rotating Selections

1. Press Command-D (Macintosh) or Control-D (Windows) to deselect.
2. Make a new selection.
3. Choose Transform from the Edit menu and examine the options there. The Rotate 180°, Rotate 90° CW (clockwise) and Rotate 90° CCW (counterclockwise) commands rotate the current selection in the direction indicated.

4. Select Rotate 90° CW; the selection is rotated to the right.
5. Select Edit>Transform>Numeric. This command allows you to enter the specific number of degrees in 1/10° increments. It works on either a selection or the entire image.
6. In the Rotate section, enter 10° in the Angle field. Then click OK.

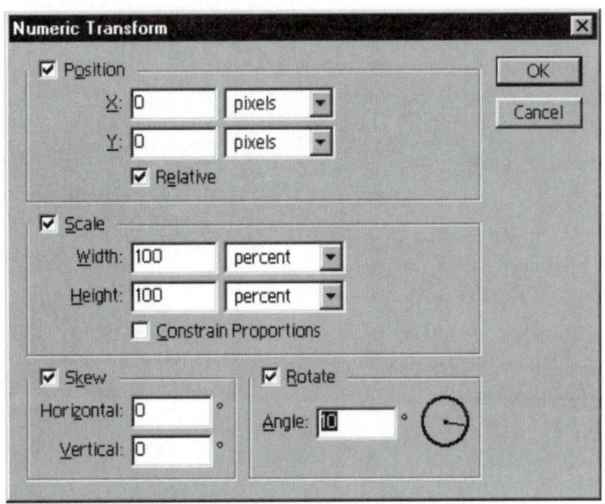

7. Select Edit>Transform>Rotate. Handles are added to your selection allowing you to rotate it dynamically.

Note that you can (and should) rotate a selection, then scale a selection by pressing the Return key after you have finished both commands, rather than after each command. This keeps the manipulated selection from becoming too distorted as the image manipulations are calculated only once.

8. Position the pointer at one of the handles; click and drag the corner to rotate your selection. When you're satisfied, press the Return or Enter key to finish the rotation.

9. Another useful pair of commands from the Edit>Transform submenu are Flip Vertical and Flip Horizontal. They create a mirror image of the selection; the effect is similar to flipping a transparency over from top to bottom or side to side. Select Edit>Transform>Flip Horizontal to see the effect.

10. Select Edit>Transform>Scale. Again, handles are added to the selection. Dragging a handle resizes the selection; pressing the Shift key while dragging constrains the scaling so that the height/width aspect ratio remains constant. Press the Return key to finish the scaling.

11. Keep the image open for the next exercise.

Copying and Pasting Selections

1. Selections can be copied and pasted using the standard Edit menu Copy and Paste features — Command-C and Command-V (Macintosh) or Control-C and Control-V (Windows). Make a new selection, then Copy the selection to the clipboard.

2. Now Paste your selection. It looks as though the selection marquee simply disappeared! Actually, a copy was pasted, but it is on a new layer, lying directly on top of your current selection. Move the selection with the Move tool and you will find that it behaves as though you had pressed Command-J (Macintosh) or Control-J (Windows) to create a New Layer Via Copy of the selection.

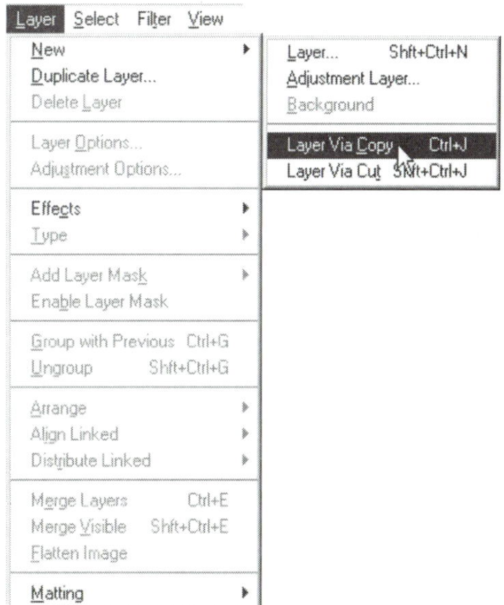

3. Make certain that Layer 1 is selected by clicking its name on the Layers palette. Click the trash can at the bottom of the palette. When a dialog box appears, click Yes to delete the layer. Paste the image again; the selection is pasted to a new layer again, but this time it is not over its original position on the image.

4. Click off the eye next to the Background layer. Notice that the pasted image is positioned precisely in the center of the image window. Click the empty box to the far left of the Background layer to turn the layer view back on. Click on Layer 1; click the trash can, then Yes to delete the layer; or simply drag Layer 1 to the Trashcan icon.

5. Create a new selection, and Cut by pressing Command-X (Macintosh) or Control-X (Windows). The selected area is deleted from the image and the selection is filled with the current background color. Notice that the marquee border is deselected, as if you'd pressed Command-D (Macintosh) or Control-D (Windows).

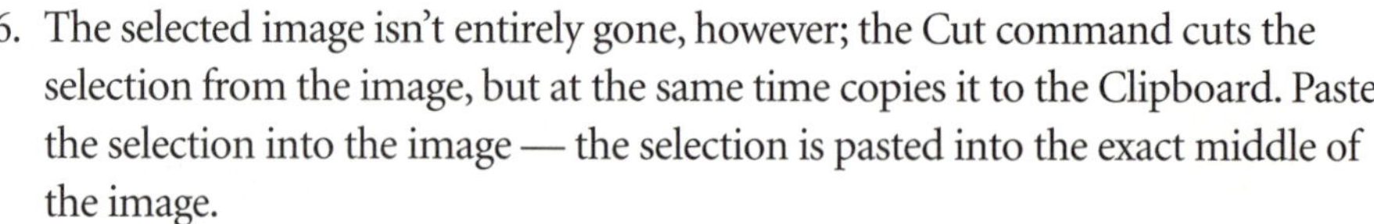

6. The selected image isn't entirely gone, however; the Cut command cuts the selection from the image, but at the same time copies it to the Clipboard. Paste the selection into the image — the selection is pasted into the exact middle of the image.
7. Copied or cut selections take up valuable RAM. Select Edit>Purge>Clipboard to clear the clipboard of image data and release that memory for other functions.
8. Keep the **Oranges.TIF** image open for the next exercise.

Filling and Stroking Selection Areas

1. Create a new selection.
2. Activate the Swatches palette and click on a color to change the foreground color. Pick a vivid color.
3. Option-click (Macintosh) or Alt-click (Windows) another color in the Swatches palette to change the background color.
4. The Edit>Fill command floods the selected area with the current Foreground or Background color, Black, White, a predefined pattern, or image data from your most recent save.

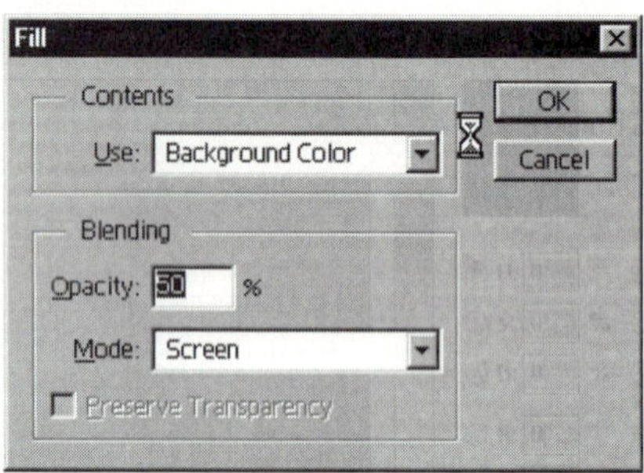

5. Select Background Color from the pull-down list in the Contents>Use section of the dialog box.
6. Set Opacity to 50% and set the Blending Mode to Screen. Click OK.

7. The Stroke command adds an outline to a selection. Select Edit>Stroke to display the Stroke dialog box.

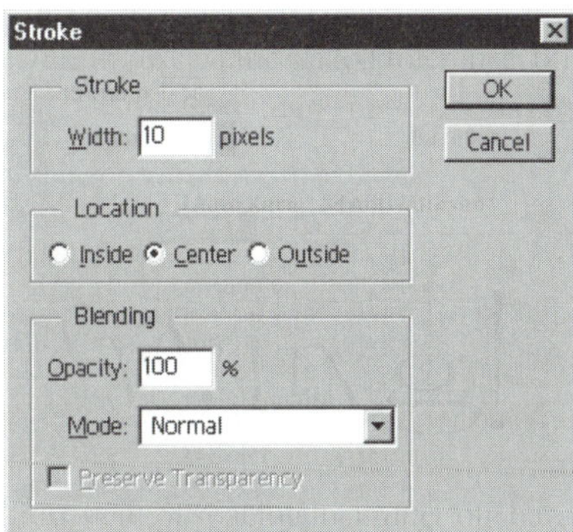

When you choose the Center option, and the Width is set to an odd number of pixels, the larger number of pixels (i.e., 2 pixels, in the case of a 3-pixel stroke) are placed inside the selection border, because Photoshop can't divide a pixel in half.

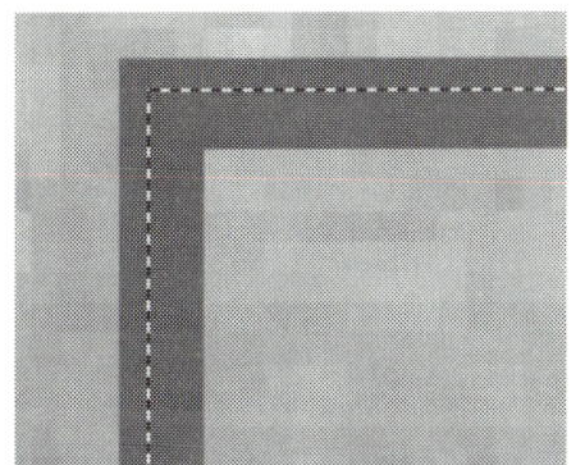

8. Enter "10" for Width to create a stroke ten pixels wide with your chosen foreground color.
9. You can choose to create the stroke Inside the selection, Outside the selection, or Center the stroke on the selection border, leaving half of the stroke inside of the selection and half of it outside. Click the Center option.
10. Leave Blending set to Opacity 100% and Mode Normal; click OK.
11. Notice that the stroke is the same width inside and outside the marquee, because 10 is an even number. If it were an odd number it would be thicker inside the marquee.
12. Close the file without saving.

Mirrored Tiles

Let's put some of your new skills to the test! Photoshop has the ability to create repeating tiles, called patterns, using the Edit>Define Pattern command. This command works only on a square or rectangular selection. Essentially, the selection is copied into a special buffer that may then be used to fill a selection or an entire image with the new pattern.

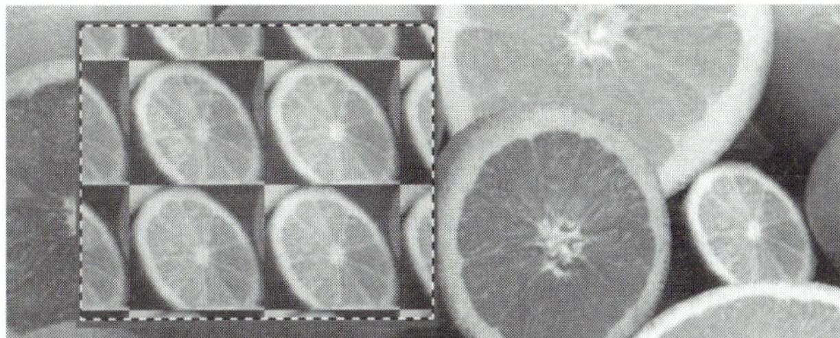

The problem with defining a pattern tile from an image is that the square edges of the image are quite evident. Instead of creating a nice, seamless background, you've simply repeated a smaller image across a larger one. Mirrored tiles solve this problem — the edges of the tile, when placed side by side, match perfectly.

Creating a Mirrored Pattern Tile

1. Open the **Oranges.TIF** file from the **SF-Intro Photoshop** folder.
2. Press the "D" key to ensure that the swatches are set to default colors.
3. Double-click on the Rectangular Marquee tool to display the Marquee Options palette. Set Style to Fixed Size. Enter "50" pixels for both Height and Width.

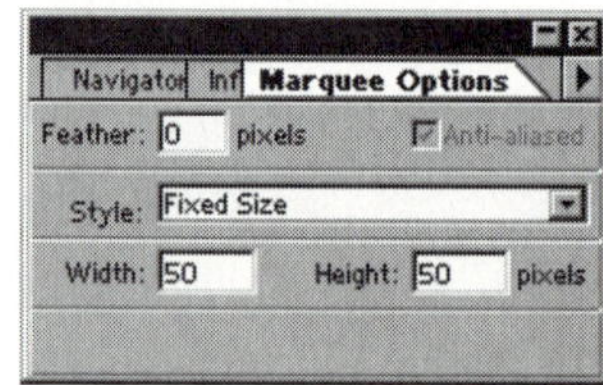

4. When you click on the image, a 50 x 50 marquee appears, which may be dragged to any part of the image. Select a visually interesting area with a lot of converging edges, such as the place where the four pieces of citrus fruit meet in the upper left corner of the image.

5. Select Image>Crop to crop the image at your selection border. Reset the Marquee tool Style back to Normal.
6. Choose Image>Canvas Size. Set the canvas size to 100 pixels by 100 pixels — exactly four times the current selection area — and click on the upper left square of the Placement grid. Click OK. You now have an image in the upper left corner surrounded by white:

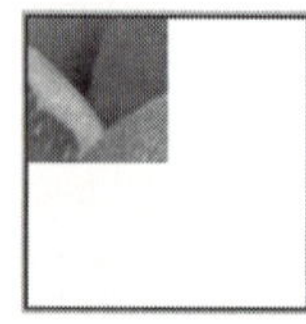

7. Press Command-A (Macintosh) or Control-A (Windows) to select the entire image, then Command-J (Macintosh) or Control-J (Windows) to create a New Layer Via Copy. Select Edit>Transform>Flip Horizontal.
8. Activate the Layers palette. The pull-down list in the upper left corner of the palette specifies the blending mode. Change this setting from Normal to Darken.

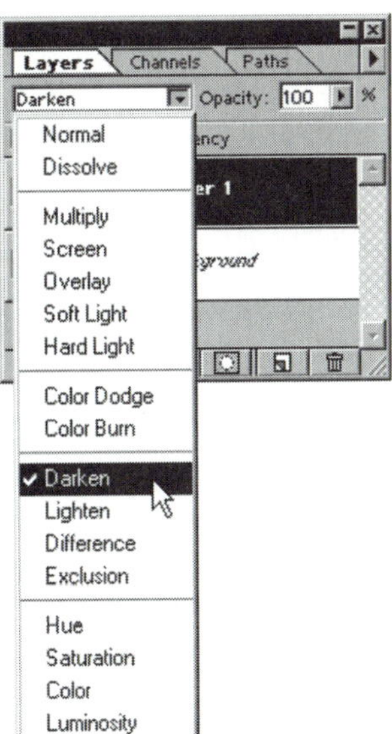

The Darken blending mode essentially turns the white transparent, as white can't darken any other color. You now have a mirrored copy of the image perfectly matched to the original.

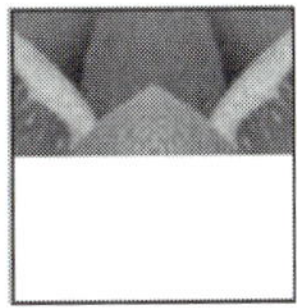

9. Press Command-E (Macintosh) or Control-E (Windows) to merge the layers back together. Press Command/Control-A to select all of the image, then press Command/Control-J to create a Layer Via Copy.
10. Choose Edit>Transform>Flip Vertical. Again, change the blending mode on the Layers palette from Normal to Darken. You've just created your first seamless tile.
11. Press Command/Control-E to merge the layers again.

12. Select>All once again, then choose Define Pattern from the Edit menu.
13. Close the pattern document; you won't need it anymore. Create a New document; this time set the dimension to 500 pixels by 500 pixels and click OK.
14. From the Edit Menu select the Fill command. The Fill dialog box appears.
15. In the Contents section, change Use to Pattern; leave the Blending Opacity at 100% and the Blending Mode at Normal. Click OK. The tiles match seamlessly!

Mirrored tiles are produced by a process called "tessellation." Variations on tessellation can create tiles of familiar-shaped elements that interlock perfectly. The most famous tessellated tiles were created by the Dutch artist M.C. Escher. You have likely see one of his most recognizable pieces depicting interlocking lizard tiles.

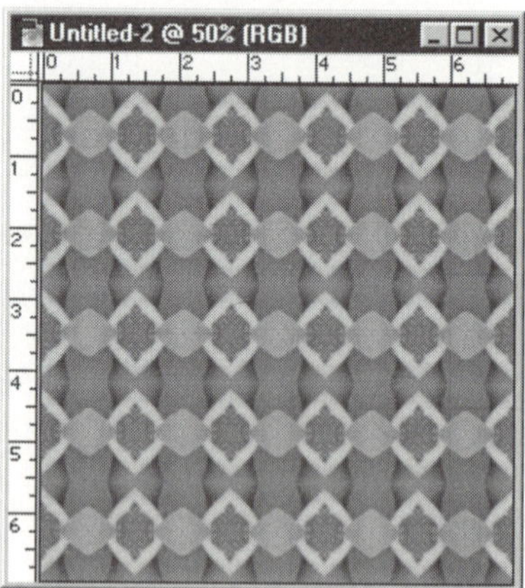

16. Rotate the filled image 90 degrees clockwise by selecting Image>Rotate Canvas>90° CW.
17. Fill with the pattern again, only this time change the Blending Mode in the Fill dialog box from Normal to Difference.

18. You can use this technique to create unique backgrounds, creating textures for textural backgrounds from almost any source. For a more subdued background, change the Opacity setting to 50% before doing the fill. Experiment with different blending modes. Create a background about 50% larger than you need and rotate 45 degrees after the Difference fill to change the diagonal of the pattern, then crop out the excess image data. The possibilities are literally endless. Close the file without saving.

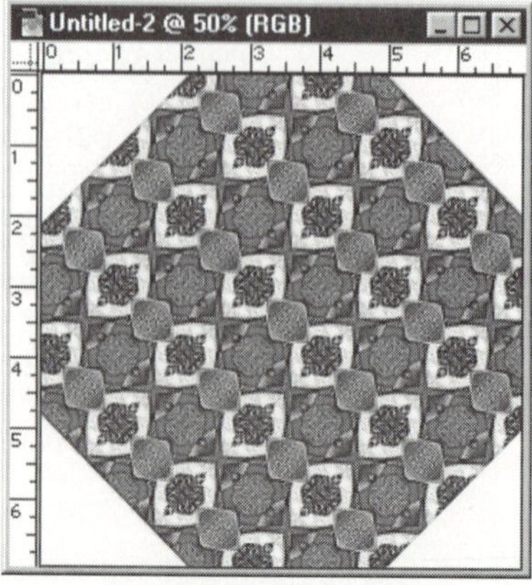

The Elliptical Marquee

Though the Elliptical Marquee is used mainly for special effects, or for images created directly in Photoshop, it can sometimes be useful for creating the *initial* selection of a round object, such as a sliced orange.

Using the Elliptical Marquee

1. Open the file **Oranges.TIF**, located in the **SF-Intro Photoshop** folder.
2. Press the "F" key once. The image window background will expand to occupy the entire screen.
3. Select the Magnifying Glass (the Zoom tool) or simply press "Z". Click and drag the tool over the sliced orange located in the middle of the image, toward the right hand side.
4. With the Rulers displayed (Command/Control-R), drag guides from the top and side rulers to exactly frame the elliptical orange slice. Use the intersections of the guides to start and end the drawing of the Elliptical Marquee. This technique can be used for very accurate placement of the selection marquee.
5. Press the "M" key to activate the Marquee tool. Press Shift-M until the Shape on the Marquee Options palette is set to Elliptical.

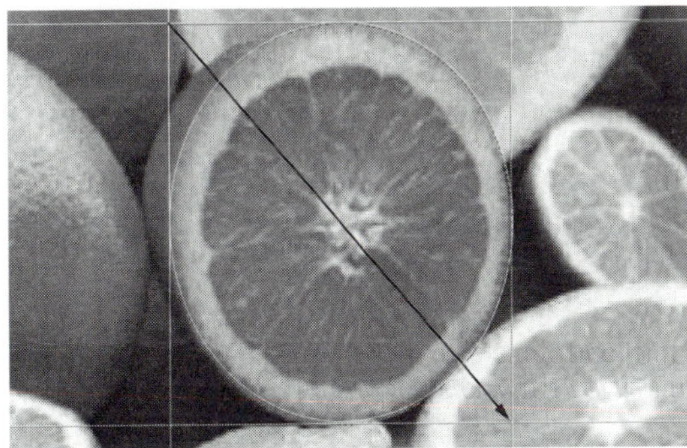

6. If the elliptical marquee is not centered properly on the orange, use the direction arrows to nudge the selection border into place.

   It is likely that you still don't have a *perfect* fit because the orange slice is not a perfect ellipse. Later in this section we'll learn to add and subtract pixels from a selection using the Lasso tool. While elliptical selections around natural objects are rarely acceptable on their own, it's a great way to make quick initial selections of round objects.

7. Leave the file open for the next exercise.

Hold down the Option key (Macintosh) or Alt key (Windows) and start your selection as close to the center of the orange as you can. Pressing the Option/Alt key draws an ellipse or rectangle from the center rather than from corner to corner.

Use the Regular Lasso tool by holding the mouse button as you draw the selection.

Use the Polygon Lasso tool by alternately holding the mouse button to draw freehand, and releasing to draw straight line segments.

Use the Magnetic Lasso tool by drawing freehand along an edge, clicking occassionally to position additional anchor points along the selection path.

Using the Lasso

1. Press Command-D (Macintosh) or Control-D (Windows) to deselect the orange; double-click the Hand tool to make the image fill the screen.
2. Select the Zoom tool again (or press Command/Control-Spacebar) and Zoom in on the three oranges in the center of the image.
3. Select the Magnetic Lasso tool from the Toolbox or press "L" for lasso (it doesn't have to be upper case — the key works with both upper and lower case). Use Shift-L to cycle through the three different lasso tools.
4. To the best of your ability, use the Magnetic Lasso tool to outline the three oranges. Don't release the mouse button until you've surrounded all three pieces of fruit. Don't worry if your selection isn't perfect; we'll refine it later.

5. Analyze the selection by zooming in and out with the magnifying glass. You will notice areas of the fruit that *should* be in the selection area (but aren't) and others that *shouldn't* be in the selection area (but are). To perfect this selection, you will learn a technique that will *add to* or *subtract from* portions of the selection area. Keep the file open and the selection active for the next exercise.

Adding or Removing Portions of a Selection

Adding and removing portions of a selection offer the only way to actually complete selections. Almost without exception, selections must be fine-tuned.

We learned the basics of this technique when reviewing options for the Rectangular Marquee. As we pointed out, however, most selections aren't rectangular. Here we'll learn how to refine "real-world" selections.

To enclose the top portion of the image with the lasso tool, drag above and outside of the upper corners of the image. The selection will shrink down to the borders of the image.

Refining Your Selections

1. Zoom in a little closer to the selection border. Make certain that the Lasso tool is still selected.
2. Locate areas that should be inside of your selection marquee. To add to your selection, start inside the selection, hold down the Shift key and carefully outline the areas you need to add, swinging back into the selection area to complete the additional selection. It is often easier to work from the top down, adding small amounts as you go. Working in small sections ensures that if you slip, you will only have to undo or redo a small amount of work.

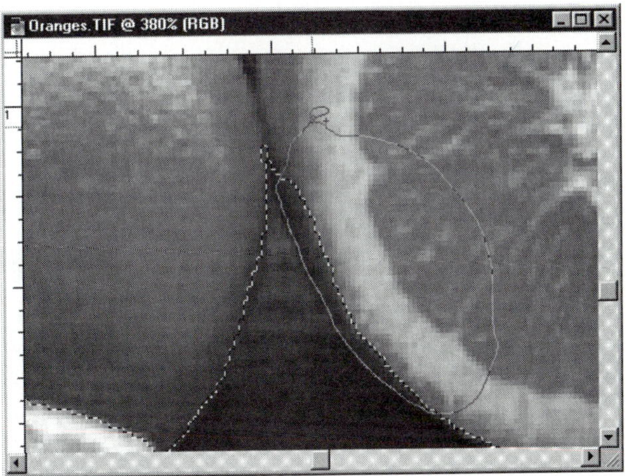

3. To move around to examine other parts of the image without zooming in and out, use the Navigator palette.
4. To remove portions of the selection, press the Option/Alt key instead of the Shift key. As you outline sections with Option/Alt-Lasso, they are subtracted from the selection region:

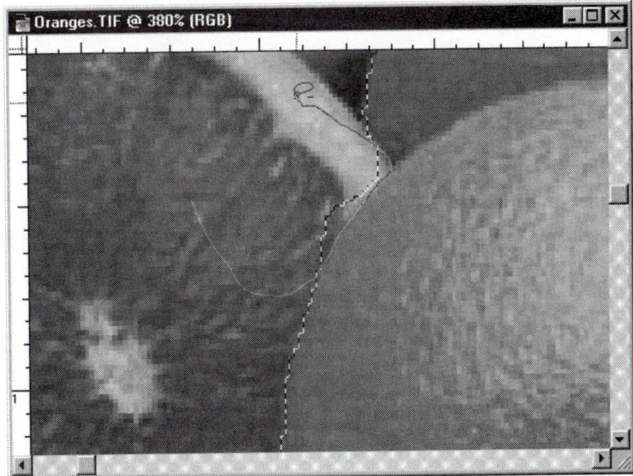

5. Close the file without saving.

Holding the space bar in any tool will temporarily convert to the grabber hand, which can be used to scroll around the image.

The Type Tools

Though the Type tool is not actually a selection tool, the Type Mask tool *does* create marquee selection borders of type; the concepts for both tools are identical, so we'll cover them both now. Generally speaking, type should be done in a program which offers more control, such as Adobe Illustrator or Macromedia FreeHand, then imported into Photoshop. For basic text, however, Photoshop's Type tool works just fine.

Creating a Type Mask

1. Open the image **Archery Target.TIF** from the **SF-Intro Photoshop** folder.
2. Press "D" to set the foreground and background colors to their defaults.
3. Select the Type Mask tool (it looks like a marqueed "T").
4. Click the upper-middle of the image to display the Type tool dialog box.

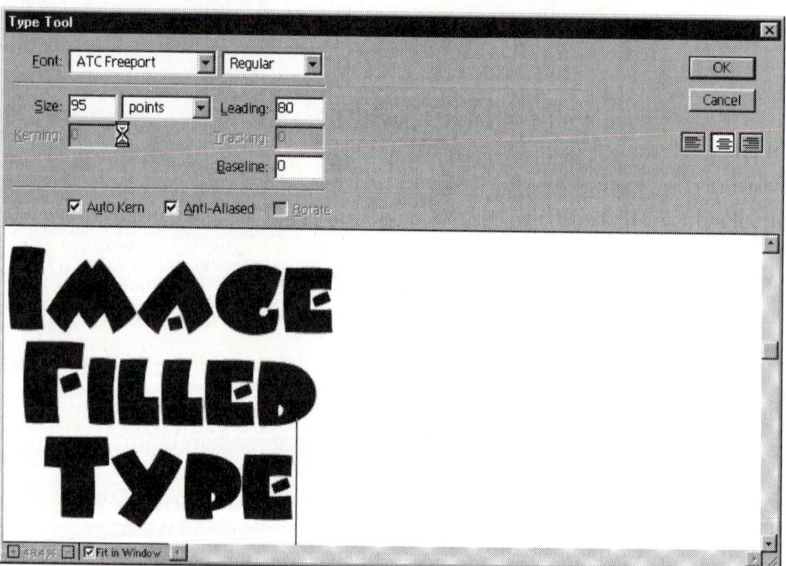

5. The Font section allows you to select a typeface from the pull-down list. Select ATC Freeport, a heavy face that will provide a lot of area for the type mask.
6. You may specify Size, Leading, and Spacing values. Leading adjusts the distance between lines of type vertically. Spacing adds or subtracts space between the letters. Change Size to 95 points, and Leading to 80.
7. In the Style area, check the Anti-Aliased box to smooth the edges of the type.
8. The Alignment icons depict the different types of alignments available: left justified, centered, or right justified. Select Centered, the middle button.
9. The open area at the bottom of the dialog box accepts the text you wish to enter. Enter the words "Image Filled Type" in this box. You may display the font using

When specifying type size, realize that Photoshop uses the height stored within the font to determine height. For example, if you specify 100-pixel type, a capital letter may be around 70 pixels high. This is because the height stored within the font includes the distance from the top of a capital letter to the bottom of a decender on letters such as j, y, or g.

the actual size or at a larger or smaller size. Clicking the Fit in Window option at the bottom of the Type Tool window allows a better preview of large elements.

10. Click OK. The new type mask selection appears in the middle of the image.
11. Open the **Tropical Waters.TIF** image from the **SF-Intro Photoshop** folder.
12. Use the Rectangular Marquee to Select and then Copy the blue-green water.

13. Close the **Tropical Waters.TIF** file without saving.
14. With the **Archery Target.TIF** window selected, and the type mask still active, select Edit>Paste Into to fill the type mask with water.

15. Close the file without saving.

Layers and Selections

Pasting anything into an RGB, CMYK, or Grayscale image, or creating type with the regular Type tool, automatically adds a *layer* to a document. Layers allow different image components to be selected independently for manipulation.

There is a comprehensive chapter on layers later in this course. For now, you only need a basic understanding of the Layers palette.

Introduction to Layers

1. Open (or File>Revert) the **Archery Target.TIF** image from the **SF-Intro Photoshop** folder.

2. Activate the Layers palette. Notice that the only layer showing in the document is called Background. This layer represents a traditional raster image such as a scan. A new scan will always default to a single Background layer.

3. The standard Type tool and pasted selections automatically add layers to an image, and moving selected areas of an image create a temporary layer called Floating Selection. To add a layer manually, click the New Layer icon (the small page) at the bottom of the Layers palette. The layer name will default to Layer 1 if it is the first new layer, Layer 2 if it is the second, and so forth.

Use Command/Control-Shift-V to easily Paste Into an object.

4. You can also create a new layer by selecting New Layer from the Layers palette pull-down menu:

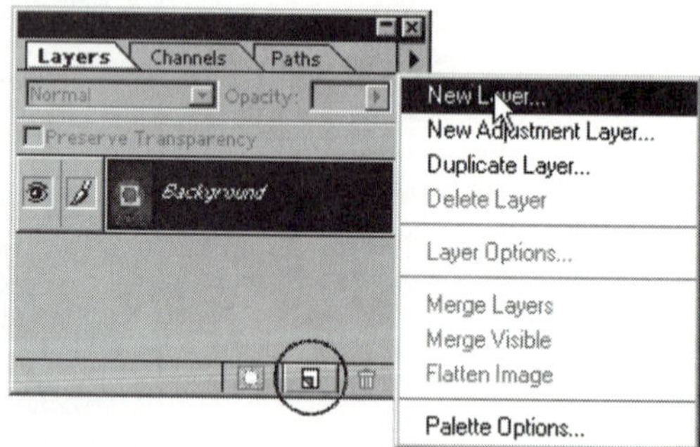

5. Press "D" to reset the foreground/background color swatches to black-and-white, then Option-Delete (Macintosh) or Alt-Backspace(Windows) to fill the layer with black.

6. The Background image is now obscured by the black layer. All of the information is still there, but you can't see it because Layer 1 is currently opaque and is above the Background layer. The Eye icon located to the left of each layer name in the Layers palette controls the display of that layer. Click on the eye next to the words "Layer 1" and the black image disappears, allowing the photo underneath to show through. Notice that the eye icon for Layer 1 has disappeared.

7. Click the space where the Eye used to be. The eye reappears and so does the black paint, again obscuring the target.

8. The paintbrush next to an eye indicates which layer is being edited. Click on the word Background in the Layers palette. The paintbrush moves to the Background layer. If you were to paint or edit the image now, you'd be affecting the actual archery target image, even though you can't see it.

9. Select the Paintbrush tool, and press "X" to paint with white paint.

10. Draw a large question mark. You cannot see anything happening because the black-filled layer is obscuring the archery target.

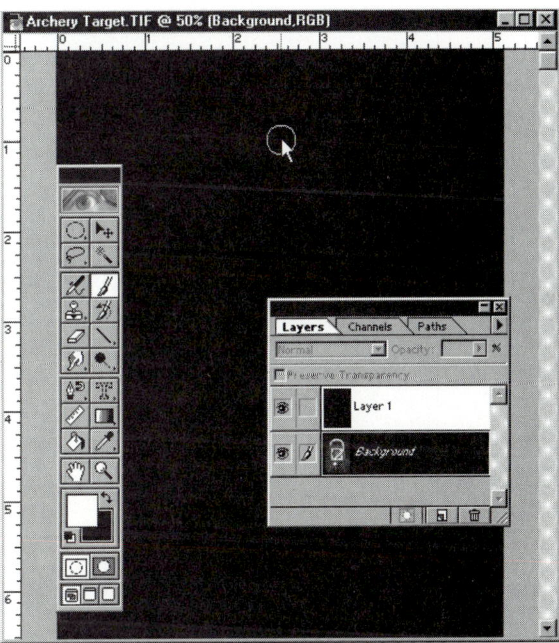

11. In the Layers Palette, click off the Eye icon for Layer 1; now you can see the painted question mark. Close the document without saving.

Selections in the Real World

So, which type tool should you use? The Type tool, which creates filled type on a separate layer, is great for type placed over an image which may need to be moved at a later time. The Type Mask tool, on the other hand, is good for special effects, such as cutting type out of an image, for filling type with a pattern or transparent color, or for creating offsets as we did in the last exercise. After some experimentation you'll easily be able to choose the right tool for the job.

CHAPTER 6

WORKING WITH TYPE

CHAPTER OBJECTIVE:

To learn about Photoshop's ability to handle type with an image; applying special effects to type. In Chapter 6, you will:

- Understand when type created within Photoshop is used to its best advantage.
- Learn about type tools and layers.
- Study the Layers panel and how it applies to a type layer; know when special effects have been applied.
- Understand the Type Mask tool, and how to use it to create a Type Mask.
- Understand the type layer and its format, and the appropriate time for rendering.

Working with Type

Since Photoshop's final result is always a bitmapped image of varying resolution, you probably don't want to include a large amount of type within an image, but there may be times when it is appropriate to add a large headline or something similar to an image. You can also use Photoshop to apply a large number of special effects to type, many of which can't be achieved by any other means.

The type on the left was created in an illustration program and looks very clear and sharp. The type on the right was created in Photoshop at a low resolution — you can clearly see the difference in the appearance of the type.

WoW! WoW!

Photoshop is not a Typesetting Program

Type created in (or imported into) Photoshop becomes a bitmapped part of the image. Once you save a Photoshop file as a TIFF image, for example, you can no longer edit the type. If you enlarge the image, the type (and probably the rest of the image) becomes blocky and unattractive. If you plan to use this type in a page layout and don't want to compromise quality, you will probably be better off creating the type in an illustration program (for example Illustrator or Freehand) or entering it directly into a page layout program (Pagemaker or QuarkXPress).

Because it is bitmapped, the type created in Photoshop is not scalable, as is most type created in publishing programs. If there is a great deal of type to input, this is not the place to do it. Small type, especially, is very vulnerable to distortion and pixelization when used in Photoshop.

The best use of type in Photoshop is for larger type sizes, combined with an image, and treated as continuous tones. If there are hard edges on the type, the pixelization effect becomes more obvious.

Anti-Aliasing is a technique used to soften the hard edges of type (and other objects) by creating a grayscale ramp in the edge. This visual trick makes bitmapped type appear to have a softer edge and helps eliminate pixelization. You can see the effects of anti-aliasing below.

WoW! WoW!

The left image was Anti-Aliased; the right was not. You can easily see the difference in the edge "hardness" of each sample.

Type Tools and Layers

Photoshop has two basic tools for entering and styling type: the Type tool and the Vertical Type tool. They don't differ much; one sets type horizontally, and the other sets it vertically. Vertical type is usually pretty hard to read, so use this one sparingly.

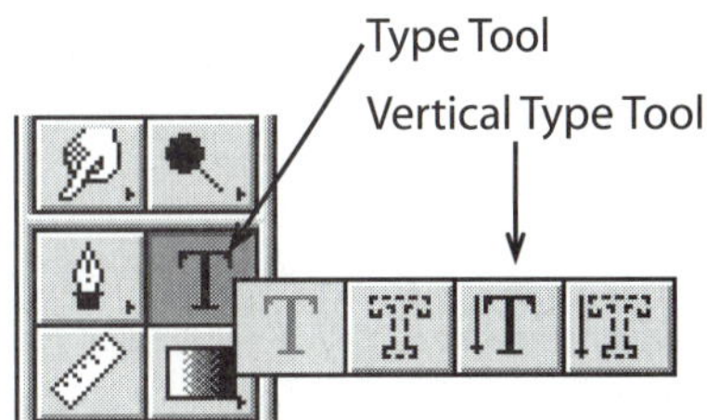

The Type tool creates type along a common *baseline*, regardless of the size of the character. Here are some type definitions to help you understand these terms:

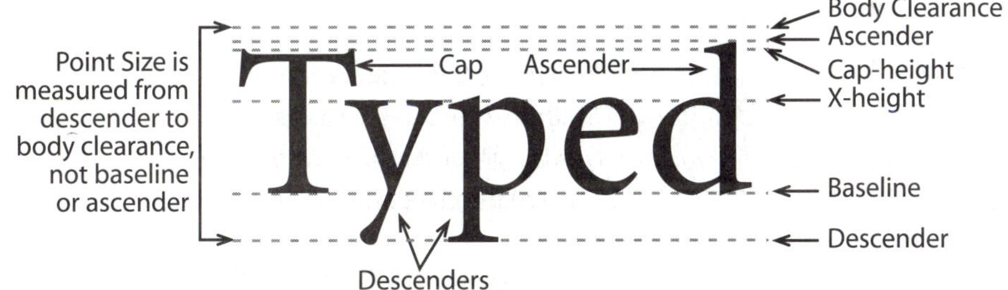

Type in Photoshop has the same options as you would get in a layout program — you can assign specific fonts, leading, size, color, and alignment. Kerning, tracking and baseline shift may be applied as well. Just remember that your ability to change these settings cease outside of Photoshop.

To use the Type tool, select it and click anywhere on the canvas. The Type Tool dialog will appear.

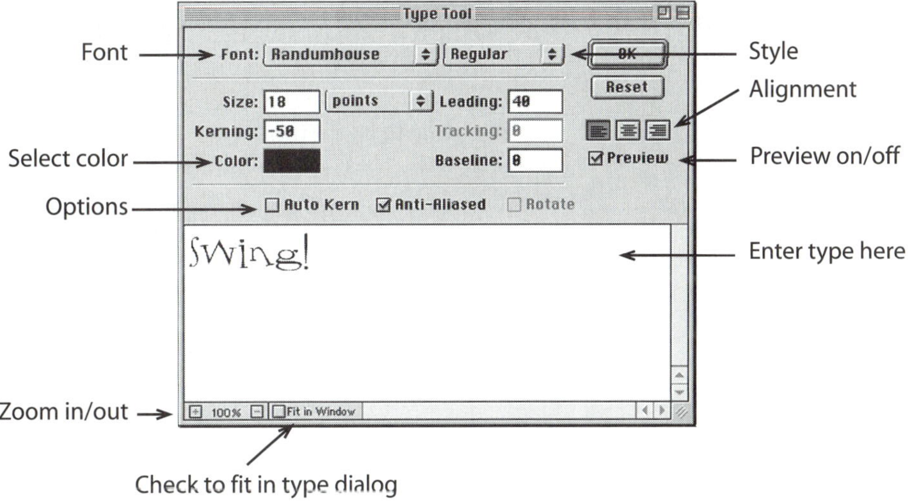

A type layer with special properties is created whenever type is placed on the canvas. Each new instance of type placement creates a new layer. If you have multiple lines to enter, you can enter all of them into the Type dialog shown here, separated by pressing the Return key (Macintosh), Enter (Windows). Type layers appear in the Layers palette, and look like this:

The Type Tool

Within the Type Tool dialog are a number of typographic tools. The most obvious are font and size; you can also adjust the following:

Type layers are not created for images in multichannel, bitmap, or indexed-color mode — these modes do not support layers.

- *Color* — clicking the color swatch presents the standard Photoshop Color Picker. By default, the current foreground color will be selected for the type. You can change this by choosing a new color from the Color Picker.

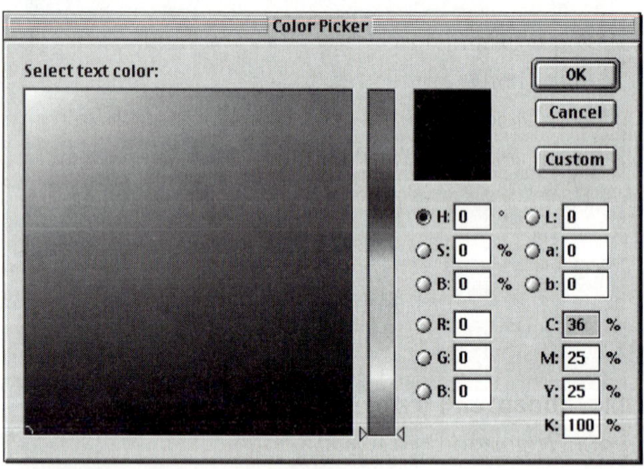

- *Alignment* of the text — left, right, or centered with relation to other lines of type that you enter, in relation to the point on the canvas that you originally clicked to show the type dialog.

- *Leading* — the amount of space set between lines of text. Typically, this is used for an entire block of text, although it can be increased or decreased to suit your needs. Increasing leading results in more line spacing; decreasing it results in tighter line spacing.

- *Kerning* — the adjustment of spacing between two letters, in units of 1/1000 of an *em space*. An em space is equal to the width of the chosen point size, so if you have chosen 36 point type, the em space for that type will be 36 points wide.

Unless your type is very small, you will usually need to enter values of at least 25 to notice any spacing difference. Enter negative values to reduce the amount of space; enter positive values to increase the amount of space.

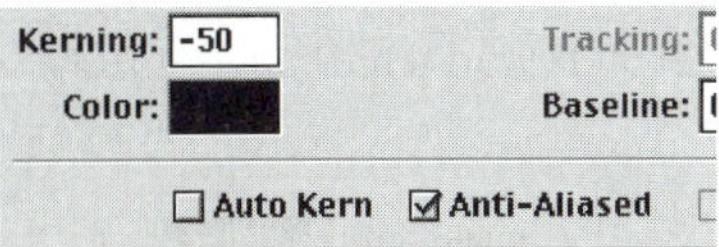

You must turn off Auto Kern to set kerning between letter pairs.

To adjust tracking, Auto Kern may be on or off.

- *Tracking* — the adjustment of spacing in a *range* of characters as opposed to just a pair of letters. Tracking is also measured in units of 1⁄1000 of an em space. Kerning applied to a pair of letters is maintained if the line or word of type is then tracked, either positively or negatively.

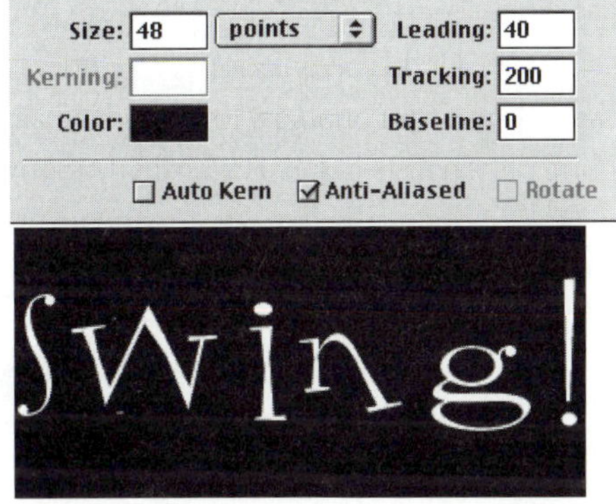

Compare the overall letterspace here with the example above.

- *Baseline shift* — the adjustment of a letter or line's baseline up or down relative to other characters or lines. Like kerning and tracking, this is specified in units of 1⁄1000 of an em space. For example, if the typeface you chose has tall ascenders, as in the example that follows, they might collide with the descenders of the line above it.

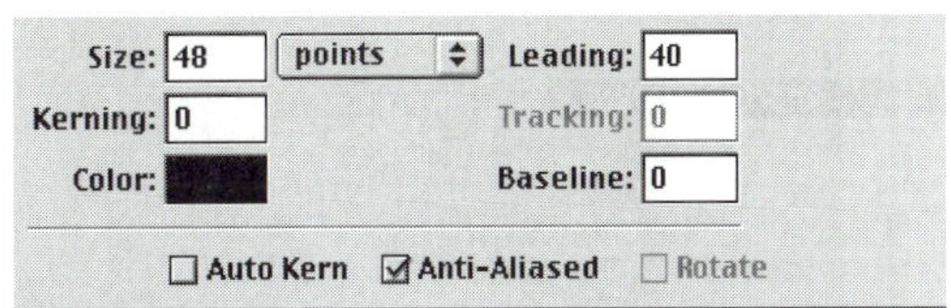

Baseline shifting moves the lower line away from the upper line:

The Vertical Type Tool

This tool presents the same options as the regular type dialog, except for two important differences: the "rotate" checkbox, and the choice of alignment. Alignment is still relative to the point at which you clicked the tool on the canvas, except that it is now vertical. The default behavior of the Vertical Type tool is to set type unrotated, so that the letters are stacked over one another:

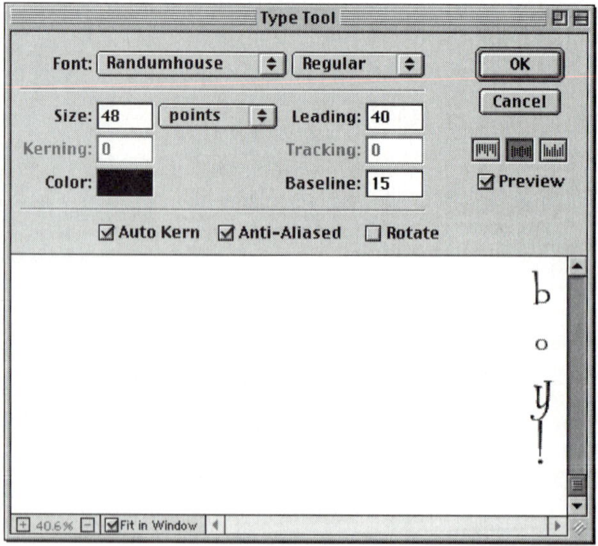

You can create rotated lines of text by selecting the text in the dialog and then checking the "rotate" checkbox. The text is now rotated 90 degrees with no stacking:

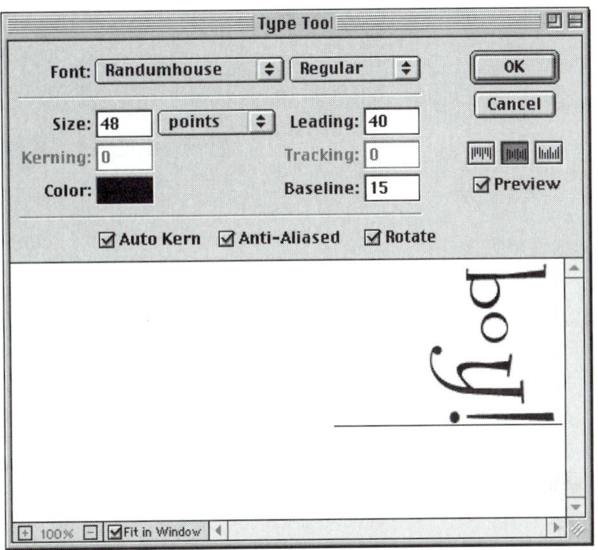

Type Layers

In most color modes, every time you use the Type tool, a new type layer is created. As you will learn in Chapter 14, layers are a powerful feature of Photoshop, and type layers behave the same way as any other layer.

Unless you're working in Multichannel, Indexed Color, or Bitmap mode, a new channel will be created whenever you use the Type tool.

A type layer retains the type in a *vector* format, and stores all of the typographical settings that you apply to it. You can go back at any time and change any of the type settings as long as you keep your file in the native Photoshop file format. If you save a file as a TIFF or EPS or any other format, or if you *flatten* the layers, all of your layers will be merged together and you won't be able to make any changes to type, which will be turned into a *bitmap*. You should always keep a copy of the file in the native Photoshop format so that you can easily make changes without having to recreate your work.

You can *render* a type layer — this will convert it to a regular layer, and also makes the type into a bitmap. You can't edit it any further with the type tools and must use the other Photoshop editing tools to make any alterations. Never render or flatten a type layer until you are certain that the type attributes (and spelling!) are correct. You can also change the orientation of a type layer from horizontal to vertical and back by choosing Layers>Type, where you can also render a type layer.

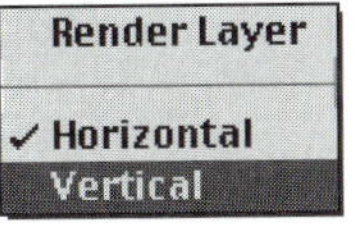

The Layers panel as it applies to a type layer:

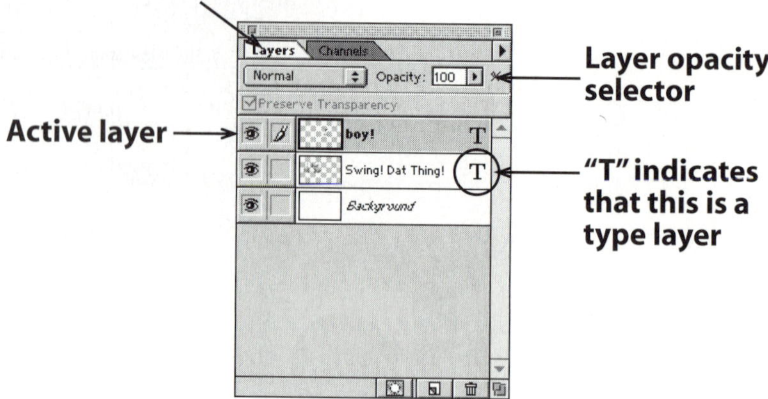

You can apply some special effects to type layers from the Layers>Effects menu:

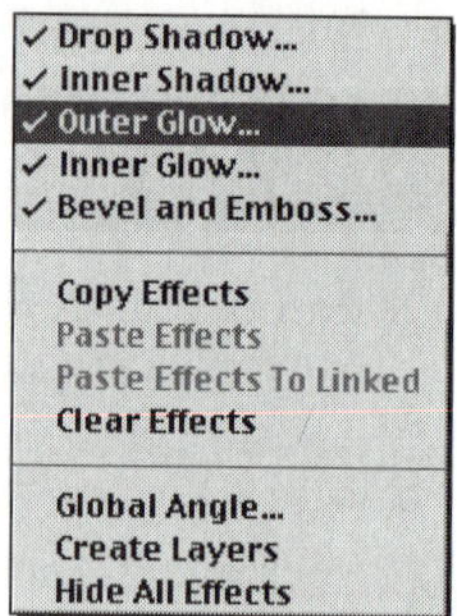

Here you can choose an effect to apply to a type layer. Effects are applied to all of the type in the layer, so if you only want part of the type modified, you need to make it a separate type layer.

A type layer that has had effects applied to it shows in the Layer palette, like this:

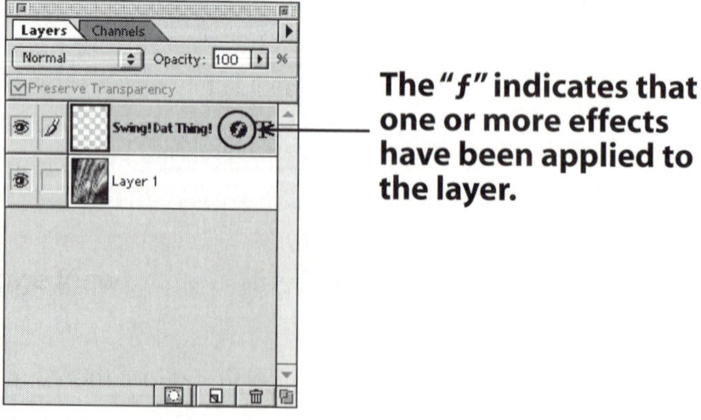

Here is an example of type effects applied to a type layer above an image:

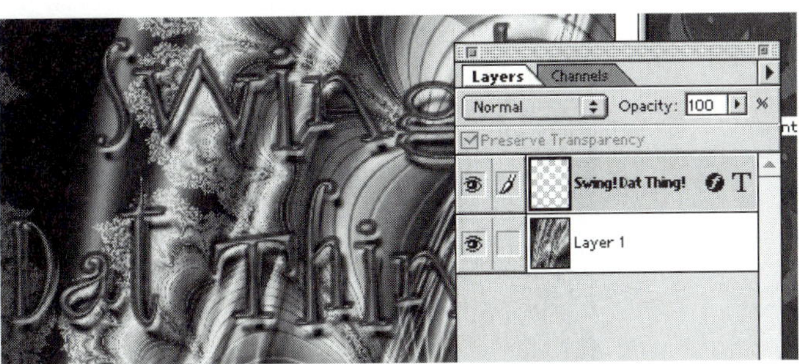

You'll create your own type effects in the following exercise.

Type Effects

1. Open the file **Colorful Flow.TIF** from the **SF-Intro Photoshop** folder.

2. Select the Type tool from the Tools palette, and click on the image to show the Type dialog. Type your first name, and style it as — Font: ATC Freeport, Size: 48, Leading: 48, Color: your choice (choose one that will stand out against the image — here we've used RGB values of 143, 31, 156), no baseline shift, turn Auto-Kerning off, turn Anti-Aliasing on. Remember, you need to select all of the text to apply some of these settings.

3. Click OK to see your name on the canvas.

4. The Layers palette will show the new type layer with your name in it:

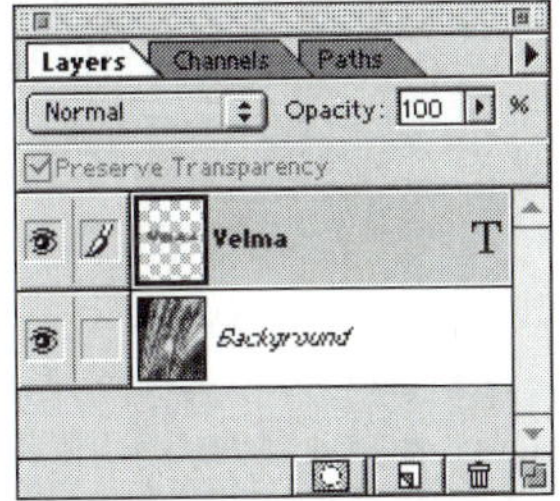

5. Double-click the type layer to open the Type dialog again. This is how you can make changes to the type if you change your mind. Select all of the text and notice that Auto-Kerning is off.

   Look at the spacing of the letters: are there any unusually large gaps or are some spaces too small? You can manually *kern* pairs of letters to improve the letterspacing and readability. In this example, the "V" and the "e" in "Velma" are too far apart, and so are the "m" and the "a." We could close up the space between the "V" and the "e" by applying *negative kerning*, but there's really no way to close up the space between the "m" and the "a" without the two letters running into each other. So in this case, we'll apply *positive tracking* to the entire word. Negative tracking would reduce the amount of letterspacing, and applying positive tracking will even out the spacing of all the letters to lessen the visually jarring gaps between them.

Kerning *is the process of adjusting the amount of space between two letters.* Tracking *is the process of adjusting the letterspacing of a complete word, sentence, or paragraph.*

6. Click the cursor between the initial two letters and enter -100 in the Kerning field. Look at the difference in the letterspacing.

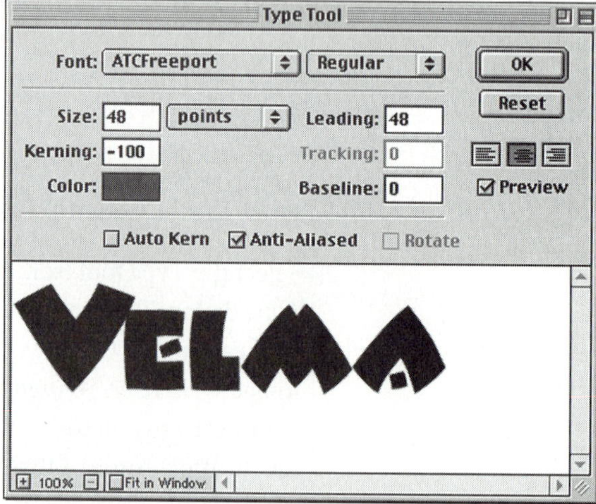

7. You could leave the type letterspaced like this, or you could apply positive tracking to better even out the gaps. Select all of the text and enter 100 into the Tracking field. Click OK to see the results on the canvas.

8. Adjust the settings further until you are satisfied with the letterspacing.

9. Save the file as "Type Example.PSD" (you can only save it as a Photoshop file because there are layers present) into your **Work in Progress** folder, but leave it open.

Applying Effects to Type

1. Continue with the open file. Select the type layer in the Layers palette and choose Layers>Effects>Drop Shadow.

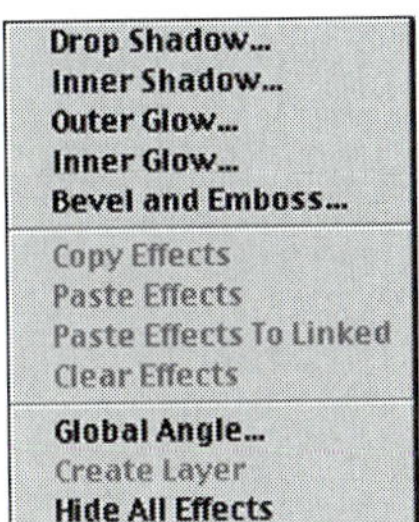

2. In the Drop Shadow dialog, you can press Command/Control-1 through 5 to change to other effects modes. Press Command/Control-5 to show the Bevel and Emboss dialog.

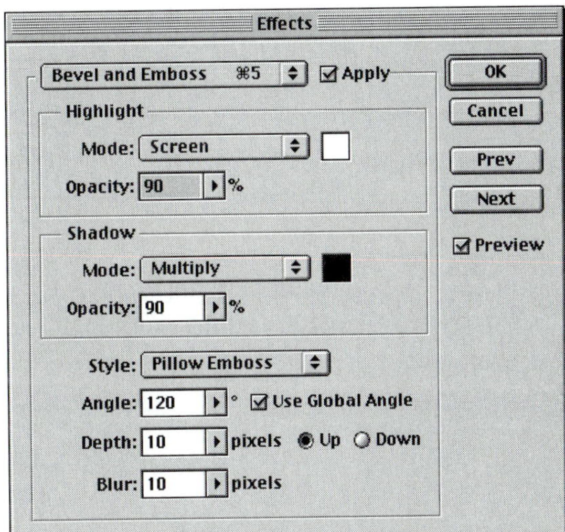

3. Apply the settings shown. Move the dialog box so you can see the results of the effect on the type (make certain that "Preview" is checked to see the results). You should end up with an effect like this:

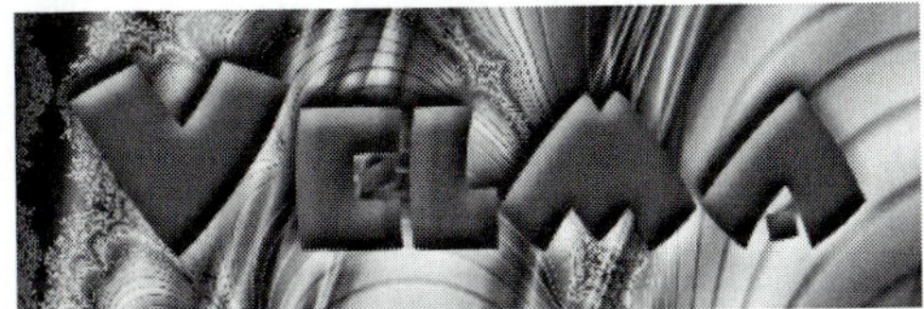

4. Experiment with the other effects available, such as Drop Shadow, Inner and Outer Glow, and Inner Shadow, and pay attention to the results of applying these effects. Save and close the file.

The Type Mask Tool

A *type mask* is the process of creating a selection area that uses the outline of the selected type as the selection border. Type masks are usually applied to an existing layer; you can create them in a type layer but they won't have any effect.

To create a type mask, select the Type Mask tool:

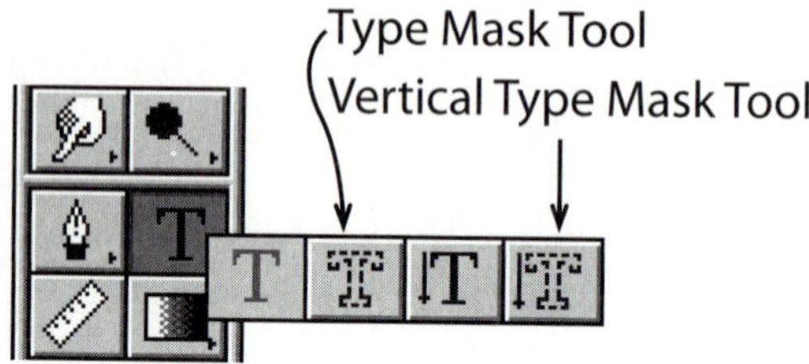

Click over a layered image to show the Type dialog. Enter your text and apply the desired style. Then click OK to create the type mask, which will appear as a selection marquee (the "marching ants"):

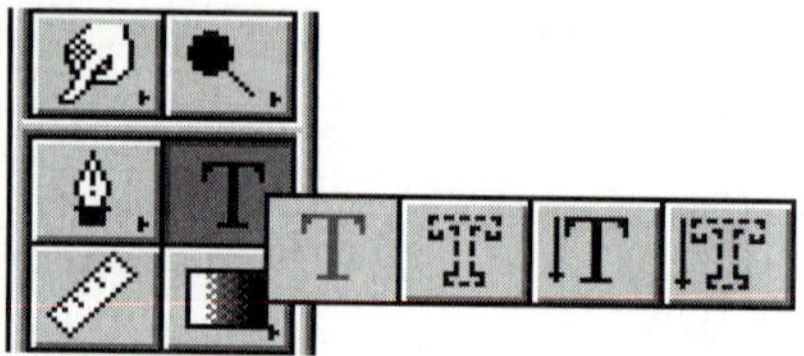

You can now apply the mask. Choosing Layer>Add Layer Mask>Reveal Selection masks the image within the type.

Choosing Layers>Apply Mask>Hide Selection creates a knockout in the layer that is the same shape as the type. Layers below the current one will show through the mask.

Type masks can also be used like any other Photoshop selection. You can apply filters, feathering, deletions, and special effects, including those found in plug-ins.

Type mask selection that has been feathered:

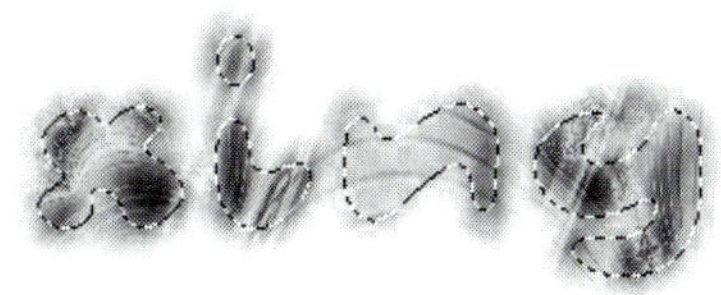

Type mask selection after applying the Pointillize filter:

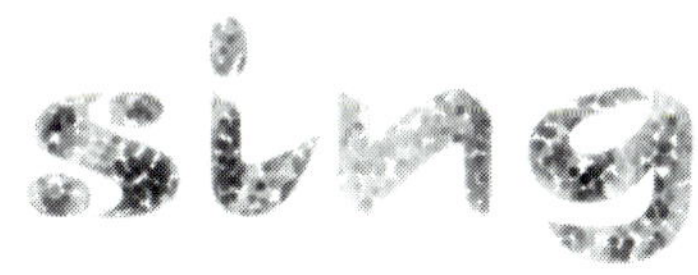

Any other filters or tools that operate on a selection can be applied to a type mask.

Exercise: Type Masks

1. Open the file **Colorful Flow.TIF** from the **SF-Intro Photoshop** folder.
2. Select the Vertical Type Mask tool, enter and style the text as shown, then click OK.

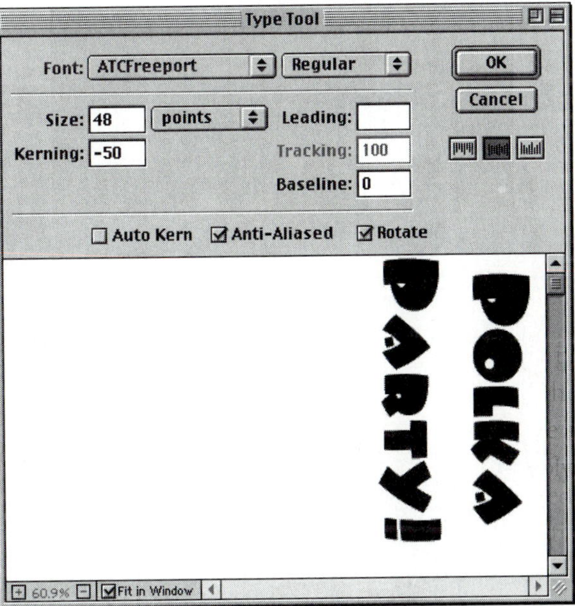

3. Move the type selection wherever you like, then choose Select>Save Selection:

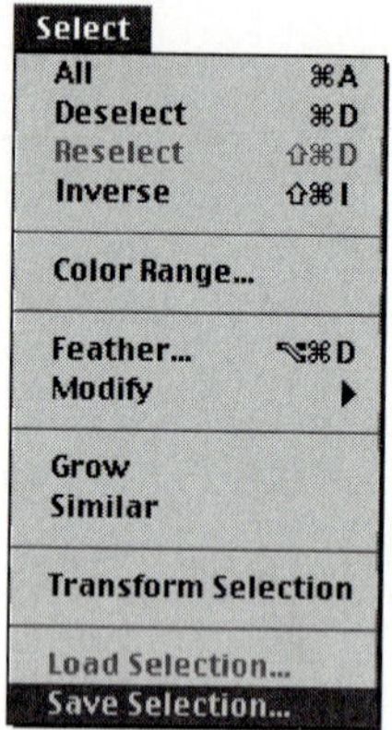

Type a name for the selection then click OK.

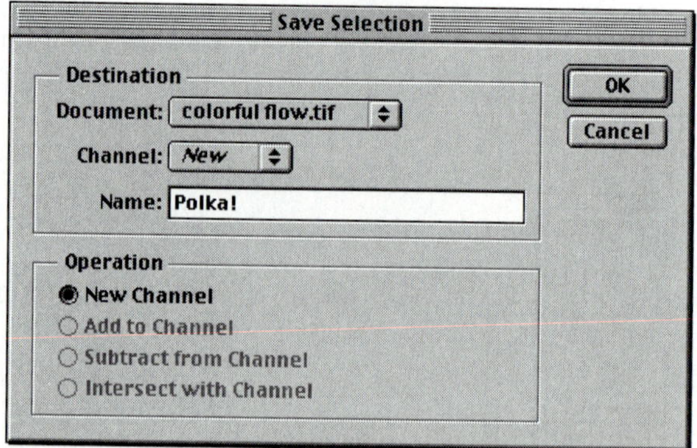

4. Choose Select>Inverse to invert the selection. This means that everything that wasn't selected before is now selected.

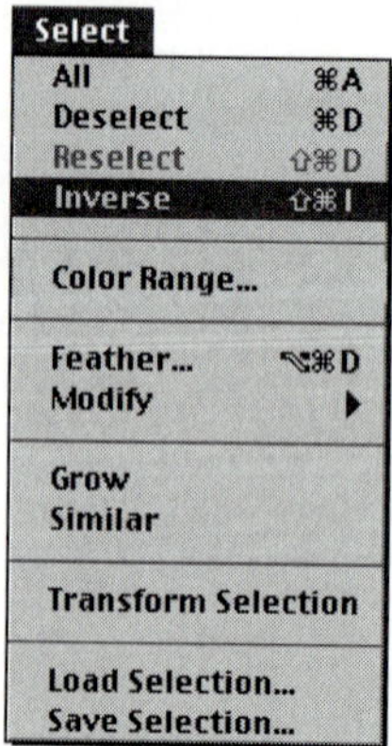

5. Choose Select-Feather…

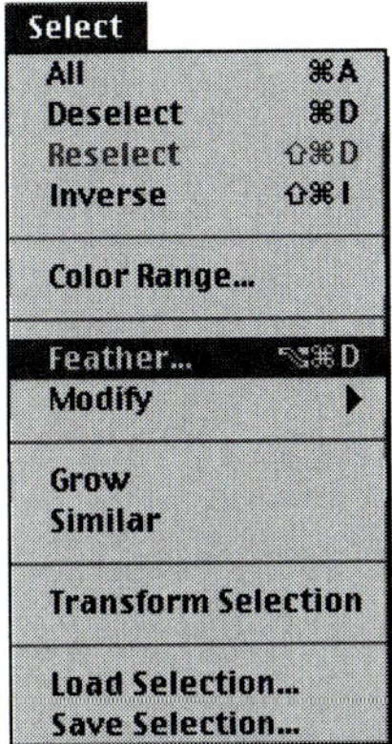

and enter "5" for the Feather Radius. Click OK.

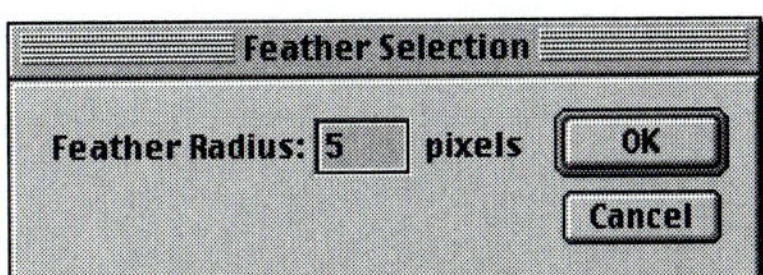

6. You won't see much on the screen until you delete the portion of the image around the type selection. Simply press the Delete key to reveal the feathered type selection, then press Command/Control-D to deselect everything.

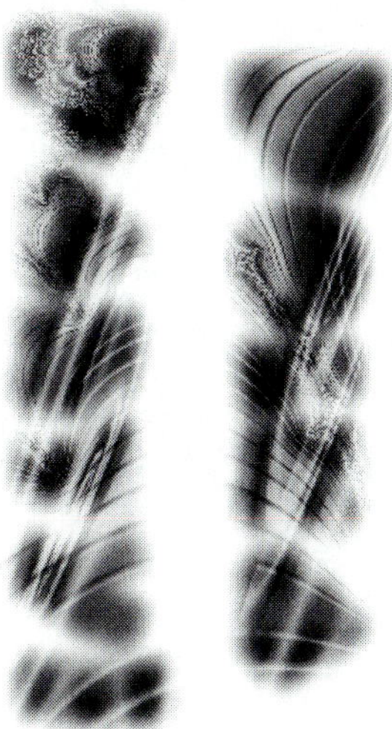

7. The Feather Radius of 5 pixels was a little too much. You could try to undo the delete, but this won't let you change the Feather Radius because Undo only works once. This is where Photoshop 5's new History feature is really helpful. Choose Window>Show History to view the History palette:

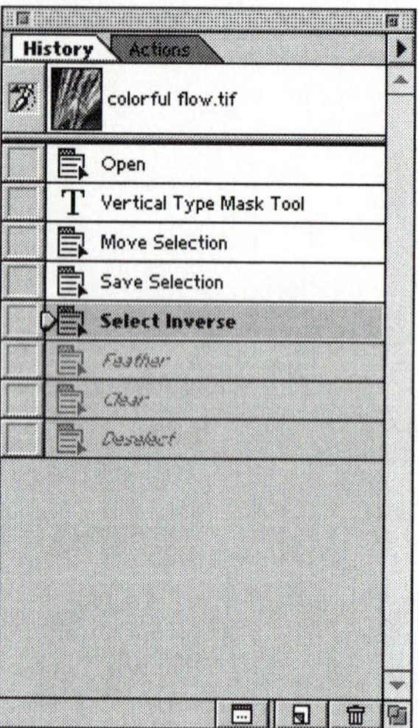

Just click on the "Select Inverse" history item to revert back to that particular point in the document's life. Now feather the selection again, but just give it a radius of one pixel. Press the Delete key again to clear the selection, deselect everything, then choose Image>Rotate Canvas>90° CCW.

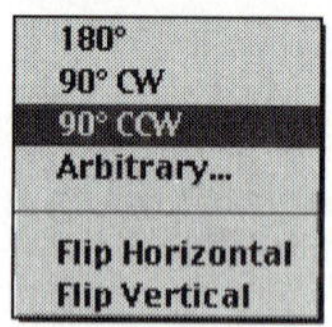

Here's the final result:

8. Name and Save the file as "Polka.TIF", in your **Work in Progress** folder, and then close it.

Chapter 7

Painting Tools

Chapter Objective:

To develop your knowledge of Photoshop's painting tools; how to adjust and apply them to retouching, special effects, and creating original artwork. In Chapter 7, you will:

- Work with the Brushes palette, learning its various sizes, shapes, angles, spacing, and hardness of available brushes.
- Learn how to add or edit brushes in the Brush Options dialog box.
- Learn to use the Pencil tool, Paintbrush, and Airbrush.
- Use the Line tool, Paint Bucket tool, and Gradient Fill tool.
- Learn about the special Eraser tool, and how to use it.
- Learn about the History brush, and how to use it.
- Learn about the Rubber Stamp and Pattern Stamp.

Projects to be Completed:

- Marinara Shelf Talker
- KSOL Rising
- Maui Travel Postcard
- Rough Riders Ad
- Gulls Poster
- Concert Poster
- Banana Boat Table Tent
- Salute to Veterans Poster

Painting Tools

Photoshop has some excellent painting tools which may be used for photo retouching, special effects, or creating original artwork.

Each painting tool has an Options setting that allows control over the way the tool interacts with the image. Most settings are unique to the specific tool being used, but the tools have some settings in common.

All the regular painting tools provide the ability to set a Blending Mode. A blending mode combines image information according to mathematical rules. One example of this is the Difference mode, which was used when filling the mirrored pattern tile. Difference calculates the mathematical value of the color of each pixel in the image (the original pattern) and in the added fill and subtracts one from the other, depending on which has the greater brightness. Blending modes will be discussed in depth later in the course.

In addition, all painting tools except the Airbrush have an Opacity slider on the Options palette. The Opacity slider allows adjustment of the transparency of the color, pattern, or effect being applied to the image. When Opacity is less than 100%, repeated applications of color are required to make the paint more opaque.

For example, if the Paintbrush is set to 25% opacity, the first stroke will combine 25% of the foreground color and 75% of the image. If the area is stroked again with the same color (after releasing and depressing the mouse button) a bit more of the image will be obscured by paint. Enough applications of the brush will eventually obscure the image entirely.

Working with the Brushes Palette

Many painting tools require the selection of a brush from the Brushes palette. Brushes vary in size, shape, angle, spacing, and hardness.

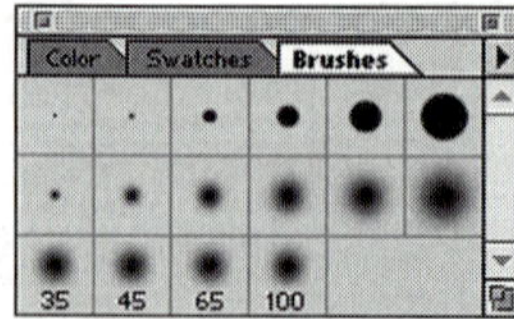

Note that the brushes in the upper row appear hard-edged, while those in the second and third rows have soft, fading edges. Generally speaking, "hard" brushes are not actually hard, except when compared to "soft" brushes. Hard brushes have a very small softened or *Anti-Aliased* edge, while soft brushes have a wide, soft edge to blend colors smoothly into the underlying image. The brushes with a number on the bottom are brushes that are too large to be dislayed in the brushes palette; the number represents the width of the brush in pixels.

Brushes may be added or edited in the Brush Options dialog box. The dialog box is accessed by double-clicking an existing brush that you wish to edit or by single-clicking the blank area at the bottom of the Brushes palette to create a new brush.

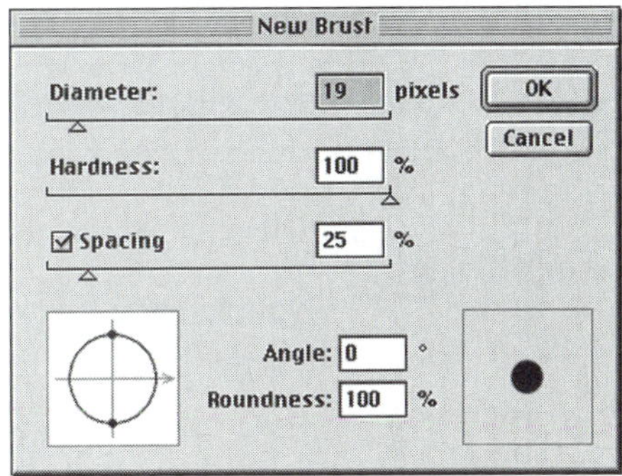

The first item in the Brush Options dialog box is Diameter, which indicates the width of the brush (at its longest dimension) in pixels.

The next item, Hardness, designates how hard or soft the edges of the brush are. Even if hardness is set to 100%, the default for Photoshop's "hard-edged" brushes, the edges are still softened slightly to create an Anti-Aliased brush. Conversely, even when a brush is softened all the way down to 0% hardness, the center of the brush is still solid.

Spacing represents how often a brush stroke repeats. The percentage listed is a percentage of the width of a brush. For example, a round, 20-pixel brush with a 200% spacing would draw a series of dots 20 pixels in diameter, with 20 pixels of space between each dot. Photoshop's default brushes have a spacing of 25%, which appears continuous except when using very large brushes. Unchecking the Spacing checkbox causes the spacing to vary according to the speed of the mouse.

Changing the Roundness value creates an elliptical brush, which can then be set at any Angle. Both the angle and roundness may be set by keying in the degree of rotation and percent of roundness, or by manipulating the graphic in the lower left of the dialog box.

Other things you should know about brushes:

- A new brush may be created by clicking anywhere in the gray area after the last brush in the Brushes palette.
- Save or Load sets of custom-created brushes, or Append one set of brushes to another by clicking on the black triangle in the upper right corner of the Brushes palette to activate the pull-down menu. Reset the Brushes palette to the defaults that initially came with Photoshop using this menu.

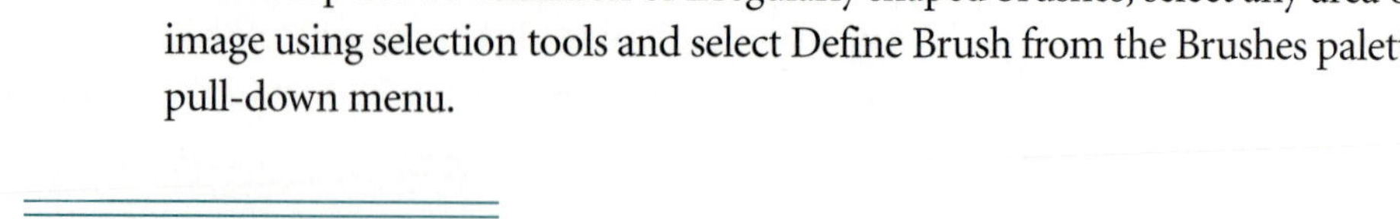

- Photoshop allows definition of irregularly shaped brushes; select any area of the image using selection tools and select Define Brush from the Brushes palette pull-down menu.

Changing Brush Options

1. Select the Paintbrush and activate the Brushes palette.
2. Double-click the brush furthest to the right in the top row of the Brushes palette to activate the Brush Options dialog box.

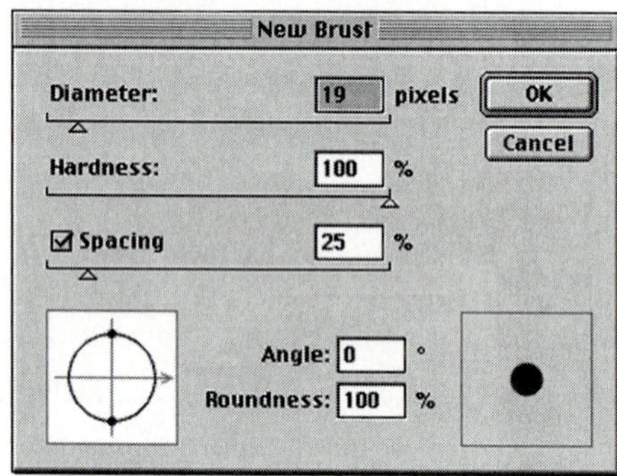

3. Move the Diameter slider to the right or left to increase or decrease the size of the brush. Notice that the preview window in the lower right corner of the dialog box changes dynamically as you move the slider. A brush may be sized from 1 to 999 pixels.
4. Move the Hardness slider back and forth and watch the brush edges change in the New Brush window.
5. Drag the dots at the top and bottom of the graphic in the lower left corner of the dialog box and watch the shape of the brush change; drag the arrow to vary the angle of the brush.
6. Note that you can also enter values directly into the boxes. Experiment with different settings using the boxes or sliders until you get a feel for how the brushes change.
7. Click the OK button to save your changes. Note how the Brush has been changed in the palette.

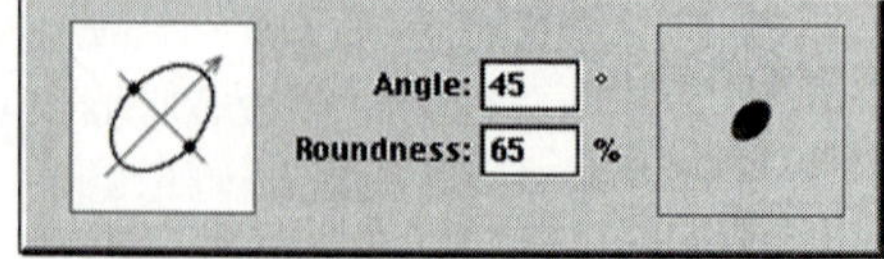

8. Select Reset Brushes from the pull-down menu that appears from the black triangle in the upper right corner of the Brushes palette. Click OK to reset the brushes to their original condition.

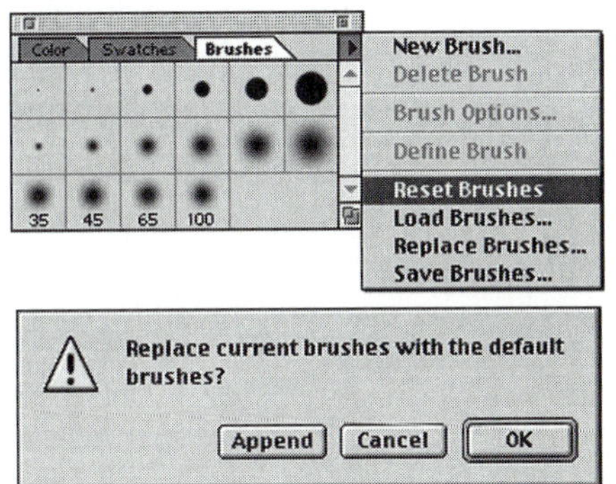

Using the Pencil Tool

1. Open the image **Coffee Alfresco.TIF** from the **SF-Intro Photoshop** folder.

2. The Pencil tool, while extremely useful for for editing bitmapped images, is rarely used with photographic images. Why? Select the Pencil tool, activate the Brushes palette, and take a look at the soft brushes in the second and third row. Notice how hard they are? A Pencil is *never* Anti-Aliased.

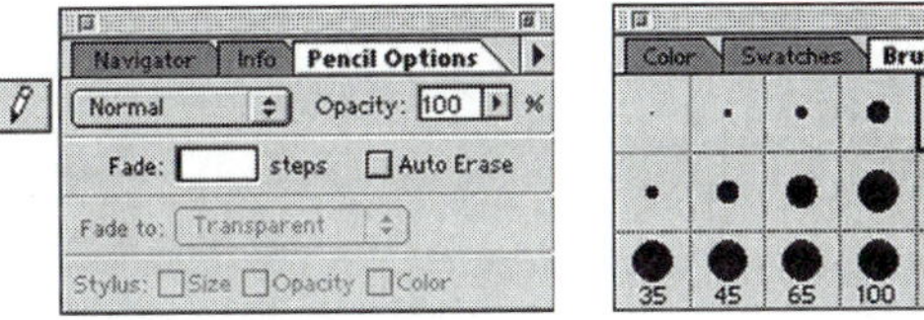

3. Select the third brush in the top row of the Brushes palette.

4. Choose a blue color from the Swatches palette.

5. Draw a few lines. The resulting lines have "jaggies," stairsteps which detract from image quality. When editing bitmaps, however, the Pencil is invaluable.

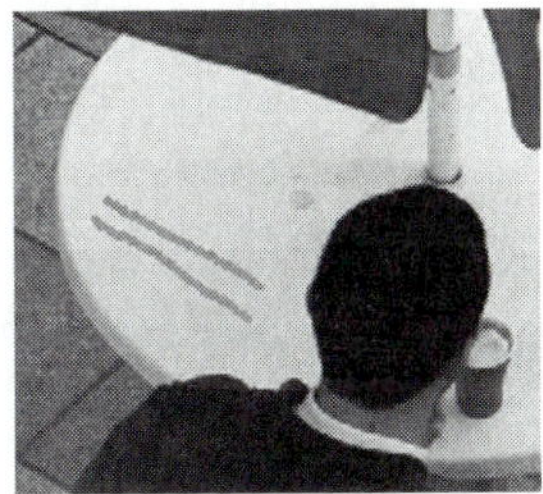

6. Keep the image open for the next exercise.

Using the Paintbrush

1. Select the Paintbrush tool and choose a green color to make it easy to tell the Paintbrush marks from your Pencil marks.

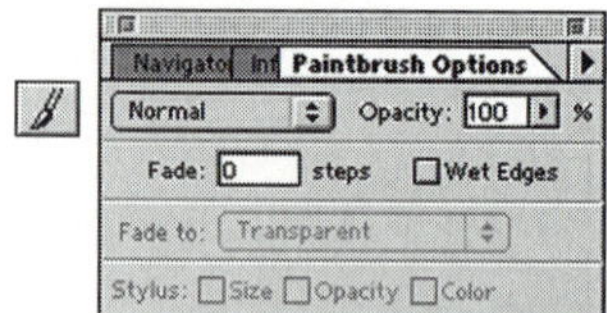

2. Select the fourth brush from the top row of brushes and paint a bit. Notice how much smoother the lines are compared to the Pencil lines.

3. Activate the Options palette and move the Opacity slider down to 25%.

4. Without removing your hand from the mouse button, paint with the Paintbrush, crossing over areas already painted.

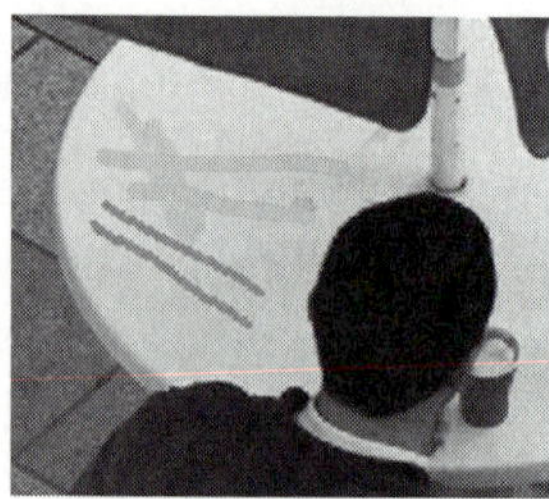

5. Notice that no matter how many times you paint over a particular area, the paint remains at 25% opacity, allowing 75% of the image to show through. Release the mouse button, then paint over the area again. Now the areas where paint overlaps become more opaque.

6. Return the Opacity slider to the 100% setting and check the Wet Edges checkbox.

7. Change the foreground color to red, select one of the large soft brushes, and paint again. The center of the stroke is partly transparent, while the paint pools up on the sides creating a watercolor wash effect.

8. Deselect the Wet Edges option. Keep the image open for the next exercise.

Using the Airbrush

1. Select the Airbrush tool.

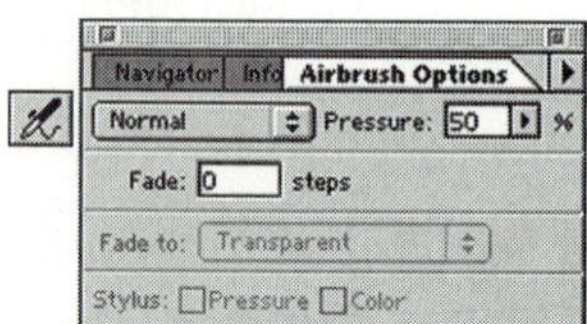

2. Instead of an opacity setting, the Airbrush palette has a Pressure slider, which makes the Airbrush behave more like its real-world counterpart. Adjust the Pressure slider to 10%.

3. Select the 65-pixel soft brush and a bright blue.

4. Hold down the mouse button over the image without moving the mouse, and watch what happens.

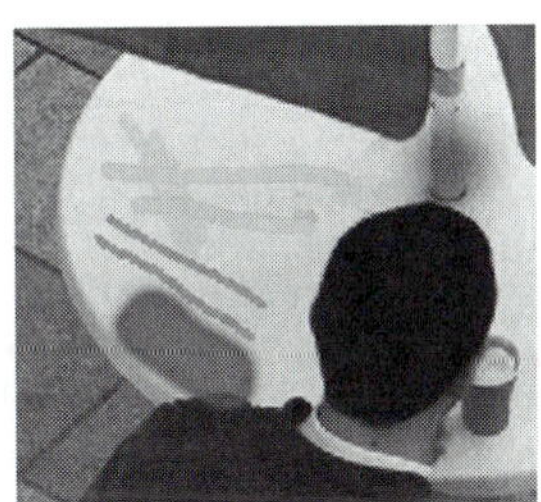

The longer you hold down the mouse button, the larger and more opaque the spot becomes.

5. Now change the Pressure setting to 90% and try it again. The end result is the same, but it happens a lot faster because the pressure is higher. Because Airbrush opacity relies upon pressure rather than a distinct opacity setting, overlaying strokes *will* result in a more opaque color. The speed with which the paint become opaque depends upon the Pressure value.

6. Select the last brush on the top row of the Brushes palette, and change the Pressure on the Airbrush Options palette to 25%. The Airbrush produces a softer edge than the Paintbrush tool unless Pressure is set to a low value and a hard-edged brush is selected; then it resembles the Paintbrush.

   The difference is that without lifting the mouse button, painting repeatedly over a given area will gradually make it more opaque. This results in a more natural painting style, making it especially useful for photo retouching.

7. Paint over your image and notice that though the lines created resemble the marks made by the Paintbrush, the paint builds up as you paint back and forth across the same area.

8. Keep the image open for the next exercise.

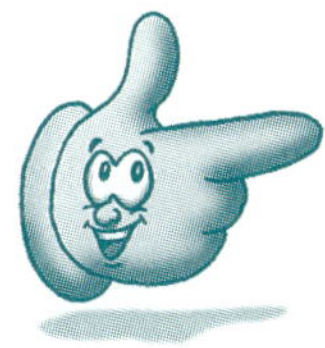

Other Painting Tool Options

1. The Paintbrush, Pencil, and Airbrush tools allow you to specify a fade-out rate. Fade allows you to fade from the foreground color to transparent, or from the foreground color to the background color. Select the Paintbrush tool and select the last brush in the second row.

2. Note the Fade box in the Options palette.

3. Steps represents the number of brush steps (according to the Spacing settings for the brush you are using) it takes to fade from the foreground color. Set Step values from 0 to 100.
4. Make certain that the pull-down list next to Fade to: is set to Transparent.
5. Select a bright red from the Swatches palette. Draw some lines on your image. Notice how the paint fades from dense red to transparent, allowing the underlying color to show through.
6. Now Option-click (Macintosh) or Alt-click (Windows) bright yellow to change your background color, and change the pull-down on the Options palette from Transparent to Background.
7. Paint a few more strokes. Now the paint fades evenly from red to yellow; if you continue the stroke beyond the 100 steps, the rest of the paint is solid yellow.
8. Choose Revert from the File menu to return to the original image. Click Revert.
9. Keep the file open for the next exercise.

Using the Line Tool

1. The Line tool is used to draw straight lines of a specified pixel width, with or without arrowheads. Double-click the Line tool.

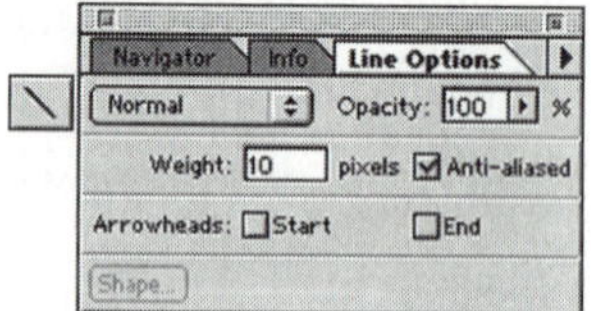

2. Set the Line Weight to 10 pixels. Keep in mind that the higher the resolution of the file, the higher the Line Weight value should be to achieve a serviceable line.
3. Draw a few lines across the image by clicking and dragging the tool. Make certain that some of them overlap.
4. Draw some more lines, but this time hold down the Shift key while dragging. This constrains the line to an increment of a 45° angle.

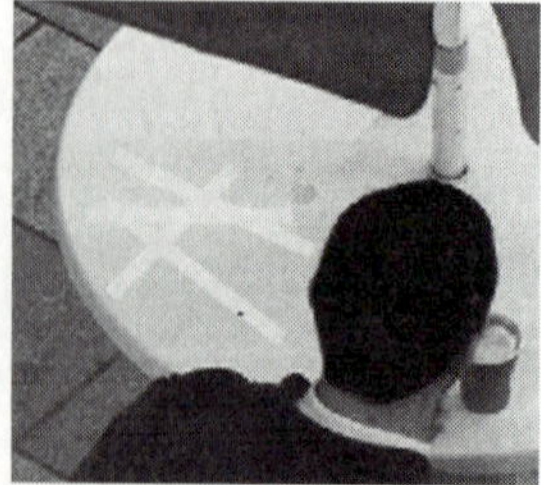

5. Keep the file open for the next exercise.

Using the Paint Bucket

1. The Paint Bucket tool fills portions of an image with either the foreground color or a predefined pattern. Tolerance on the Options palette specifies how close adjacent pixels must be in color to be filled with paint. Select the Paint Bucket.

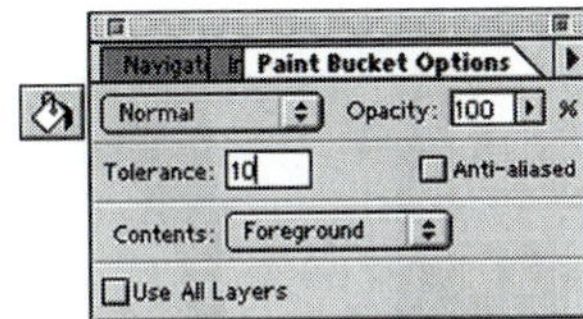

2. Set Tolerance to 10 and change your foreground color to bright blue.
3. Click a few times on the sidewalk. Parts of the sidewalk are filled with variable-sized spots of color.
4. Raise the Tolerance value to 30 and click the sidewalk again. A much larger area is filled with color.
5. Click on the lines created with the Line tool.

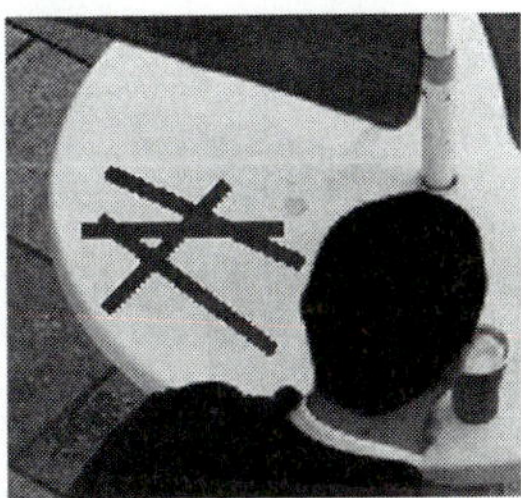

Since the lines are made up of the same color, they are easily filled, even if the Tolerance value is set very low. Tolerance may be set anywhere from 0 to 255. Zero (0) will fill only pixels identical in color to the pixel you click on; 255 will paint every pixel in the image.

6. Keep the image open for the next exercise.

Using the Gradient Fill Tool

1. Select the Gradient Fill tool. This tool creates circular (Radial) or Linear blends between foreground and background colors, or foreground and transparent, which allows the image to gradually show through the blend, or rotate around the spectrum between the foreground and background colors, creating a rainbow of color.

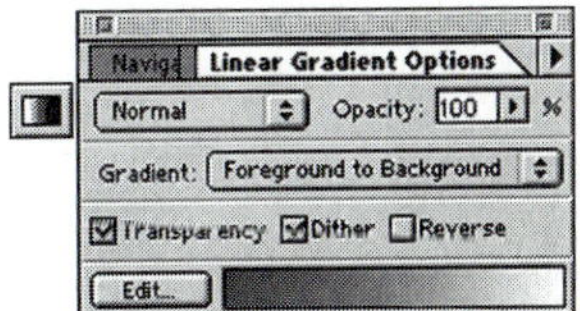

2. First we'll try a Linear fill. Make certain that Linear Gradient tool is active.

3. Change the Gradient to Foreground to Transparent.

4. Select a purple for the new Foreground color, and click and drag the mouse across the image, leaving about an inch on each side. If you hold down the Shift key while dragging, the fill is constrained to a 45° increment.

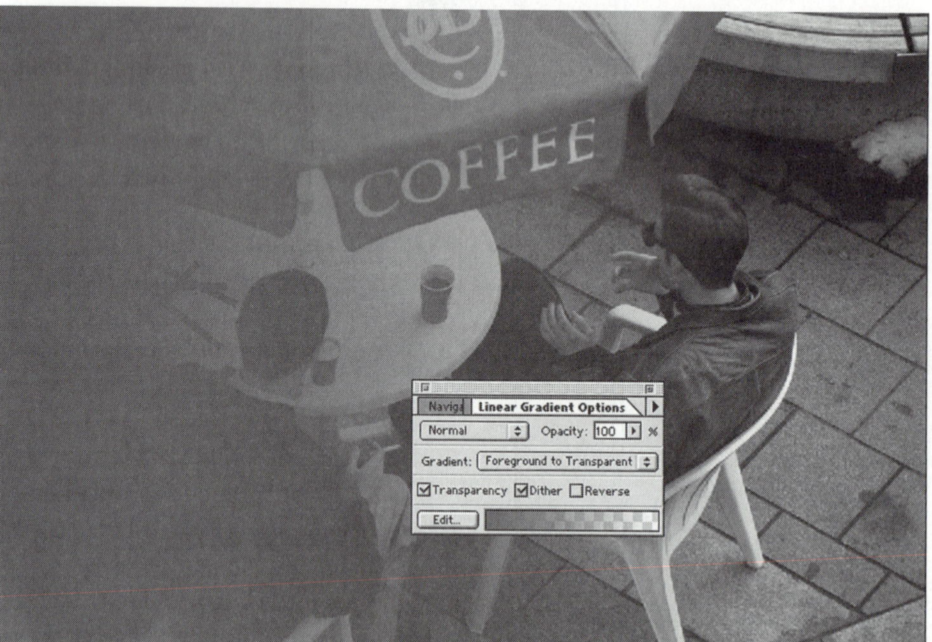

The image is filled with 100% foreground color at the beginning of the fill, and fades to transparent (0%) at the end of the fill. Note that the area outside the beinning of your gradient is filled with 100% foreground color, and the area outside the area of the end of the fill is 100% transparent. The blend occurs only between the starting and ending points.

5. Select Command/Control-Z to Undo the previous fill, or delete the Gradient state in the History palette.

6. Change to the Radial Gradient tool.

7. Click the Reverse button in the Options palette.

8. Click in the center of the image and drag to any corner. The image shows through in a circular area in the center of the image and fades to the foreground color at the outside edges. Press Command/Control-Z to Undo the fill.

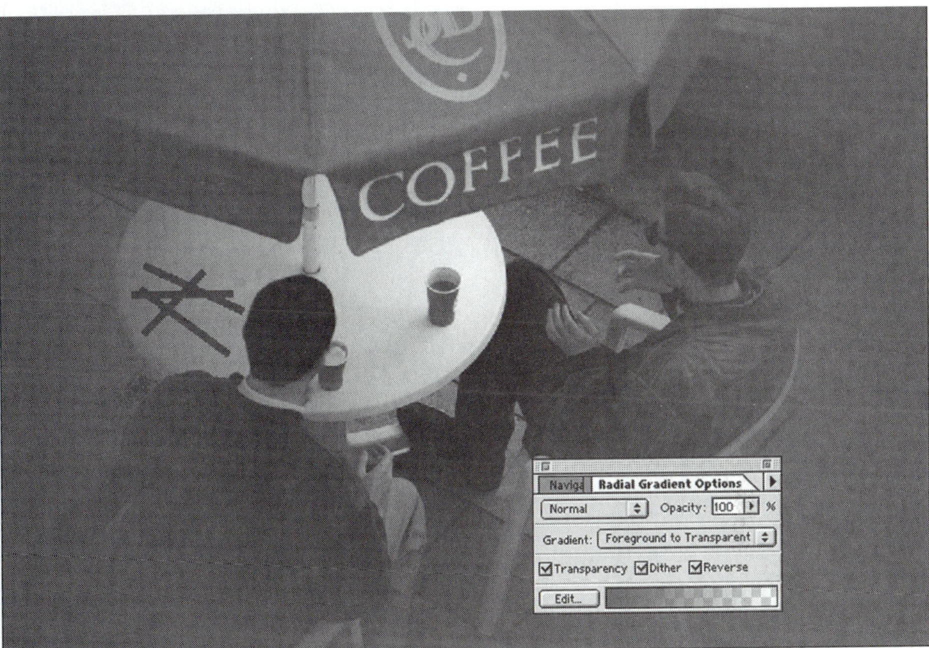

9. Keep the image open for the next exercise.

Creating a Sphere

1. Make certain that the Radial Gradient tool is still selected.
2. Change the foreground color to a very light blue; Option/Alt-click a much darker blue to change the background color.
3. Change Gradient Type to Foreground to Background in the Options palette.
4. Select the Elliptical Marquee tool. Create a circular selection by holding down the Shift key while dragging the mouse.
5. Activate the Radial Gradient Fill tool again. Deselect the Reverse button. Create a gradient beginning in the upper right area of the circular selection; don't get too close to the edge of your selection. Drag down to the lower left area of the selection. Again, don't get too close to the edge of the selection.

6. Release the mouse button — you've created a perfect sphere. You can create a sphere with a different light source by beginning and ending the gradient in a different place. Always remember, however, to keep a little distance between the starting and ending points of the gradient and the edge of the circular selection. Deselect (Command/Control-D) the active selection.

7. Keep the image open for the next exercise.

Multi-Color Gradients

1. Change to the Linear Gradient tool.

2. In the Gradient Options palette, select the Gradient pull-down. Choose Yellow, Violet, Orange, Blue.

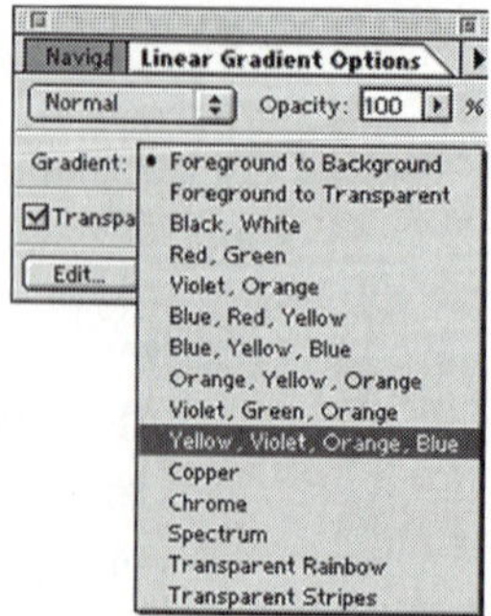

3. Draw a gradient across the image. Notice that the bands are very even, and the colors match those displayed in the Options palette. Press Command/Control-Z to Undo the gradient.

4. In the Linear Gradient Options palette, click the Edit button, to the left of the gradient preview.

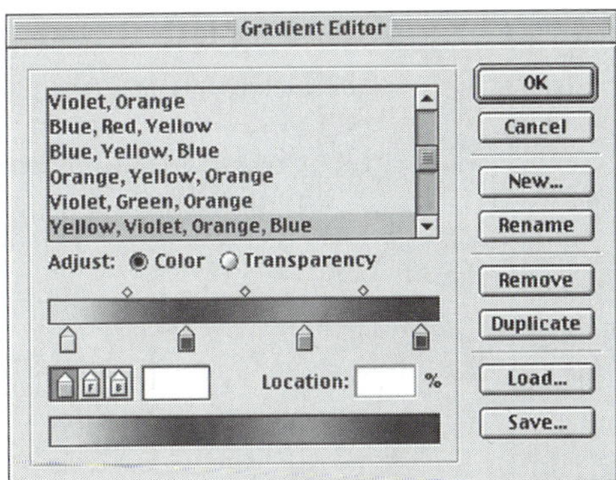

5. The diamonds at the top of the gradient bar in the center of the dialog box determine the midpoint between the two colors specified in the small colored boxes below the gradient bar. Use the mouse to drag one of the diamonds right or left; notice the change in the preview in the bottom of the dialog box; the preview looks exactly the same as the gradient bar used for editing.

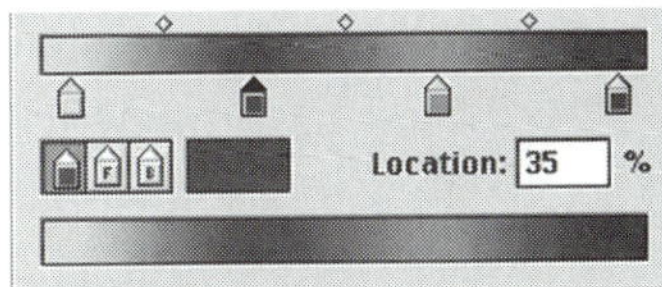

6. The color swatches at the bottom of the gradient bar used for editing represent the colors used in the blend; click and drag one of the color swatches, and observe the effect.

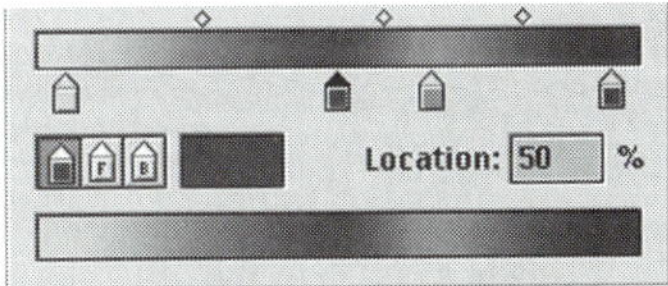

7. The icons at the bottom left (the box, the "F," and the "B") represent color choices. If the color point resembles the solid box, an actual color may be selected in the color picker; otherwise, "F" stands for foreground color and "B" stands for background color. Click one of the boxes below the center gradient bar, then click on the "F" icon.

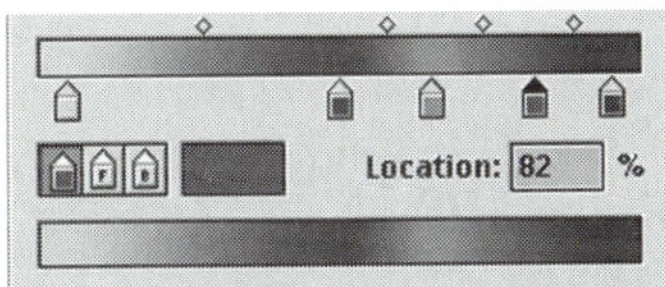

Note: Creating a gradient with foreground or background colors doesn't permanently store those colors. When using such a gradient in the image, these colors will be replaced with the *current* foreground and background colors.

8. Select another color square and click in the color swatch between the icons at the lower left and Location input box to select a new color from the Color Picker.

9. Add a new color by clicking between any two colors, or either end of the center (editable) gradient bar. Use the Color Picker to change the color. Select a color and click OK.
10. Delete a color by clicking and dragging it off the palette.
11. To create a transparent area in the gradient, click the Transparency radio button in the Adjust section. The center gradient bar will turn black.

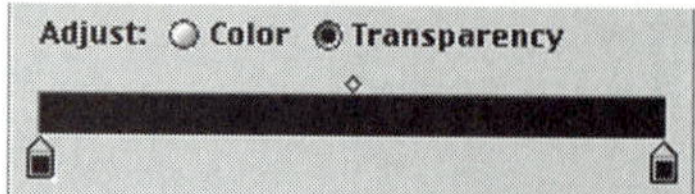

12. The black bar is the *gradient mask*. This mask may be turned on or off in the Options palette. You can add, delete, and edit transparency boxes using the same methods used to add and subtract color boxes to vary the transparency of the gradient. The difference is that instead of entering a color, you enter in a percent that represents how opaque you want the gradient to be at different points in the blend.

    Click on the left box, drag it right, and change Opacity to 25%. Notice that parts of the mask have turned more transparent (less opaque). Observe the effect on the preview gradient at the bottom of the palette; the preview displays the gradient with the chosen transparency options.
13. Experiment with different opacities and colors in the gradient, then click OK. Draw a gradient across your image.
14. Press Command/Control-Z to Undo the gradient. From the black triangle at the upper right of the Gradient Options palette, choose the Reset tool to restore the default gradients.
15. Keep the image open for the next exercise.

The Magic Eraser

At this point, it's probably difficult to see your original image. To correct this problem, it's time to introduce a special tool: the Eraser tool.

The Eraser can behave like any of the brush painting tools (the Paintbrush, the Airbrush, or the Pencil) or can be used with a simple square block. The type of tool it emulates is selected from the pull-down list on the Eraser Options palette.

Instead of painting with the foreground color, the Eraser paints in one of three ways. If you are on a *Background* layer, a layer which contains no transparency, the Eraser paints with the background color. If you are on a layer which *does* allow transparency, the Eraser removes all image data, making the area transparent. Finally, if the Erase to History box is checked, the tool will actually restore image data from the state you have designated in the History palette.

Using the Magic Eraser

1. Select the Eraser tool from the tool bar.

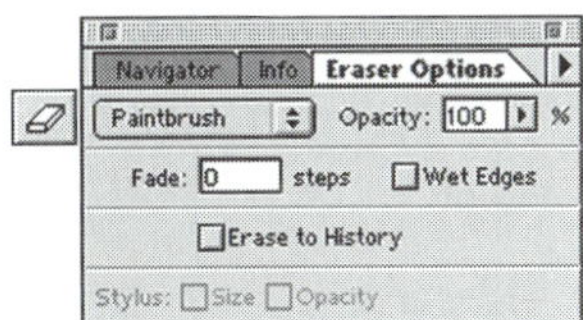

2. Choose the Airbrush from the pull-down on the Options palette (not the Toolbox) and change to a 65-pixel soft-edged brush.
3. In the History palette, click on the box to the left of the Elliptical Marquee state.
4. Select the Erase to History checkbox in the Eraser Options palette.
5. Begin painting on the image. As you paint, more and more of the older information appears.

6. Uncheck the Erase to History option. Paint the image a little more. Note that now the Eraser paints with the background color instead of the original image.
7. If white is not the current background color, press "D" to restore the Swatches to the default colors.
8. Check the Erase to History option again, and paint on the image.
9. The Erase to Saved option works only when the file is the same size and color mode as the original file. Select the Cropping tool and crop the image. Change back to the Eraser tool. The Erase to History option is unavailable in the Options palette.
10. Leave the file open for the next exercise.

The History Brush

This tool works opposite of the Magic Eraser. Instead of erasing *to* a point in history, it paints *from* a point in history.

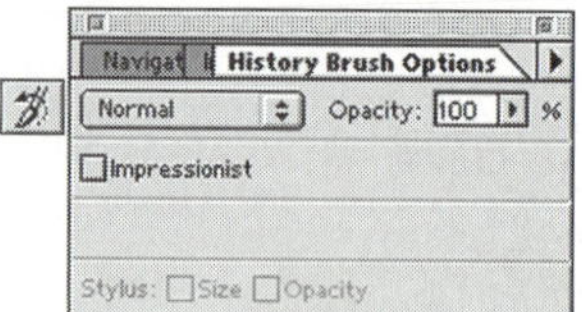

Using the History Brush

1. In the History palette, select the second Gradient state, then select New Snapshot. Accept the default name of Snapshot 1.
2. From the Options pull-down, clear the history.
3. Select the History Brush, click the box next to the Snapshot and begin painting.

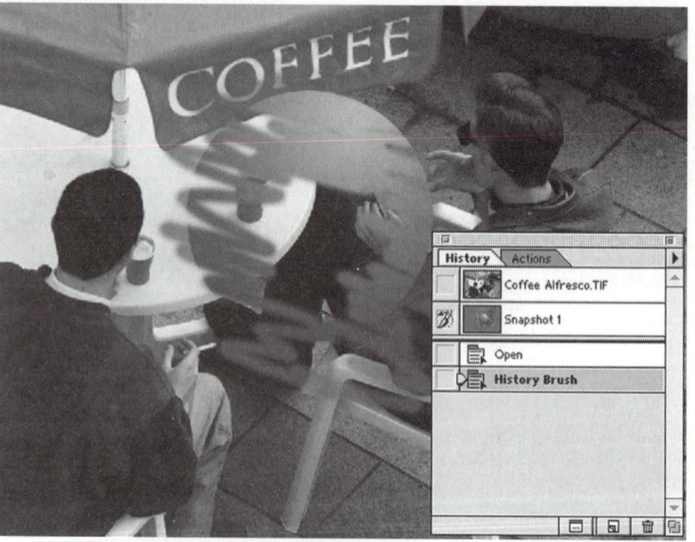

4. In this manner, you can selectively "reinstall" information for selected points in an image's history.
5. Close the file without saving.

The Rubber Stamp and Pattern Stamp

One of the most exciting tools available in Photoshop is the Rubber Stamp tool. This tool permits cloning of information from elsewhere in the image or from another image entirely.

The Rubber Stamp tool will copy image data from one area of the image (defined by Option/Alt-clicking on the the area to be copied) or from another document. Aligned mode always copies images relative to Option/Alt-clicked areas when beginning a new stroke. When the button is not selected, the reference is always returned to the Option/Alt clicked area as an absolute position.

The Pattern Stamp tool copies image data from a predefined pattern. With Aligned checked, it will copy the pattern contiguously, regardless of the number of strokes; non-aligned will start at the same point in the pattern with every stroke.

Using the Rubber Stamp

1. Open the image **Coffee Alfresco.TIF** again. Activate the Rubber Stamp and select a medium-sized soft brush.

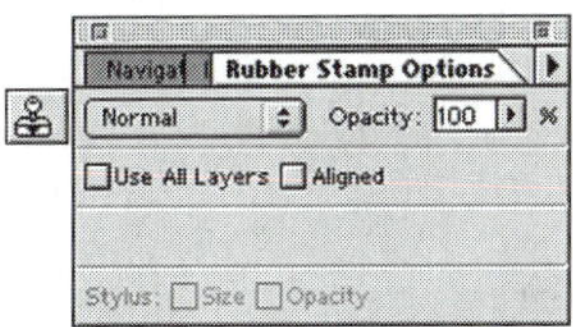

2. From the Options palette, be certain that Aligned is not selected.
3. Depress the Option/Alt key and click on the red cup on the side of the image. This defines the *source area*, the part of the image you wish to copy from.
4. Release the Option/Alt key and begin painting somewhere else on the table. Don't release the mouse button until you see an entire cup. When you've painted a complete cup, begin another one elsewhere in the image.

5. Select Aligned and Option/Alt-click the original cup again.

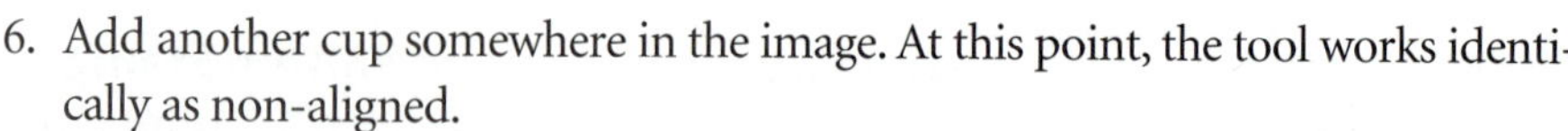

6. Add another cup somewhere in the image. At this point, the tool works identically as non-aligned.
7. Now start painting elsewhere in the image. Instead of painting cups, the tool copies existing image data relative to the first cup you painted in aligned mode.
8. Select Revert from the File Menu. Leave the file open for the next exercise.

Using the Pattern Stamp

1. Using the Rectangular Marquee, select a cup from the image to use as a repeating pattern.

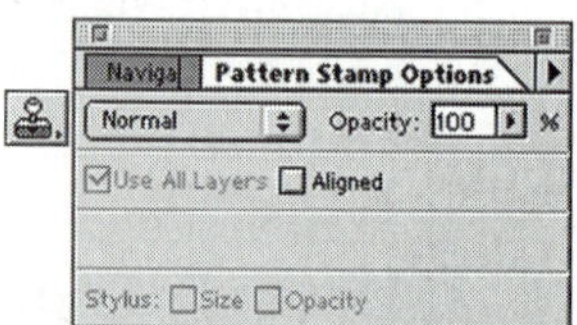

2. Choose Edit>Define Pattern. Deselect the image area. (Otherwise this will be the only area that you will be able to paint into.)
3. Select the Pattern Stamp tool.
4. Drag to paint with the tool.

5. Close the file without saving.

In Summary…

Clearly, the painting tools provide Photoshop users a variety of means to modify or to create images. The variety of approaches each tool affords allows for filling selected areas with color having a variety of transparency, and interacting differently with underlying areas. The next chapter explores the interaction between different layers in an image, and how they react when they are blended.

Complete Project A: Marinara Shelf Talker

Chapter 8

Blending Modes

Chapter Objective:

To learn how Blending modes will affect your image; the use of Blending modes in the Layers palette. In Chapter 8, you will:

- Understand how each Blending mode affects a layer's interaction with the layer beneath it.
- Become familiar with Normal and Dissolve modes.
- Learn to use modes that work with Highlight and Shadow.
- Learn to use the Lighten, Darken, Difference, and Exclusion modes.
- Learn to use Color Dodge and Burn.
- Learn when it is practical to use Blending modes.

Projects to be Completed:

- Marinara Shelf Talker
- KSOL Rising
- Maui Travel Postcard
- Rough Riders Ad
- Gulls Poster
- Concert Poster
- Banana Boat Table Tent
- Salute to Veterans Poster

Blending Modes

As previously explained, blending modes specify how Photoshop combines image information from two different sources. Most of these modes are available when using painting tools, when using the Edit>Fill command, and when compositing layers. Don't worry about the math, but it *is* important to understand how blending modes will affect your image.

Blending Modes and Layers

Blending modes are located in a pull-down menu in the upper left corner of the Layers palette if you're not on the Background layer, and in the upper left corner of the Options palette when a painting tool is selected. Select a painting tool and activate the drop-down list. Notice that the blending modes are separated into five groups (designated by a horizontal line) according to the type of blending operation they perform.

Most modes are available on both the Options and Layers palettes; the exception, Behind is available only when using painting tools. It simply allow you to paint only the transparent areas in an image — similar to painting on the back of a piece of acetate.

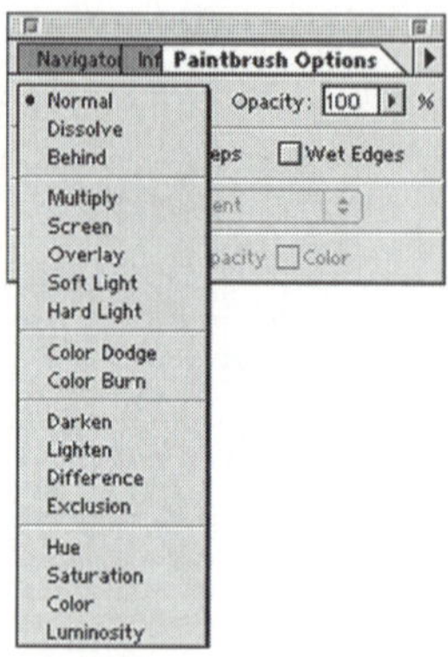

For most of this lesson, we'll be discussing the use of blending modes in the Layers palette. The concepts are the same whether using a tool, the Fill command, or the Layers palette. We won't get into an in-depth discussion of layers right now, but there are a few things that you should know.

By default, layers work as though two photographs are stacked on top of each other; anything on the upper layer will obscure what is on the layer below it. When using blending modes, however, each mode affects the way a layer interacts with the layer beneath it.

Layers and Blending Modes

1. Open the **Archery Target.TIF** image from the **SF-Intro Photoshop** folder.

2. You'll need a new layer to blend with. Select the New Layer option from the Layers palette submenu, accessible by clicking on the black triangle in the upper right corner of the palette. Click OK to automatically create a layer with the name "Layer 1". The new layer will be the active layer. Notice that you can set the blending mode for the layer from this dialog box.

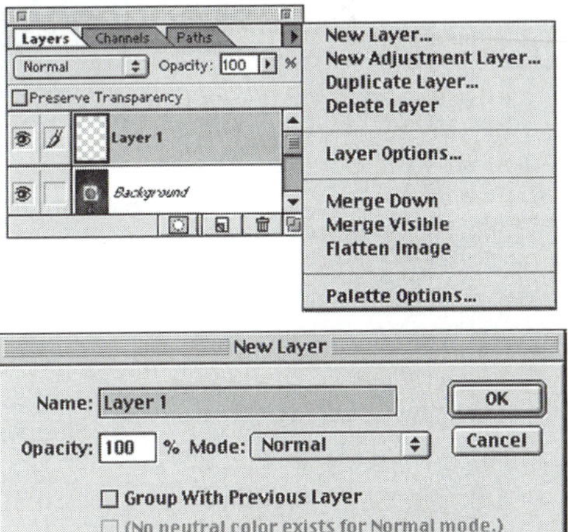

3. Press "X" to toggle between foreground and background colors.

4. While depressing the Shift key, select Filter>Render>Clouds. The layer will be filled with a cloud texture. (Holding down the Shift key while selecting this command creates very high contrast clouds; i.e., clouds with lots of very light and very dark areas.)

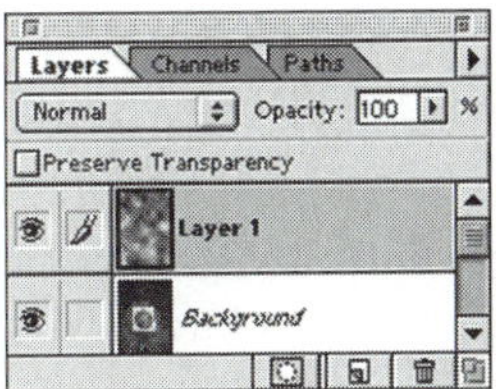

5. The *Background* is now obscured by the black-and-white image. Note the word Normal on the Layers palette. Clicking here will display the list of blending modes. Click the list now, but just look at it; leave the blending mode set to Normal.

6. Notice the word Opacity on the Layers palette. The slider below Opacity adjusts the transparency of the layer. Adjusting this slider left makes the layer more transparent. Moving the slider right makes it more opaque. Move the slider back and forth to get a feel for how opacity can affect a layer.

7. Name the file "Blending Practice.PSD", and save it into your **Work in Progress** folder before closing.

Foreground and background colors remain in the palette once a document is closed. If you had previously worked on a document that had blue as a foreground color and orange as a background color, those are the colors that would initially appear for the next document you worked on.

The Blending Modes

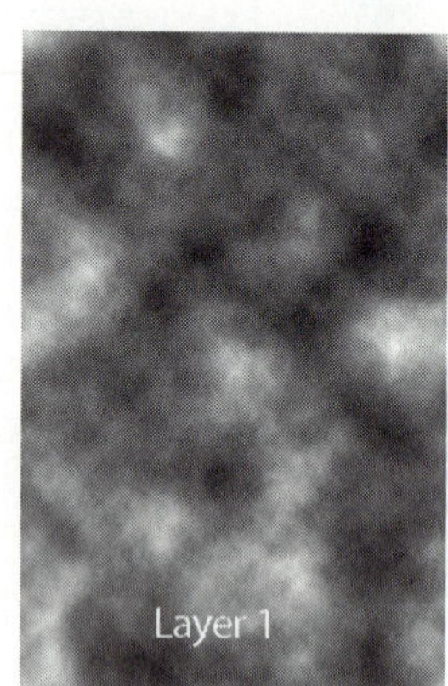

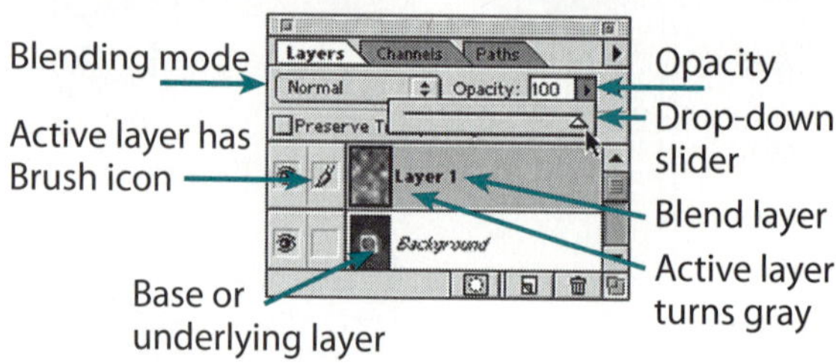

- A layer set to Normal, when set to 100% opacity, will obscure the layer below it, except where the upper layer is transparent. If the layer opacity is reduced, the upper layer fades into the lower layer.

- Dissolve behaves identically to Normal at 100% opacity. If the blend layer is partly transparent, Dissolve mode will randomly make the layer pixels either 100% opaque or 100% transparent. The ratio of pixels which become 100% transparent is determined by the pixel opacity. A layer with 30% opacity set to Dissolve will turn about 30% of the pixels opaque and the remaining pixels transparent.

- Multiply literally multiplies the values of the pixels on the upper layer and the underlying layer to produce a new color. The color produced is always darker than the original color. White pixels, which have a value of 0, are transparent. Multiplying any color by black will produce black. Adjusting the opacity softens the effect.

- Screen mode is the opposite of Multiply mode; it always creates a color *lighter* than the original color. Screening with black leaves the underlying pixels unchanged; screening with white will produce pure white.

- Overlay multiplies or screens the blended layer with the underlying layer, depending upon the color of the base layer. The upper color is blended with the lower color, not replaced, which preserves the highlights and shadows of the image.

- In Soft Light mode, the closer the blend layer pixel is to white, the more the underlying image is lightened; the nearer to black, the more the base layer is darkened. Using black-and-white on the blended layer will create a color much lighter or darker than the original, but will never change to pure black or pure white.

- Hard Light behaves almost like Soft Light does, except that instead of simply lightening or darkening, the mode *adds* black or white to the image. If pixels in the blend layer are 100% black or white, then the resulting color will be totally obscured by black or white. In both Hard Light and Soft Light modes, 50% gray is transparent.
- Color Dodge brightens the base color based on the blend color. 100% black is transparent.
- Color Burn darkens the base color based on the blend color. 100% white is transparent.
- Darken will display the pixels of the upper layer only when they are darker than the pixels on the underlying layer; otherwise, the base layer pixels are displayed.
- Lighten displays the blend layer pixels if they are lighter than the pixels on the underlying layer; if they're not, the base layer image is displayed.
- Difference, which we used in our mirrored tile exercise, compares the pixels on the upper layer to the pixels on the lower layer; it subtracts the value of whichever is the darker of the two from the brighter. Since black has a brightness value of 0, it will not affect the underlying image. White will invert the colors in the underlying image.
- Exclusion behaves in much the same way as Difference mode; it simply produces a softer effect.
- Hue mode uses the *hue* (the "named" color) of the blend layer, but preserves the luminance and saturation of the original image. It allows you to preserve the highlights and shadows in the image while changing the color.
- Saturation uses the *saturation* of the blend color and the hue and luminance of the base image. It is the *intensity* of the color that changes, not the color itself. Grays have 0% saturation and, therefore, are transparent. Very bright colors, such as pure reds and greens, will oversaturate areas of the image.
- Color mode blends the hue *and* saturation of the image. It's extremely useful for tinting or colorizing images since it maintains the grays, and therefore, much of the detail of the base image.
- Luminosity is the opposite of Color mode. The grays, or luminance, of the blend layer are used with the hue and saturation of the base image.

Blending is more easily understood when seen; let's try some blending!

When creating a new layer with a special blending mode, you can ask Photoshop to automatically fill the layer with a neutral color — one that is transparent in that blending mode. For example, if you create a layer in Hard Light mode, you can ask Photoshop to fill it with 50% gray. The layer will appear transparent, but filters such as the noise filter can be run on it without filling it first.

Using Normal and Dissolve Modes

1. Open the file **Blending Practice.PSD** from the **SF-Intro Photoshop** folder. When you created a layer, the blending mode defaulted to Normal. Reduce the opacity by moving the Opacity slider to the left, allowing some of the lower image to show through.

2. Click on the layer name, Layer 1. Slide the Opacity setting down to 60%. Layer 1 is now 40% transparent — 60% of the image data on the layer is visible, blended with 40% of the layer underneath.

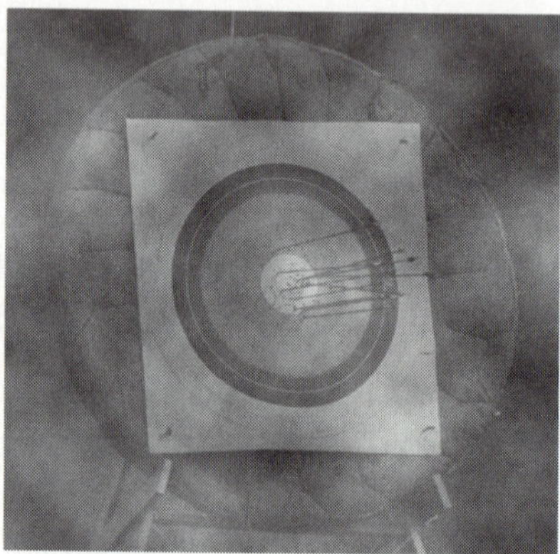

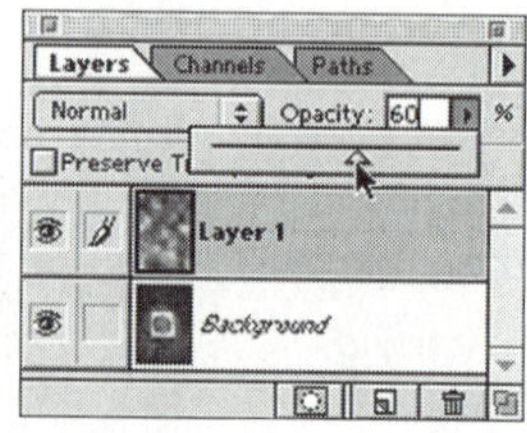

3. Return the Opacity slider to the 100% position. Click on the word Normal to bring up the Blending Mode pull-down list. Select Dissolve. The image stays the same; when a layer is set to 100% opacity and there are no partially transparent pixels, Dissolve mode behaves identically to Normal.

4. Move the Opacity slider down to 50%.

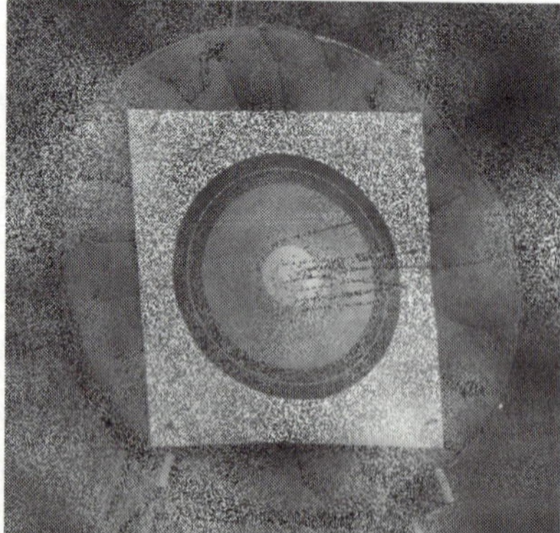

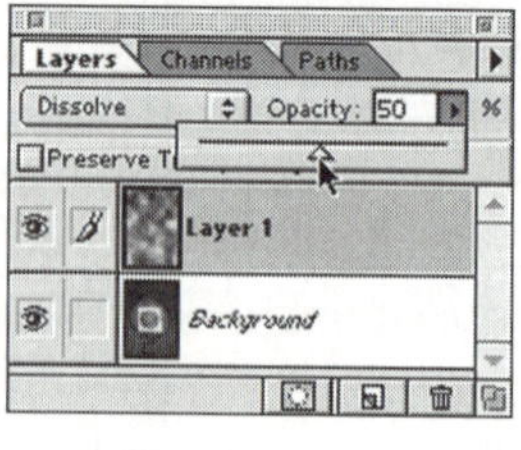

Half of the pixels display the image on the *Background layer*; the other half display portions of the black-and-white blending layer. Spend a minute adjusting the slider back and forth to get a feel for how Dissolve affects your image.

5. Move the Opacity slider back to 100%.

6. Keep the file open for the next exercise.

Using Modes that Work with Highlight and Shadow

1. Change the layer mode to Screen and adjust the Opacity slider down to about 50%. The underlying image looks as though it is being viewed through fog.

2. Change the blending mode to Multiply and the Opacity to 50%. The black portion of the blended layer darkens the image, as if that portion of the picture were in deep shadow. The white portions of the blend layer allow the brighter underlying base layer to show through. The end result is an effect much like sunlight dappled through trees.

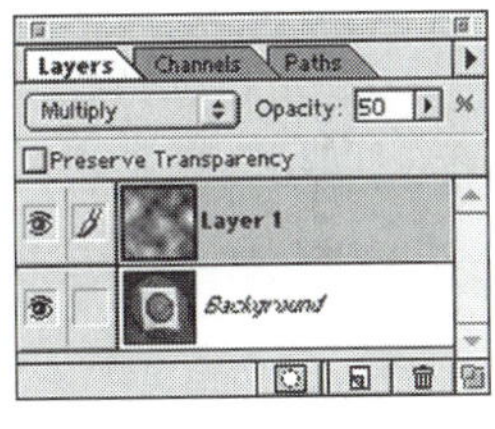

3. Set the blending mode to Overlay. The image is darkened or lightened (multiplied or screened) according to the information in Layer 1, the blend layer. Compare this blend with the opacity at 50% to the Multiply and Screen results.

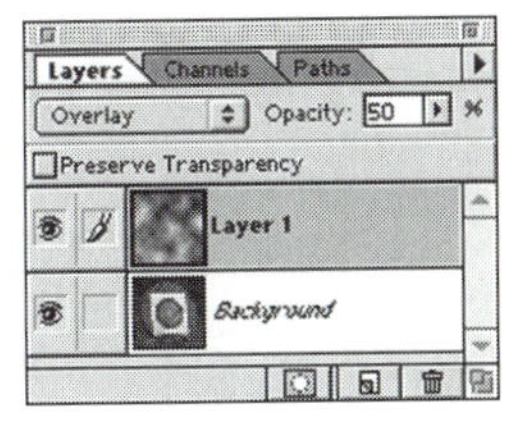

4. Soft Light and Hard Light behave in a similar manner, but with markedly different results. Change the blending mode to Soft Light and set the opacity at 100%. The image is lightened or darkened according to the blend layer, but never changes to pure black or pure white.

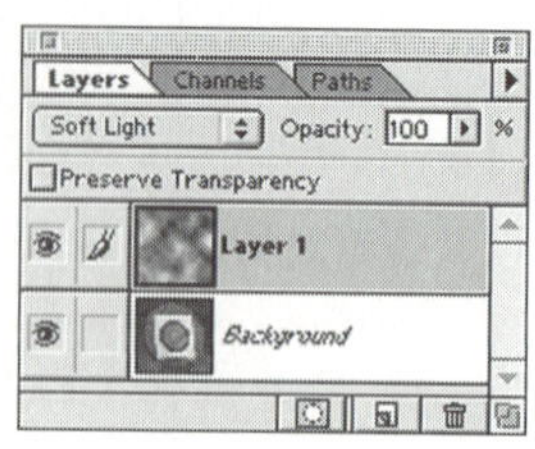

5. Change to Hard Light. See the difference?

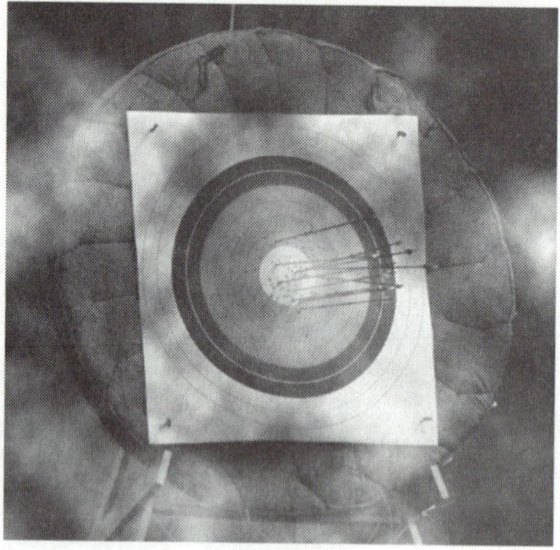

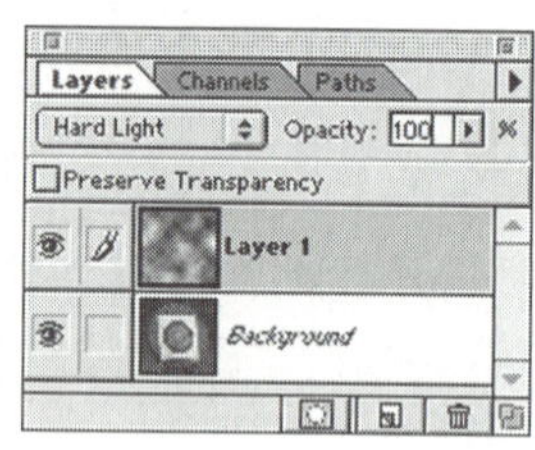

6. Where Layer 1 is 100% white, the image is obscured with white; black in the blend layer turns the image black. Hard Light and Soft Light are especially useful for adjusting the highlights and shadows in an image.

   In addition, Hard Light can be used for special effects such as compositing a texture onto a grayscale image and creating buttons used in multimedia and Internet graphics. Reduce the opacity to about 20%; notice that the effect now resembles Soft Light.

7. Set opacity to 100% and leave the image open for the next exercise.

Using Lighten, Darken, Difference, and Exclusion

1. Change the mode to Lighten. Because much of the layer is pure black-and - white, Lighten shows only the area that was painted with black spots.

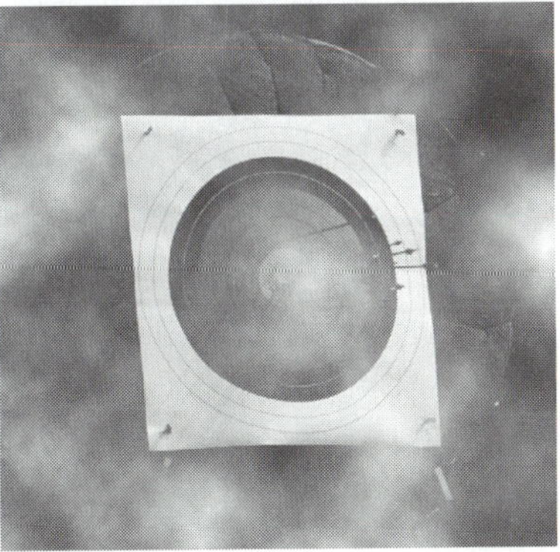

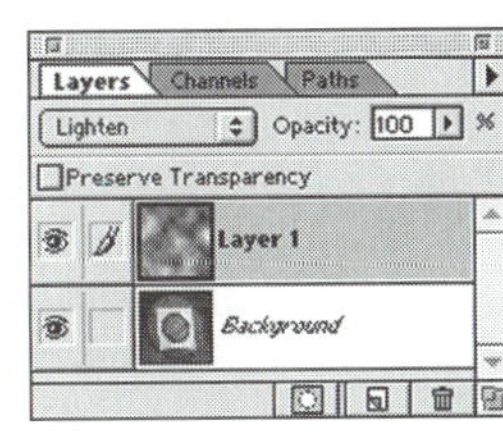

2. Now change the mode to Darken. Darken allows everything *but* the spots to show through.

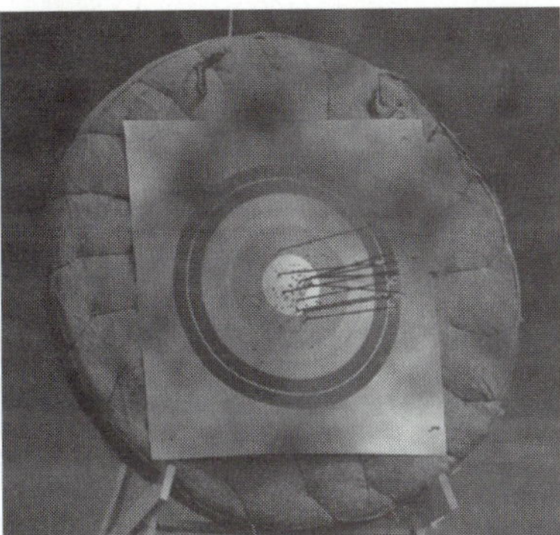

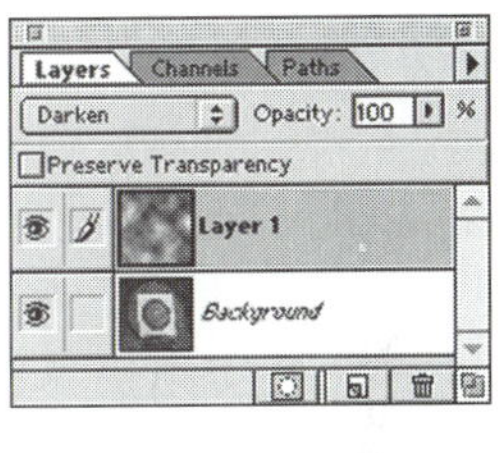

3. Change the blending mode to Difference. This mode is used primarily for special effects. Since black has *no* brightness, it will not affect the underlying image. White pixels invert the pixels underneath.

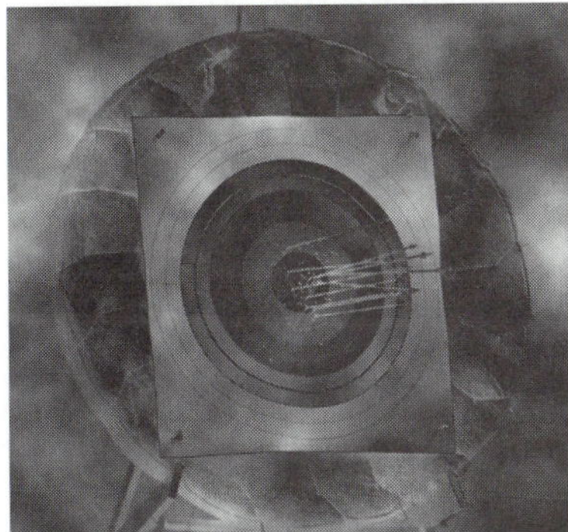

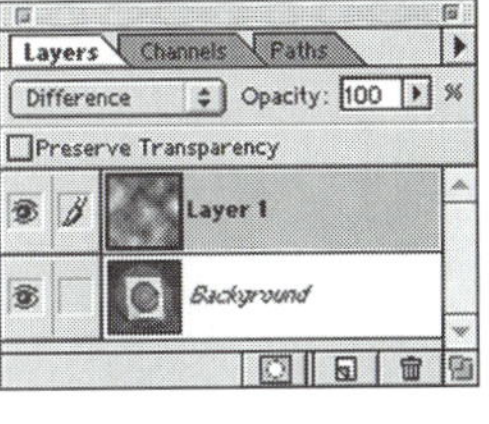

4. If Layer 1 contains colored pixels, Difference subtracts the mathematical value of one *color* from the other. Click on Layer 1 to activate it and select the Paint-

brush. Choose a bright foreground color such as red. Paint a bit on Layer 1 to see the effect.

5. Change the blending mode to Exclusion. Notice that it is very similar to the Difference mode, only not as harsh.

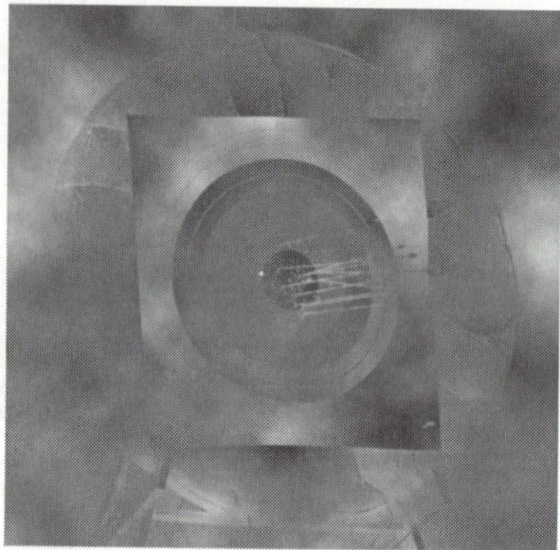

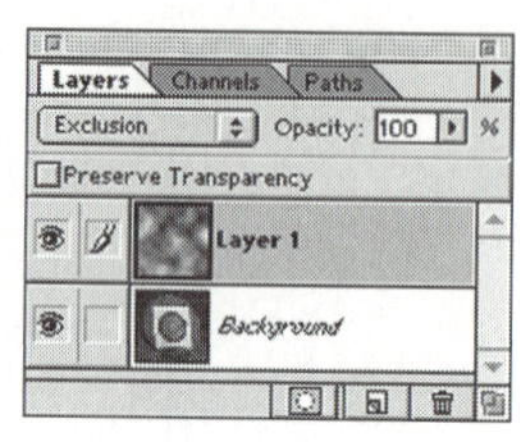

6. Delete Layer 1. Leave the image open for the next exercise.

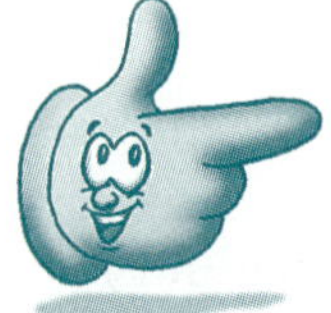

Using Color Dodge and Burn

1. Many modes manipulate the *color* of an image, so our clouds layer really isn't appropriate for demonstrating these effects. Click Layer 1 to make certain that it is active, press Command-A (Macintosh) or Control-A (Windows) to select all, and press the Delete key. This erases all the data on the layer, setting the entire layer to transparent. Set Opacity back to 100% and change the blending mode to Normal.

2. Open the file **Spectral.TIF** from the **SF-Intro Photoshop** folder. Select All, and drag the contents of the Background layer of **Spectral.TIF** to **Blending Practice.PSD**. This will create a new layer. Try to make the image fill the window completely. Close **Spectral.TIF**.

3. Change the blending mode to Color Dodge. The image is brightened according to the pixels in the blend layer.

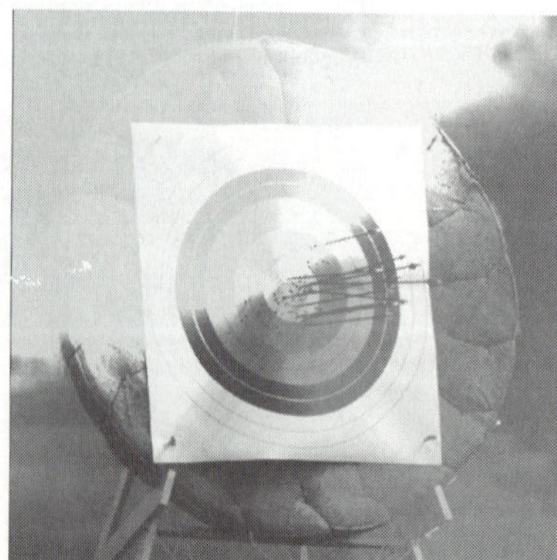

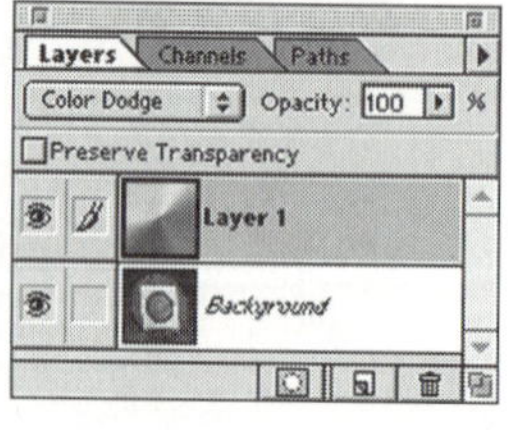

4. Change the blending mode to Color Burn. This mode is essentially the opposite of Dodge mode; the pixels are darkened according to the blend layer. Both of these modes also work well in black-and-white.

5. Leave the image open for the next exercise.

Using Color Blending Modes

1. We're going to use the Clouds filter for the next exercise. Click Layer 1 to make certain it is active, press Command-A (Macintosh) or Control-A (Windows) to select all, and press the Delete key. From the Filter menu, select Render>Clouds. Be certain that Opacity is set to 100%, change the blending mode to Hue and watch.

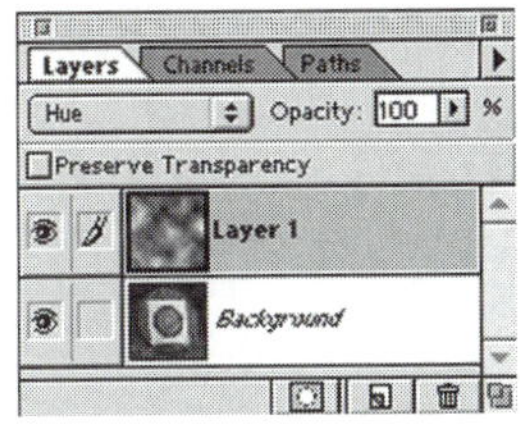

Hue preserved the luminance and saturation of the original, while replacing the hue (red, blue, yellow, etc.). Highlights and shadows are preserved. Click the eye next to Layer 1 on and off for comparison.

2. Now change the blending mode to Saturation. This time, click the eye next to the *Background* on and off. Notice that it is the *intensity* of the color that changes to match the intensity of the pixels in Layer 1 rather than the color of the underlying image.

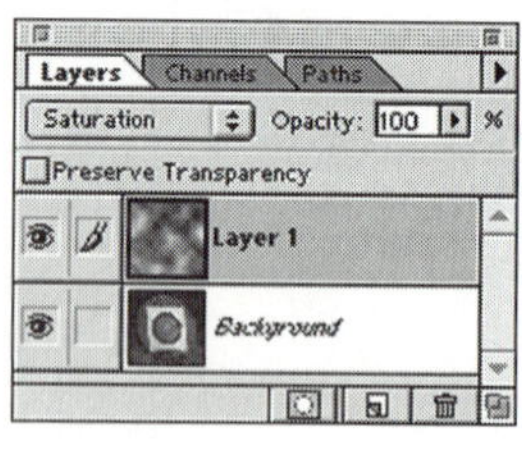

3. Color mode blends both the hue and saturation of the image. Switch the blending mode to Color. The black-and-white components of the colors in Layer 1 are replaced by the black-and-white of the image.

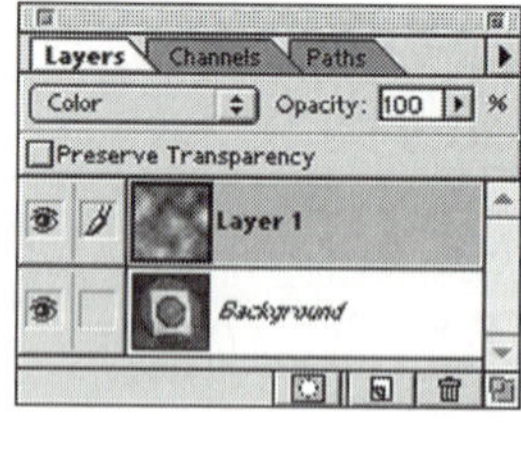

4. Change the blending mode to Luminosity. This mode is the opposite of Color mode. The brightness, or luminance, of the blending layer is used with the hue and saturation of the base image.

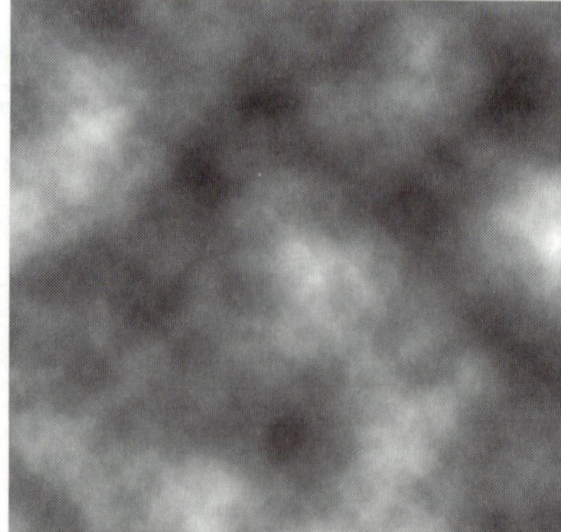

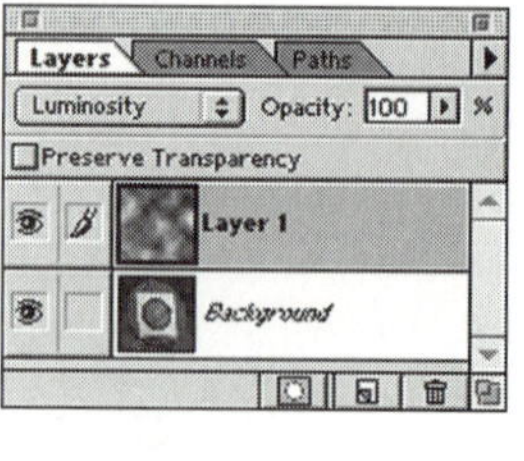

5. Close the image without saving.

Practical Usage

At first glance it may seem that the blending modes are useful only for surrealistic special effects. There are many real-world Photoshop problems, however, that can't be easily handled in any other way.

For example, colorizing grayscale images is a snap using painting tools and the Color mode. Hard Light may be used to intensify highlight and shadow areas of low-contrast images. Darken makes it simple to superimpose black line art onto an image. And Hue allows you to recolor items in an image without changing the saturation or brightness of a color.

Notes:

Review #1

Chapters 1 Through 8:

In Chapters 1 through 8, we learned the basic operations necessary to build advanced Photoshop documents, including an understanding of how images may be used, a familiarity with Photoshop's working environment, navigation of this environment, sizes and resolutions, basic selection techniques, working with type, painting tools, and blending modes. Through this series of discussions and hands-on projects, you should:

- Know that all images must be in a digital format for work in Photoshop. You should also be comfortable with the many devices used for capturing and converting images. You should know about resolution, and its effect on images.
- Understand the Photoshop Toolbox palette, and the variables it offers. You should also be aware of the importance of Photoshop's preferences, and know how to adjust and save them.
- Know how to navigate in Photoshop, and how to use navigational control to its utmost efficiency. You should also have developed an initial understanding of Selection tools and their functions.
- Know the difference between PPI and line screens, and their relevance to the printed piece. You should also understand how to resize an image, and how tones and bit depth affect a mechanical's quality.
- Be familiar with the basic selection tools, and have a working knowledge of their use. You should also know how to create a Type Mask, and have a basic understanding of Layers.
- Be comfortable with Photoshop's type handling abilities, and know how and when to use type for special effects. You should also have gained additional knowledge of Layers and how they apply to type.
- Know how to work with Photoshop's painting tools, and understand how to adjust and apply them to your artwork.

Chapter 9

Complex Selections

Chapter Objective:

To learn additional methods of creating and manipulating selections that would be extremely difficult using the manual selection tools. In Chapter 9, you will:

- Learn how to use the Magic Wand tool, and to smooth a selection.
- Learn how to Preserve selection information, and how to load and save these selections.
- Learn about Feathered selections, and when to apply them.
- Understand how to create vignettes.
- Understand how to create a Composite with selections.

Projects to be Completed:

- Marinara Shelf Talker
- KSOL Rising
- Maui Travel Postcard
- Rough Riders Ad
- Gulls Poster
- Concert Poster
- Banana Boat Table Tent
- Salute to Veterans Poster

Complex Selections

So far we've learned to make selections using the Lasso and Marquee tools. While these tools can be very useful for many types of selections, Photoshop provides other ways to create and manipulate selections that would be difficult to create using the manual selection tools.

The Magic Wand

The Magic Wand allows you to create selections based on the nearness in color of contiguous pixels, similar to the way the Paint Bucket tool chooses areas to paint. The Magic Wand uses a Tolerance setting which behaves identically to the Tolerance setting in the Paint Bucket Options palette.

The Eyedropper Options palette allows setting the sensitivity of data sampling to a Point Sample (one pixel), 3 x 3 Average, or 5 x 5 Average. The 3 x 3 Average is generally best.

Working with the Magic Wand

1. Open the image **Champagne.TIF** from the **SF-Intro Photoshop** folder.
2. Double-click the Magic Wand tool to activate its Options palette.
3. Set Tolerance to 5. Click on the gloved hand. Irregular areas of adjacent pixels are selected according to how closely they are related in color. In this instance, since the Tolerance is set to such a low value, only a few pixels are selected.

This setting also affects the way other Photoshop tools and commands work, including the Magic Wand Tolerance setting and the color.

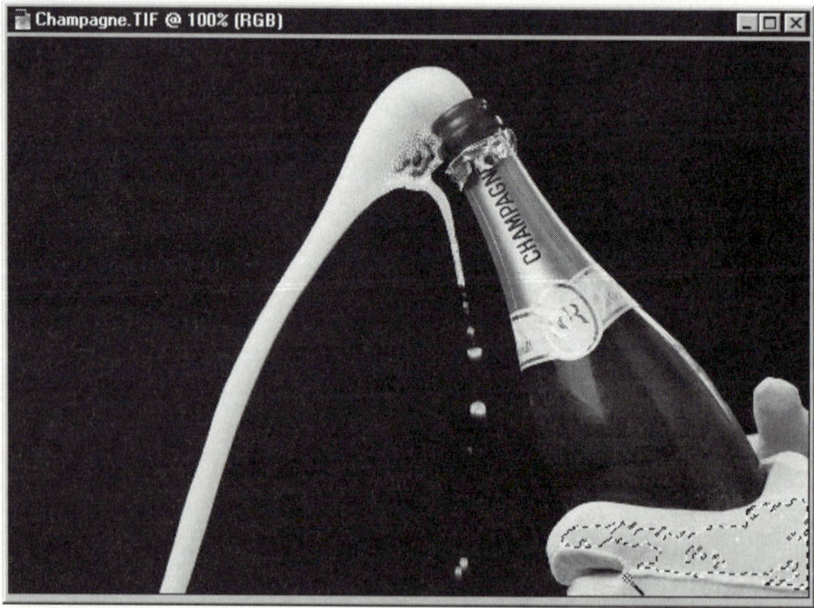

As you learn about Channels and Selections, it can become confusing. When instructed to "Load" a channel, you should Select> Load Selection; when instructed to "Activate" a channel, click on the channel in the Channels palette.

4. Shift-Select a few more areas; it would take some time to select the entire hand using these settings. Press Command-D (Macintosh) or Control-D (Windows) to deselect the area and change the Tolerance value to 180. Click on the hand again.

Be cautious. Sometimes it is difficult to make an accurate selection without zooming in to see individual pixels.

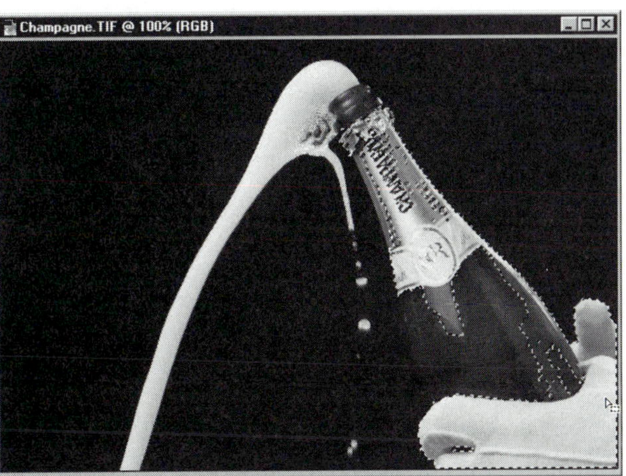

Now, too much is selected. Though you have selected all of the gloved hand, much of the bottle is selected as well. Press Command/Control-D to deselect the area, and change Tolerance to 16. Click on the gloved hand, then Shift-click some of the larger, unselected areas. Make certain that you click on shadow areas, such as the thumb, as well as highlight areas.

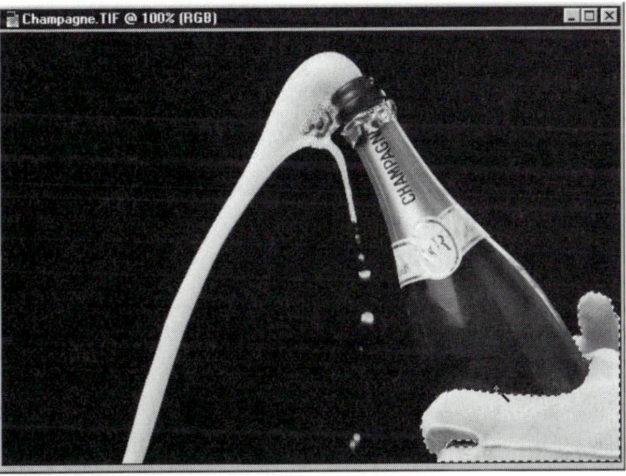

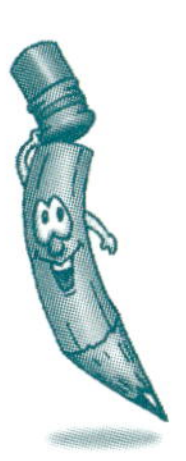

Grow and Similar commands use the Tolerance value set in the Magic Wand Options palette. Repeated application of these commands will expand your selection incrementally, depending on this value.

5. You probably still have some small, unselected areas on the glove, especially around the edges. The Select>Grow command expands the current selection based on the Tolerance setting on the Magic Wand Options palette. Choose Select>Grow; more of the glove is encompassed by the selection border.

6. Choose Select>Grow several times, until the selection border has expanded all the way to the black background. You will likely still have a few unselected areas in the glove, and the edge may be a bit rough in some places. If we were to use this selection, it would probably be easiest to tidy it up using the Lasso tool.

7. What if you want to select all of a range of color in an image, not just pixels adjacent to each other? You could Shift-Select the different areas, though it could be a tedious process. Select>Similar selects pixels within the specified Tolerance throughout the image, not just adjacent to the current selection. Choose Similar from the Select menu. Parts of the bottle and the stream of champagne are selected. Choose Select>Similar.

Similar and Grow work on any active selection.

8. Activate the Similar command again, and the entire stream of champagne is selected. If you wished to select just the glove and the champagne itself, you could deselect the bottle highlights using the Lasso tool.
9. Close the image without saving.

Smoothing a Selection

1. Open the image **Champagne.TIF** from the **SF-Intro Photoshop** folder.
2. Activate the Magic Wand and set Tolerance to 2. If this selects only a few pixels, increase the tolerance to 12.
3. Click on the black background on the left hand side of the image.
4. Shift-click on large unselected black areas around the image to increase the selection area. You probably have most of the background selected, but there are areas missing along the edges and a few unselected pixels in the black area.
5. Choose Modify>Smooth from the Select menu. Set Sample Radius to 4 and click OK. The Smooth command removes stray pixels outside of the selection and adds selected pixels that are isolated within the selection to the inside of the selection.
6. By now, your selection should be fairly accurate. If there are stray groups of unselected pixels not picked up by the Smooth command, use the Lasso tool to add them to the selection. Areas which are not needed can be removed by using the Lasso tool along with the Option/Alt key.

Accurate selections of complex images are often more easily accomplished using a combination of the Freehand, Polygon, and Magnetic Lasso tools, in conjunction with judicious application of the Magic Wand tool set to the appropriate tolerances.

7. Smooth can adversely affect the existing edges of a selection; it can smooth the edges of the selection, drawing it away from the edge of the item being selected. Use the Magic Wand to reselect the already selected background area to tighten up your selection.
8. Carefully review your entire selection, fine-tuning as necessary. This selection will eventually be composited with another image, so it is important that it is as accurate as you can make it.
9. Keep this image open and its selection intact; you'll need it to complete the next section.

Preserving Selection Information

You've just completed a rather complex selection. What happens if you need to work on another job or if it's time to go home? Photoshop's Select menu includes tools for saving and loading selections you have created.

Saving and Loading Selections

1. With the selection of the champagne bottle background still active, choose Save Selection from the Select menu to display the Save Selection dialog box.

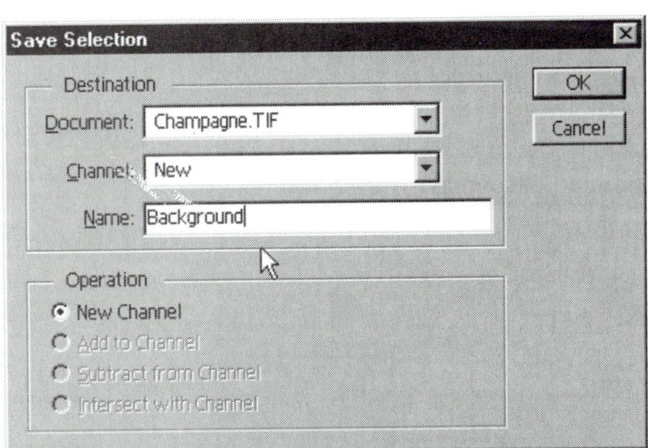

2. If you don't change the dialog box settings, Document defaults to the current document and Channel defaults to New. The Channel will automatically default to a number representing the next available channel. For this example, leave these fields at their defaults, and type "Background" into the Name field. Click OK.
3. Press Command/Control-D to deselect. Activate the Lasso tool and draw a loose selection anywhere in your document to entirely obliterate the current selection.

If you do not name the selection, it will assume the default name of "Alpha 1."

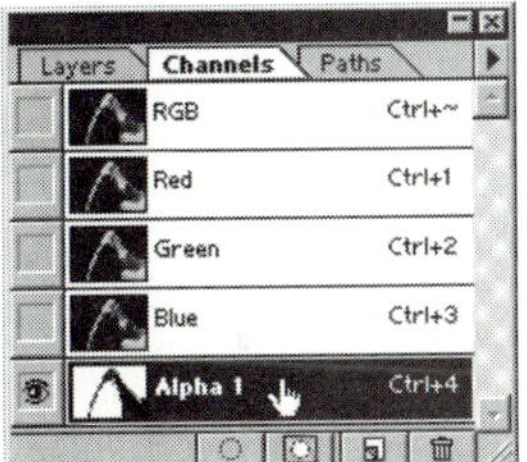

4. Choose Load Selection from the Select menu.

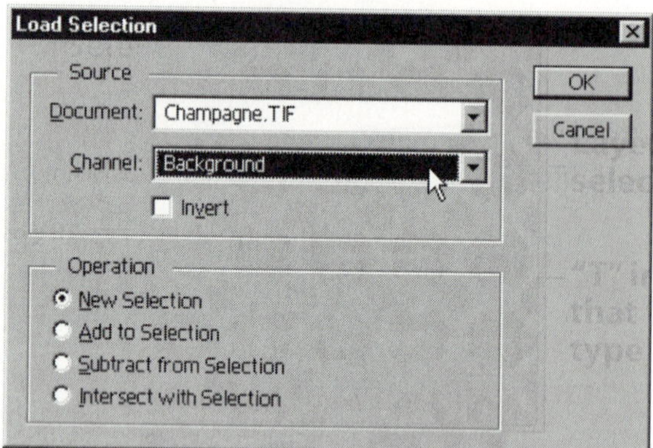

Leave the Document set to Champagne.TIF. The Channel should default to Background. When you saved your selection, it was saved into an alpha channel; since there are already three channels in your RGB document (red, green, and blue) the new channel is the fourth in the Channels palette. Click OK to restore your champagne bottle selection.

5. Press "D" to reset the default foreground/background color swatches. Press Delete to silhouette the champagne and bottle.

The History palette can be used to restore an earlier version of the Champagne image.

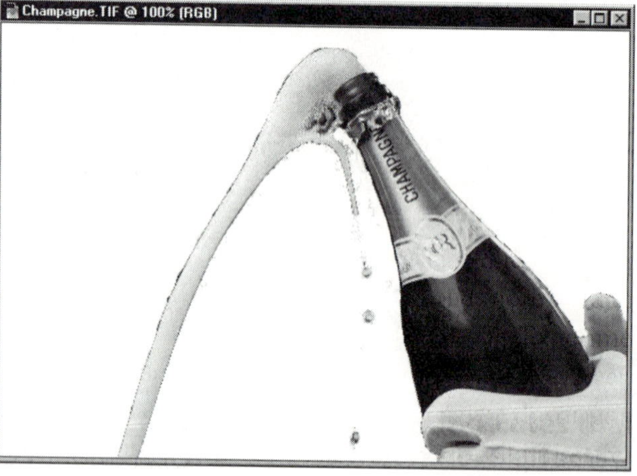

6. Press Command/Control-Z to undo the deletion of the black background.

7. Choose Load Selection from the Select menu again. This time, make certain that the Invert box is checked. Click OK.

The bottle itself is selected instead of the background; that is, everything that was selected is now deselected and everything that was not selected, is selected.

Save even simple selections; it's easier to throw away an alpha channel when you are finished than to recreate your selection from scratch.

8. Press Command/Control-D to deselect. Using the Lasso tool, draw another loose selection. Make certain that you include both parts of the image (background and part of the bottle).
9. Load Selection from the Select menu. Leave the first three settings at their defaults, but in the Operation box, select Intersect with Selection. Click OK.
10. Press Delete. The random selection minus the champagne and bottle is removed. Undo the delete.

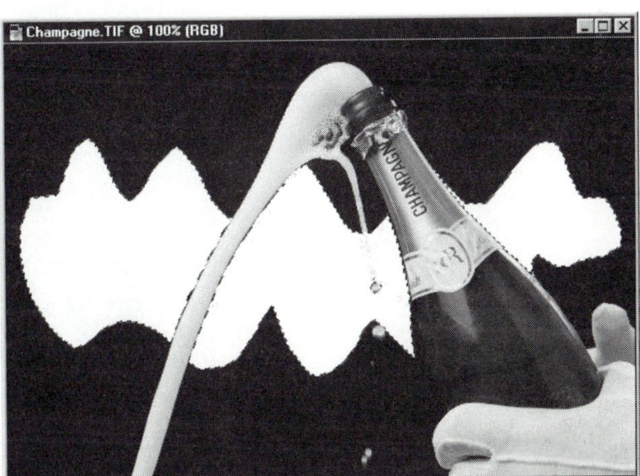

The new selection is made of the part of your Lasso selection that intersected with the saved selection of the background; the selected area which included the bottle is deselected because it wasn't included in the saved selection of the background and, therefore, did not intersect with the Lasso selection.

Try the Polygon Lasso tool to make a starburst selection with rays that cross the champagne and bottle.

11. Deselect the current selection and create another loose selection with the Lasso. Make certain that the selection includes part of the champagne bottle.

12. Choose Select>Load Selection, and change the Operation to Add to Selection. Click OK to load the bottle background. The new selection includes both the Lasso selection and the saved background. Press delete to see exactly which areas are selected. (Keep the selection intact while we continue.)

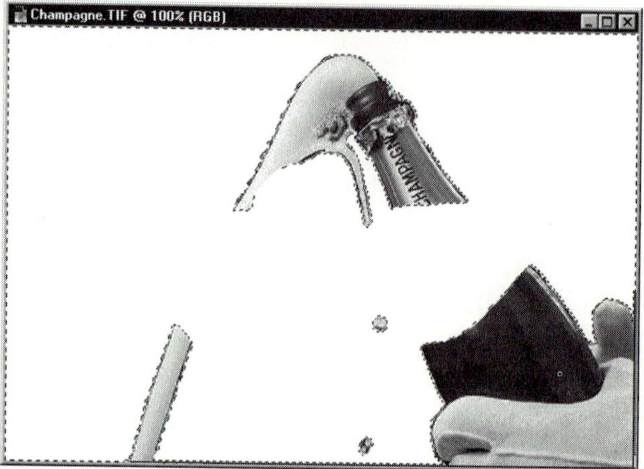

13. You can also Subtract from Selection. Undo the Delete step and choose Select >Load Selection and change the Operation to Subtract from Selection. When you click OK, the saved selection is subtracted from the current selection. Press Delete.

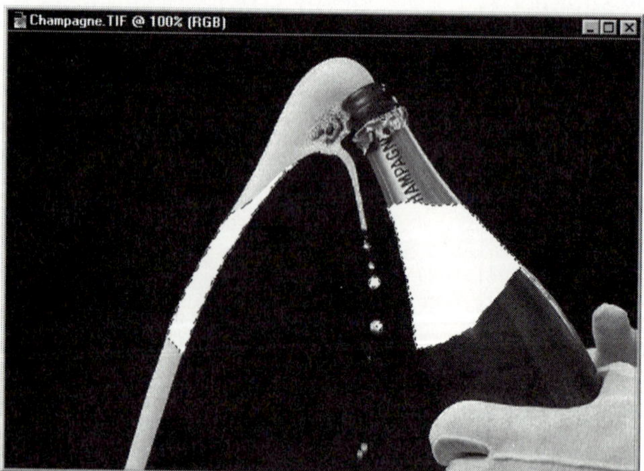

14. Undo the Delete and save the image as a Photoshop file named "Champagne Selection.PSD" before closing. We'll be using the alpha channel selection you saved a little later.

Feathering

A *feathered* selection is one that blends gradually between the selected data and the unselected background. It is especially useful for smoothly blending pasted selections into other images.

Selections may be feathered while drawing a selection or by specifying a feather amount in the Options palette for selection tools. Most of the time you'll want to feather your selection after you have created it. The "soft" edges of a feathered selection can be difficult to locate precisely when using Shift to add to your selection.

Feathering Selections

1. Open the image **Picnic.TIF** from the **SF-Intro Photoshop** folder.
2. Using the Lasso tools, carefully select the woman's head; include the entire head, and finish the selection with a straight line across the neck.

The selection marquee for a feathered selection assumes the position of the 50% point, so that the actual pixels selected will extend beyond that selection border.

3. Choose Select>Save Selection, name it "Woman's Head" and click OK to save your selection.
4. Press Command-J (Macintosh) or Control-J (Windows) to create a layer containing the woman's head. Select Edit>Transform>Numeric and rotate the selection -30 degrees. Click OK.
5. Use the Move tool to position the second head so it is resting on her shoulder, next to her original head.

If you zoom in on the newly placed head, there is probably an obvious edge where the neck was cut off, as well as some "dirt" where the second face overlays the first.

Why expand before feathering? Feathering affects both sides of the selection border. It adds a soft halo of pixel information from the area outside of your image, but it also softens the area just inside the selection. This will affect the clarity and sharpness of the selection edge. Expanding the selection by a number of pixels equal to the feather radius ensures that the feathering occurs outside of your selection, without affecting the data inside.

The Modify menu also has a command to Contract a selection, or make it smaller by a specified number of pixels, and to create a selected Border around your existing selection edge.

6. Click the trash can on the Layers palette, then click OK to delete Layer 1. Choose Select>Load Selection and click OK to load the saved selection of the head.

7. Choose Select>Modify>Expand. Enter "3" to expand the current selection by 3 pixels; click OK. Now choose Feather from the Select menu, and set the Feather Radius to 3 pixels.

8. Press Command/Control-J to turn the selection into a layer. Use Edit>Transform>Rotate to rotate the layer about 30 degrees counterclockwise. Again, use the Move tool to position the second head so it is resting on the woman's shoulder. Zoom in and examine the edges — they should blend almost perfectly with the original image.

9. Close the file without saving.

Vignettes

Vignettes, soft-edged images which fade out into the paper, used to be produced photographically, using a stencil and an enlarger. The stencil was oscillated above the photographic paper, usually by hand, to vary the exposure on the edge of the image.

Today, this technique is produced digitally; using Photoshop to create a vignette is quick and easy. Vignettes may be produced using any shape; the most common border of this type is rectangular.

Creating a Vignette Border

1. Open the image **Picnic.TIF** from the **SF-Intro Photoshop** folder.

2. Using the Rectangular Marquee, select the couple. Make sure you leave a little extra room around the edges.

3. Choose Select>Modify>Smooth, and set Sample Radius to 10 pixels.

The maximum Sample Radius value for Expand, Smooth, and Contract is 16 pixels.

What is the difference between feathering and Anti-Aliasing? Mostly it's a matter of degree. Anti-Aliasing is designed as an automatic feature to blend just a few pixels to soften an otherwise jagged edge. Feathering allows you to specify blended edges in amounts from 1 to 250 pixels. A feathered edge of 1 or 2 pixels is almost identical to an Anti-Aliased edge.

The Smooth command creates radius corners on sharp angles. The radius of the curve is equal to the number of pixels used in the expand.

4. Choose Select>Feather and set Feather Radius to 10 pixels.

5. Invert the selection by choosing Inverse from the Select menu. Press "D" to change foreground and background colors to black-and-white. Press Command-H (Macintosh) or Control-H (Windows) to hide the selection border.
6. Press the Delete key; the background is filled with white and blends smoothly into the image.

7. Vignettes aren't always white; press Command-Z (Macintosh) or Control-Z (Windows) to Undo the fill, then press Option and Delete keys (Macintosh) or Alt and Delete keys (Windows) to fill the background with black.
8. Save the image into your **Work in Progress** folder as "Picnic With Vignette.TIF". Keep the file open.

Creating a Composite with Selections

1. Open the **Champagne Selection.PSD** image from your **Work in Progress** folder that you created. Choose Select>Load Selection, check the Invert checkbox and click OK.
2. Press Command-C (Macintosh) or Control-C (Windows) to Copy the image to the clipboard. Close the champagne image.
3. Open the image **Picnic With Vignette.TIF**. Press Command-V (Macintosh) or Control-V (Windows) to Paste the champagne bottle into the image.
4. Use the Move tool to position the champagne bottle so that the champagne in the picnic image is between the large bottle and the stream of champagne.

The best selections are made using a combination of tools rather than just one.

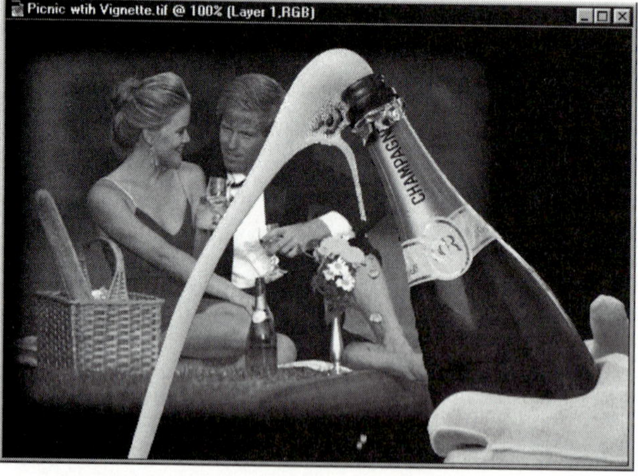

5. Close the image without saving.

Chapter 10

Channels and Masks

Chapter Objective:

To learn and understand the manner in which image information is arranged in specialized components known as Channels. In Chapter 10, you will:

- Understand the differences between Color and Alpha channels.
- Learn how to manage channels.
- Learn how to use a Quick Mask channel, and understand its limitations.
- Learn how to mask a portion of an image with a channel.

Projects to be Completed:

- Marinara Shelf Talker
- KSOL Rising
- Maui Travel Postcard
- Rough Riders Ad
- Gulls Poster
- Concert Poster
- Banana Boat Table Tent
- Salute to Veterans Poster

Channels and Masks

Making selections can be a complex, difficult task. As you learn more about selections and how they affect the interaction between various tools, filters, and techniques and the image itself, you will begin to gain an appreciation for the control over the look of your work that well-developed selection skills can give you.

When a new Photoshop document is created, or when you open a scanned image file, the image information is arranged in specialized components known as *Channels.*

Color Channels

Think of a light table covered with piles of film. Each pile contains either one, three, or four pieces of film. Each piece of film contains a component of the image. Black-and-white images have only one channel — the black one — and therefore would have one piece of film. An RGB image has three channels: one containing the red component, one containing the green component, and one containing the blue component. A CMYK image has four channels, one for each ink color.

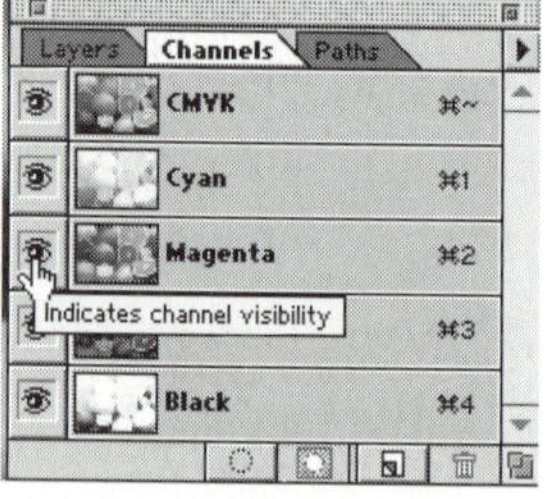

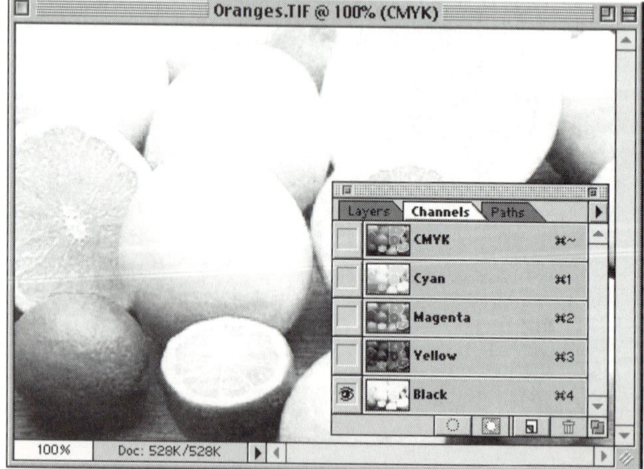

Here, all of the channels in the CMYK image except for black have been turned off.

You might ask, "Where's the film pile for a duotone?" A duotone in Photoshop is treated internally as a grayscale image and still only has one channel. You can force a duotone (or tritone/quadtone) to split into two or more channels by choosing Mode>Multichannel, but this is a fairly advanced topic, so we'll leave that for the Advanced Photoshop 5 book.

Alpha Channels

These are a special type of channel that only stores selections. If you choose Select > Save Selection and give the selection a name, an *alpha channel* is created with that same name. Then you can use the alpha channel to create a *mask* in your image. A mask is simply an area that shows or hides specific areas of the image. You can create up to 24 channels, color and alpha, in one Photoshop document.

Understanding Alpha Channels

1. Open the image **Dendrobium.TIF**, located in the **SF-Intro Photoshop** folder.
2. Open the Channels palette. It contains three channels, since this is an RGB image. Click on each of the channels to see the individual red, green, and blue components. To view the composite image (all three color channels), click on the RGB channel, or press Command/Control-Tilde (~).

   You can save a selection as you work to avoid losing lots of careful clicking and dragging. Additionally, you will need to save selections to execute many high-level effects that we will be practicing within the course of our lessons.

Adding alpha channels can make your file size grow dramatically, so you might want to delete unnecessary channels as you work on or finish a document.

3. Using the Magnetic Lasso tool, carefully select the orchid in the center of the image.

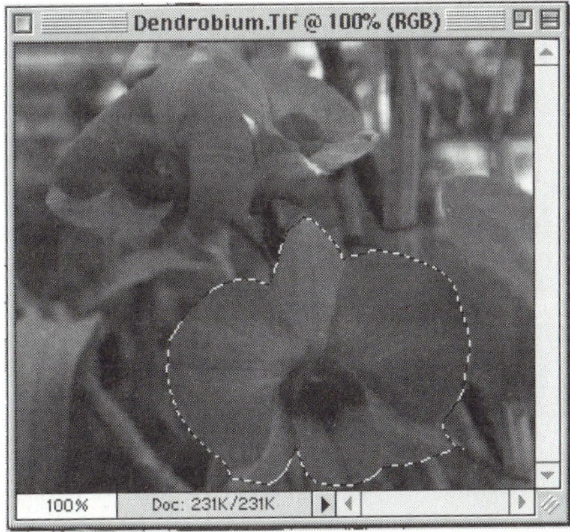

4. Once you've made the selection and are satisfied that the entire flower (without any of the background) has been selected, choose Select>Save Selection. When the Save Selection dialog box appears, type "Orchid" for the channel name and click OK.

As you create channels, they will be named, by default, Alpha 1, Alpha 2, and so forth.

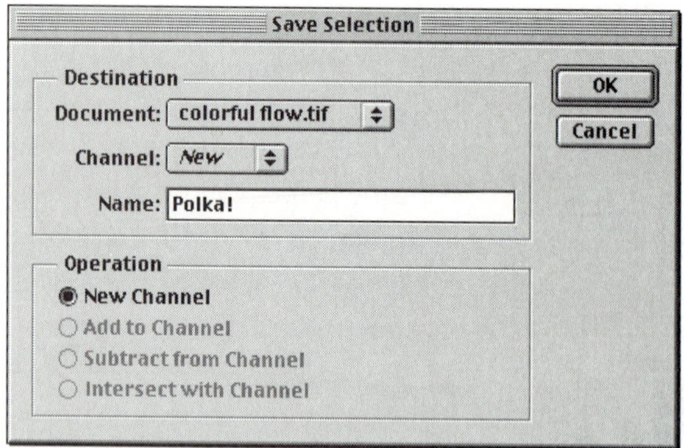

5. Look at your Channels palette. A new alpha channel has been created in addition to the three image channels and is called "orchid" (Red is #1, Green is #2, Blue is #3). If you hadn't named the channel, it would have been assigned to Alpha 1(#4). Photoshop will continue to sequentially number the new channels that you add to the document. The channel contains all the necessary information to recreate your selection.

6. Double-click the new channel's name in the Channels palette.

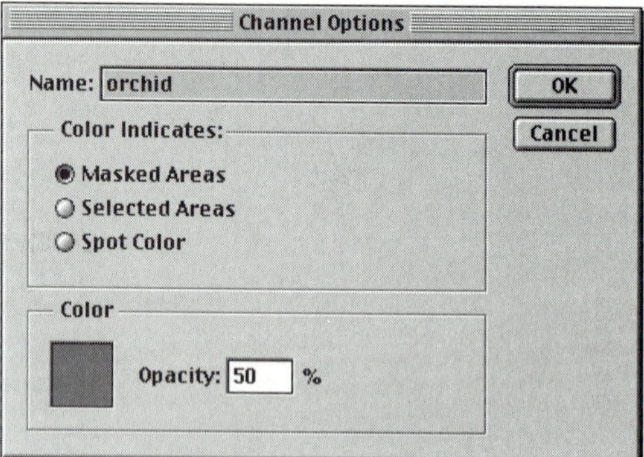

The default behavior for an alpha channel is a mask. The color you choose is only used to display the mask — it has no effect on the image. Click OK. To see the mask in action, turn the alpha channel on in the Channel palette by clicking the left columns to turn on the eye.

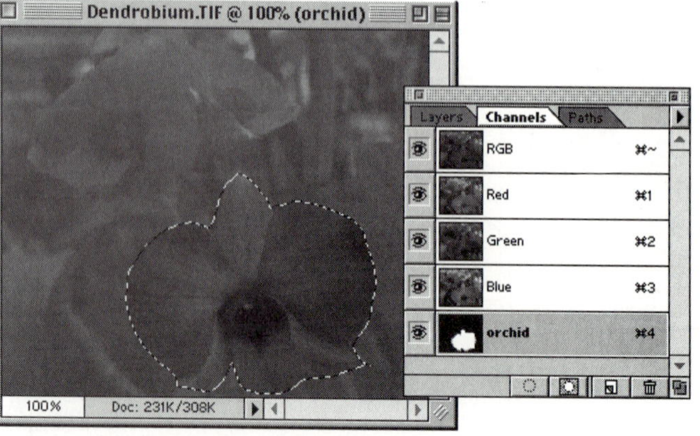

7. The alpha channel is now *masking* the rest of the image. A mask works to protect portions of an image — if you print this image with the alpha channel enabled, only the area within the mask will be visible. It can also be used to protect the area outside of the mask from accidental changes during editing.

   Now turn off all the other channels except for the orchid mask. Click the Eye icon next to the channel names to turn them off.

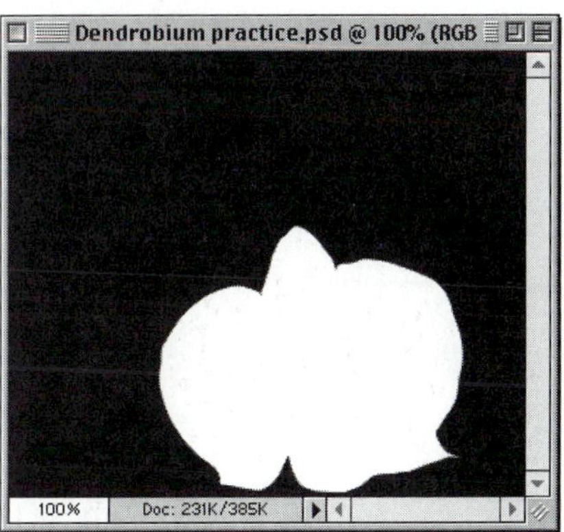

   The white areas are clear, or unprotected. The black areas are solid and protected from change. Click once on the RGB channel eye. Keep the image open and the selection active for the next exercise.

Managing Channels

Let's create another alpha channel. You can have as many alpha channels in a document as your system can handle — usually many more than you will need. Even in very complex applications you will normally never have more than eight or nine total channels (counting the first three or four). When you've finished developing an image, and you're getting ready to ship the file somewhere for output, you should eliminate any extra channels the document might contain.

Using a Channel to Mask a Portion of the Image

1. Press Command/Control-Shift-I. This is the Inverse Selection option, which turns the current selection inside out:

2. Choose Select>Save Selection, rename it "Background", then click OK.

3. Save the image as a Photoshop file in your **Work in Progress** folder, and name it "Dendrobium Practice.PSD".

4. There are four icons at the bottom of the Channels palette.

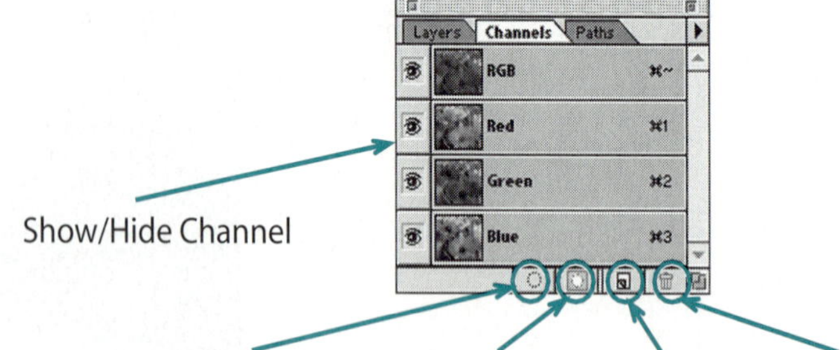

The first, a little dotted circle, is the Load Channel as a Selection icon. Click on the RGB channel name in the Channels palette and deselect any selected portions of the image by pressing Command/Control-D. Drag the Background channel to the Selection icon. Be careful not to click on the Background channel, or this will change the view to the Background mask.

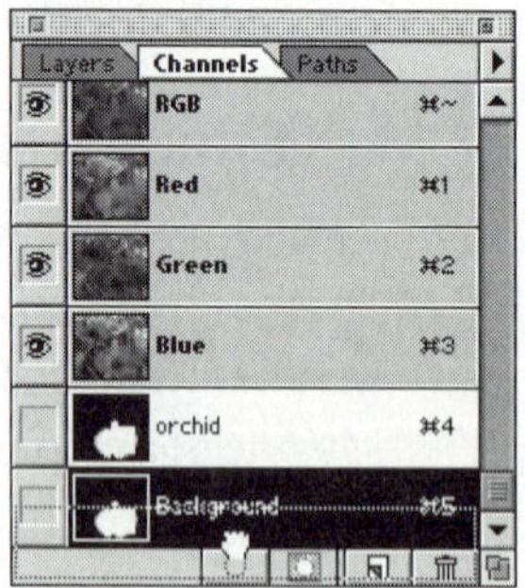

If you have done this correctly, the selection will be loaded onto the view of the color flower image.

5. Press "D" to load the default color swatches, black and white. Press Option/Alt - Delete to fill the selection area with the foreground color. The selected area of the image turns black:

6. Press Command/Control-Z to Undo the filling of the background.
7. Save the file. Now load the Orchid selection by dragging its channel name onto the Load Selection icon. Pick the Paintbrush tool, open the Brushes palette and pick a very large brush. Paint across the image.

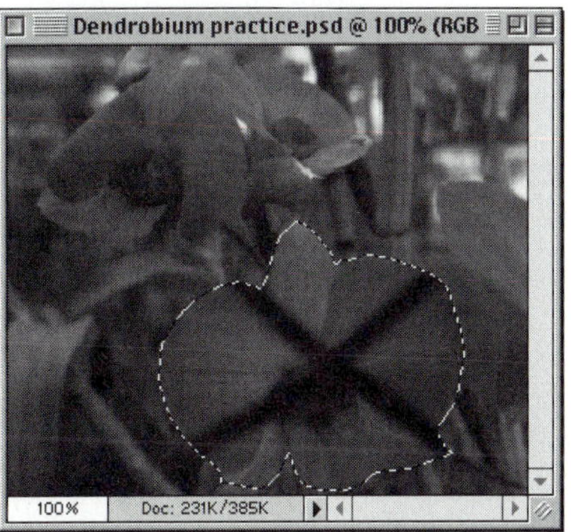

The background is masked and only the selection area is active. Remember — pixels outside the selection are protected in the image, and vice versa. Only when the brush crosses the flower does the "paint" appear. Press Command/Control-Z to Undo the painting, or use the History palette to revert to the last Load Selection.

Red is the default display color for masks because it simulates the use of rubylith, a transparent red sheet that is cut out and used to mask images that are prepared photomechanically for printing.

8. If a selection is active, press Command/Control-D to deselect it. Now click in the box to the far left of the Background channel. An Eye icon appears to the left of the channel name, and the areas of the image which are not included in the selection have turned transparent red.

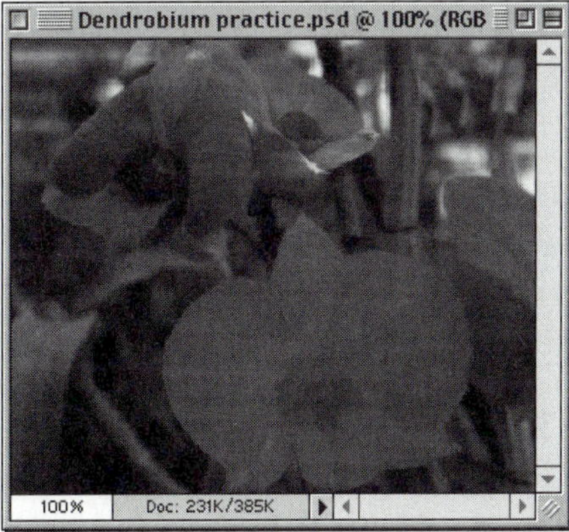

When working with extremely complex selections or with multiple channels, it can be difficult to tell what is selected and what is not. Checking your selection with the Eye icons will help to isolate problem areas.

9. Leave the image open for the next exercise.

Duplicating and Deleting Channels

1. The third icon on the Channels palette (the one with the folded corner) is the New Channel icon. Drag the Orchid channel to the New Channel icon. A new channel will appear named "Alpha 1." Double-click on this channel, rename it "Orchid copy" and click OK.
2. Drag "Orchid copy" to the Delete Channel icon when you're done.
3. Save and close the file.

More Channels Techniques

Here's a three-dimensional, cut-paper effect that works well with text and line art.

Building Cut Paper

1. Create a New document as grayscale, 400 pixels wide, 150 pixels high, and 72 pixels per inch.
2. Using the Rectangular Marquee, create a wide rectangular selection near the upper left corner of the image. Save the selection.
3. Press Command/Control-D to deselect the rectangle. Switch to the Elliptical Marquee. Create a circular selection in the center of the image by holding the Shift key while making the selection. Try to make the selection overlap the area where the first selection was made. Save the selection.
4. Press Command/Control-D to deselect, then activate the Lasso. Make a random selection near the lower right corner of the image. Again, try to make the selection overlap the area where the circular selection was made. Save the selection.
5. Activate the Channels palette. Double-click on each channel name, renaming the channels "Rectangle", "Circle", and "Lasso", respectively. Duplicate all three channels by dragging each one over the top of the New Channel icon. Rename them as "Rectangle Copy", "Circle Copy", and "Lasso Copy". You should now have seven channels in your document, including the Black channel, like this:

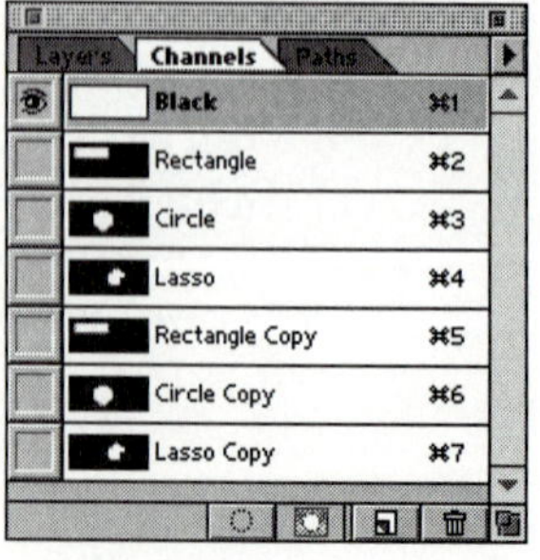

6. Activate the Rectangle Copy channel. Press Command/Control-D to make certain that nothing is selected. Choose Filter>Blur>Gaussian Blur; set the Radius to 3 pixels, and click OK.

7. Activate the Circle Copy channel. Press Command/Control-F to run the Gaussian Blur filter on the channel using the same settings as the Rectangle Copy channel. Do the same for the Lasso Copy channel.

8. Activate the Rectangle channel. Select Filter>Other>Offset. Set both Horizontal and Vertical to -2 pixels, and click Repeat Edge Pixels. Click OK and the offset filter will shift the image 2 pixels up and 2 pixels left.

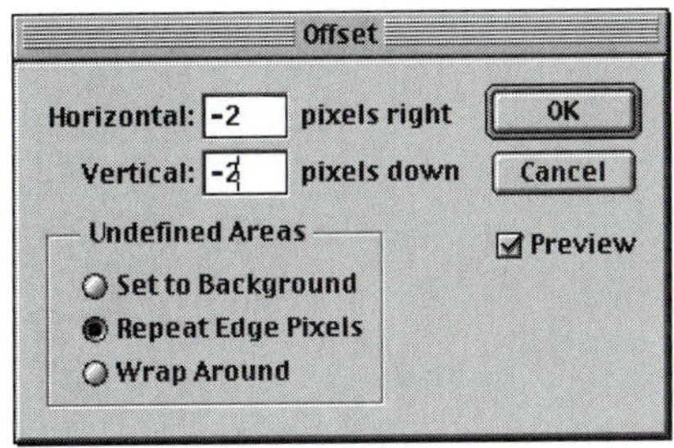

9. Activate the Circle channel. Select Filter>Other>Offset again. This time, set Horizontal and Vertical to -4 pixels. Run the filter on the Lasso channel, using -3 for the horizontal and vertical offsets. We offset the shapes at different amounts to simulate different distances from the "paper" surface to yield a more realistic 3-D effect. Now you're ready to build Cut Paper.

10. Press Command/Control-Tilde (~) to activate the Black channel. Press "D" to set foreground and background colors to the defaults. Command/Control-click the Rectangle Copy channel; Command/Control-Shift-click the Circle Copy and Lasso Copy channels to add them to the current selection. Press Option/Alt-Delete to fill the composite selection with black.

11. Command/Control-click the Rectangle channel; Command/Control-Shift-click the Lasso channel to add them to the current selection. Press Delete to fill the selection with white.

12. Command/Control-click the Circle Copy channel. Press Option/Alt-Delete to fill the selection with black.

13. Command/Control-click the Circle channel. Press Delete to fill the selection with white.

    Here's what the final result should look like. Yours will obviously not match exactly, but it should exhibit the same drop shadow effect.

14. Save the file as "Papershads.PSD" into your **Work in Progress** folder and then close it.

Using Quick-Mask Mode

Quick Mask lets you make any selection into a mask without accessing the Channels palette and while you have your image in front of you. It does not allow you to save your selections like the alpha channel method does, so it is not very helpful for complex selections. A Quick Mask channel will appear in the Channels palette if you have it open, but it goes away as soon as you finish with the mask. You use the Quick Mask mode to alter a selection area; once you have the selection you want, you can then save it as a standard alpha channel selection once you exit Quick Mask mode. You can also start a Quick Mask by loading an alpha channel selection.

Making a Quick Mask

1. Open the file **Dendrobium Practice.PSD** and load the Orchid channel you created earlier from the **Work in Progress** folder.

2. Click the Quick Mask mode button at the bottom of the toolbar.

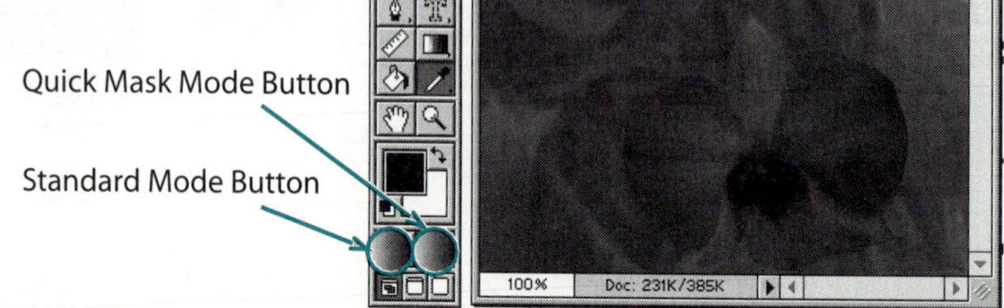

When you have made a selection, clicking the Quick Mask button lets you modify the mask with almost any standard filter or tool. The masked area is shown as transparent red, or rubylith.

3. Select the Paintbrush tool and choose a large, soft brush. Press "D" to revert back to the default colors. Paint around the edge of the mask.

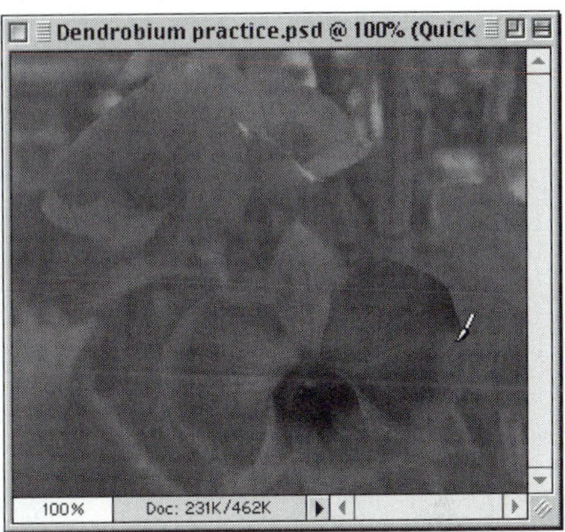

It might be a little hard to see, but here we've almost painted around the edge of the mask with the Paintbrush.

4. When you've painted all the way around, click the Standard Mode button. You'll see that by painting around the mask, you've changed the selection. It's smaller now. Painting (or using any tool or filter) on a Quick Mask only affects the selection; it does not affect the image.

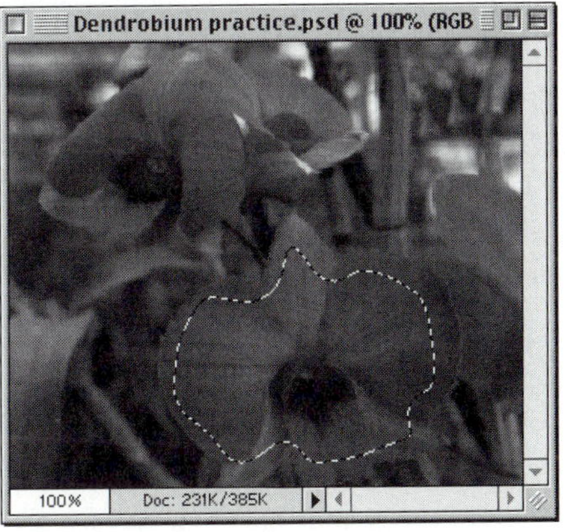

Be careful to select the painting color after you switch to Quick Mask mode. The color selection you might have in Standard mode may not carry over to Quick Mask mode.

5. Press Command/Control-D to deselect, and repeat steps 1, 2, and 3, only this time choose white as your paintbrush color for painting around the mask.

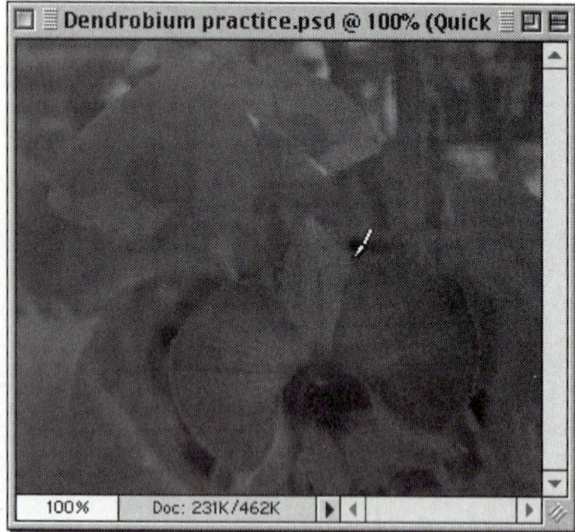

Switch back to Standard mode. What's different about this new selection?

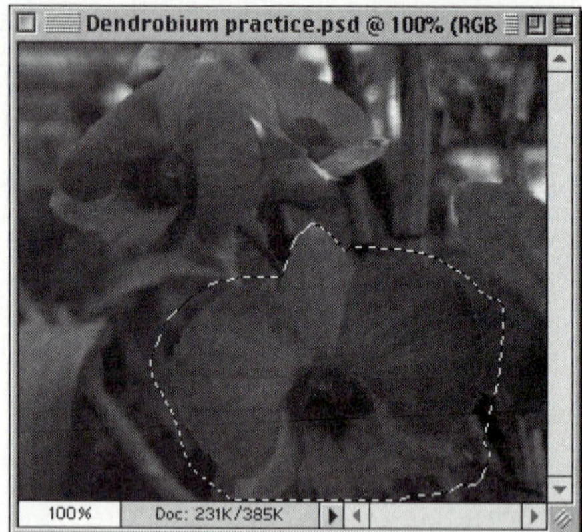

Painting with white reduces the mask and adds to the selection; painting with black adds to the mask, shrinking the selection.

6. Repeat the same steps again, only this time, choose a neutral gray color as your paint color from the Color Picker. Paint around the edges, then switch to Standard mode. Press Delete to see what painting in a non-black or white color does; it creates a feathered selection. The degree of feathering will vary depending on which color you choose.

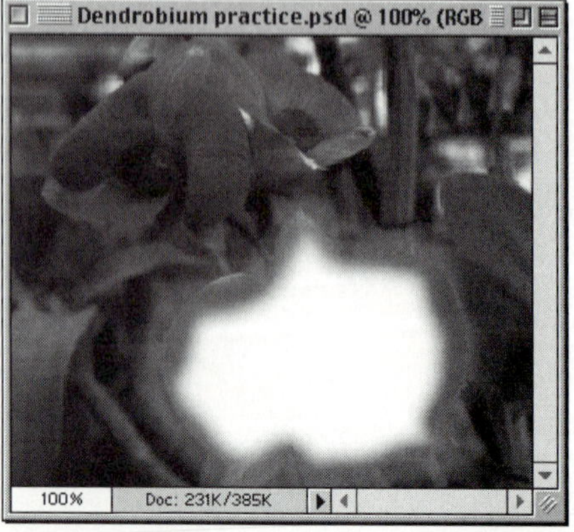

Quick Mask Options

Double-click the Quick Mask Mode button to show the options panel.

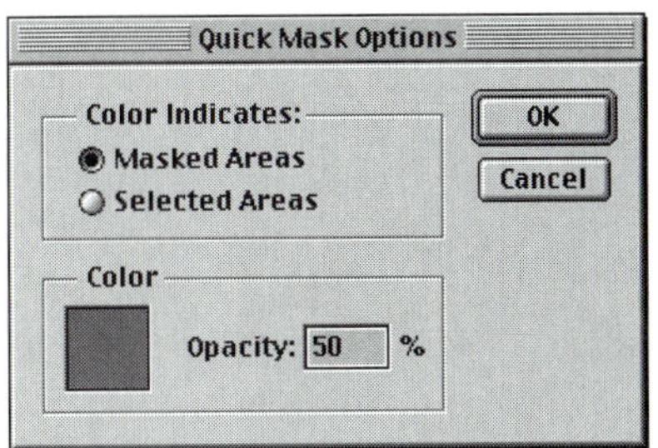

Choosing "Masked Areas" (the default) causes the Quick Mask to behave as you've already seen: Painting with white reduces the mask and adds to the selection; painting with black adds to the mask, shrinking the selection. Choosing "Selected Areas" causes the Quick Mask to behave exactly opposite from what we've used: Painting with black reduces the mask and adds to the selection; painting with white adds to the mask, shrinking the selection.

You can also choose another color or tint value instead of 50% red to represent the mask. Clicking the red patch will show the Color Picker, and you can choose a new color there. Type a new opacity percentage to change the mask opacity.

Notes:

CHAPTER 11

WORKING WITH LAYERS

CHAPTER OBJECTIVE:

To build on the knowledge of layers that you developed when learning about type, blending modes, and pasting selections. This chapter will expand that knowledge with discussions and hands-on activities. In Chapter 14, you will:

- Learn that layers can contain colors.
- Learn how to create layers.
- Learn how to work with multiple layers.
- Learn how to create a new layer from a selection.
- Learn how to create a Multimedia button.
- Learn how to create a composite using layers.
- Learn how to distort elements and layer effects.
- Learn more about applying various blending modes to individual layers.

PROJECTS TO BE COMPLETED:

- Marinara Shelf Talker
- KSOL Rising
- Maui Travel Postcard
- Rough Riders Ad
- Gulls Poster
- Concert Poster
- Banana Boat Table Tent
- Salute to Veterans Poster

Working with Layers

We've already learned a little about layers while using blending modes, creating type, and pasting selections. Layers are one of the most powerful tools that Photoshop has to offer. Among other things, they give you the ability to composite images in real time, and to test special effects and color correction before permanently applying them to your image.

Layers, unlike channels, can contain colors. They are actually entire images that are lying on top of, or underneath other images. Layers can be transparent. This means that you may "cut" the background out of one image and place it atop another, allowing part of the bottom image to show through.

Photoshop's layers create versatile artwork. You could, for example, create a standard advertisement with an image and logo, and then add several different layers of text. You can colorize the logo or background according to the current marketing plan. This way, whatever text, logo, and background are needed for a particular publication, all versions of the advertisement would reside in a single file.

Let's create a multi-layer document.

Creating Layers

1. Create a New document. It should be 5″ × 5″ at 72 dpi, in RGB mode, with White selected in the Contents section. Name the document "Layers Practice", and save it into your **Work in Progress** folder.

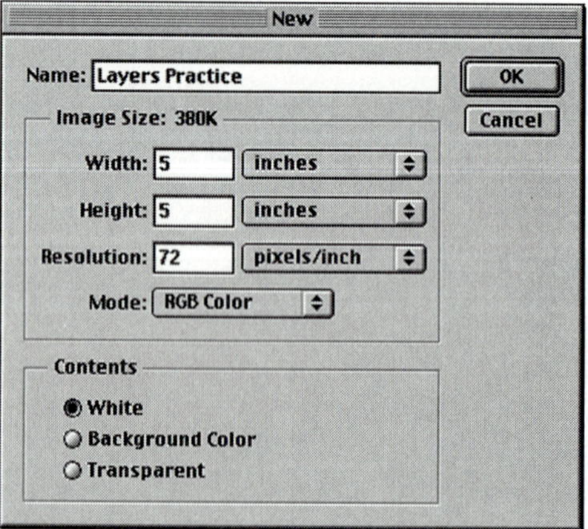

2. Notice the default *Background* layer on the Layers palette. We're going to create a texture on this background that looks a little like handmade paper. From the Filter menu, choose Noise>Add Noise. Move the slider until the figure reads somewhere around 115. Click OK.

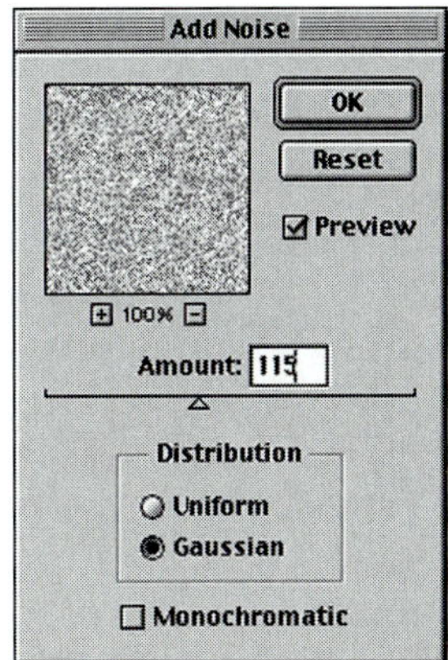

3. Choose Filter>Blur>Gaussian Blur. Enter 1.0 for the pixel radius.

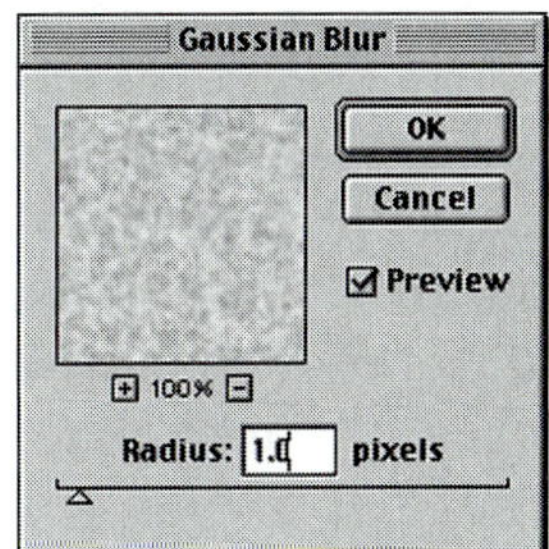

4. Next, choose Filter>Pixelate>Facet. Run the filter again by pressing Command-F (Macintosh) or Control-F (Windows), or choosing it from the Filter menu (it will be at the top of the Filters menu once you run it). Next, choose Filter>Stylize>Emboss and enter the following numbers before clicking OK:

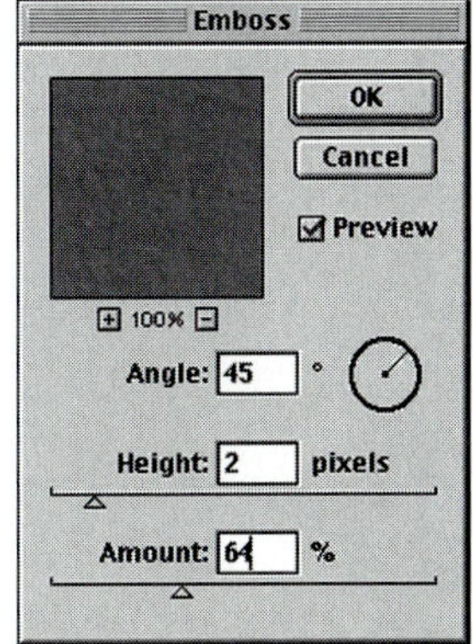

5. Choose File>Place and select the **Type.EPS** file from the **SF-Intro Photoshop** folder. Hold the Shift key and size the artwork (using the handles at each corner) and position it until it resides in the upper left corner.

6. Press Return to finish placing the image. Notice that a new layer is created with the same name as the placed file, Type.EPS.

7. At this point, both the *Background* layer and the Type.EPS layer are visible. Turn the *Background* layer off by clicking the little eye to the left of its name. Now you can see what a transparent layer actually looks like.

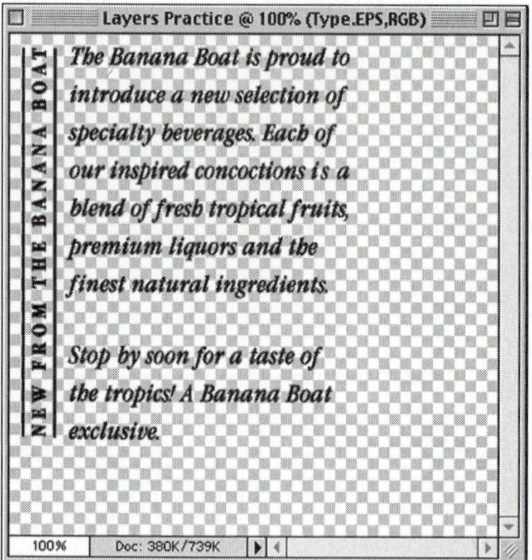

When using the Canvas Size command on an image with a Background layer, the background canvas will be filled with the current background color. If the image contains layers, the added canvas for each layer will be transparent.

8. In the Layers palette, make the *Background* layer visible and active by clicking once on its name in the Layers palette. Draw a rectangular marquee around the type box. Select Image>Adjust>Brightness/Contrast. Move the sliders as shown to lighten the selection area (+31). Notice that even though the type is within the selection area, its contrast and brightness aren't affected.

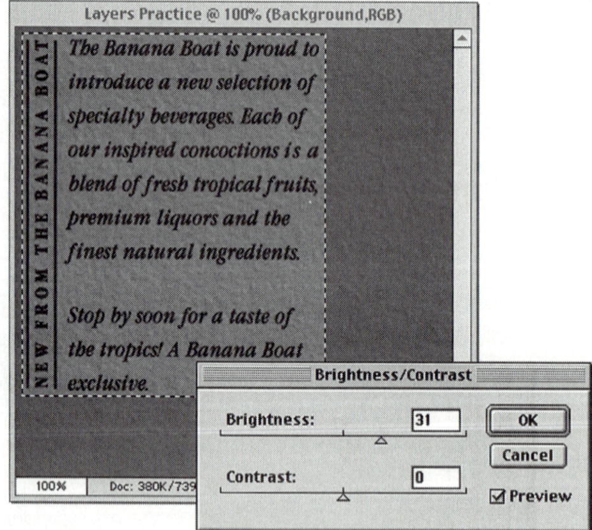

Why? Because the active layer is the only one that's affected by painting, filters, or other actions.

9. Click OK and choose Save Selection from the Select menu. When the dialog box appears, click OK to let the selection name default to New, which will name the channel Alpha 1.

   Press Command-D (Macintosh) or Control-D (Windows) to deselect the selection.

10. Save the file and leave it open for next exercise.

Working with Multiple Layers

Once the layers are in place they may be duplicated, edited, or reordered. This gives you the ability to experiment on some portions of an image without affecting others, and without having to create a selection.

Creating a New Layer from a Selection

1. In the Layers Practice file, make certain that the *Background* layer is active by clicking on it once in the Layers palette. Choose Select>Load Selection. Click OK to load the saved, lightened rectangle.
2. Press Command-J (Macintosh) or Control-J (Windows) to turn the selection into a layer.
3. Hide the other layers by turning off the Eye icons to the left of their names.
4. The layer name defaulted to Layer 1. Drag Layer 1 to the top of the list. Activate the Blending mode list and select Dissolve.

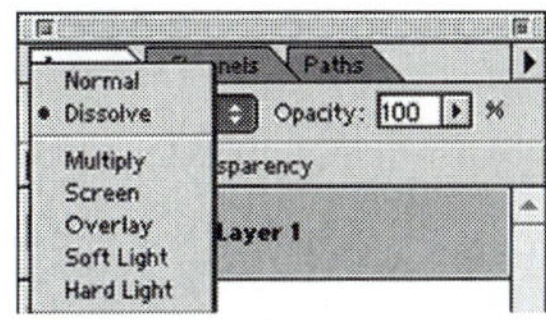

5. Turn on the Type.EPS layer so that both it and Layer 1 are visible. Change the layer opacity of Layer 1 to 50% to allow it to dissolve into the Type layer.
6. Select the *Background* layer. Select Image>Adjust>Hue/Saturation. Click the Colorize box and enter the figures shown below:

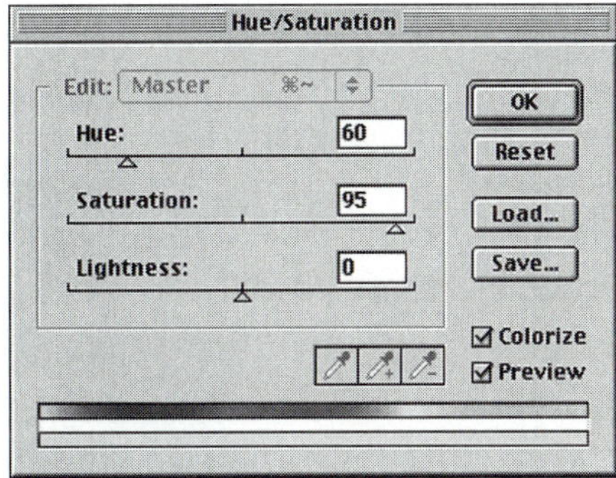

7. Adjust the Opacity of Layer 1 and the Type.EPS layer to get a feel for the interaction between layers.

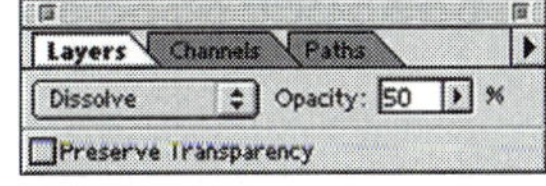

8. Save the file before closing.

Creating a Multimedia Button

1. Open the file called **Rock.TIF** from the **SF-Intro Photoshop** folder.
2. Activate the Channels palette, and click the New Channel icon to create a new, empty channel. Make sure that this is the active channel.
3. Choose Place from the File menu, and select **Go.EPS** from the **SF-Intro Photoshop** folder. Place the graphic and size it as shown by dragging the corner handles. Press Return to place the graphic.

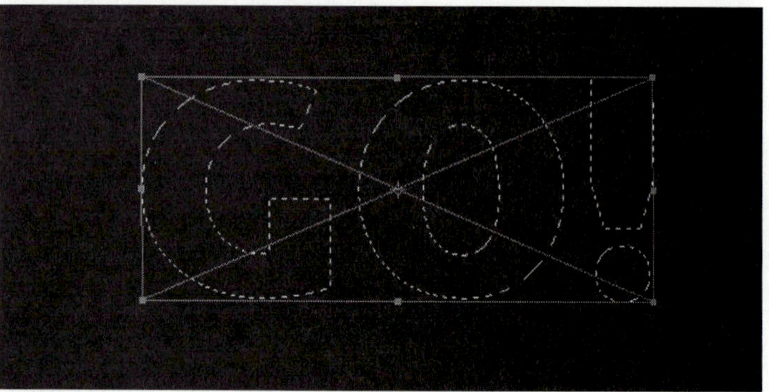

4. Press Command/Control-X to cut the type, then Command/Control-V to paste it back into the image. This will center the type perfectly inside of the image.
5. Press "D" to change the foreground color to white. Press Option-Delete (Macintosh) or Alt-Backspace (Windows) to fill the type with white. Press Command/Control-D to drop the selection.
6. Press Command/Control-A to select the entire image, then Copy it to the clipboard. Press Command/Control-Tilde to change to RGB composite mode, then activate the Layers palette. Paste the type into the document.
7. Select Filter>Blur>Gaussian Blur and set Radius to 5.0 pixels.

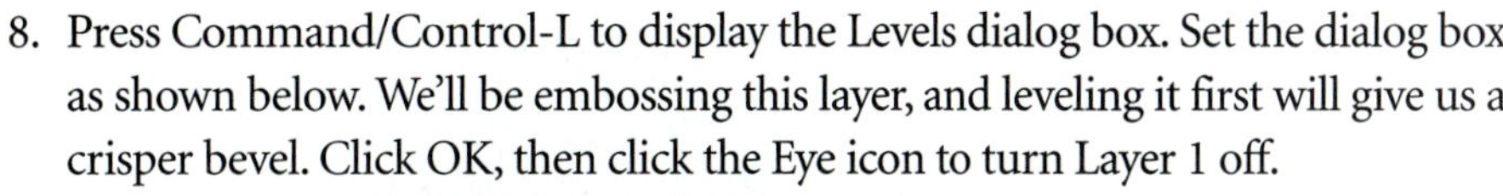

8. Press Command/Control-L to display the Levels dialog box. Set the dialog box as shown below. We'll be embossing this layer, and leveling it first will give us a crisper bevel. Click OK, then click the Eye icon to turn Layer 1 off.

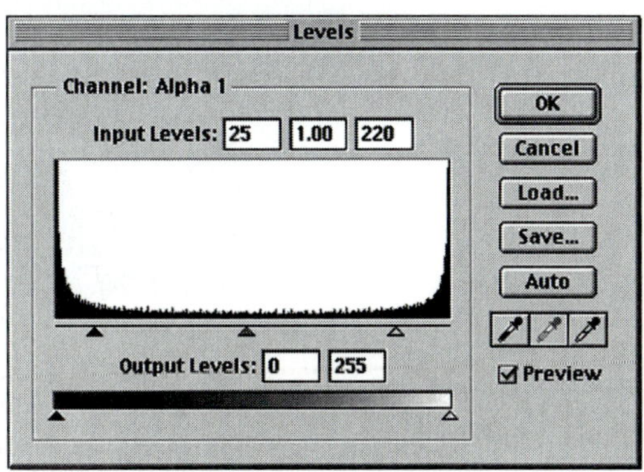

When the Move tool is active, you can use the arrow keys to move a layer or selection one pixel at a time. Holding the Shift key while using the arrow keys will move the object 10 pixels at a time.

9. Make certain that the foreground color is set to white. Click the New Layer icon at the bottom of the Layers palette to create another new layer. Press Command/Control-A to select the entire layer. Press Option-Delete or Alt-Backspace to fill the layer with white.

10. Choose Select>Modify>Border. Set the Width to 36 pixels, and click OK. The Border command adds a feathered selection border to the image. Press "X" to make the foreground color black again, Option-Delete or Alt-Backspace to fill the selection with black, then press Command-D or Control-D to drop the selection.

11. Select Filter>Stylize>Emboss. Set Angle to -50, Height to 4, and Amount to 200%. Click OK. Click the layer's Eye icon to turn it off.

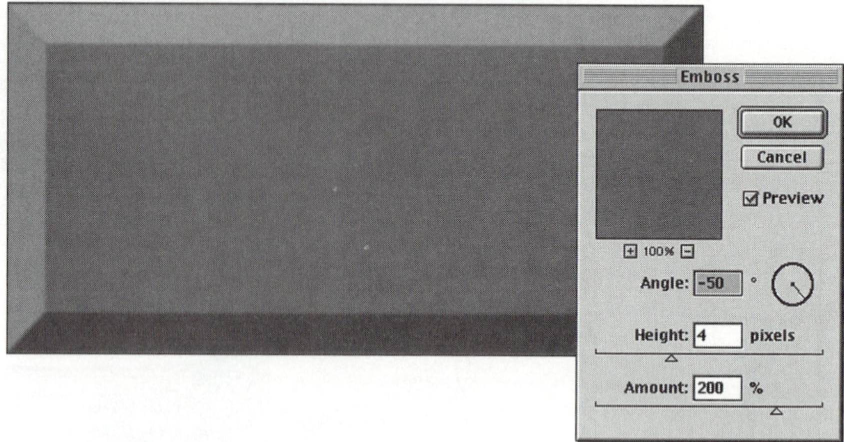

12. Click Layer 1 in the Layers palette to activate it. Select Filter>Stylize>Emboss. Set Angle to -50, Height to *3* (notice that we've changed the height), and Amount to 200%. Click OK.

13. Turn Layer 2 back on. Set the blending mode for *both* Layer 1 and Layer 2 to Hard Light.

14. Close the file without saving.

Photo Composites with Layers

The real strength of layers lies in the compositing of photographs. Remember the champagne bottle we composited against the picnic scene when learning about complex selections? What would happen if you needed to change the vignette from white to black? You'd have to start over, that's what.

Let's try the same exercise again, only this time using Photoshop's layers. It will give you an idea of just how powerful they really are.

Creating a Composite

1. Open the image **Picnic.TIF** from the **SF-Intro Photoshop** folder.
2. Double-click on the *Background* layer, and click OK when the dialog box appears. This changes the *Background* layer to Layer 0, a normal layer which can contain transparent areas. Click OK.
3. Use the Rectangular Marquee to select the couple in the image. Choose Select>Modify>Smooth, and set Sample Radius to 10 pixels. Click OK.
4. Choose Select>Feather and set Feather Radius to 10 pixels. Click OK. Pick Inverse from the Select menu to turn your selection inside out, and press the Delete key to create a border which fades to transparent.

5. Click the New Layer icon at the bottom of the Layers palette to create a new layer called Layer 1. Drag this layer below Layer 0. Press Command/Control-A to select all. Set your foreground color to white, and press Option/Alt-Delete to fill the layer with white.

Now you can change the color of the vignette background any time you want without redoing this part of the image.

6. Open the image **Champagne Selection.PSD** from your **Work in Progress** folder. Choose Load Selection from the Select menu, and load the Background selection. Use Select>Inverse to turn the selection inside out. Press Command/Control-C to copy the selection to the clipboard.
7. Close the Champagne image. Press Command/Control-V to paste the bottle into the picnic image. Position this layer at the top of the layers list.
8. Activate Layer 2, the Champagne bottle layer, and use the Move tool to adjust the champagne bottle wherever you like.

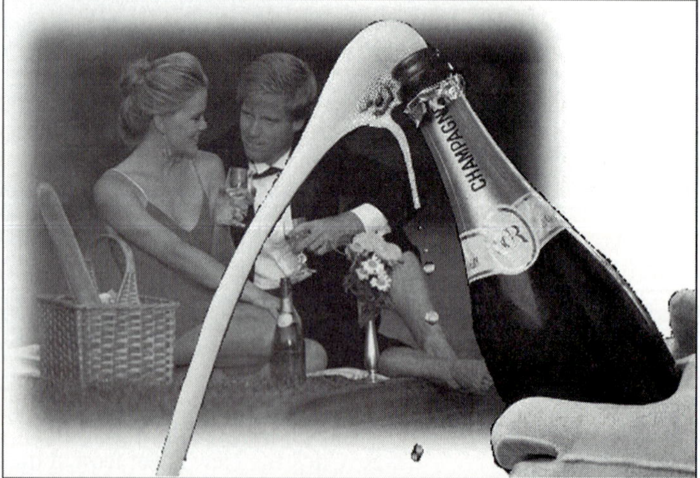

9. Add a new layer, Layer 3, and fill it with white. Move the layer to the bottom of the Layers palette and turn off Layer 1, the white background layer.
10. Create a handmade paper background using the methods outlined in our Layers Practice exercise at the beginning of this chapter. Save the image as "Picnic.PSD." You now have a single file with two decidedly different looks for an advertisement.

11. Select File>Save a Copy. Make certain that Flatten Image is checked. (Flattening collapses all layers back into the *Background* layer.) Save the file as a Tiff image called "Picnic Ad 1.TIF". Turn on Layer 1. Use File>Save a Copy again to save a flattened Tiff version with a white background; call the image "Picnic Ad 2.TIF". The flattened versions of this file could be cropped and placed into QuarkXPress or PageMaker, while the original image can be saved for later adjustments.

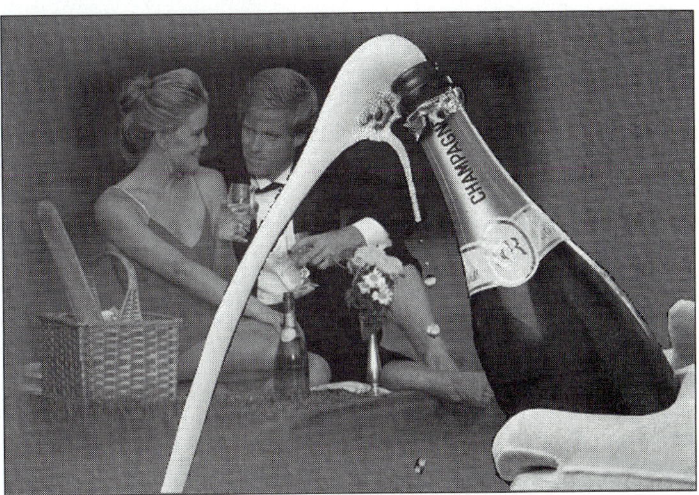

12. Close the file without saving.

Distributing Elements and Layer Effects

1. Create a New document 5 inches square at 100 ppi, in RGB mode, with White selected in the Contents section. Name the document "Photo Wall.PSD".

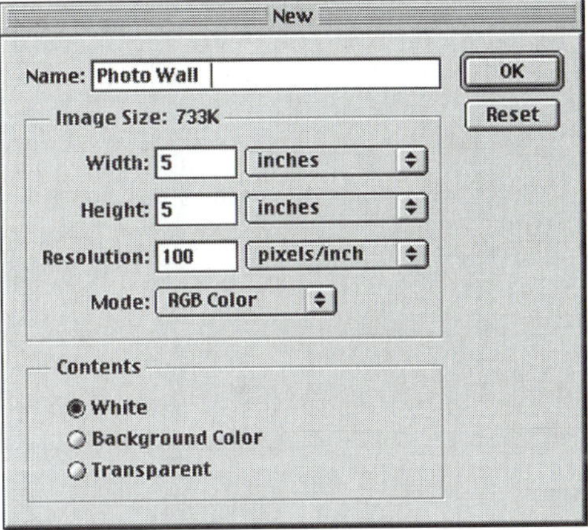

2. From the View menu, select Show Rulers. Click on the top ruler and drag a guide down to the 1/4 inch mark.

3. Create five new layers. Allow them to have the default names Layer 1, Layer 2 and so forth.

4. Click on Layer 1 to select it.

5. Open the file **Portrait1.TIF** from the **SF-Intro Phtoshop** folder. Select All and Copy the photo.

6. Switch to the Photo Wall document and press Command/Control-V to paste the photo into Layer 1. Holding down the Shift key to constrain the movement to only a vertical direction, slide the photo up until it "grabs" the guide you placed.

7. Activate Layer 2. Copy and Paste the photo named **Portrait2.TIF** onto the layer. Position it so it just overlaps the bottom of the photo above, with its right edge approximately in the middle of the page (2 1/2 inches).

8. On Layer 3, Paste **Portrait3.TIF**, slightly overlapping **Portrait1** on the right; paste **Portrait4.TIF** on the left, also slightly overlapping. Paste **Portrait5.TIF** about 1/4 inch to the right of **Portrait2**. At this point, your photo grouping should look something like this.

9. With Layer 1 activated, click on the box to the right of the eye on layers 3 and 4. This will link these layers.

10. Let's align the centers of these portraits. Select Layer>Align Linked>Vertical Center.

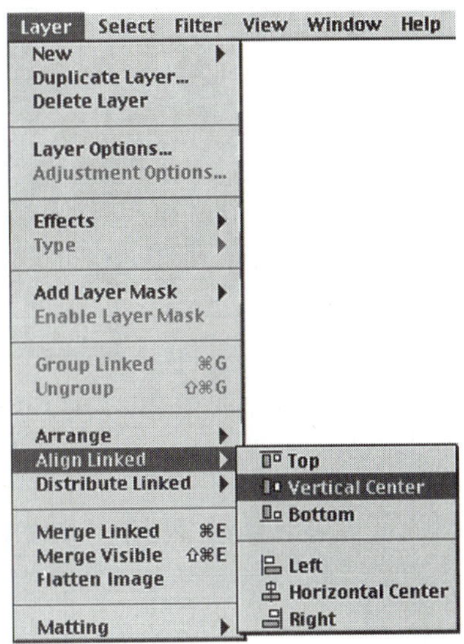

11. Repeat the process with the two bottom photos. Activate Layer 2, then click on the box to the left of Layer 5 to link them.

12. Select Layer>Align Linked>Vertical Center.
13. Activate Layer 1. From the Layers Menu, select Layer Effects>Drop Shadow and set the effect as you see below. Repeat for all five layers.

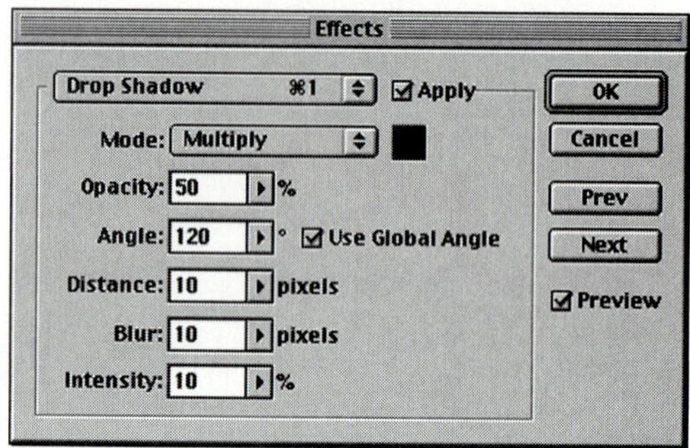

These settings will give us a soft effect with very little effort on our part.

14. As a final step, we're going to Activate Layer 5, then select Layer>Arrange>Send to Back. If you wish, you can also select View>Hide Rulers and View>Hide Guides.

15. Save and close the document. Close all other open files.

Complete Project B: KSOL Rising

Complete Project C: Maui Travel Postcard

Chapter 12

Calibrating Your System

Chapter Objective:

To develop a basic understanding of Color Calibration by learning the intricacies of the process of fine-tuning your system to achieve acceptable output. In Chapter 11, you will:

- Understand how to predict output color, and compensate for the many variables involved in the printing process.
- Understand factors that affect color display, such as ambient lighting, monitors, video cards, the ability of the scanner operator adjusting your scan, and a plethora of other variables that can affect the printed piece.
- Understand how to use the gamma program to compensate for the visual difference in your perception of color on a monitor.
- Understand how critical gamma correction is to visualizing how an image will reproduce.

Projects to be Completed:

- Marinara Shelf Talker
- KSOL Rising
- Maui Travel Postcard
- Rough Riders Ad
- Gulls Poster
- Concert Poster
- Banana Boat Table Tent
- Salute to Veterans Poster

Calibrating Your System

Before we investigate a few of Photoshop's advanced functions, a discussion of a crucial topic is necessary to achieve acceptable output — calibration.

WYSIWYG — What You See Is What You Get is a term used in the industry to describe the hope that what you see on your monitor will be the same as the output you receive.

What is Calibration?

Very often, what we see on our screen or from your printer isn't anywhere *close* to what is output at the service bureau. There are good reasons for this, which we'll explain. The important thing to know is that there *is* something you can do about it.

Calibration is the process that brings a monitor's image closer to what is produced on the printed page. We'll never get an exact match; the idea is to create a consistent working environment from which you can reliably predict output color, and to compensate for differences in different *printing methods* and *personal interpretation* and other factors.

It's more than just a case of the monitor not matching the printer. There are many factors that affect a person's perception of color, *including* hardware.

*You can use the three major color modes in the industry (RGB, CMYK, and CIE L*a*b) to view different areas of the color spectrum. You should understand that each one of these modes can only represent a confined area of the spectrum, and none of these modes can represent all colors that your eye can see.*

- Perception of color can be affected by your mood, your age, the time of day, physical conditions, medication that you are taking, as well as other factors.
- A stable and correct lighting system may be the most important factor in color calibration. If the lighting changes constantly or adds color casts, there is no consistent basis from which to begin.
- Every monitor, including monitors of the same make and model, is different. A monitor which has not "warmed up" will produce a different display than one that has been on for a while. Phosphors, or the standard that a particular monitor uses to represent colors, vary between screens.
- Video cards and driver sets can produce different sets of colors.
- An image scanned on different scanners will contain different image information. In addition, there are vast differences in scan quality between reflective scans such as those done on a flatbed scanner, and scans of transparencies, such as slides.
- Everyone's perception of color is different. One of the places where the color consistency equation can break down is the ability (or lack of ability) of the scanner operator who will be adjusting your scans.
- Different software packages have differing calibration abilities, ranging from excellent, as in Photoshop, to none, as in older versions of PageMaker. The available color management systems are good, but they're not perfect. These

RIP — Rasterized Image Processor is software that interprets files into a format that an output device can produce.

systems attempt to present a unified view of color on screen to be matched to various output devices.

- All output devices are different. To further complicate matters, two *identical* printers may have different output characteristics, printing darker, bluer, etc. Many printing devices have their own color control systems (RIPs, color correction software, etc.) that can also affect color consistency.
- The color, density, absorption quality, grain, and finish of the paper stock used all affect output quality and color.
- The properties of the different materials used to output Photoshop images can vary greatly between manufacturers; in addition, many manufacturers offer more than one grade of their ink, toner, or film, and the hue usually varies from one grade to another. Impurities in inks or toners, as well as the photo-sensitive material (emulsions) used in film, can cause the same image to appear differently. That makes it impossible to match colors exactly between the two sets of inks or film.

Steps to Calibration

There are many factors to deal with when attempting to calibrate a computer and/or applications to produce consistent output results. Photoshop 5 has many tools that will allow the user to work closer with whatever printing device or outside vendor is chosen.

This is a process that takes time; it's not something that can be completed in a class session. Here are the basic steps to calibrating a computer system and monitor.

Color Setting options are: RGB, CYMK, Grayscale, and Profile.

- Stabilize the lighting system. Fluorescents having 5000°K (Kelvin) color temperature (also called "full spectrum" fluorescents) don't add color casts to documents the way other light sources can.
- Calibrate when you're alert and the monitor is warmed up (at least 30 minutes). If the home or office has windows, either calibrate with shades closed, or try to calibrate at the same time of day in consistent lighting conditions.
- Adjust the monitor with the panel controls. Adjust the brightness and contrast, and if the monitor is so equipped, pick an appropriate color temperature. If it has individual controls for color, adjust according to the manufacturer's specifications. When the monitor is looking good, tape down the controls. We're not kidding!
- The Adobe Gamma utility calibrates the monitor and defines the RGB color space that the monitor can display. This utility should have been installed in the control panel during the installation of the Photoshop application. The monitor must be calibrated prior to displaying colors accurately on it. Once the monitor is calibrated, Photoshop will compensate for differences between the color space

in which the image resides and the color space in which the monitor displays images. Setting the Adobe Gamma will be discussed later in this chapter.

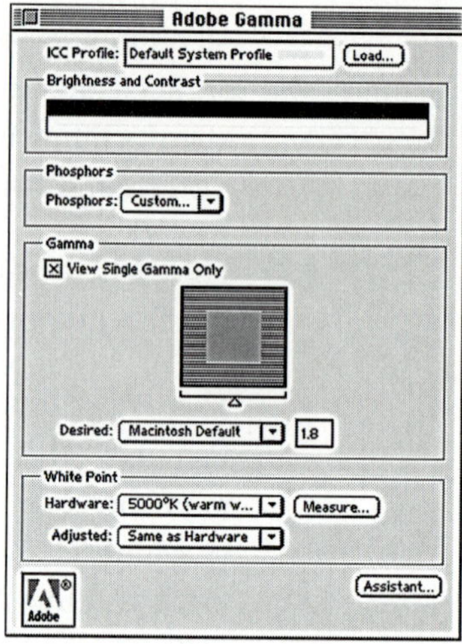

Adobe Gamma

The Color Setup screens will allow you to match the parameters of your output devices, or the output devices of the printing vendor that you are using.

- Depending on the color mode that you are going to work in, select the proper Setup window by going to the File>Color Settings dialog box. If the monitor is not listed, get the specifications from the monitor manual or the manufacturer. The target gamma is usually 1.8 if you deal mainly in print media, or 2.2 for video. If the monitor is listed, the default gamma, which can be as high as 2.5, should be fine.

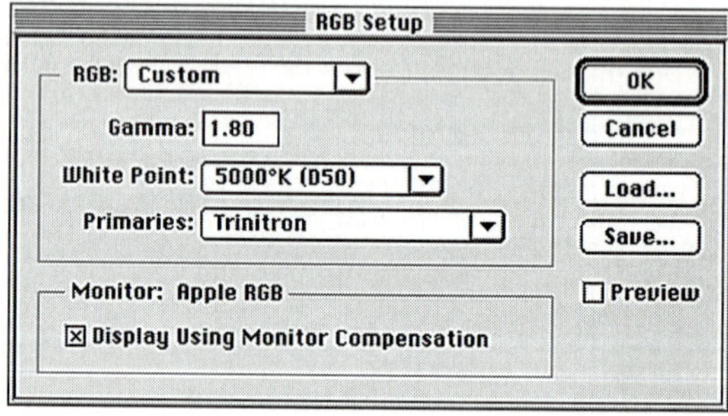

RGB Setup

- Choose File>Color Settings>RGB Setup. Under the RGB pull-down menu, there are options for many standards used in the industry such as:
- RGB — A standard used by many hardware and software manufacturers. This is the default setting for Photoshop.
- Apple RGB — A standard used in earlier versions of Adobe Photoshop as well as other desktop publishing applications. This is the best choice for images that will be displayed on Mac OS systems.

- CIE RGB — An RGB color space defined by the Commission Internationale d'Eclairage. While it has a fairly large color gamut, it doesn't represent cyan well.

- Other settings are Color Match RGB (for Radius monitors), NTSC (1953) (for standard television), SMPTE-240M (for high definition television), Custom, as well as others.

Use the **RGB Setup** to set parameters in how Photoshop represents images in the RGB color mode.

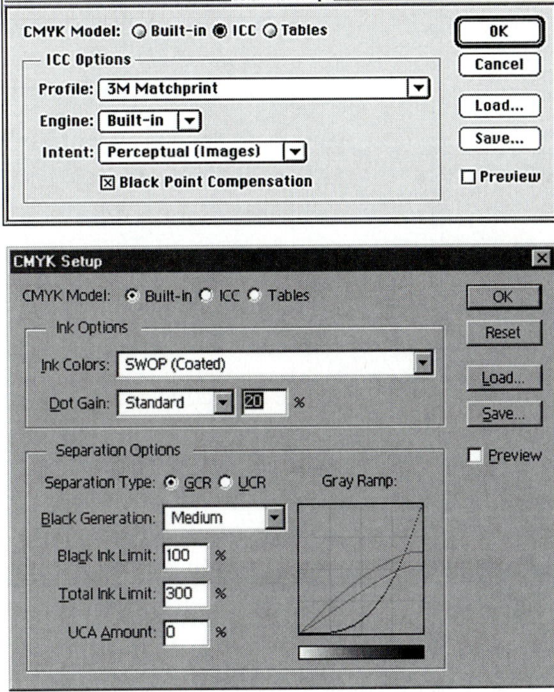

CMYK Setup for Macintosh (top) and Windows (bottom)

- Use the CMYK Setup screen to define the CMYK color space for a variety of inks, paper stock, and color management profiles. Choose File>Color Settings>CMYK Setup. This setting affects the way RGB documents are converted to CMYK. If an ink set runs heavy in magenta, for example, the program takes that into consideration when converting the document. Depending on what CMYK color profile is worked in, choose controls either in the Built -In settings, an ICC profile, or other tables as designated by the printer that you are using.

  The default setting in the Built-In mode is SWOP (Coated). SWOP stands for Specifications for Web Offset Printing, which are inks common in the U.S. This is fine in most instances. Other ink sets are listed if needed; in addition, a custom set can be created, or an existing set can be modified to more closely match the output.

ICC — International Color Consortium. For more information, visit their web site: www.color.org

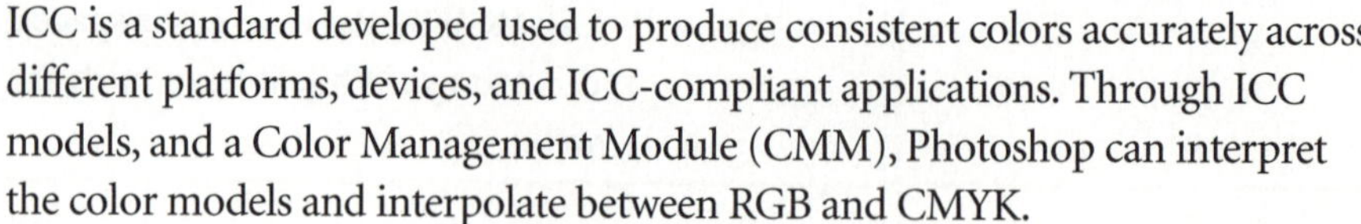

ICC is a standard developed used to produce consistent colors accurately across different platforms, devices, and ICC-compliant applications. Through ICC models, and a Color Management Module (CMM), Photoshop can interpret the color models and interpolate between RGB and CMYK.

- Get a color proof from a CMYK service bureau or output device, and compare it with the screen image. Additional adjustments may need to be made to the Gray Balance to remove unwanted color casts, or compensate for dot gain, wherein a halftone dot grows larger on the press, darkening one or more of the CMYK primaries in your image.
- Repeat until the results are satisfactory.

Using the Gamma Program

Gamma is defined as contrast between midtones. Monitors display gamma in a linear fashion; we humans see logarithmically. The purpose of the gamma program is to compensate for the difference between the way we see images and the way the monitor displays an image; it also corrects color casts — hints of blue or green visible in most monitors. Even if other calibration tasks are skipped, gamma correction is critical to accurate reproduction of images.

Before correcting a monitor's gamma, make certain that everyone in the class has Photoshop set up the same way. When Macintosh users gamma-correct, it affects all applications; for Windows users, only Photoshop is affected.

Before We Correct Gamma

1. If Photoshop is open, exit the application. Locate and open the System folder (Macintosh) or locate and open the Photoshop application folder, then locate the Adobe Photoshop Settings folder (Windows).
2. Open the Preferences folder within the System folder and find Adobe Photoshop 5.0 Prefs (Macintosh) or open the Adobe Photoshop Settings folder within the Photoshop folder and find Adobe Photoshop 5 Prefs.psp (Windows).
3. Drag the Prefs file to the trash can (Macintosh) or the Recycle Bin (Windows), and empty it.
4. That's it! Relaunch Photoshop; it will take a little longer than normal to load while it builds a new preferences file.

Setting Your Monitor

The Adobe Gamma Wizard is one way to calibrate a monitor. This program takes you step by step through the calibration procedure. There are some minor differences between Macintosh and Windows setup screens. Not all screens are shown.

We're going to make the assumption that the room lighting is at the level we wish to regularly calibrate in, that the monitor has been turned on for at least 30 minutes, and that the display is a neutral gray.

1. Launch the Adobe Gamma utility from the Photoshop>Goodies>Calibration folder (Macintosh) or the Photoshop>Goodies>Calibrate folder (Windows).
2. The first screen selects the method of calibration that will be used. The Adobe Gamma Wizard gives the option of either a step by step method (by using the Adobe Gamma Wizard), or using the control panel (as previously shown). For this example, we will use the Wizard.

For more information on SWOP, visit the SWOP web site: www.swop.org

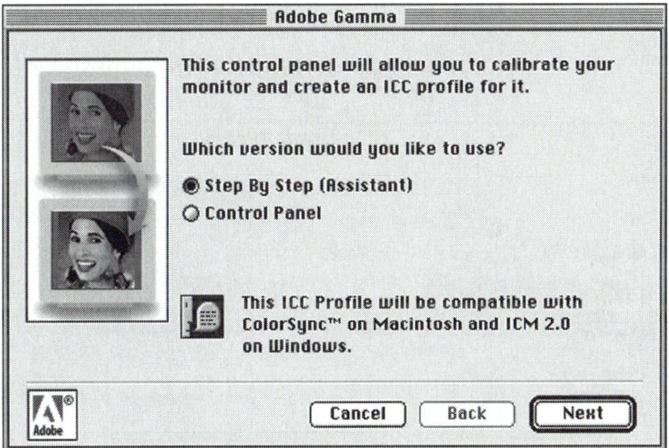

3. The first step is to adjust the monitor to the maximum setting. Change the Contrast control to the highest setting, and adjust the Brightness control to make the center box as dark as possible (but not black), while keeping the frame around it a bright white.

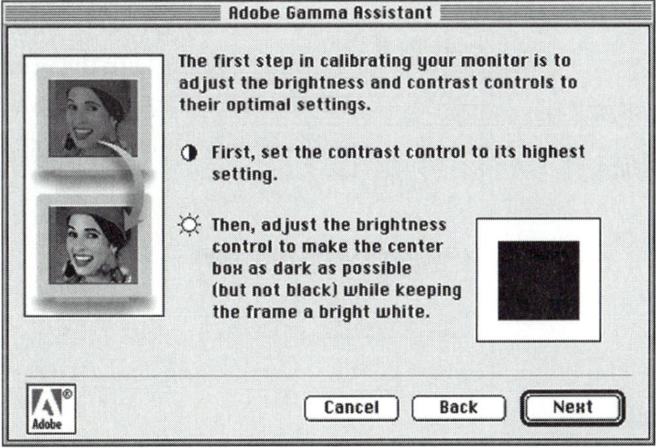

Phosphors — how a monitor produces the red, green, and blue color on the screen.

4. The next step will set the Phosphors. Phosphers vary between different manufacturers. The Gamma Wizard will attempt to measure phosphor levels. If this setting is incorrect, obtain the correct setting from the monitor's owner's manual, and record it on this screen.

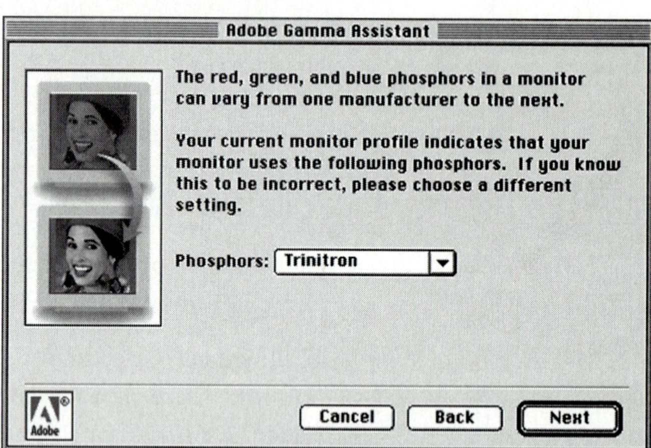

5. To set the midtone levels, adjust the midtone level inside of the gray box until the center solid gray box fades into the pattern box. Then choose the proper gamma for the monitor (either Macintosh, Window, or Custom). Deselecting the *View Single Gamma Only* option allows for the adjustment of the midtone levels for the red, green, and blue colors.

You can deselect the "View Single Gamma Only" option, and adjust your midtone levels for the red, green, and blue colors independently.

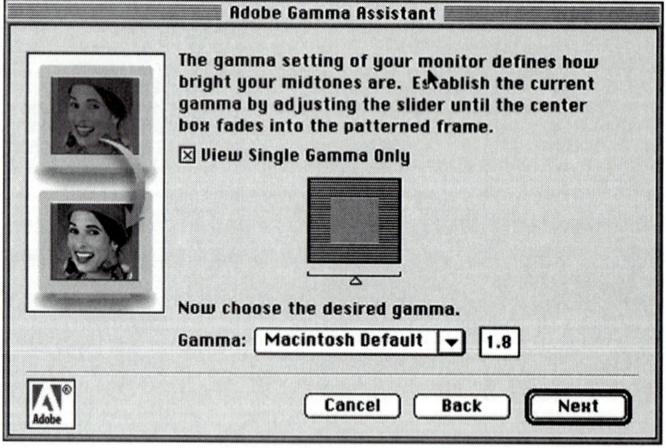

6. The next step is to determine whether the monitor is using a warm or cool white point. As with the previous steps, the Wizard will determine what it feels is the current temperature at which it believes the monitor is representing the color white. If this in incorrect, reset it.

The setting available are:

5000°K (warm white)

5500°K

6500°K (daylight)

7500°K

8500°K (cool white).

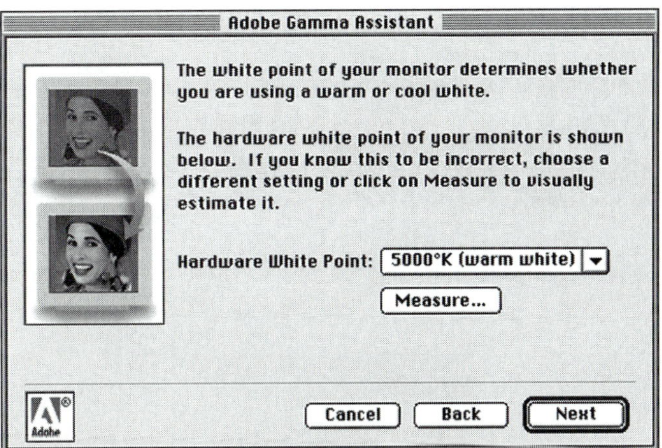

7. Upon the completion of these settings through the Wizard, save them to the computer. This will allow you to recall them, if it becomes necessary to adjust them, or if other factors cause the need to change the settings. Name a new folder, Photoshop Gamma Setting, within the Photoshop program folder, and save these settings to that folder. Windows users, just Save.

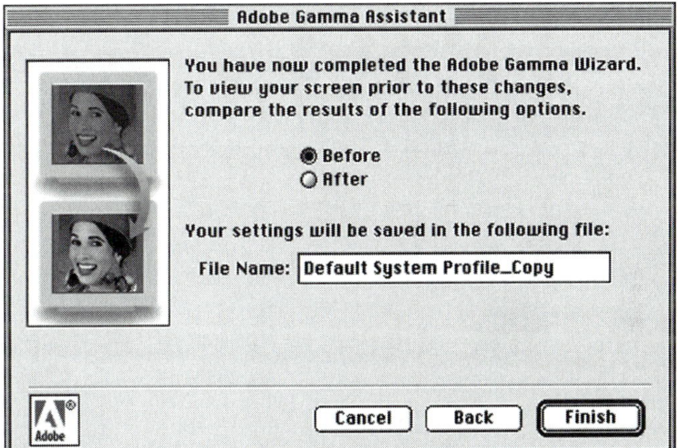

Summary

The proper working environment, combined with a calibrated computer system, can be the greatest first step in the production of high-quality Photoshop images. Since many factors can affect the image, Photoshop has included many tools to meet the needs of the graphic design and production professions.

Now that the monitor has been calibrated to the work environment, it's time to understand the concept of color, its effects on the images, and how we can improve work through the tools available in Photoshop 5.0.

Notes:

CHAPTER 13

ADJUSTING BRIGHTNESS AND CONTRAST

CHAPTER OBJECTIVE:

To understand the relationship between Brightness and Contrast, and how these two values affect the quality of reproduction in digital images. In Chapter 12, you will:

- Become familiar with the many tools available for tonal correction and color adjustment.
- Learn the three-step process for adjusting brightness and contrast.
- Become familiar with the tools for adjusting brightness and contrast: the Histogram, Brightness and Contrast, Levels, and Curves commands, and how the Info palette shows the value of the color.
- Learn how to choose highlights and shadows from an image.

PROJECTS TO BE COMPLETED:

- Marinara Shelf Talker
- KSOL Rising
- Maui Travel Postcard
- Rough Riders Ad
- Gulls Poster
- Concert Poster
- Banana Boat Table Tent
- Salute to Veterans Poster

Adjusting Brightness and Contrast

Highlight — The lightest area of the image.

Shadow — The darkest part of the image.

Gamma — Contrast in the midtone range.

In a perfect world, all photographs would be crisp and clear, and all scans optimally balanced with beautiful, accurate color. The reality of the situation is quite different. With digital images coming from a variety of sources, many are far from perfect. To reproduce your images with the best quality, no matter the quality of the input, is one of the greatest reasons to know Photoshop's many tools and controls.

The Photoshop arsenal includes many tools for tonal correction and color adjustment. The first step in correcting an image is adjusting brightness and contrast.

What is Contrast?

Contrast is defined as the difference between the lightest and darkest areas of an image. A low-contrast image will look washed out, and lacking in detail thorough the image. A high-contrast image lacks detail in the shadow areas and highlights; in some high-contrast images, the midtones can be nearly nonexistent.

Adjusting brightness and contrast is a three-step process:

- Determine the highlight areas within the image.
- Determine the shadow areas within the image.
- Adjust the gamma — the contrast in the middle grays or midtones of an image. The gamma adjustment determines the proportion of darker grays to lighter grays.

Use the Histogram tool only as a review tool.

Remember, use Brightness and Contrast tools only for overall correction of an image.

Tools for Adjusting Brightness and Contrast

There are many tools available for brightness and contrast adjustment in Photoshop. The differences between them are mainly a matter of the degree of accuracy and amount of control each command can produce. In this chapter we will concentrate on four.

The Histogram command shows the distribution of pixels from the darkest to the lightest portion of the image. This distribution can be shown for the entire image, or for each of the individual color channels.

The Brightness and Contrast command can be used to make gross corrections, changing all of the pixels in an image. This is really only appropriate for special effects. You can't adjust the highlights, shadows, and gamma separately.

The Levels command will give you most control over the brightness/contrast and midtones of your image. Use the Curves command for the finer correction of midtones.

The Levels command allows you to adjust highlights, shadows, and gamma individually. In addition, you can either work on all the channels in a document at once, or just work on an individual channel. The Levels command uses a Histogram, a graph of the brightness levels within an image, to allow you to *see* the distribution of pixels in an image.

The Curves command, while usually used for color correction, can also be used to correct the brightness and contrast of an image. While the Levels command is usually more than adequate for the task, occasionally you'll find a particularly difficult image that needs different midtone adjustments in various ranges of midtone values. For example, Curves allows you to make light midtones darker and dark midtones lighter in each individual color channel. Adjusting the brightness and contrast for this type of image is usually done while performing color correction, covered in the next section.

The Info palette shows the value of the color in a particular point on an image. Photoshop 5 allows you to map two different points on an image. This, as you shall see, will assist you in judging the best point to choose for your highlight or shadow area. The Info palette will be explained, in more details, in a later chapter.

Using the Brightness and Contrast Command

1. Open the image **Poolside_GS.TIF** from the **SF-Intro Pshotoshop** folder. This is an especially low-contrast image.
2. Select Image>Duplicate to make a copy of the grayscale image. Name this copy "Poolside_GS_BC.TIF".
3. Select Image>Adjust>Brightness/Contrast.
4. Move the Contrast slider to the right to about 25 to increase the contrast.
5. Move the Brightness slider to the left a little, about -10, to darken the image.
6. While these adjustments have improved the image overall, there is still a lack of contrast in areas such as the palm fronds at the top. If you adjust the contrast high enough to correct the contrast in the palm fronds, the white around the pool and the shadow areas lose *all* detail.

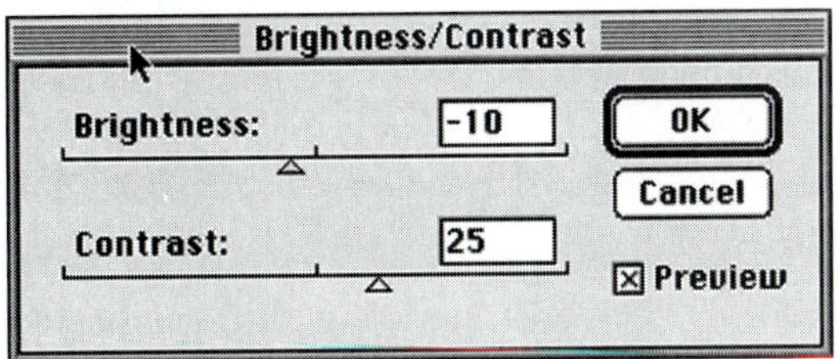

7. Play with the Brightness and Contrast sliders until you feel you've achieved the best looking image possible. Notice that while you can make overall brightness and contrast corrections, the highlight and shadow will still lack detail. Click OK.

8. Leave both images open, and continue on to the next exercise.

Using Levels to Adjust Brightness and Contrast

1. Activate the **Poolside_GS.TIF** image, and select Image>Duplicate again. Name the duplicate "Poolside_GS_Levels.TIF".

2. Select Image>Adjust>Levels, or Command/Control-L.

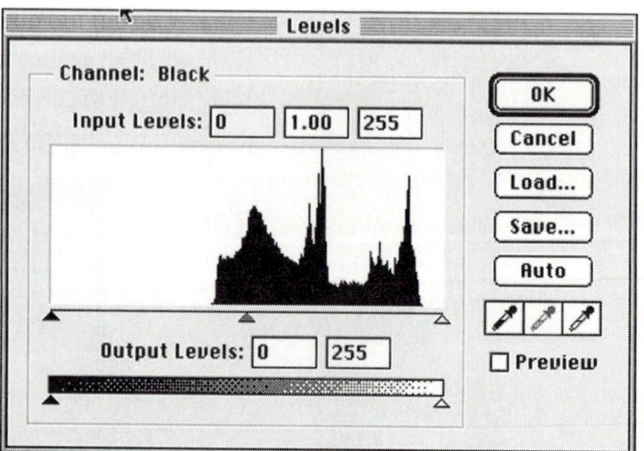

Check the small box that says "Preview." This will provide you instant feedback as you make changes to the values in the histogram. The histogram (the graph in the center of the dialog box) is typical of a low-contrast image. Most of the image data is bunched together in the middle, indicating a lack of distinct highlights and shadows.

3. The first set of sliders, the Input Levels, are used for increasing contrast and adjusting gamma. The Output Levels are used to decrease contrast in an image. Move the black slider of the Input Levels control bar to the right so that it just touches the rise on the left edge of the graph.

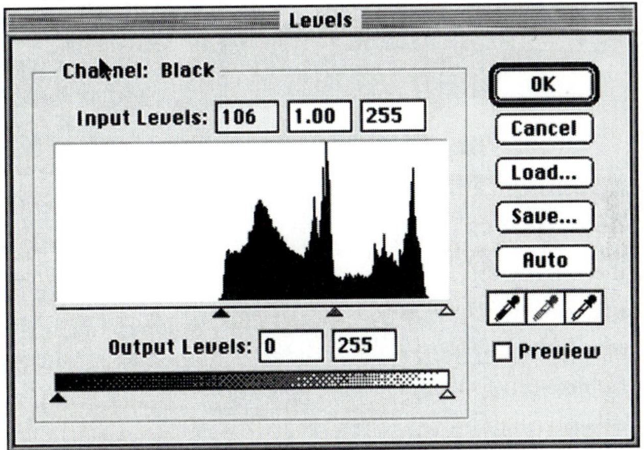

Notice that the first of the numbers listed above the histogram changes as you move the slider. Essentially, any pixel with a brightness value *lower* than that number (or any pixel to the *left* of the slider) will be remapped to black.

4. Repeat the process with the white slider. Move the slider left until it touches the rise in the graph on the right. The image should now appear similar to the one you corrected using Brightness and Contrast.

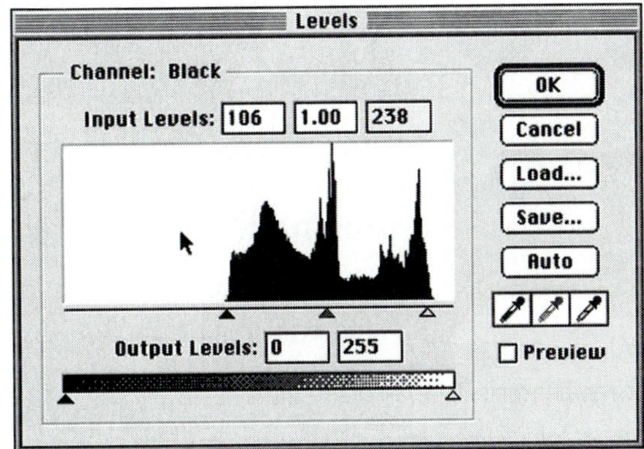

5. The contrast isn't quite high enough. Move the black-and-white sliders toward the center a little more (but not too far!) to increase the contrast. Remember

that only the pixels between the two sliders will maintain color; the remainder will turn either black or white.

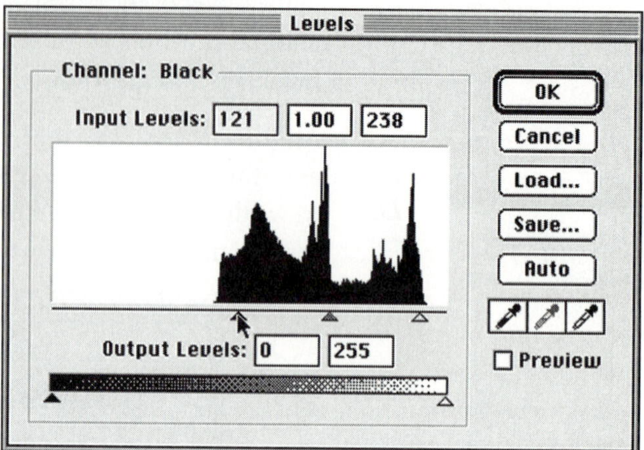

6. The slider in the middle is the gamma slider. Moving it to the right increases the distance between the black and gamma sliders, and reduces the distance between the white and gamma sliders. The result is *darker* midtones, because the ratio of dark pixels (the pixels between the gamma slider and the black slider) is higher. Move the gamma slider left to about 1.35 to lighten the image. Click OK.

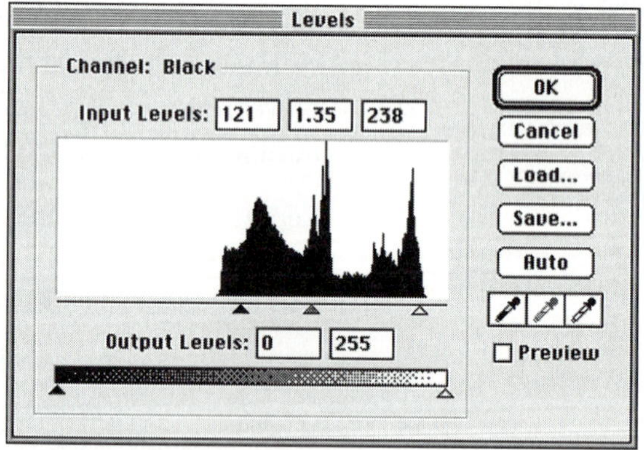

7. Leave the file open while you proceed to the next exercise.

You can review and revise saved brightness and contrast settings in the History palette.

Choosing Highlights and Shadows from the Image

The result of using Levels in the previous exercise is slightly better than what was achieved using Brightness/Contrast. Generally speaking, most images don't have a contrast problem this severe, and the type of leveling used above is sufficient to achieve excellent depth and results far superior to using Brightness/Contrast.

By moving the black-and-white sliders in the previous example, you were changing the *black point* and *white point* of the image, the point at which pixels become black or white. Occasionally, you'll find an image, such as the one we're working on, that doesn't respond well to leveling according to the histogram. With this type of image it is necessary to pick the black-and-white points directly from the image.

Setting black-and-white points manually takes a little extra thought and care. You could rely on your eyes to find highlight and shadow points, but there's a better way. With the use of the Color Sampler tool, the Video LUT setting in the Preference window, and the multiple sampler option in the Info palette, you can determine the black-and-white points quickly.

Leveling with Black and White Points

1. Activate the **Poolside_GS.TIF** image agan, and select Image>Duplicate. Name this duplicate "Poolside_GS_ManualLevel.TIF". Click OK.
2. In Photoshop Display & Cursors Preferences, be certain that Video LUT Animation is selelcted.

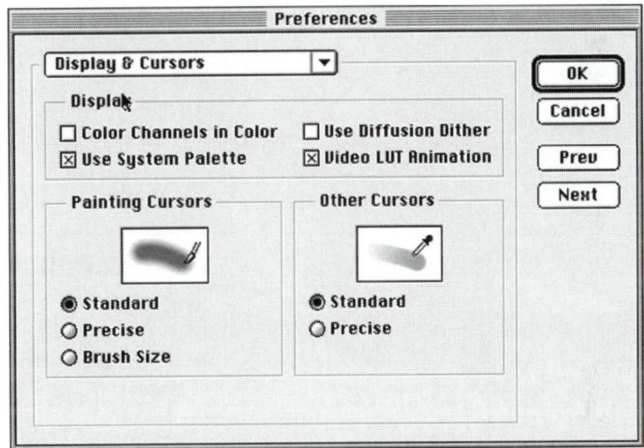

3. Open the Color Sampler tool in the Eyedropper tool. Double-click the Eyedropper to activate its Options palette. Set Sample Size to 3 x 3 Average.

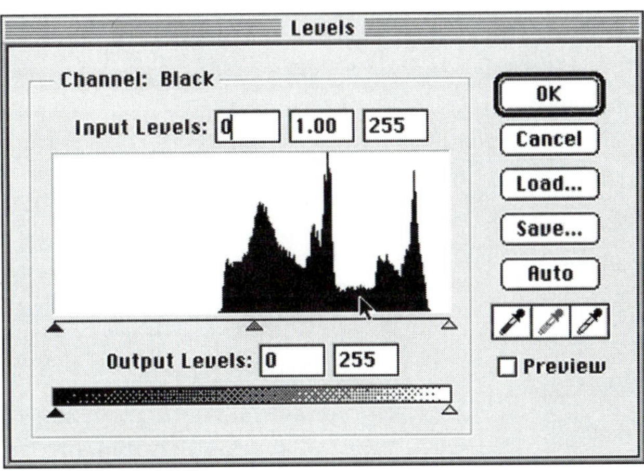

You can also make professional tonal changes with the Adjustment Layers tools in Photoshop, which will be explained in a later chapter. Adjustment Layers allow you to adjust color and contrast adjustments to an image without permanently applying them to the original data.

When you're using the Levels eyedropper, pay particular attention to detail — both in shadow areas as well as in the highlights. The color of the area that you choose also affects the results. Click on several different areas to see what we mean. Keep resetting the image with the Command/Alt-Reset option.

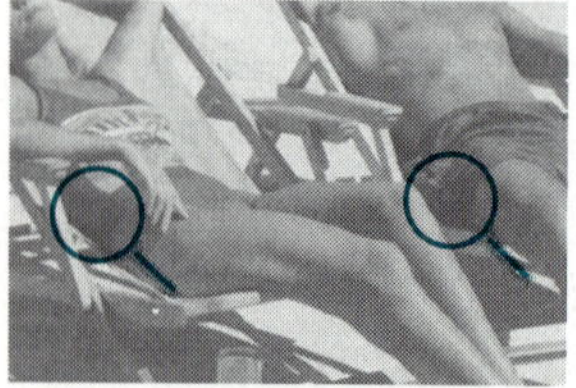

Another good location from which to select the shadow dot was in the darker areas of the swimsuits. The woman's shadow was best, with the shadow on the man's suit almost as good. While you're picking and resetting the shadow, pay particular attention to the detail under the left side of the woman's lounge chair. You'll see detail appear and get lost as you pick from different areas.

4. Select Image>Adjust>Levels (or Command/Control>L) to activate the Levels dialog box. Make certain that the Preview is not activated in the Levels palette.

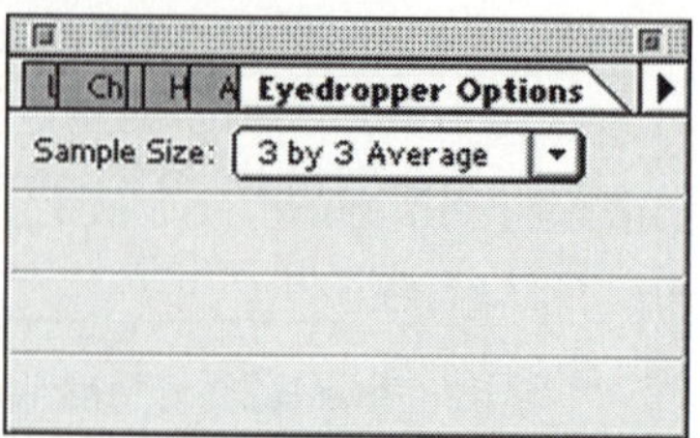

5. Hold down the Option/Alt key, and drag the Input Shadow pointer (the pointer on the left) to the right, and back again. The area that becomes visible first is the lightest point in the photo.

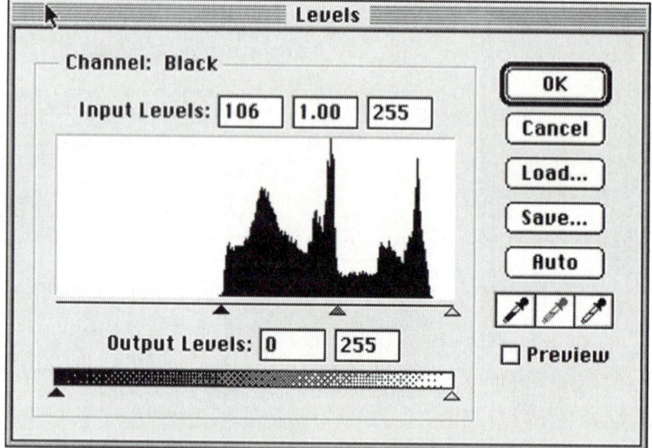

6. Repeat with the Highlight pointer. That is the darkest part of the image.

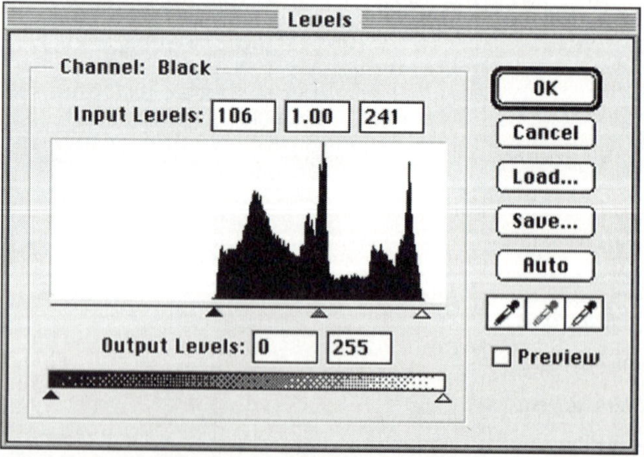

7. The idea is to find a highlight and shadow point that maintains detail. Choosing a point that has no detail will cause the area to go totally white (highlight) or black (shadow), with no detail reproduced. Look for a good highlight and shadow point; for example, details in the texture of the pool's surface, or folds in the bathing suit. These details should be printable, meaning that a halftone dot should be able to distinquish the changes in the grayscale of the image.

8. Save and name the file "Poolside_GS_ManualLevel.TIF" into your **Work in Progress** folder.

Summary

Understanding the relationship between brightness and contrast, and how these two values affect the quality of reproduction in digital images, is the first, and possibly the most critical factor, in creating a high-quality image. An image that has too much contrast (a "sharp" image) or not enough contrast (a "flat" image) will produce an unsatisfactory print. Photoshop's Brightness/Contrast, Levels, and Curves tools make a process that used to take hours in a photographic darkroom, and reduces it to minutes on a computer.

Complete Project D: Rough Riders Ad

Notes:

CHAPTER 14

FILTERS

CHAPTER OBJECTIVE:

To learn about filters, an important and extremely functional set of processes built directly into Photoshop; to learn the effects of various different inherent filters, and how to apply them to you images. In Chapter 14, you will:

- Learn how to access filters.
- Learn about Photoshop's Filter menu's thirteen groups, divided by the type of function that the filters perform.
- Know when filters will and won't work.
- Learn to create buttons, an important tool when employing Photoshop for use in interactive projects such as building web pages or multimedia CD-ROMs.

PROJECTS TO BE COMPLETED:

- Marinara Shelf Talker
- KSOL Rising
- Maui Travel Postcard
- Rough Riders Ad
- Gulls Poster
- Concert Poster
- Banana Boat Table Tent
- Salute to Veterans Poster

Filters

Filters, located in the Filter menu of the Photoshop menu bar, are like small programs to create special effects in images. Photoshop comes with 98 built-in filters; other manufacturers also create filters for Photoshop called *Plug-ins*, which expand the program's functionality even further.

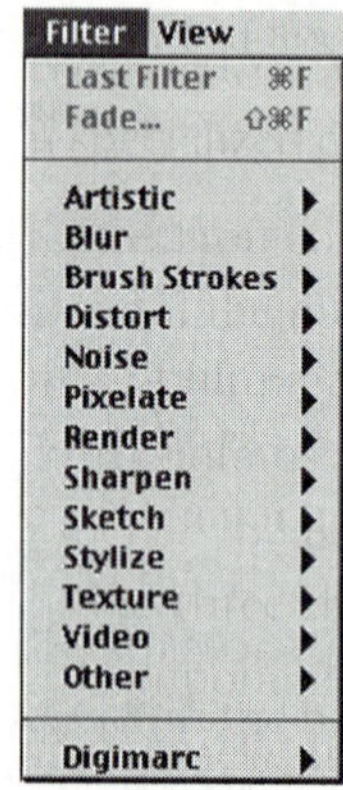

You've already used some of Photoshop's filters in exercises and projects throughout this book: Gaussian Blur, Emboss, and Noise to name a few. Entire books have been written about Photoshop filters alone. We're coming to the end of this book, so for now, we'll cover the basic filter types. In the exercises at the end of this chapter we'll actually use several more of these filters to create complex textural backgrounds.

There are many wonderful third-party plug-ins available, but it's good to remember that plug-ins are not a substitute for knowing the program and using it skillfully. Be judicious in your use of filters.

The Filter Groups

Photoshop's Filter menu is divided into thirteen groups, according to the type of function the filters perform:

- The Artistic filters apply effects to images that emulate artistic or other organic textures. Examples are the Watercolor filter, which creates a passable watercolor effect, and the Plastic Wrap filter, which makes the image look as if it hass been wrapped in bubbled plastic.

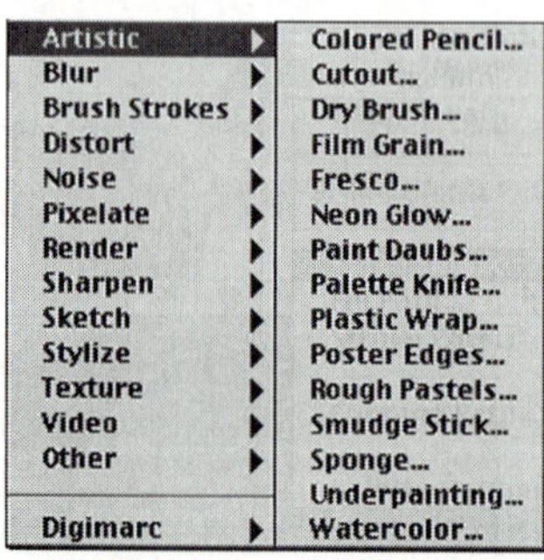

- The Blur filters include filters such as Gaussian Blur, which you've used several times already, as well as other blurring filters which allow different degrees of blurring, and special effects such as Radial Blur and Motion Blur.

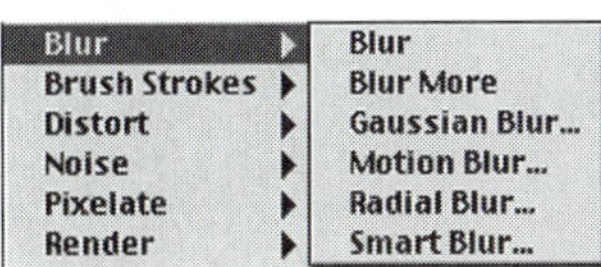

- The Brush Strokes filters add painterly effects, such as Cross Hatching, which is especially good on grayscale images.

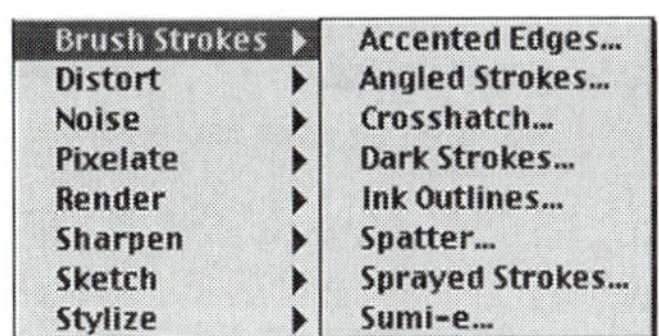

- The Distort filters section contains commands to warp an image into spheres, waves, ripples, and other convoluted shapes.

- The Noise filters allow the addition and removal of noise from an image or graphic. Many complex backgrounds begin with a simple noise fill.

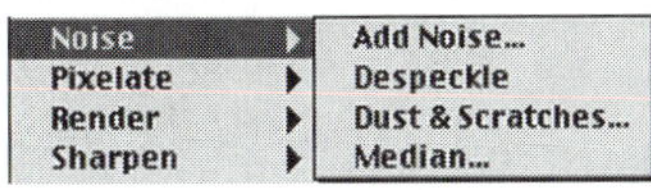

- The Pixelate filters produce a variety of impressionistic effects, such as Mezzotints and Pointillization.

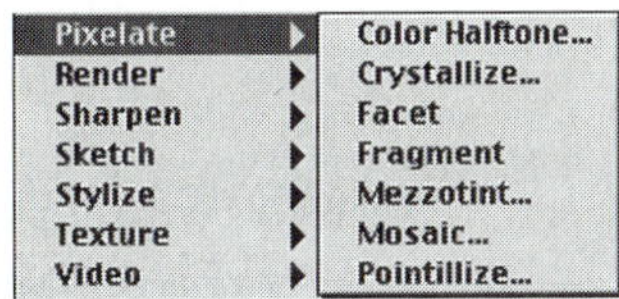

- The Render filters are a special group of filters to create complex textural effects. Some of these filters work only on RGB images. From the Render menu, clouds can be created, 3-D lighting effects are built, or an effect similar to the flare of a camera lens may be added.

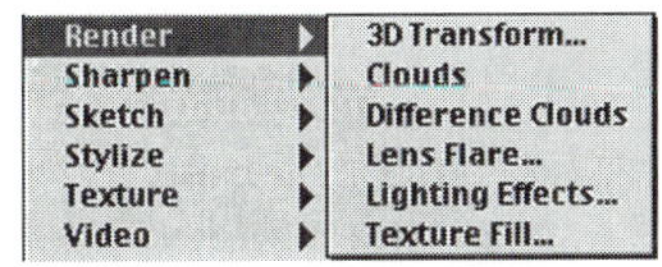

Relying heavily on third-party plug-ins can be dangerous. When Windows 95 was first released, most third party plug-ins no longer worked with Photoshop. Users who relied solely on plug-ins for special effects were stuck until Adobe released a software patch to correct the problem.

In addition, some plug-ins don't work with newer versions of the program.

- The Sharpen filters include commands to make images appear sharper or grainier.

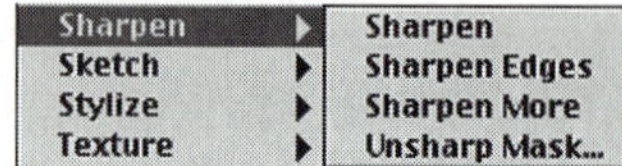

- The Sketch filters make images look hand-drawn with various art media, such as Chalk & Charcoal.

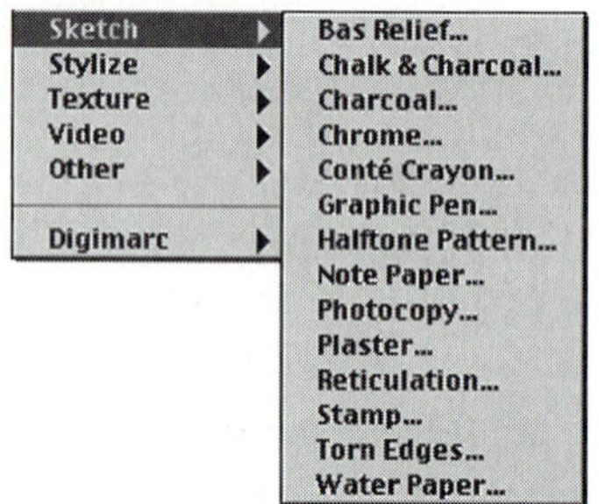

- The Stylize filters section is made up of wild special effects such as Extrude, which turns an image into cubes or pyramids, Emboss, which you used when making a multimedia button, and Wind, which "blows" pixels in your image to the right or left.

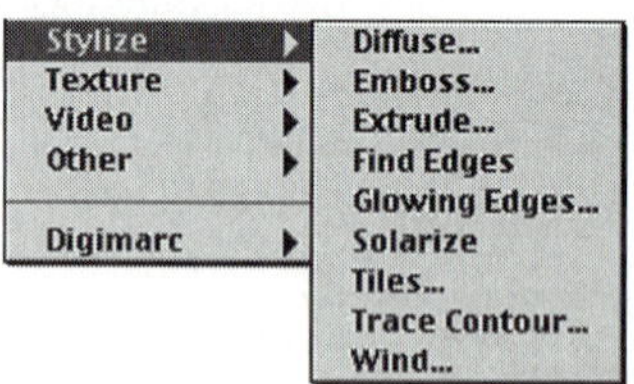

- The Texture filters add three-dimensional texture to images. These filters often emulate something in the physical world, such as Stained Glass, or Texturizer>Burlap. You can even texturize an image with another Photoshop image.

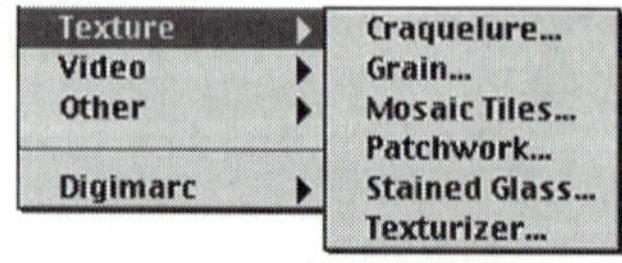

- The Video filters adjust image color and image data to make Photoshop files more acceptable for inclusion in video formats.

- The Other section contains filters which don't really fit in any other group, such as the Offset filter, which shifts an image horizontally or vertically a specified number of pixels, and Custom, which allows technophiles to create specialized filters.

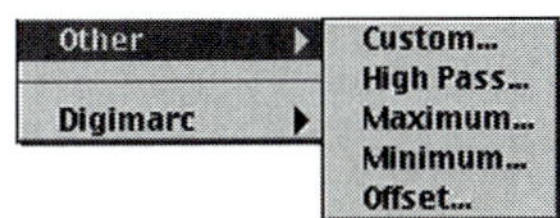

- The Digimarc filter, while technically a third party product, ships with Photoshop. It allows the creator of an image to embed a digital watermark, or for a user to read a digital watermark, and locate the author for copyright purposes.

Experimenting with Filters

1. Open the file **Mountain Child.TIF** from the **SF-Intro Photoshop** folder.
2. Apply a variety of effects from the Artistic and Sketch palettes, returning each time to the original image (select the first state after Open in the History Palette, and delete, or select Revert to Saved from the File Menu.) Notice that minute changes in the filter application can drastically affect the image.
3. Save the image as a grayscale image and apply effects from the Brush Strokes palette to get a feel for how these filters affect the image.
4. When you are finished, close the image without saving.

More Experimentation with Filters

1. Open the file **Closeup.TIF** from the **SF-Intro Photoshop** folder.
2. Zoom in to 200% and select the iris and pupil of both eyes (the green part with the black center) using the Lasso.
3. From the Filter Menu, select Sharpen>Unsharp Mask. Set the effect to match the dialog box that follows. Click OK and deselect the right eye (hold down the Option key and loosely draw around the eye).

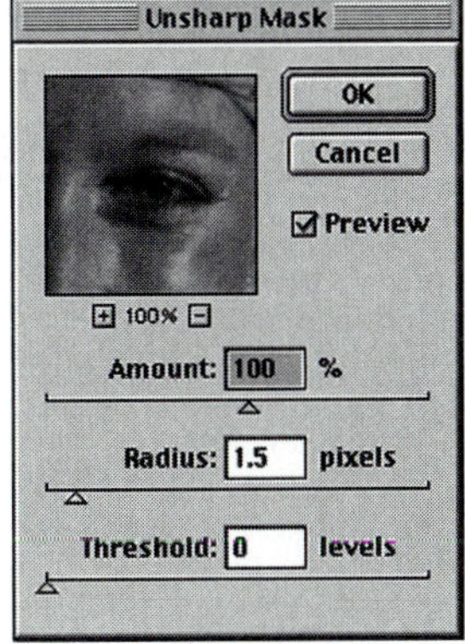

In the Sharpen filter group, the Unsharp Mask filter is the only one that gives you hands-on control over the sharpening of an image.

Now that we've given her penetrating eyes, we're going to put some sparkle in the left eye.

4. From the Filter Menu, select Render>Lense Flare. Set the effect at Brightness 100%, Flare Center at the lower right of the eye, and use the 35mm Prime lense. Click OK. Deselect the eye and zoom to 100%.

   Her shirt has a number of fine wrinkles that we'd like to remove.

5. Using the Lasso tool, select a wrinkled area on the front of the T-shirt.

6. From the Filter Menu, select Noise>Dust & Scratches. Set the Radius at 4 pixels and the Threshold at 0. Click OK.

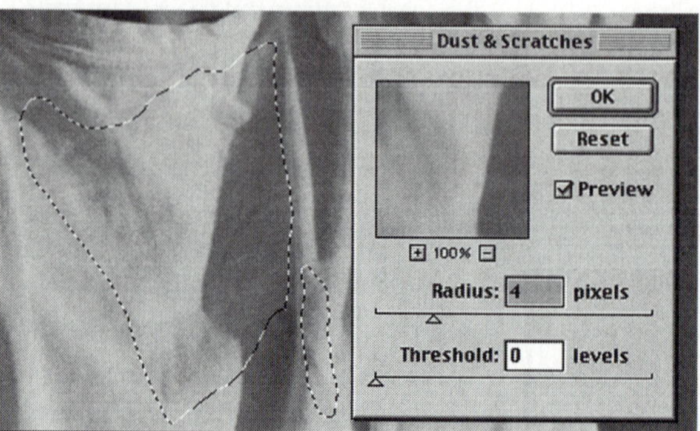

   In this Noise filter group, Despeckle has only one setting, giving you no control over the action. Median gives control only over the pixel radius. The most control over the image lies with the Dust & Scratches and Noise filters.

7. Close the file without saving.

Having Fun with Filters

1. Once again, open the file **Closeup.TIF** from the **SF-Intro Photoshop** folder.

2. Using the Lasso tool, select the cluster of umbrellas and save the selection.

3. Apply filters from the Pixelate, Stylize, and Texture filter groups, reverting to the photo's original state each time — or combine some effect to see how they interact.

4. Close the file without saving.

Other Things to Know About Filters

- Many filters include a preview image which gives the ability to zoom in on areas of the image to see the effect of the filter before it is applied. Unchecking the Preview checkbox (preview causes the entire image to show the filter effect) can really speed things up, and the effects of the filter are still visible in the dialog box.

- Filters don't work on Bitmap or Indexed Color images; some filters don't work on CMYK or Grayscale images.

- A layer must contain information for many filters to have any effect. In other words, with most filters, a newly created layer must be filled with white or another color before the filter is applied; otherwise, Photoshop will generate an error message or the filter will simply be unavailable.

- Depending on the blending mode, a new layer may be able to be automatically filled with a neutral (transparent in a particular mode) color. For example, the neutral color for Hard Light is 50% gray; noise may be added to the layer without taking an extra step to paint the layer with a color. Modes which don't have a default transparency color cannot be filled automatically.

In the following section, you'll have an opportunity to test your new skills. The hands-on exercises that follow contain the minimum amount of information necessary to complete each task. Except for the final image in each exercise, we'll be using a minimum of screen shots. Don't be afraid to refer back to previous sections in the book if there's something you don't understand.

Creating a Round Multimedia Button

1. Create a New RGB document 2 inches by 2 inches, 200 ppi, with a transparent background.
2. Fill the layer with white. Make a large circular selection in the middle of the image.
3. Draw a radial gradient with white in the center and black on the outside. Build the gradient so that the white center is located in the upper left of the circle.
4. Deselect, and choose Filter>Distort>Pinch. Set the Pinch filter to -100, and click OK. Press Command-F (Macintosh) or Control-F (Windows) to apply the filter again with the same settings.
5. Use the Levels command to adjust the image. Adjust the black and white sliders, and move the gamma slider to the center of the hump in the histogram.

6. Set the layer mode to Hard Light.
7. Save and name the image "Round Button.PSD."
8. Keep the image open for all of the exercises in this chapter.

Creating "Grass"

1. Turn off Layer 1 in the document **Round Button.PSD**. Create a new layer.
2. Fill the layer with white, and Add Noise with an amount of 600; make it Gaussian and Monochromatic. Gaussian Blur the noise 1 pixel.
3. Select Filter>Stylize>Wind. Change the settings to Stagger and From the Left. Apply the filter again with the same settings. Select All, then Rotate the layer 90 degrees clockwise.
4. Apply the Wind filter again. Rotate the layer 90 degrees clockwise.

5. Level the image a little to bring out the highlights and shadows, then select Image>Adjust>Hue and Saturation. Colorize the document; change Hue to 100, Saturation to 70, and Lightness to -40.
6. Save the image.

Making Granite

1. Create a new layer in the Round Button.PSD document and name it "Granite".
2. Fill the layer with white, and add Gaussian, Monochromatic Noise at 100.
3. Select Filter>Stylize>Diffuse. Diffuse with the Darken Only setting. Run the filter a second time to strengthen the effect.
4. Save the document.

Creating a Wood Texture and Autumn Leaves

1. Create a new layer in the Round Button.PSD document and name it "Wood Leaf". Fill the layer with white, and Add Gaussian Monochromatic Noise with an amount of 600.
2. Select Filter>Blur>Motion Blur; set Angle to 0 and Distance to 30 pixels.

3. Use the Levels command to add some strong shadows to the texture, and increase the contrast. Move the black and white sliders so they just touch the rise on the left and right edges of the histogram.
4. Colorize the layer using the Hue and Saturation command. Settings of Hue 20, Saturation 30, and Lightness -35 work well for wood.
5. Duplicate the layer. Run Filter>Pixelate>Crystalize with a cell size of 10 pixels on the new layer.
6. Save the image.

Creating Orange Peel

1. Create a new layer in the Round Button.PSD document and name it "Orange Peel". Fill the layer with white.
2. Add Gaussian Monochromatic Noise, at about 600.
3. Filter>Stylize>Diffuse the layer, with the Lighten Only option. Apply the filter a second time with the same setting.
4. Gaussian Blur the image about .5 pixels, and emboss it to a height of about 4 pixels. Choose whatever amount and angle looks good to you.
5. Use Hue and Saturation with Colorize selected to color the background orange.

6. Keep the image open and available for the next exercise.

Viewing the Buttons

1. Turn off all of the layers in the **Round Buttons.PSD** document.
2. If it isn't already at the top, move the Button layer to the top of the document and turn it on.
3. Turn each layer on and off in turn to see the effects of the background on the button.
4. Turn on the Orange Peel layer and the Granite layer and adjust the layer opacity so that the background looks like golden granite, or sawdust.
5. Adjust the blending modes for different layers to see what kinds of interesting effects you can achieve.
6. Reset all layers back to normal. Keep the file open and available for the next exercise.

Making a Photo Button

1. Open the image **Couple on a Rock.TIF** from the **SF-Intro Photoshop** folder.
2. Select All and Copy. Close the image after copying.
3. Activate the **Round Button.PSD** document and Paste the image to create a new layer.
4. Move the layer with the Couple image until the two people are positioned within the button to your satisfaction. Save the file.

Trying Other Button Effects

1. Create another layer with your initials and a drop shadow (see Chapter 11).
2. Create a mirrored tile from one of your student images and use it as a background (see Chapter 5).
3. Create a composite of elements from two or more of your student images, cut out with the Lasso tool (see Chapter 9).

Complete Project E: Gulls Poster

Complete Project F: Concert Poster

CHAPTER 15

BASIC COLOR CORRECTION

CHAPTER OBJECTIVE:

To learn how colors interact, or complement, one another. To understand the relationship between the two basic color models: RGB and CMY. In Chapter 15, you will:

- Learn the theory of the Color Wheel, a visual tool to help you understand the relationship between color and color modes.
- Learn how to create a Color Wheel.
- Learn how to mix colors.
- Learn about subtractive primary and subtractive secondary colors.
- Learn how to manipulate color in an image. Learn how to create and use a Full Spectrum Color Wheel.

PROJECTS TO BE COMPLETED:

- Marinara Shelf Talker
- KSOL Rising
- Maui Travel Postcard
- Rough Riders Ad
- Gulls Poster
- Concert Poster
- Banana Boat Table Tent
- Salute to Veterans Poster

Basic Color Correction

It's not unusual for color in an image to be slightly out of true. No matter what method is used to acquire an image, there are many factors that can influence the color and tonal ranges. And unfortunately — due to the difference in RGB and CMYK color — an image can look terrific on screen, yet when output to film and printed it may contain too much or too little of a particular color. Photoshop has many useful tools to correct these problems in images. Each is suitable for a particular task.

Before starting to color correct an image, an understanding of how colors interact, or *complement*, each other, is needed. The two basic color modes, RGB and CMY, have a relationship that we use to maximize our efforts.

Please note that, while learning the comparison of CMY, K (Black) is added to the printing process to create a better quality image. The combination of only C, M, and Y will produce a muddy brown in areas that should appear black. Printing inks contain pigments, which, unlike natural light, contain impurities. Black ink adds definition to the image, compensates for the impurities in the inks used, and enhances the overall contrast of the image.

The Color Wheel

Clicking on the Image>Mode menu in Photoshop will show a long list of different options. Each of these modes has its benefits. However, for working in color, there are two standard modes that are used almost universally: RGB and CMYK. Scanning, input, outputting to photographic materials (such as slides and light-sensitive paper), and preparing images for web publication, is done in RGB. Output for printing is generally done in CMYK. Although they handle color differently, these two color modes are definitely linked. In digital display, RGB colors are *directly inverse* to CMY colors. Their relationship is the primary basis for all on screen color.

The words *directly inverse* refer to positions on a color wheel. To illustrate this concept, let's create one.

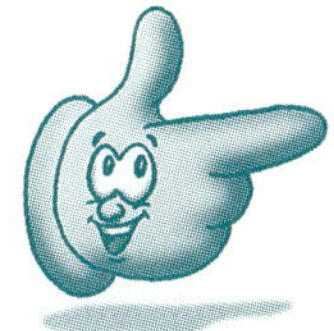

Try to use a process color book that matches your job in paper stock (matte, gloss, dull, etc.) as well as ink type. The absorption qualities (how much ink is absorbed into the paper) and color of the paper stock can greatly affect final ink color.

While it may seem odd that red and green together produce yellow, it's not as strange as you might think. If you mix red and green paint together, you get an icky brown; if you reduce the saturation and lightness of yellow in Photoshop, you'll get a very similar color.

Creating a Color Wheel

1. Open **Color Wheel Template.TIF** from the **SF-Intro Photoshop** folder.

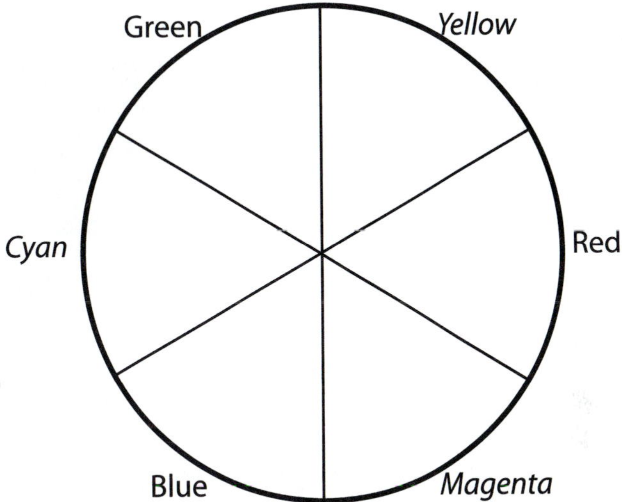

2. Click on the foreground color to open the foreground color picker, and find the box labeled R.
3. Type "255" in the R box. Make certain that the values in both the G and B boxes are 0. Now you have pure red. Click OK.
4. Activate the Paint Bucket tool and click in the sector marked Red on the Color Wheel to fill it with the color.
5. Repeat for the blue and green sectors. Type "255" in the B box, and "0" in the R and G boxes; then fill the blue sector with the Paint Bucket. Type "255" in the G box, and "0" in the R and B boxes; then fill the green sector with the Paint Bucket.

   Now you have half of the colors you need to complete your Color Wheel. It's time to add the CMY colors.

6. Open your foreground color picker, and find the box labeled Y. Type "100" in the box, making certain that the values in the other CMYK boxes = 0. Click OK.
7. Use the Paint Bucket tool to fill the sector labeled Yellow.
8. Repeat for the magenta and cyan sectors. Type "100" into the box corresponding to each color (M = magenta, C = cyan) and make certain that all other CMYK values are 0. Use the Paint Bucket tool to click on the appropriate sector.

The table below lists the different combinations of RGB and CMY primaries and the colors that result.

RGB:	*CMY:*
R= M+Y	*C= B+G*
G= C+Y	*M= B+R*
B= C+M	*Y= R+G*

Complements:

Red and Cyan

Green and Magenta

Blue and Yellow

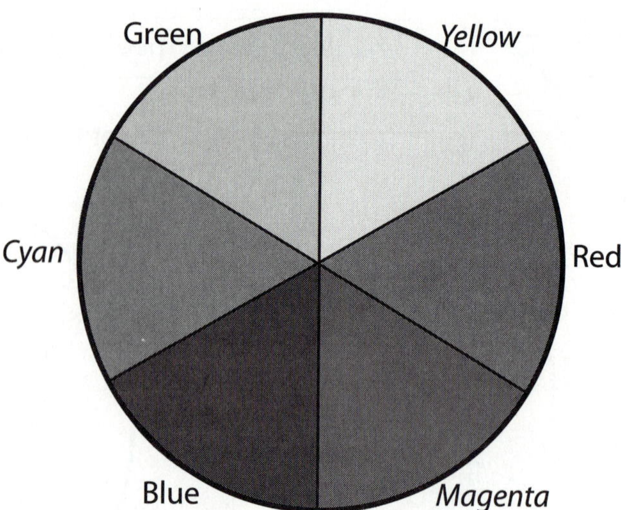

9. You have now completed your Color Wheel. Save the image as a TIFF file; and name it "Color Wheel.TIF." Keep it open; as we'll be using it in the next section.

Understanding the Color Wheel

Now we can refer to the color wheel and use it to understand how the RGB colors relate to the CMY colors. If you take any two colors in a triangle (for example, red and blue from the RGB triangle) and add them together, the resulting color will be the CMY color located between the two RGB points. In this example, red and blue combine to form magenta. This is what we mean when we say the two color modes are *directly inverse*. Each CMY color is made up of two RGB colors and vice versa. Vary the proportions of the primaries and add black to the equation, and you have the millions of colors in the digital palette.

A color complement is the color located directly opposite on the wheel. For example, find green on the wheel. Green is the complement of magenta, because green is the one color in the RGB triangle that is not included when making pure magenta. Adding the complement of a color neutralizes its brilliance, causing the color to become grayish.

Mixing Colors

Assuming you could work only in RGB mode, how could you *make* yellow? Believe it or not, the answer is "adding red and green." This seems confusing when you think of mixing red and green paints together. Paint is another example of *subtractive* color. When additional colors are applied to a surface, the amount of light that is reflected to your eye in reduced, or subtracted, from the original light that is hitting the subject.

Additive color is working with light, the RGB mode. The additive primaries are red, green, and blue. When added together at full intensity these colors make white light. The additive secondaries are yellow, magenta, and cyan — the colors that fall between the primaries on the color wheel. That means, to form a color, blend its complementary colors.

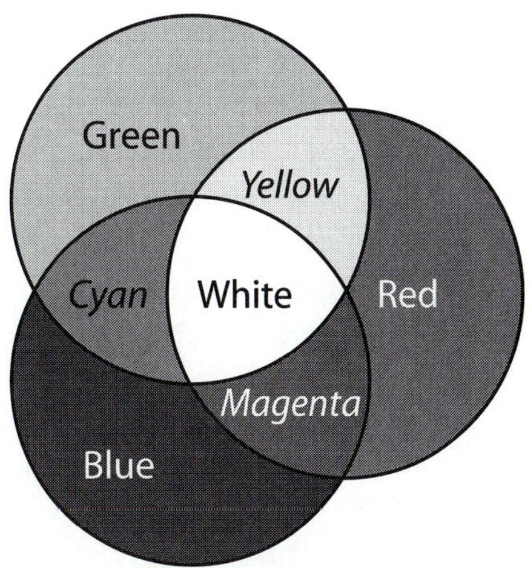

Subtractive color is working with pigment, such as paint or inks, the CMY mode. The subtractive primaries are cyan, magenta, and yellow. When all pigments are subtracted from an image, white remains; when they are added, they create black. The subtractive secondaries are red, green, and blue, the additive primaries.

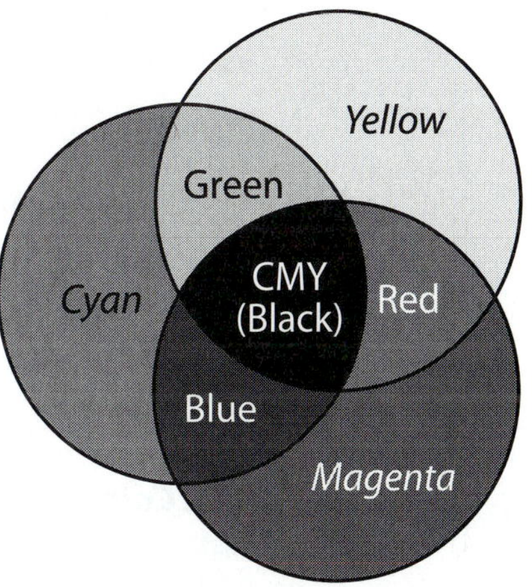

Since colors made with light are *additive* (meaning you add colors to produce other colors when the light is transmitted to your eye, the same as with a monitor) red and green together make yellow. Yellow is the CMY primary the two RGB primaries have in common; red is made of magenta and yellow, and green is made of cyan and yellow. By the same token, magenta is created by adding blue and red, and cyan is created by adding blue and green.

To manipulate color in an image, you need to take advantage of the relationship between color complements. If you want to add a specific color to an image, you have three options: add the color, add equal parts of its constituent colors, *or* remove some of its complement. For example, to add magenta to an image, you could add magenta, add more blue and red, or remove green. Conversely, this means that to remove a color from an image, you can remove the color itself, equal parts of its constituents, or add its complement.

While it may seem that it would be easiest to add or subtract the color in question, better results may be achieved by adding one color and subtracting another. For example, if an image needs less blue, simply removing blue may cause reds to go pink or cyan to lean toward green. Instead, adding red and green may be a better solution. Subtracting all three colors, or subtracting blue and adding amounts of red and green may result in the best image. Ideally, work with just the primary colors in a given model to achieve best results.

Shortly, we'll be learning how to make these types of corrections in images. For now, it's important that you understand the relationship between colors.

Pop Quiz

Here's a quiz for you to test your color mixing skills. (It's okay to refer to the Color Wheel you have open.)

1. To take out red, either remove ________and _______ or add _______.
2. To add green, either add ________ and ________ or remove ________.
3. To remove cyan, you can add _______ and ________ or remove _______ .
4. To increase blue, you may add _______ and _______ or remove _______.
5. To take out yellow, either remove ________and _______ or add _______.
6. To add magenta, either add ________ and ________ or remove ________.

Close the Color Wheel image.

Hue and the Color Wheel

1. Open the file **Lemon.TIF** from the **SF-Intro Photoshop** folder.
2. Choose Image>Adjust>Hue/Saturation (Command/Control-U) from the menu bar.

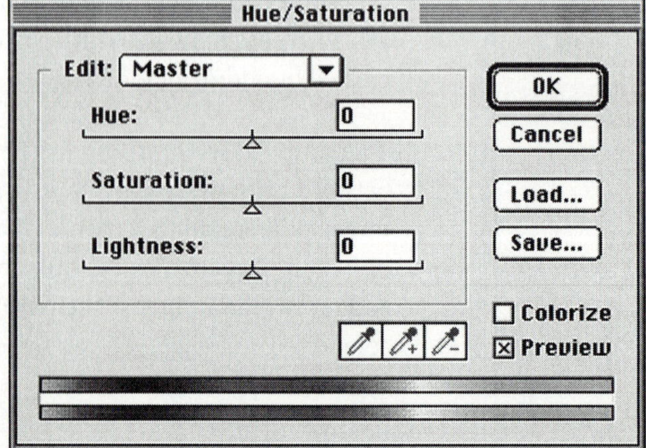

3. Moving the Hue slider, in either direction, actually rotates the color around the color wheel. Notice that the bottom bar of the Hue/Saturation palette is a representation of the color spectrum, like your color wheel. When you move the hue slider, this strip will also change, showing you the shift in the color spectrum. Move the Hue slider in the Master option to the far right. All of the colors in the image shift to their complements.

   We've essentially rotated the colors in the image 180 degrees around the wheel.

4. Move the Hue slider back to 0.
5. We'd rather not affect any of the other colors in the image except those used in the lemon. Click on the drop-down menu, and scroll down to Yellows (Command/Control-2). Each color, whether in the RGB or CMY palette has its own controls in the Hue/Satuation window.

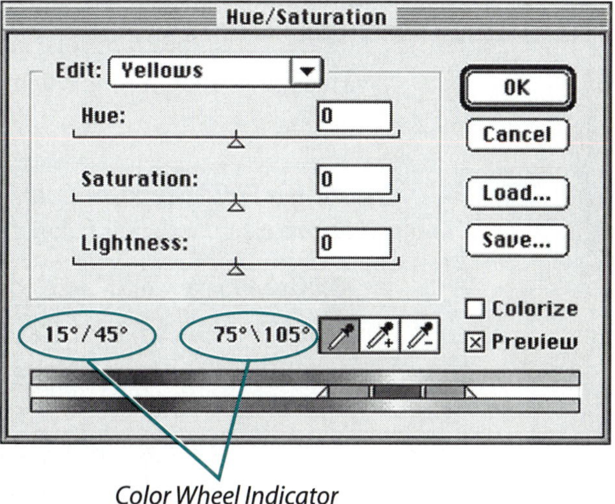

Color Wheel Indicator

Notice that the indicators above the color spectrum bar also show the current placement of the selected color in reference to the color wheel. (See above).

If you're printing your job to a short-run color printer, such as a Canon Laser Printer or a Xerox Docutect, make certain that the service provider calibrates their equipment on a regular basis. The color balance on these systems is affected by many factors, including temperature and humidity. Your service provider should be able to provide you with a process color chart for checking color.

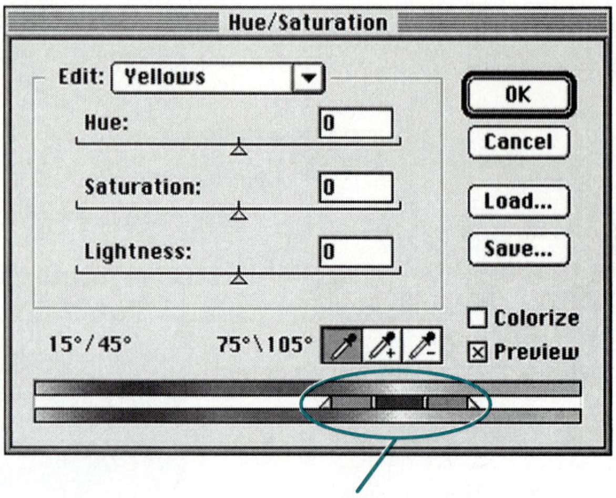

Range Indicator

The Range Indicator is a tool that will help you judge the degree of change in relationship to the overall image. This will show you whether a change will affect just the colors within this range, or if it will cause the color to drastically fall off.

6. Reduce Lightness to -30 or so, and drag the Hue slider at the top roughly halfway to the right. Move the slider back and forth until you find a good lime-green.

7. Close the file without saving.

Full Spectrum Color Wheels

The color wheel we created in the previous section is useful for understanding the relationship between CMY and RGB. There are a lot more colors than these six, however. A full spectrum color wheel will allow you to locate the complement of virtually any color in your system.

Creating a Full Spectrum Color Wheel

1. Create a New file 5″ × 5″ square, RGB Color Mode, Contents White, and 100 pixels/inch.

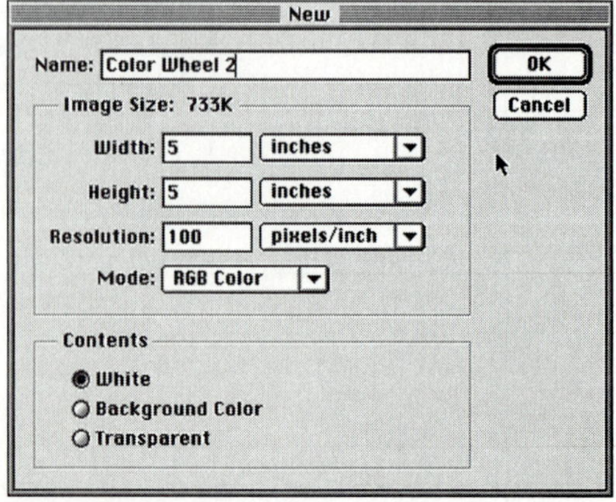

2. From the View menu, select Show Rulers.

3. Select the Elliptical Marquee tool (click and hold on the Marquee tool, slide the pointer to select the ellipse).

4. Position the cross hairs of the Marquee tool exactly in the center of the square (at 2.5″ on both rulers).

5. Hold down the Option-Shift (Alt-Shift) keys, and drag from the center until the edges of the circle are just inside the edge of the square.

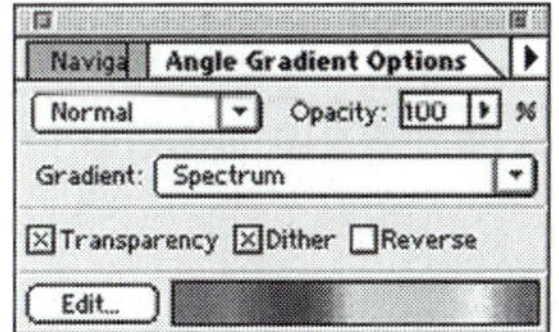

6. Click the Gradient tool in the Tool palette, and slide over to the Angle Gradient. Set the Gradient to Spectrum. Make certain that the Reverse option is not selected. Keep the Opacity at 100%.

7. Create a blend from the center to the right. Hold the Shift key down while dragging the mouse to the right. When completed, your image should look like a circle of color, with red to the right, and the balance of the colors in a clock-work direction, similar to the original color wheel that we made in the first example.

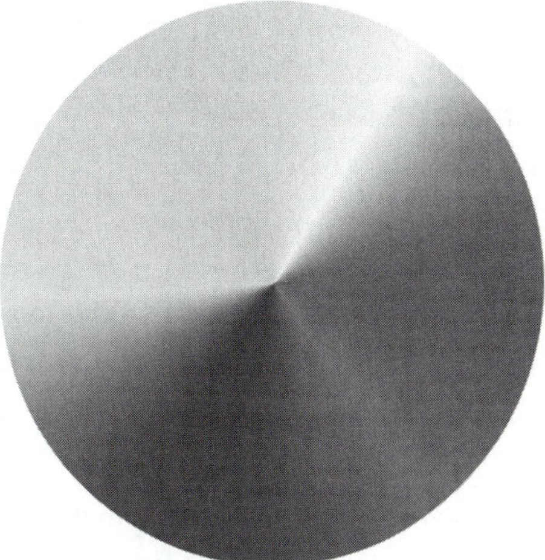

8. Save the image into your **Work in Progress** folder and name it "Color Wheel 2.TIF".

Using a Full Spectrum Color Wheel

The manner in which the wheel works is quite simple. Imagine a triangle inscribed in a circle, positioned over the color wheel. A point that lies between any two corners of the triangle is the corresponding color in the opposing model. For example, if you add red (one corner of the RGB triangle) and green (the other corner), you get yellow, which is positioned between them on that side of the triangle. Red and blue add up to magenta, while green and blue add up to cyan, just as in the simplified version of the wheel we used before.

A full spectrum wheel, however, allows you to find a complementary color for *any* color, not just primaries. To clarify things somewhat, let's add a triangle to the color wheel.

Using the Wheel to Determine Complementary Colors

1. If it isn't already open, open the image **Color Wheel 2.TIF** from your **Work in Progress** folder. Select File>Place, and place the **Com Pointer.EPS** file, located in the **SF-Intro Photoshop** folder. The EPS file might place slightly off-center from your color wheel, so align the vertical line through the middle of the wheel. Press Return or Enter to finish placing the image.

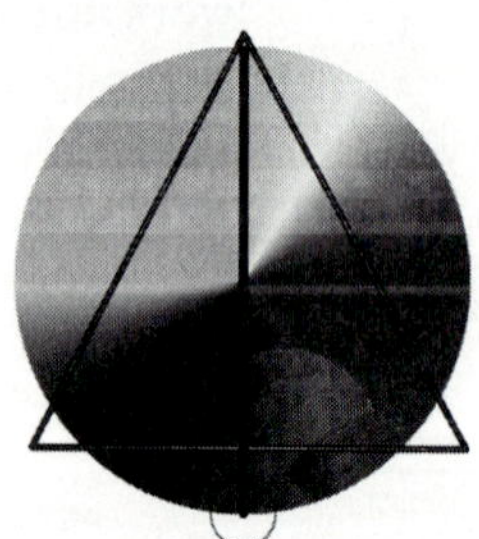

2. The top of the triangle is placed on the color you want to match. The center of the circle at the bottom represents the exact complement, while the entire bottom bar represents closely complementary colors. To find a complement for pure yellow, for example (which lies 30° away from the point at which the triangle is right now), activate the Com Pointer.EPS layer.

3. Make certain that the Info palette is visible. Select Edit>Transform>Rotate. Drag a handle to rotate the triangle image to the right about 30 degrees, until it is pointing at yellow. Press Return or Enter to finish the rotation.

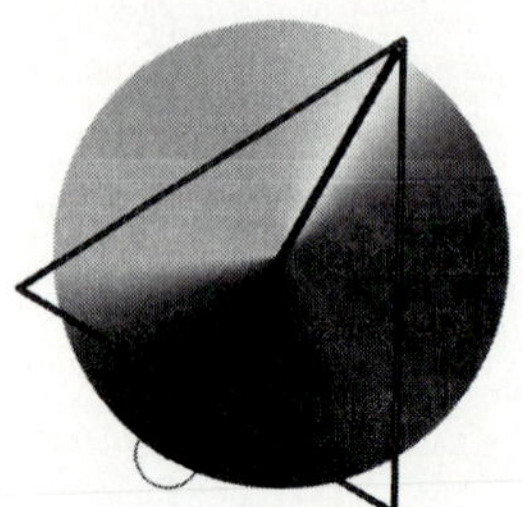

By simply estimating the degree of rotation from its current position to the color you need to match, you can use this tool any time you need to find a color's complement.

4. Save the file as a Photoshop document and name it "Color Wheel.PSD" before closing.

The Color Correction Tools

Color Balance is the most basic of color correction tools. It's easy to use, but lacks the fine adjustments necessary for proper color correction. The Color Balance tool is best used to correct an overall color cast on an image.

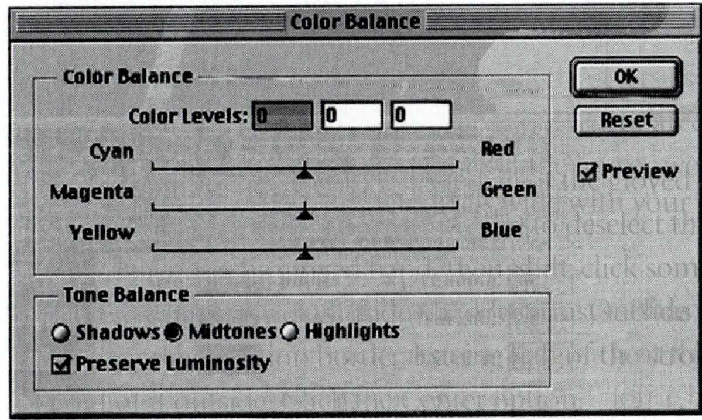

You can adjust the highlights, shadows, or midtones of an image. The Preserve Luminosity checkbox ensures that only the colors shift and that the tonal balance of the image is unchanged. Color Balance is fine for special effects such as adjusting artificial textural backgrounds created in Photoshop, but shouldn't be used for everyday color correction.

While the Levels command allows you to work on individual color channels, it lacks the control of the Curves palette. It's great if you're trying to limit your adjustment to midtones, but lacks fine control in highlight and shadow areas.

The Curves command, on the other hand, gives you exactly the type of precise control you need to adjust every area of the image individually, from the lightest highlights to the darkest shadows. It is the preferred tool for color correction. You can set individual points along the grayscale representation of each color, thereby making more accurate adjustments to an image. The Curves command will be discussed in a future chapter.

The Hue/Saturation command, which we used to change the color of the lemon, can be very useful in some situations. For example, an improperly calibrated scanner will sometimes shift the colors around the color wheel, making cyan too green, magenta too blue, and yellow too red. A quick adjustment with the Hue/Saturation command will easily correct this problem. It will also allow you to adjust individual primaries in an image, as we saw when turning the lemon into a lime.

Designers are supposed to have an unerring sense of color, right? Well, there are times when the perfect complement to the color you're trying to match doesn't just jump out at you. You can use the color wheel to identify ranges of complementary colors to use in your matching efforts. Complementary colors lie opposite each other on the wheel. We've supplied an EPS file that will match the dimensions of the file we created, and will point out a range of colors that work together.

The Variations command is interesting, though not useful for color correction for offset printing. It allows you to make adjustments based strictly on visible information by showing you the original image, plus the image with every variation of primary color added.

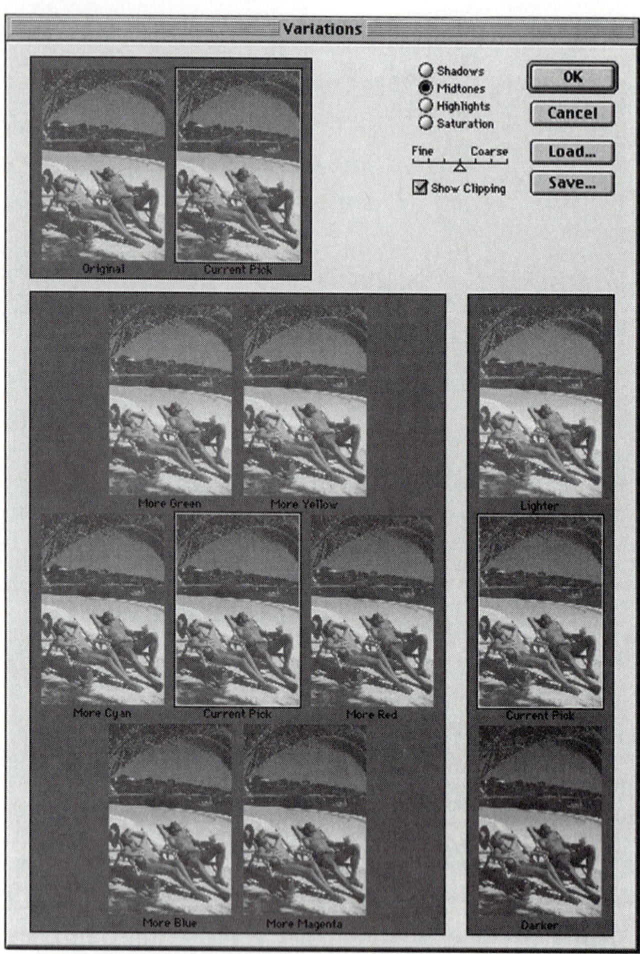

If the upper right image, which adds yellow, looked better than the center image, clicking on it would move it to the center, then recolor the surrounding images. You could then decide to add some magenta, which would move *that* image to the center. It's easy and fun, but it lacks the fine control of other correction methods. As you've learned, you *can't* judge printed output color based on monitor color. Variations also allows adjustment of saturation and brightness. It can be useful for "quick and dirty" correction for RGB graphics, but once you understand adjusting with Curves, curves are usually quicker.

The final color correction tool available is Selective Color replacement. This command allows you to edit the amount of ink produced in *only* the neutrals, blacks, whites, or individual primary colors without affecting other components of the image.

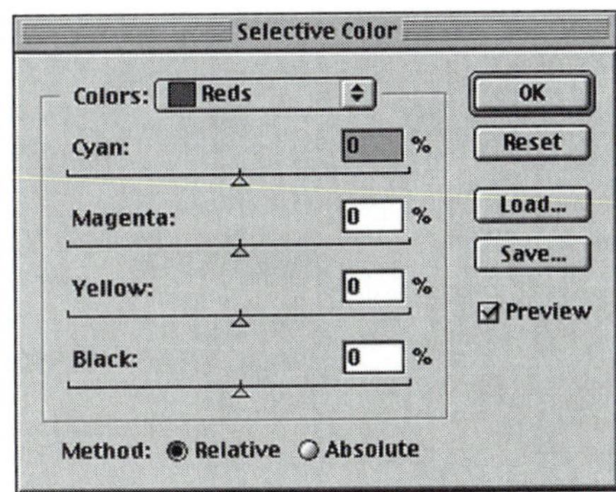

For instance, if a red car looks too magenta, you probably want to remove magenta from the image to produce a truer red. Unfortunately, magenta is a component of blue, as well as a color in its own right. If you reduce the amount of magenta, you might give your deep-blue sky a greenish cast. Selective Color allows you to adjust *only* the red, without affecting magenta, yellow, or any other range of primaries in the image. Though similar to Hue/Saturation with regard to editing a range of colors, Selective Color allows you to adjust the actual *ink* values, and can isolate and adjust the blacks and whites in your image.

Summary

Understanding how the additive and subtractive colors works and complement each other is the basic theory behind color correction. Through the use of the color wheel, mixing colors to achieve the proper blend can be achieved.

Please remember that the combination or deletion of certain colors can form the total spectrum that is visible to the output and display devices used. The principles discussed in this chapter will be a great asset in future chapters dealing with selections, and color correction.

Complete Project G: Banana Boat Table Tent

Notes:

Chapter 16

Creating and Managing Paths

Chapter Objective:

To learn to use the Pen tool for the creation of paths. To understand that line segments connected by points are objects that can be saved, edited, and converted to special purposes. In Chapter 16, you will:

- Learn how to create selections and clipping paths.
- Become familiar with the Paths palette.
- Learn to draw simple paths.
- Learn some useful tips for using the Pen tool.

Projects to be Completed:

- Marinara Shelf Talker
- KSOL Rising
- Maui Travel Postcard
- Rough Riders Ad
- Gulls Poster
- Concert Poster
- Banana Boat Table Tent
- Salute to Veterans Poster

Creating and Managing Paths

The Pen tool is for the creation of Paths. It differs from the Pencil, which draws lines of pixels, and Brushes that draw soft-edged strokes. The Pen tool produces line segments connected (and defined in the computer) by points. The paths are not bitmapped lines; rather, they are objects that can be saved, edited, and converted to special purposes. They are very similar to Adobe Illustrator's paths. They can even be copied and pasted between files.

If you use Adobe Illustrator or Macromedia Freehand, then you already know how to use Photoshop's path creation tools. Photoshop's path creation tools behave like the Pen, Path, or Spline tool in other vector-based applications.

The Paths are not part of the image itself. They are available to the Photoshop file for other work. The paths serve as a stencil, border, or a route that the other Photoshop commands and tools can follow.

Among other things, paths are used for two extremely important functions:

- To create selections. A path can be converted to a selection. For certain types of objects, the Pen tool is perfect — much better than the Lasso tool. Examples include equipment and product images which contain very well-defined curves and shapes.
- To create Clipping Paths (which is one way to save a silhouette). The clipping path strips out (will not print) the pixels outside of the defined clipping path. Without a clipping path (which are defined in Photoshop and saved within most image formats), backgrounds knock out any objects that they are on top of. This is vital when creating images that will be exported to a page layout application such as QuarkXPress or PageMaker where objects are frequently layered.

There is a close relationship between paths created in Illustrator and Photoshop. Exporting, Copy/Pasting, and drag and drop sharing of paths is supported between the two applications.

The Pen tool has seven icons:

The Pen tool draws paths by placing corner points or curve points.

The Direct Selection tool is used to move path points and reshape curves after a path has been drawn.

The Add Anchor Point tool permits the *addition* of a point to a drawn path.

The Delete Anchor Point tool permits you to *remove* a point from a path.

The Convert Point tool changes a corner point to a smooth point and vice versa. (A corner point is produced when the Pen tool is clicked without dragging. The line between two corner points is straight.)

The Freeform Pen tool creates a path by clicking and dragging the desired shape as would be accomplished with the Lasso tool. It automatically sets anchor points and direction lines to match the shape drawn.

The Magnetic Pen tool traces an object in the image with a path. It automatically sets anchor points and direction handles that create a path along the edge of an object.

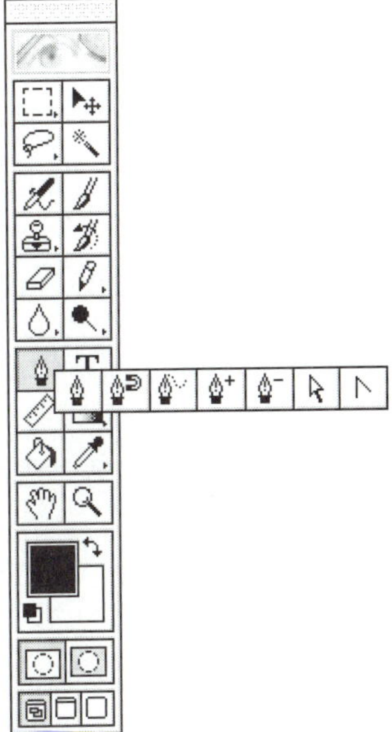

Holding the Shift key and pressing the "P" key will cycle through each of the pen tools.

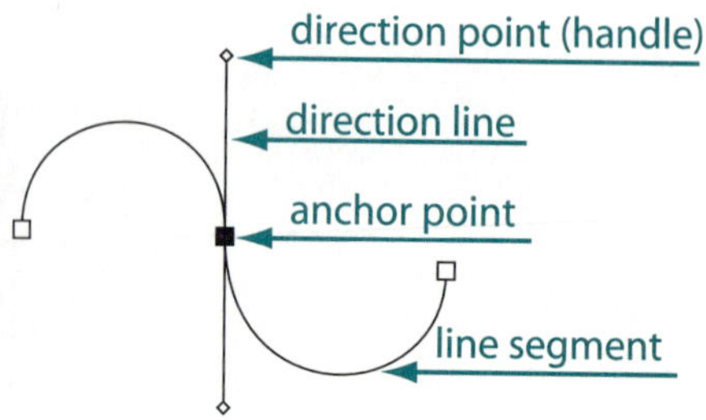

The Paths Palette

The pop-up menu in the upper right of the Paths palette holds most of the commands available for creating and applying paths.

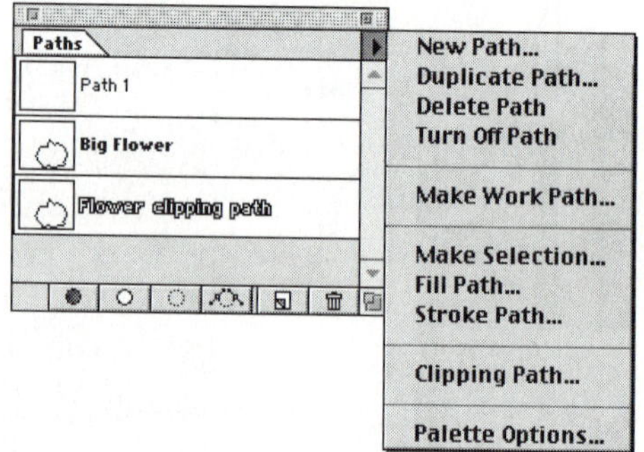

The palette also has icons along the bottom which serve as shortcuts to the most commonly used commands. The icons are shortcuts for the following:

The first will Fill an active path with the foreground color by default, or with the last used settings from the pop-up menu command.

The second will Stroke (trace) it with the active painting tool (or the last painting tool used to stroke a path if a painting tool is not selected) using the foreground color.

The third turns an active path into a selection (marching ants).

The fourth will turn an active selection into a path.

The fifth will create a new empty path.

The last will delete the targeted path.

Drawing Simple Paths

1. Open the **Dendrobium.TIF** file in the **SF-Intro Photoshop** folder. Activate the Paths palette by clicking on its tab. If the Paths palette is not visible go to the Window menu and select Show Paths. Click on the Pen tool in the Toolbox.

2. Move the cursor to the top of the big flower at the tip of the tallest petal. Click and hold down the mouse button and drag slightly down and to the left — toward the intersection of the flower's petals. Release the mouse button. Notice that a new Work Path appears in the Paths palette. You have just set an anchor point with direction lines.

3. Move the mouse to the corner where the two petals meet. Click, hold down the mouse button, and drag to pull the handle down and to the right until the curve fits the edge of the flower. Release the mouse button.

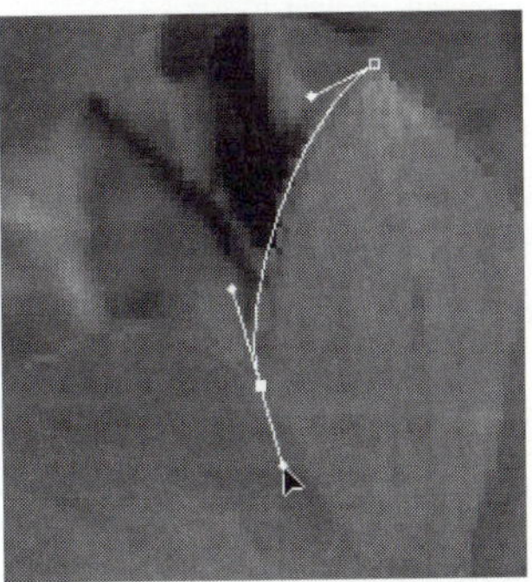

4. The curve comes out of this anchor point in a different direction than it entered the point. You have to make a sharp turn — also called a *corner point.* Option-click (Macintosh) or Alt-click (Windows) and hold the mouse button down on the anchor point you just set, and drag a handle up and to the left. Release the mouse button.

If you find the Pen tool difficult to work with, don't worry! The tool requires quite a bit of practice before it works naturally. Every expert user of paths struggled the same way you may be struggling. The payoff is big! Hang in there, it will suddenly become easy!

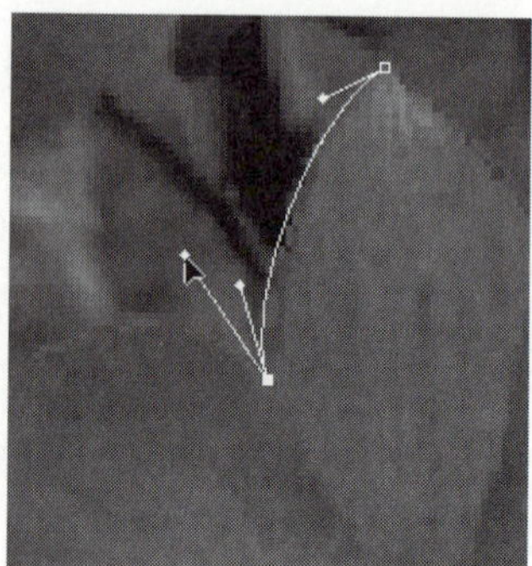

You can see how the path changed direction. This is a good image to practice on with the Pen tool, since it contains lots of curves and corners. Do not worry or fuss to make the path conform perfectly as you draw. After the path is closed, you can edit it with the other pen tools (Direct Selection, Add Anchor, Delete Anchor, and Corner tools).

5. The direction lines for the next two anchor points are shown below. Create those two points according to the illustration.

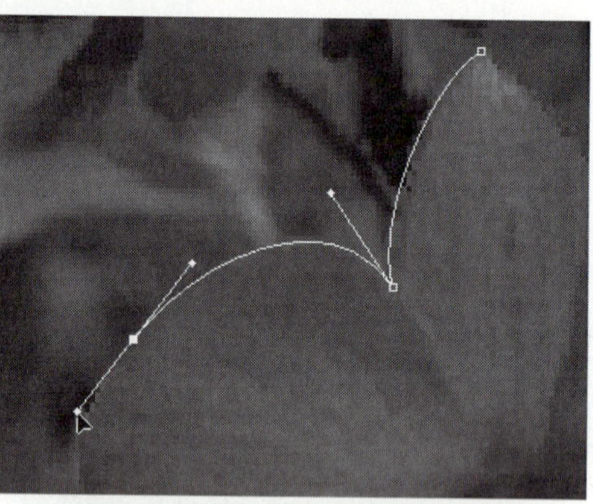

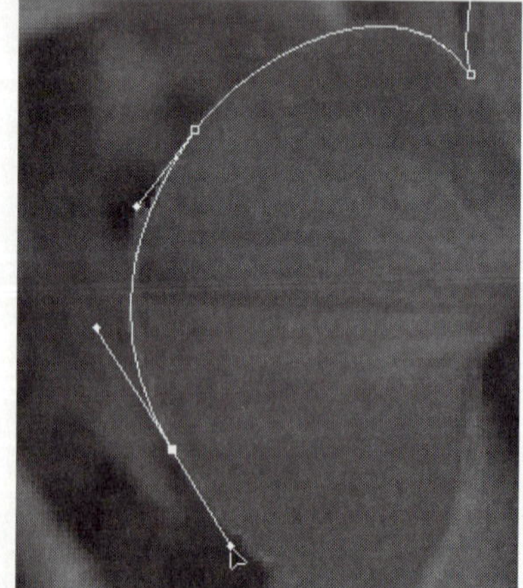

6. Keep the image open for the next exercises.

A completed path has been included in the file as a reference. Click on the "Reference Path" in the Paths palette to see an efficient path shape. Select the Direct Selection tool from the Pen tool cluster and click on the path itself — the anchor points will appear. Click on an anchor and its direction lines will become visible.

Practicing with the Pen

1. OK. You're on your own. Create a path for the entire flower. As you are about to close the path, you will notice the icon for the pen change slightly.

   This Closing Path icon appears automatically as you end the path by placing the cursor over the first anchor point.

2. After the path has been closed, edit the path with the Direct Selection tool to improve its shape. Get the Direct Selection tool from the pen tool cluster in the Toolbox.

   - Click on an anchor point to activate its direction lines. You can adjust their length and direction by clicking on and dragging the direction handles.
   - You can also click and drag on an anchor point itself to edit the path shape.
   - Finally, you can click and drag on the line segment itself to improve your path.

3. You will also need to add and delete points before the path is just right. Delete extraneous anchors by clicking on them with the Delete Anchor tool. Add lacking anchors by clicking on the path at the point you would like to add an anchor.

4. When you're done, double-click the name "Work Path" in the Paths palette and name the Path "Large Flower". Click and hold on the Paths palette pop-up menu in the upper right corner of the palette and select Clipping Path. Change Path "*None*" to "Large Flower". Set the Flatness to 1 pixel. If your path is very complex, you may want to set it to 2 device pixels to prevent output problems. Save the file as a Photoshop file and call it "Orchid Paths".

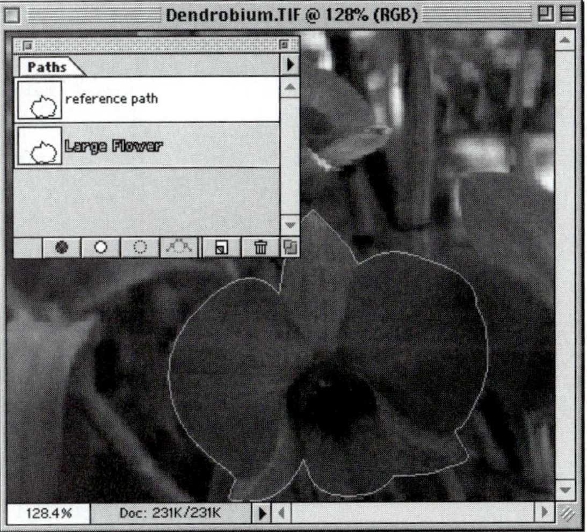

5. Keep the file open for the next exercise.

Some Tips about using the Pen Tool

- The direction handles indicate where the line segment is coming from and where it is headed. The best way to know which direction to drag the handles is to simply drag along the edge of the object you are trying to trace.

- The length of the direction handles control the torque applied (the bend strength) to the line segment by the handle. The general rule for determining the length of direction lines is to make it about one third the length of the segment you are about to create.

- Simplify. The fewer points the better. You could use twenty points to draw a circle, or two. Always try to figure out the most economical way to develop a shape. The fewer points the better.

- Don't scrimp, though. When you're making a tight, round corner, use a point going in and another going out.

- Pull, look, and pull some more. Get in the habit of pulling your curves around once you've placed the anchor points. Adjusting is easier than making it perfect the first time.

Working with Paths

Clicking on the icons at the bottom of the Paths palette is just like using the same command from the popup menu, but no dialog box appears. This is a time saver if you want to apply the last settings used for that command. To force the icon buttons to provide a dialog box, hold the Option (Macintosh) or Alt (Windows) key down as you click on the desired icon.

1. The Large Flower path should be active (highlighted in the Paths palette). Click the pull-down menu in the upper right corner of the Paths palette and examine the options. Most of them are self-explanatory. For example, Turn Off Path deactivates it so that it's out of the way (clicking on it reactivates the path). For now, choose Make Selection. You can accomplish the same thing by clicking the third icon in the bottom row of icons (the one with the dotted circle). Make no settings. Click OK.

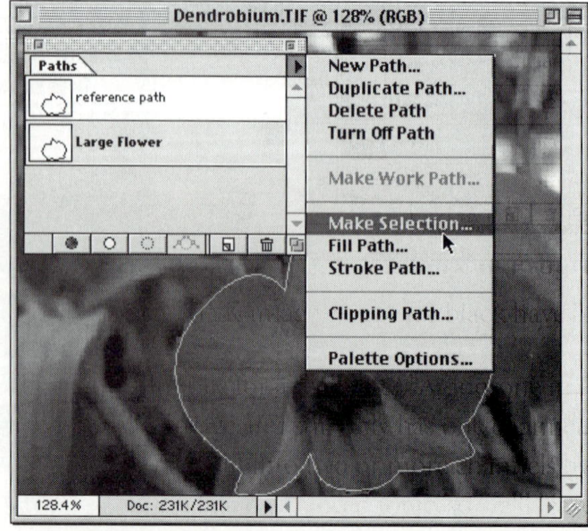

The program creates a selection region that matches the path's shape. You can also stroke a path with any of Photoshop's many brushes. Try this next little experiment:

2. Copy the selection to the clipboard. Press Command-D (Macintosh) or Control-D (Windows) to deselect.
3. Select a bright yellow as the foreground color, and choose the Airbrush tool. Make certain that no fade is set. Pick a large soft brush (the illustration below used a 45 pixel diameter brush at 0% hardness). Activate the Paths palette again and click the icon with the dark black ring around a white circle, the second icon. This is the Stroke Path icon. Watch what happens.

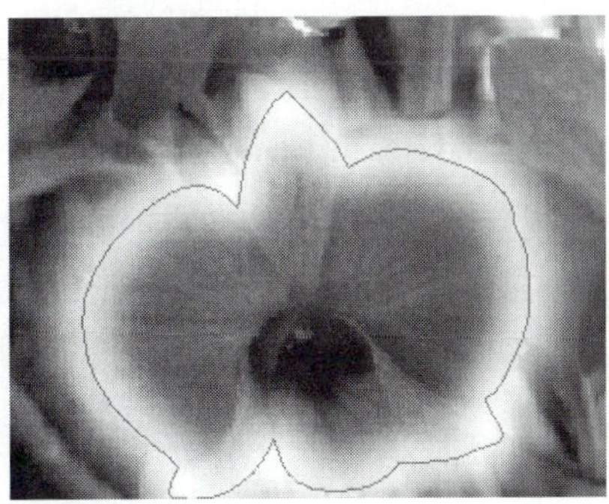

4. Click the Load Paths as a Selection icon and press Command/Control-V. The inside image restores, leaving the neon glow around the outside edges. This is a particularly useful technique when you want to create neon type, glowing lines or shapes, or when you want to otherwise paint paths.
5. Turn off the path and deselect the object. Take a look.

6. Close the file without saving.

There are many ways to restore the inside of the flower other than copying and pasting. One such method is to use Layer Via Copy from the New Layer command under the Layers menu while the flower is selected (at the end of step #1). Then deselect, reactivate the path, target the lower layer, and stroke the path as described in step #3.

A second method is to skip step two and use the use the "From History" option in the Edit >Fill... command after you restore the selection at the start of step #4.

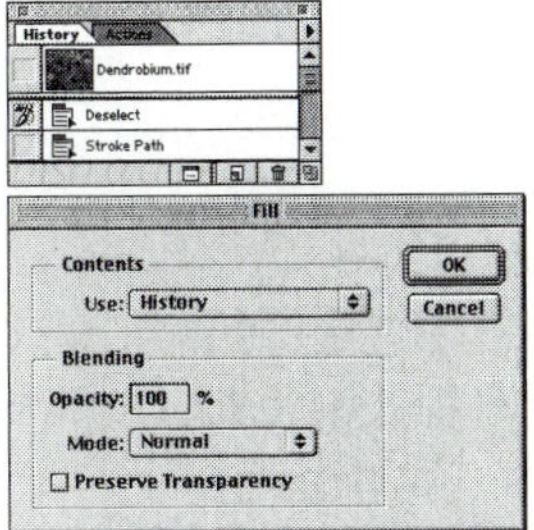

Writing with Neon

1. Create a New RGB document, 5″ x 1.5″ at 200 ppi. Fill the background with black.

2. Activate the Channels palette and create a new channel. Use File->Place to import the image **Sale.EPS** from the **SF-Intro Photoshop** folder into the new channel. Press Enter or Return. Click on the RGB composite layer.

3. Activate the Paths palette. Click the black triangle at the upper right corner of the palette to activate the pull-down menu, and select Make Work Path. Use a Tolerance of .5.

4. Select the pull-down menu from the Paths palette again, and choose Save Path; name the path "Neon". Edit the path to tidy up the letters.

When specifying the image size in pixels, the resolution setting does not matter. The resolution setting will not affect the file size.

5. Create a New RGB document 200 pixels wide by 50 pixels high, at 200 ppi, with a white background; name the document "Blue Gradient". Click on the Swatches palette and Option-click (Macintosh) or Alt-click (Windows) to select a very dark blue for your background color; click to select a very light blue for the foreground.

6. Select the Linear Gradient Fill tool in the Tool palette. Press the Return key to bring the Linear Gradient Options palette forward. Set 100% Opacity, and Foreground to Background. Draw a gradient in the new document from left to right. This will give you a complete range of blues from which to select your colors.

With a path active, you can select any painting tool and press Enter on the number pad of the keyboard (not Return) to stroke the path with that tool at its last used settings.

If you have a selection tool selected, with an active path, the Enter key will change the path into a selection.

7. Make certain that both documents are visible on screen. Select the Airbrush. Set Pressure to 15%, and select a 100-pixel soft brush. Option/Alt-click in the lightest blue area of the Blue Gradient image. Stroke the path by clicking on the circle with the solid outline at the bottom of the Paths palette.

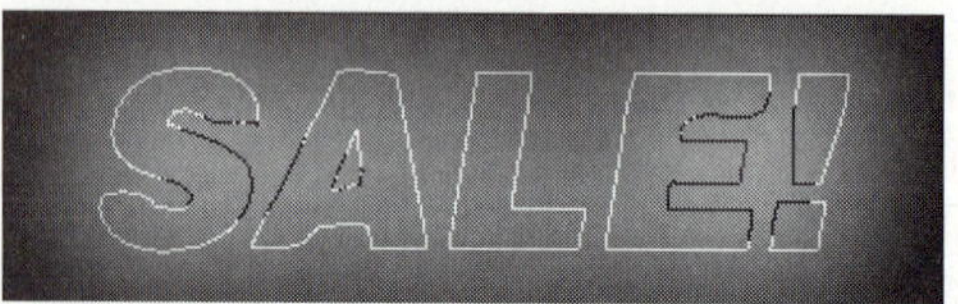

8. Change the Airbrush to 50% pressure. Select the 45-pixel soft-edged brush, and Option/Alt-click to select a dark blue from the far right of the Blue Gradient image. Click the outlined circle again to stroke the path.

9. Change to the next smallest brush (35 pixel) and select a little lighter blue, about 3/4 of the way across the Blue Gradient image. Stroke the path again. Continue working this way with smaller brushes and lighter colors until you've reached the lightest area in the Blue Gradient image.
10. Select the smallest soft brush and change the foreground color to white. Stroke the path once more. Activate the Paths palette pull-down menu by clicking on the black triangle, and select Turn Off Path.
11. Now you can put your name up in lights! Close both files without saving.

Complete Project H: Salute to Veterans Poster

Notes:

Review #2

Chapters 9 Through 16:

In Chapters 9 through 16, we used the knowledge developed through the first half of this course to further our ability to create complex Photoshop mechanicals. We delved deeper into the importance of Selections by studying Complex Selections. We also acquired a more advanced understanding of Channels. We learned about Calibration, Brightness and Color, and Paths and Filters. After completing the second half of this course, you should:

- Know how to use the Magic Wand tool. You should know how to preserve selection information for later use. You should have developed a working knowledge of Feathered selections, and when to apply them. You should also know how to create vignettes, and understand how to create a Composite with Selections.
- Understand Channels, and the manner in which image information is arranged. Know how to use Color and Alpha channels, and understand their different qualities. You should also be familiar with the limitations of a Quick Mask channel.
- Understand the basics of calibrating your system. You should know how to predict color output, understand the factors that affect color display, and be aware of the critical nature of gamma correction.
- Know the relationship and effects between brightness and color in the quality of the reproduction of digital images. You should be familiar with the tools for tonal correction and color adjustment.
- Understand how colors interact with one another. You should know the relationship between the two basic color models: RGB and CMY.
- Know how to create the Color Wheel, and understand its theory. You should know how to mix colors. You should also have learned how to create and use a Full Spectrum Color Wheel.

Project A: Marinara Shelf Talker

Shelf talkers are produced in large quantities, so they are printed using the lithographic process. This document will have only the one application.

Select and Delete the Background

1. Open the image **Salad Vegetables.TIF** from the **SF-Intro Photoshop** folder.
2. Press the "F" key to view in full screen mode.
3. Use the Lasso and Polygon Lasso tools to encircle the lettuce and cabbage; your selection should include all of the picture from the top of the image to the top of the tomato, peppers, and leeks.
4. Zoom in and use the techniques you have learned to analyze and refine your selection. You'll need to pay special attention to the roots on the leeks and the dark area beneath the whole head of cabbage.

Press "L" to toggle between the Lasso and the Polygon Lasso.

5. When you feel it's just right, press "D" to reset the foreground and background colors.
6. Press Command/Control-H to hide your selection border.
7. Press Option/Alt-Delete to fill the selected area with black, the current foreground color. At this point, if you're not happy with your selection, you can undo by pressing Command/Control-H again to refine it a little more.

To deselect an area (or drop it, press Command/Control-D or click anywhere else on the image with the Lasso or Marquee tool.

8. Save the image into your **Work in Progress** folder as a Photoshop document named "Marinara Shelf Talker.PSD".

Duplicate Elements

1. Press Command/Control-D to deselect the background. Use the Elliptical Marquee to do a loose selection on the tomato, using the Option/Alt key to draw the marquee from the center.
2. Refine your selection and Copy the tomato to the clipboard.
3. Choose Inverse from the Select menu or press Command/Control-Shift-I. Now everything *but* the tomato is selected.
4. From the Edit menu, select Paste Into. This is a special paste command. At first glance, there doesn't seem to be any difference from the regular paste command. However, if you move the pasted tomato on top of the original, the difference will soon become apparent.

   Paste Into creates a *Layer Mask* that allows the pasted graphic to show only *inside* the selection that is active. This effectively allows you to use one tomato to mask the other.
5. Use the Move tool to position the second tomato to the upper left of the first, so that part of it is going outside of the image border, and about half of it is obscured by the first tomato.
6. The pasted tomato looks a little unrealistic, since it is at exactly the same angle as the original. Use the Edit>Transform>Numeric command. Rotate the image to the right 15 degrees, then reposition the tomato again to cover a little more of the stem.

Inverting a selection and filling a background with black and/or white is a great way to check a complex manual selection for accuracy.

Be aware of the light source on the original image when pasting and rotating objects; if the light source is too obviously different from the rest of the image, the pasted item will look unrealistic, making or rendering the image useless.

Press Command/Control-E to merge a single layer into the layer beneath it, or Command/Control-Shift-E to merge all visible layers.

7. Press Command/Control-E to permanently merge the tomato into the background.
8. Press "L" to activate the Lasso tool. Use the Lasso to carefully outline the three mushrooms (be certain to include the shadow).
9. Refine your selection, then Copy the mushrooms to the clipboard.
10. Deselect the mushrooms. Press Command/Control-V to paste a copy of the mushrooms into the document.
11. With the Move tool, position them to the right of the first group of mushrooms. The new mushrooms should cover as much of the carrots as possible. (It's all right if the mushrooms are chopped off at the side of the image.)
12. Use Edit>Transform>Numeric to rotate the selection to the right fifteen degrees, and reposition if necessary.
13. Paste another copy of the mushrooms into the document. Position them in the foreground to cover the rest of the carrots on the right, and to cover both sets of mushrooms.
14. Use the Rotate command again to rotate the mushrooms, this time 12 degrees to the left (–12°). Adjust if necessary.
15. Press Command/Control-Shift-E to permanently merge both the mushroom layers into the background image.

16. Save the image.

Adding Type

1. Press"D" to make certain that the foreground and background colors are set to their defaults, then press "X" to exchange the foreground and background colors.

2. Select Image>Canvas Size.

3. Change Height to 5 inches, and click the bottom middle square in the placement grid.

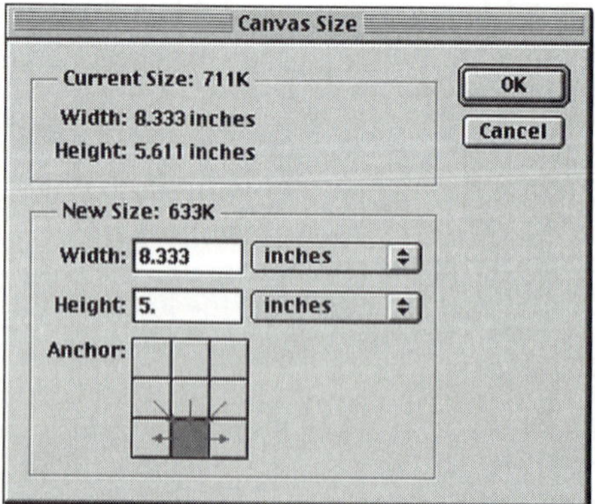

Click Proceed, then click OK.

4. Press "D" to return the foreground and background colors to their defaults.

5. Let's match the color of the tomatoes for the new foreground color. Select the Eyedropper tool and click on a bright red spot of the foremost tomato. Set the background to a mushroom color by holding down the Option/Alt key when clicking on one of the mushrooms.

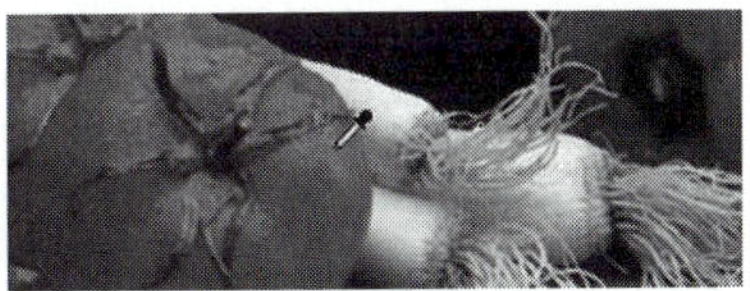

6. Select the Type tool, and click in the upper left corner of the image.
7. Change the Font to ATC Bahama, the Size to 32 points, Leading to 36, Tracking at –35. Make certain that Alignment is set to left.

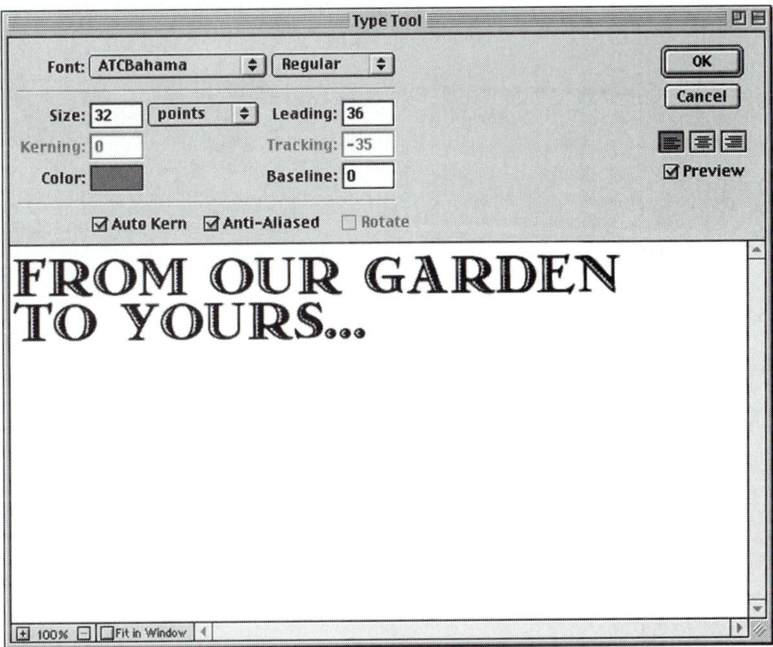

Press "T" to toggle between the Type and Type Mask tools.

8. In the type box, type (without the quotes):

   "FROM OUR GARDEN
   TO YOURS…"

   Make sure you press the Return key between the lines. Click OK.
9. You'll probably notice that the YO in YOURS is very spacey. Double-click on the type layer, place the cursor between the Y and the O, and change Kerning to –130. Click OK.
10. Reposition the type, if necessary, to the position below.

Press "V" to activate the Move tool.

11. Since we want to make the headline a gradient, we need to change the Type Layer to a regular layer. Select Layer>Type>Render Layer.

12. With the Magic Wand tool, select any letter, then Select>Similar.

13. While holding down the Shift key to constrain to 90 degrees, drag the Linear Gradient tool from the stem of the F to the right stem of the N and release.

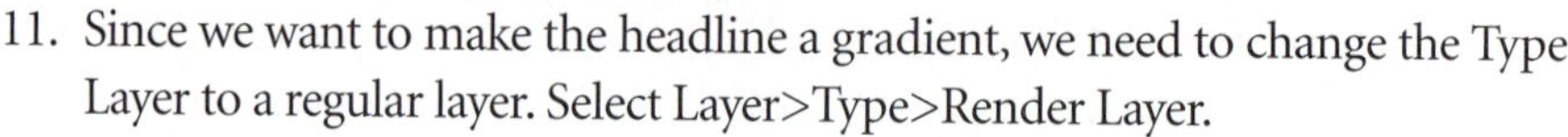

14. Press Command/Control-D to deselect.

15. Select the Background layer and click the Type tool in the lower right corner of the image.

16. Set the Font to ATC Plantation and the size to 24 pixels. Make certain that the Alignment is centered, that Leading is 27 point and that Tracking is set to –20.

17. Type the following text into the text box (without the quotes):

    "Angelina's
    Pasta
    Sauce"

    Press Return between the lines. To type the apostrophe, press Option-Shift-Right Bracket (Macintosh) or Alt-0146 (on the numeric keypad in Windows). Click OK.

18. Reposition the type, if necessary, to look like the example below, then press Option/Alt-Delete or Option/Alt-Backspace to fill the type. Render the layer as before.

19. Press "X" to exchange foreground and background colors.
20. Select Edit>Stroke. Set Width to 3 pixels and Location to Outside.

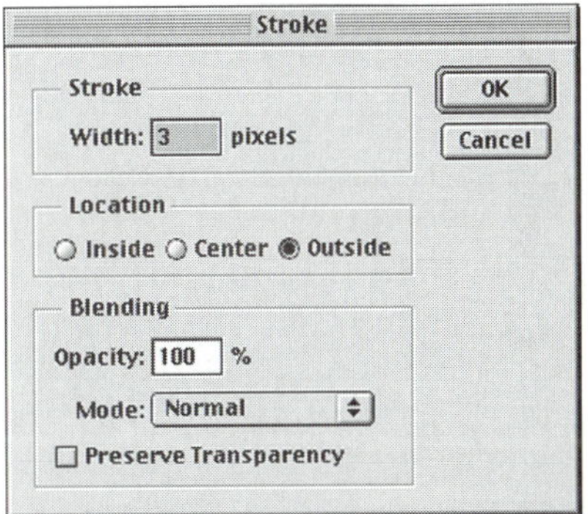

Click OK.

Prepare Files for Output

Now that you have a Photoshop file, you need to prepare a file for the printer.

Preparing Files for Printing

1. Merge all visible layers.
2. Select File>Save As…>TIFF. Name the file "Marinara.TIF".
3. Close the file.

Project B: KSOL Rising

This ad will appear in magazines and in newspapers.

Color Correct the Original Image

1. Open the image **SkyWater.TIF** from the **SF-Intro Photoshop** folder.

2. Save the file as "KSOL.PSD". This creates a new file, so that your original resource file remains unchanged. Since you know that you will be using layers, save it as a Photoshop file, the only format that allows layers.

3. Press Command/Control-A to select the entire image. (Since this image has only one layer, and you want to select everything on that layer, this is not strictly necessary. Most functions in Photoshop effect everything in the current layer, unless you have selected a smaller section of the layer.)

4. Pull down the Image menu to Adjust, and then to Variations on the sub-menu. Be sure the Midtones button is selected.

Setting Preferences>Saving Files to Always Append File Extensions is a great time saver. You never have to type in the three file extension letters, just pick the file type from the drop-down menu.

With almost every action in Photoshop that requires you to click OK, you can accomplish the same result by hitting the Return key. One exception is the Type mode, in which the Return key, logically enough, behaves like the Return key in a word processing application - it begins a new line of type.

5. Click on the "More Cyan", look at the result in the "Current Pick" window, and then click on "More Blue". To finalize the change, click OK. Deselect the image.

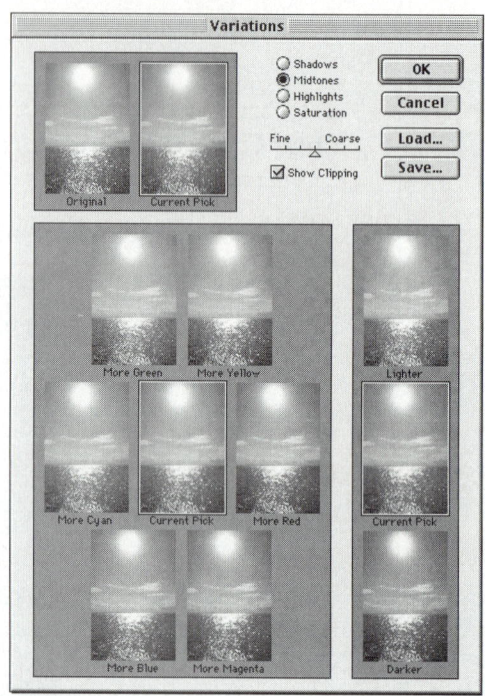

6. If the LAYERS window is not already showing, pull down the WINDOW menu and select SHOW LAYERS.

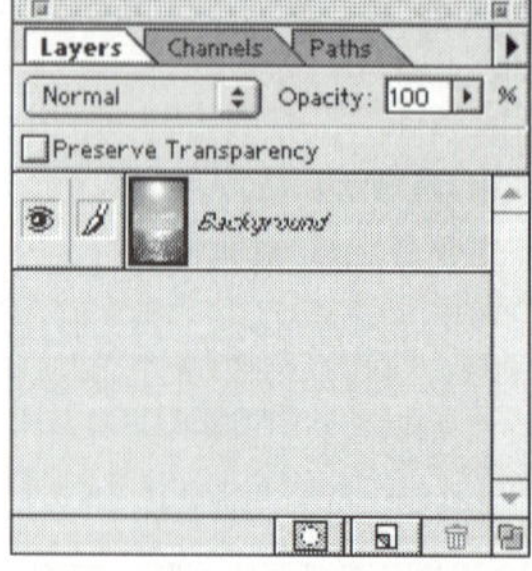

7. This image only has one layer so far, so by default, it is named "Background". It is helpful to keep track of where the various elements are, so double-click in the area that contains the word "Background". A new dialog box will appear, giving you several options. Type the word "SkyWater", then click OK.

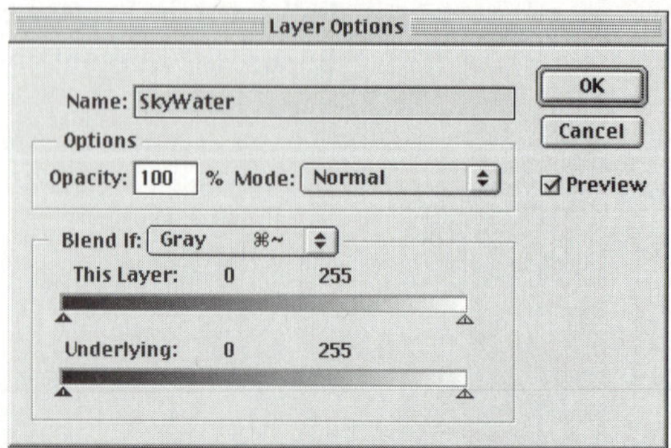

8. Click on the arrow at the top of the LAYERS window, and select NEW LAYER.
9. Type in "Radio", and click OK.
10. It is smart to save your work along the way, so that if something should happen (computer freeze, power failure), you haven't wasted much time. Since you have already saved this image once, all you need to do it press the Command (Macintosh) Control (Windows) key and the S key simultaneously. (This is true for most applications, not just Photoshop.)

Adding a New Element

1. Open the image **Radio.TIF** from the **SF-Intro Photoshop** folder..
2. Click the Magic Wand tool on the while background. With the background selected, go to the SELECTION menu and choose INVERSE. This will result in just the radio itself being selected.

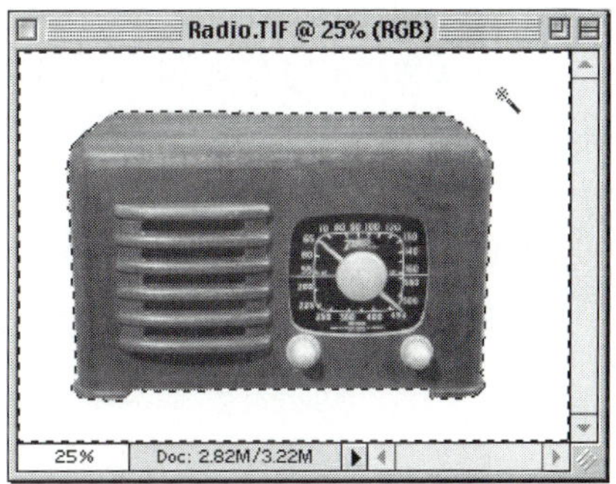

3. Press Command/Control-C to COPY the radio, then paste it into the KSOL.PSD document with Command/Control-V. Or, drag it from the Radio.TIF document into the KSOL.PSD document.
4. Close the Radio.TIF document, and work with the KSOL.PSD document. Notice that, if you pasted the Radio image, it is now perfectly centered, and in the Radio layer. If you dragged it, it is somewhere in the image, superimposed over the water and sky.
5. Using the MOVE tool, drag the radio until the top of it is just barely above the horizon, where the water meets the sky. The line where the front of the radio becomes the top should fall approximately along the horizon.

6. Press Control-S to SAVE again at this point.

Blending the Radio Into the Water

1. The illusion we want to create is that the radio is "rising" up from the depths. If that were happening in the real world, our vision of the radio would fade, the deeper underwater it was. So we are going to fade this radio, so that it looks as though the water is coming up almost to the tuning knobs.

2. From the SELECT menu, choose LOAD SELECTION. The CHANNEL box should say Radio Transparency, then click OK.

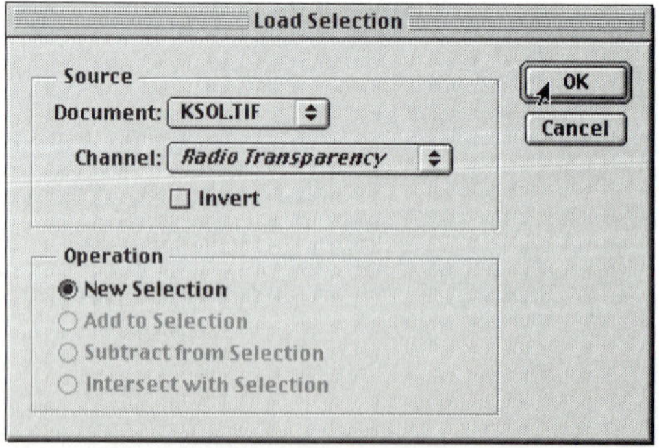

3. Select the Eraser tool. You will be using it almost like an airbrush, except that it will fade the bottom of the radio. The selection border (Marching Ants) will be a distraction, so press Command/Control-H to hide it.

4. Choosing the right size of brush, and the right pressure, will be trial and error. You will definitely need a larger brush than the 100 pixel model, which is the largest default.

5. Click on the arrow at the top of the Brushes palette, and select New Brush. Drag the slider for Diameter until it reads 150 pixels. Be sure that Hardness is set to 0%. Click OK.

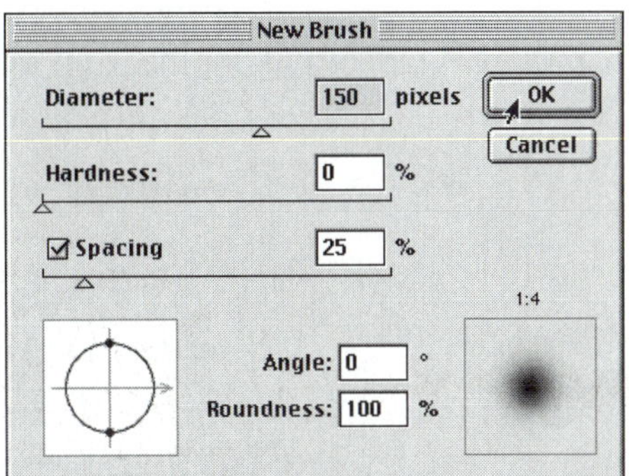

6. Click on the new 150 pixel brush to select it, and in the Options palette, choose Airbrush for the Tool and 100% for the Pressure.

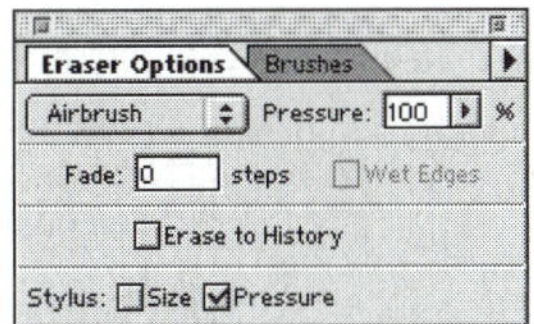

7. Place the Eraser cursor just slightly to the left of the bottom left corner of the radio. Press and hold the Shift key to constrain your movement to a straight line, as you click and drag the cursor across the bottom of the radio. The resulting image will be a clean fade, making it look as though the water is coming up to just over the radio's tuning knobs.

8. Press Command/Control-D to deselect the radio.

9. Press Command/Control-S to SAVE.

Adding Type

1. In two steps, you will add the phrase "KSOL Rising". The layout of this piece calls for the word "KSOL" to be tall and narrow, while the word "Rising" beneath it is smaller, with more normal proportions.
2. Click on the arrow at the top of the LAYERS window, and select NEW LAYER.
3. Type in "Type", and click OK.
4. Click on the white watch in the Swatches palette to select white as your foreground color, or type D to select the Default colors, then X to exchange the background and foreground colors.
5. Choose the Type tool, and click it just above the top left of the radio.
6. The Type Dialog box will appear. Select ATC Caribe for the font, and 45 points entered for the size. Type the word "RISING" in all caps. Click the Fit in Window box, so you can see the entire word before making any final decisions.
6. Deselect Auto-Kern. Set a Tracking value of 300. Adjust kerning between letters as appropriate to match the sample following step 16. Click OK.

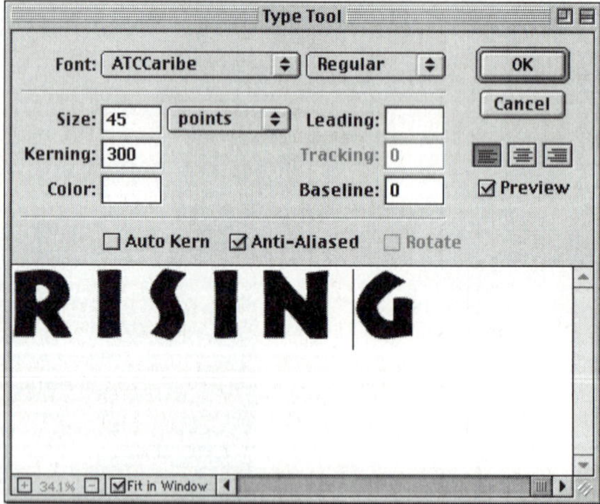

7. If the type is not centered above the radio, use the Move tool to reposition it.
8. In the Layers palette, click the arrow at the top right, and select MERGE DOWN. The new type will then be in the Type layer.
9. Command/Control-S to SAVE again.
10. Click on a yellow in the Swatches palette, to select yellow as the foreground color.

11. Select the Type tool again, and click it above the left edge of the word "Rising". This time you will type in the call letters KSOL. The size will be 200 points. Allow Auto Kern.Set tracking to 0. Click OK.

12. You won't see the entire word, but it still be editable.

13. Pull down the EDIT menu, and select TRANSFORM: NUMERIC. In the Scale: Width field, enter a value of 40%. Click OK.

14. Center it above the word "Rising", using the Move tool.

15. In the Layers palette, click the arrow at the top right, and select MERGE DOWN. The new type will then be in the Type layer.

16. Command/Control-S to SAVE.

Creating a Drop Shadow

There are many ways to create a drop shadow, using Photoshop or using third party filters. This is a simple way that gives you a lot of control over how soft and feathered the shadow appears.

1. Select the Type layer. Click on the arrow at the top of the LAYERS window, and select DUPLICATE LAYER. Type in "Shadow", and click OK.
2. Click on the new Shadow layer in the Layers palette, and drag it down below the Type layer.
3. From the SELECT menu, choose LOAD SELECTION. The CHANNEL box should say Shadow Transparency, then click OK.
4. Choose black as the foreground color, then press Option/Alt-Delete to fill the type with black. Because this is obscured by the Type layer, you won't see the results until you . . .
5. . . . use the Move tool to drag the black type slightly down and to the right. Press Command/Control-D to deselect.
6. Under the FILTER menu, go the BLUR: GAUSSIAN BLUR. Input a value of 10 pixels, then click OK.
7. The type reads much better with this improved contrast, appears to pop off the page, but the shadow is a bit harsh, too dark. You can improve that by reducing the Opacity of that layer to 60%. Either use the slider (by clicking the arrow), or click in the numeric box and type 60.
8. Since that Opacity slider improved the look of the Shadow layer so nicely, let's activate the Type layer, and change its Opacity to 75%. The type looks more modeled, not so bright.

9. Command/Control-S to SAVE.

Prepare Files for Output

Now that you have a Photoshop file, you need to prepare a file for the printer and for the newspaper.

Preparing Files for Traditional Litho

1. Merge all visible layers.
2. Select Image>Mode>CMYK.
3. Select File>Save As…>TIFF. Name the file KSOL.TIF
4. Leave the file open for the next operation.

Preparing Files for the Newspaper

1. Select Image>Mode>Grayscale.
2. Save the file as TIFF with the name KSOLG.TIF. The "G" lets you know that it is a grayscale image.
3. Close the file.

Project C: Maui Travel Postcard

Colorize with Layer Opacity & Blending Modes

1. Four stock images need to be customized for use in the postcard. Open the file **Scuba.JPG**, located in the **SF-Intro Photoshop** folder.

2. Choose Image>Image Size. Make certain that Resample is checked. Enter 2.5 inches for the height, keeping width proportionate and resolution at 300 ppi. Click OK.

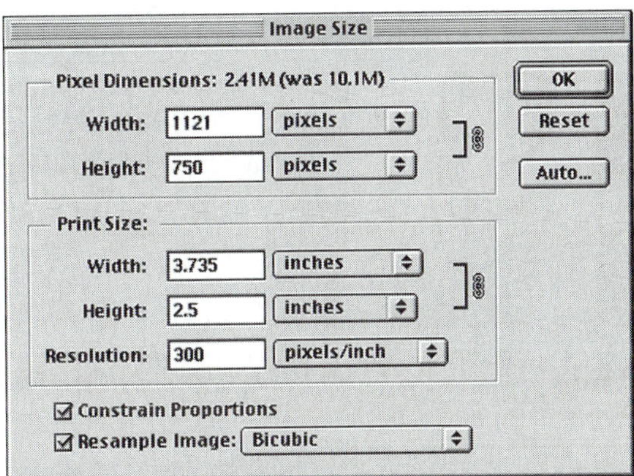

Crop the image as shown.

Press Shift-Command/Control-N to create a new layer or click the center icon at the bottom of the Layers palette.

3. For a special iridescent effect, add a new layer by choosing Layer>New>Layer. Name it "Cyan Boost". It should be the active layer.

4. Change the Foreground color to 100% cyan by selecting it in the Swatches palette (2nd row, 4th from the left). Press Command/Control-A to Select All. Fill the area with cyan (Edit>Fill choosing Foreground).

Press Option-Delete to fill with the current foreground color.

5. Change the Opacity of the layer to 30% and choose Overlay as the Blend mode.

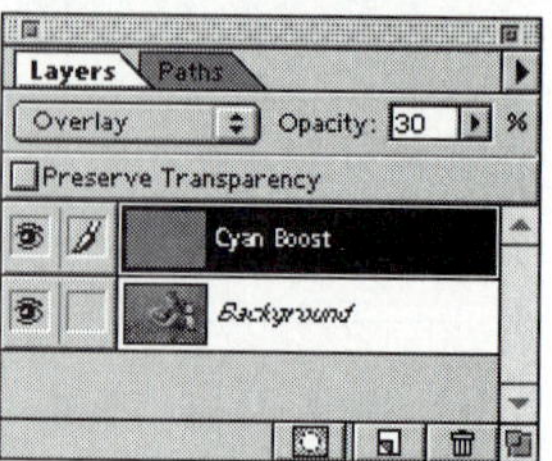

6. Choose Layer>Flatten Image. Save this file to your **Work in Progress** folder as "Scuba1.TIF" and close the file.

Use a Channel as a Special Effects Layer

1. Open the **Biker.JPG** file, located in the **SF-Intro Photoshop** folder. Choose Image>Image Size. Height should be 3.5 inches. Click OK. Crop the image as shown.

2. For a neon effect, we'll use one of the channels as a color mode layer. Select the Red channel from the Channels palette. Select All, then Copy just the red channel.

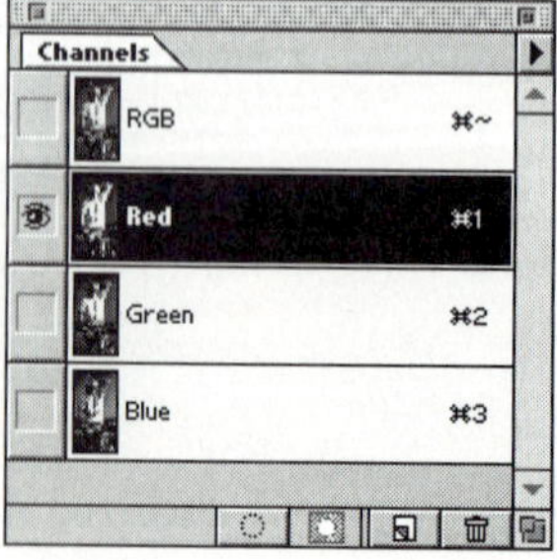

Select the RGB channel so that you are viewing a color image before proceeding.

3. Create a New Layer by clicking on the center icon of the Layers palette. Double-click to name it "Red Dodge". Change Color Mode to Color Dodge and Opacity to 50%.

Flatten Image is also available from the Layers palette menu.

If you want to merge two adjacent layers, select the upper layer and choose Merge Down from the palette menu.

If unselected areas are not in red, double-click the Quick Mask tool and choose "Color Indicates Masked Areas". You can also change the color of the mask here to better differentiate it from certain image colors.

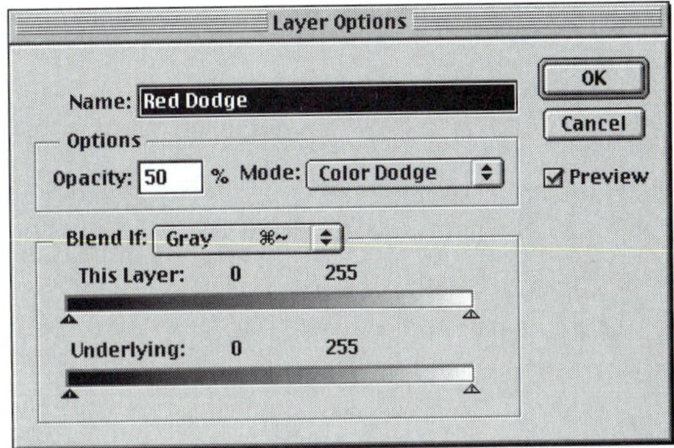

Press Command/Control-V to paste the Red channel (grayscale) into this layer.

4. Flatten the image. Save it as "Biker1.TIF" into your **Work in Progress** folder. Close the file.

Create Sky Mask using Magic Wand and Quick Mask

5. Open the **Hikers.JPG** file, located in the **SF-Intro Photoshop** folder. Choose Image>Image Size. Enter new width as 3 inches. Click OK.

6. With the Magic Wand tool (tolerance = 32, Anti-Aliasing not selected) click in the center of the sky. Hold Shift and click again on the left side to include lighter blues. Repeat until only stray areas remain. If other areas not in the sky become selected, Undo. Don't forget to select the area under the bar of his backpack. Your selection should look something like this:

7. To clean up the selection, turn Quick Mask on (in the tool bar). The areas not selected should be in red. Select the Brush tool and a small, hard edge brush. Make the foreground color white, and paint over areas that should be included in the selection, for instance in front of her mouth. Press "X" to switch colors (black is now foreground) and paint areas that should be excluded from the selection, possibly the poles on his backpack. Change brush sizes as needed and repaint mistakes with the other color (black or white). When you're satisfied, turn off Quick Mask.

8. Choose Select>Save Selection to save all this hard work. Name it "Sky". It will appear in the Channels palette.

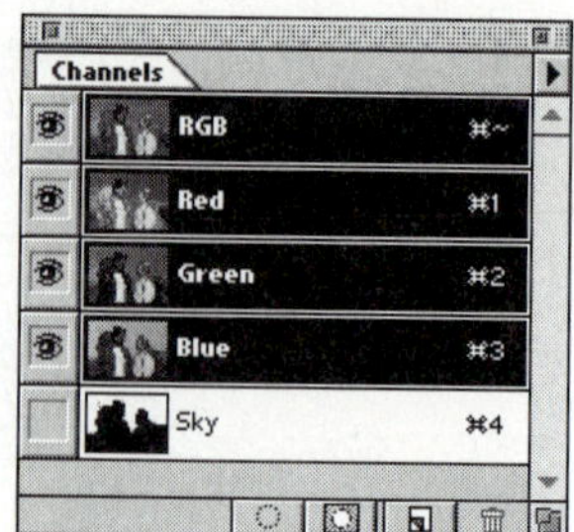

Recall Channel to alter sky and drop a shadow behind People

1. Blend the selection into the background a bit by choosing Select>Feather. Enter "1" pixel. Copy the selection and Paste it into a new layer. Name the layer "Sky" and change its Blend Mode to Screen.

2. Activate the Background layer again. Select>Load Selection choosing Sky and check Invert to end up with a selection that includes everything BUT the sky.

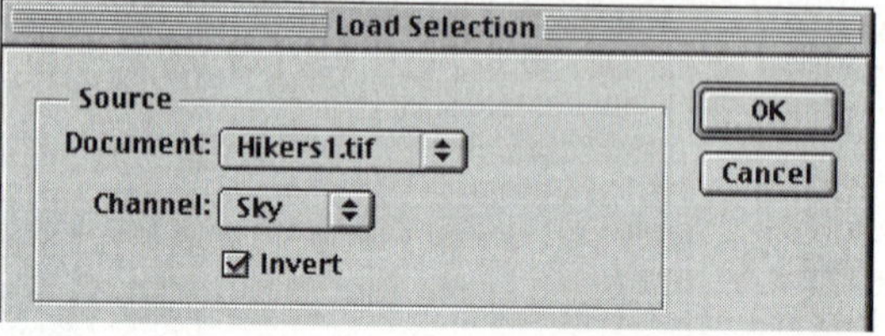

3. The people and ground should be selected. Press Command/Control-C to copy the selection and Command/Control-V to paste the selection. Name the new layer "People". Drag this layer above the "Sky" layer.

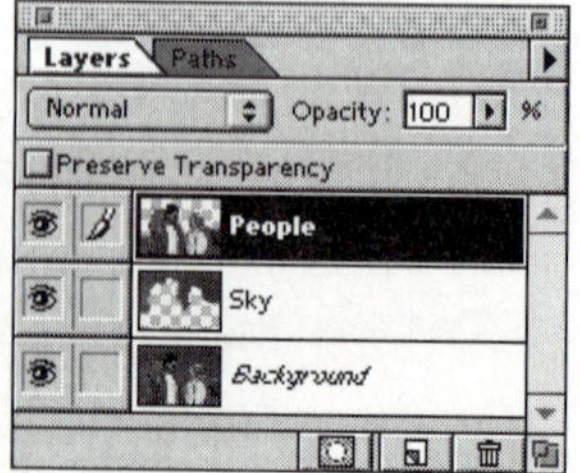

4. Select>Load Selection again (Choose Sky and Invert). Press the up arrow 4 times and the right arrow 4 times to offset just the selection. Select>Feather and type "5" pixels. Make the foreground color black by pressing "D" and choose

The Behind Mode is only available from the Fill dialog when a transparent layer is active.

Edit>Fill. In the pop-up menu choose "Foreground color" and 50% Opacity. Choose Behind Mode. Deselect.

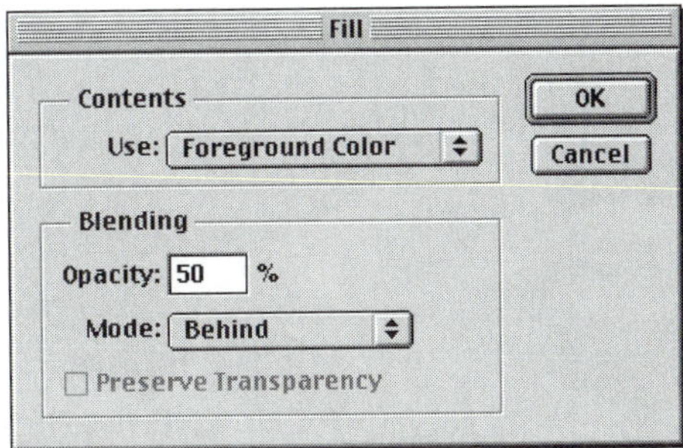

5. Flatten the image. Save the file to your **Work in Progress** folder as "Hikers1.TIF". Close the window.

Change Color of Sail Stripes by Selecting with the Magnetic Lasso

6. Open the **Boat.JPG** file, located in the **SF-Intro Photoshop** folder. Choose Image>Image Size. New width is 2.75 inches. Click OK.
7. Go to Image>Rotate Canvas>Flip Horizontal. Crop image as shown.

8. Choose the Magnetic Lasso tool. Double-click the tool to change its options to match the following dialog box:

"Add to Channel" saves complex selections in progress. If at any time new additions to the selection go astray, Select>Load Selection and continue on.

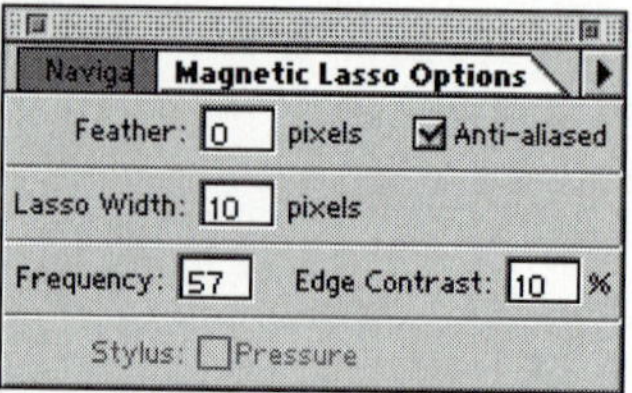

Magnify the image and drag around one of the blue stripes in the sail to select it. You don't have to be exact since this tool will snap to pixel edges that contrast. When you complete the stripe, Select>Save Selection and name it "Stripes".

9. Without deselecting, hold the Shift key and drag around the next blue stripe to add it to the selection. Select>Save Selection again to update it. Select Stripes from the Channel pop-up menu and click on Add to Channel.

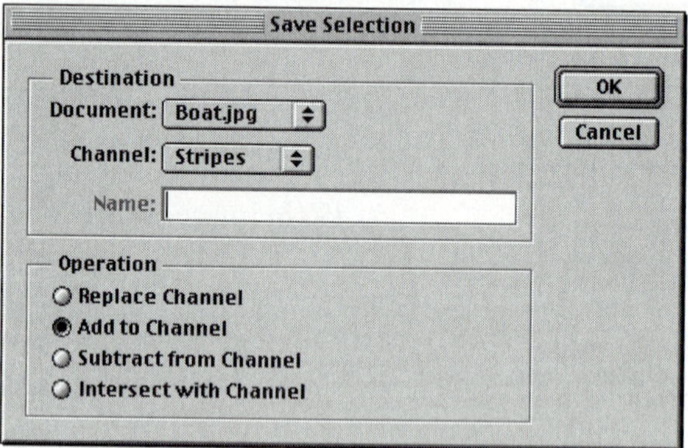

You don't need to hold down the Magnetic Lasso tool while dragging. In tight spots, click to anchor a point so it won't snap as you drag.

When complete, your selection should look like this:

10. Use Quick Mask again to fine-tune the selection. Clean up tight areas and large sections of the rigging by painting in with white or painting out with black. Turn off Quick Mask and Save Selection by Adding it to the existing "Stripes" Channel.

11. With the Stripes selection loaded, choose Image>Adjust>Levels. Choose the Green Channel in the pop-up menu and drag the left slide toward the center. This adds Magenta to the blue stripes making them purple. Click OK and deselect.

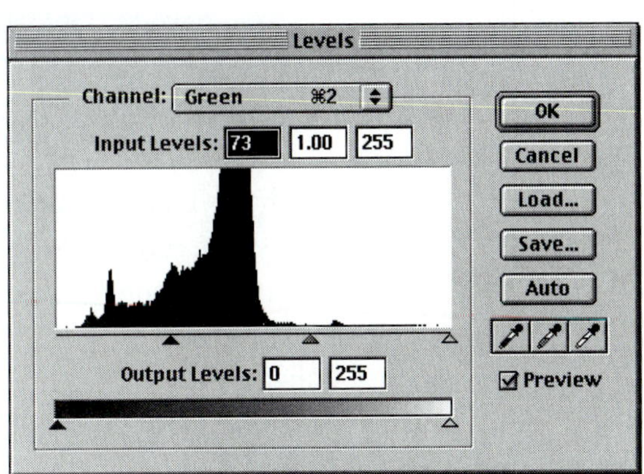

12. Sample a purple area in the image with the Info palette open. Write down the RGB values here. You'll use them later to make a glow.

    Red _________ Green _______ Blue ________

13. Save this file to your **Work in Progress** folder as "Boat1.TIF" and close the window.

Paste Images into Letters for the Postcard

1. Start a new document named "Maui".

   Width = 6.75″
   Height = 5.25″
   300 ppi Resolution
   RGB color mode
   White background

2. View>Show Rulers, if necessary, and drag guides to 1/8″ inside all four borders. Use these guides as the edge of your image area. (Guides mark 1/8″ bleed.)

3. Choose black as the foreground color (Default). With the Type tool, click in the center top of the image area. In the Type dialog choose
   Font : ATC Tequila
   Size: 60 point
   Alignment: Centered
   Type the word "EXPERIENCE" in all caps without the quotation marks.
   Select all the type and work with tracking to stretch the headline across the postcard. Click OK.

   Drag the letters into position.

Hold the Command key at any time to temporarily use the Move tool.

4. With the Type Selection tool, click below the word EXPERIENCE on the left side of the card. In the Type dialog box, make the following selections:
   Font: ATC Typhoon
   Size: 200 pt
   Alignment: Left
   Type the letter "M" upper case without the quotation marks.
   Click OK.
   Drag the selection near the left edge of the image area.

5. Open **Hikers1.TIF** from your **Work in Progress** folder. Select All, then Copy. Close that window and return to your document. With the "M" shape selected, choose Edit>Paste Into. A new layer is automatically created. Rename it "Layer M". With the Move tool, shift the image inside the M so that both faces are visible and the picture fills the entire shape.

6. In the Layers palette, click between the small icon of the picture and the "M" Mask icon. A Link icon appears to indicate that the mask and the image will move as one.

7. Press Command/Control-D to make certain that nothing is selected. Choose Edit>Free Transform and rotate the layer (the "M" and image) counterclockwise about -22°. Shift the image up as indicated. Press Return.

Before Transforming, open the Info palette. It will indicate the scale, dimensions, angle of rotation, and skew as you modify the layer.

8. Create a type selection for "A" using 200 pt. ATC Nassau and position it. Paste into it a copy of the file **Scuba1.TIF** from your **Work in Progress** folder. Position the image inside the letter. Link the image and mask to move them both. No rotation. Rename it "Layer A".

9. Create a type selection for "U" using 200 pt., ATC Typhoon. Paste into it a copy of the file **Boat1.TIF** from your **Work in Progress** folder. Position the image inside the letter as shown. After linking the image and the mask, Edit>Free Transform to rotate both into position. Move them into position with the Move tool. Shoot for about 22° clockwise. Rename this layer "Layer U".

Press Command/Control-T for Free Transform. Position the pointer outside the box and drag to rotate. Drag the center point inside the box to change its pivot anchor of rotation.

10. Create a type selection for "i" using 250 pt, ATC Nassau. Paste into it a copy of the file **Biker1.TIF** from your **Work in Progress** folder. Position the image inside the letter. Link the mask and image before moving it into final position. Rename the layer "Layer i".

File>Save a Copy... allows you to flatten layers and save in several file formats with one step. It's a good idea to also save a Photoshop version of the file with layers intact for further editing.

Your Layers Palette should now look like this:

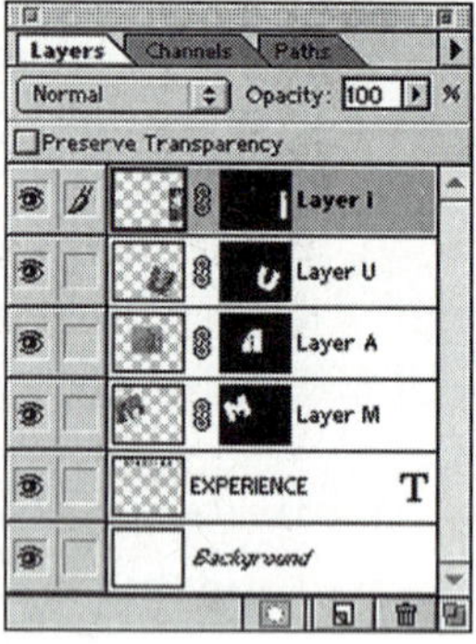

Add Layer Effects to Image Masks

1. Make Layer M active. Command/Control-click on the mask icon of Layer M to get the selection around its perimeter. Choose Layer>Effects>Drop Shadow. Duplicate the following settings in your dialog box:

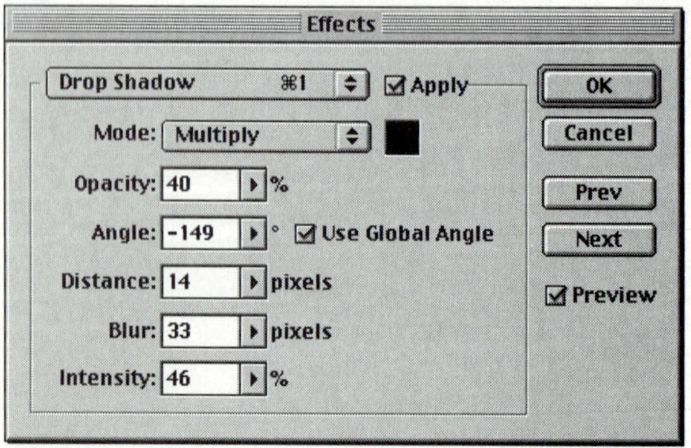

2. Make Layer A active. Command/Control-click on the mask icon for the selection. Choose Layer>Effects>Drop Shadow again. Enter settings for the Drop Shadow, then choose Inner Shadow from the pop-up menu. Check Apply to activate it and uncheck Global Angle, then enter the settings shown.

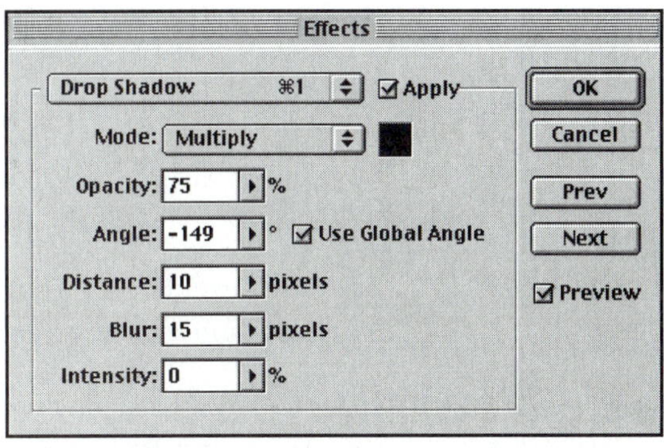

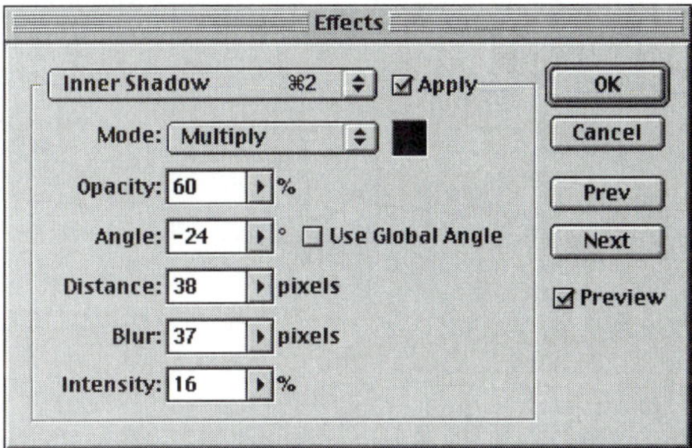

Press the Tab key when you're in a dialog box to quickly move and enter values in each successive field.

3. Make Layer U active. Command/Control-click on the mask icon for the selection. Choose Layer>Effects>Inner Glow. Click on the swatch and enter the RGB values for purple you wrote down in step 24. Complete the settings as shown below, then choose Outer Glow from the pop-up menu. Check Apply to activate it and enter the settings shown. Change the color of the Outer Glow to the same purple.

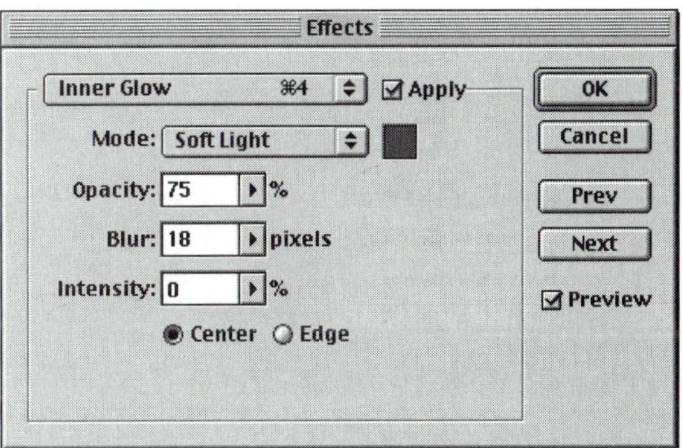

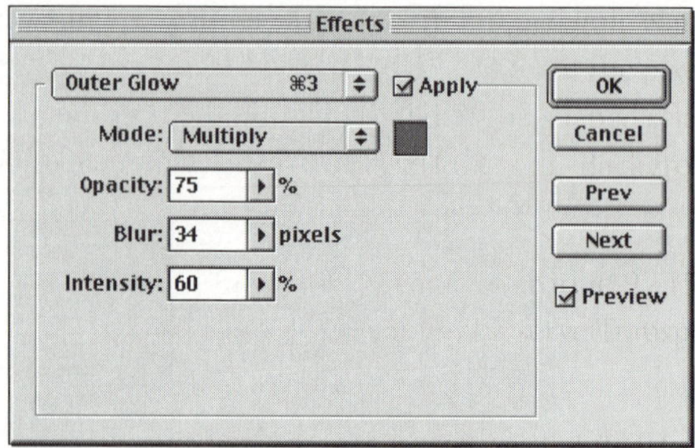

4. Make Layer i active. Command/Control-click on the mask icon for the selection. Choose Layer>Effects>Bevel and Emboss. Enter the information as shown below:

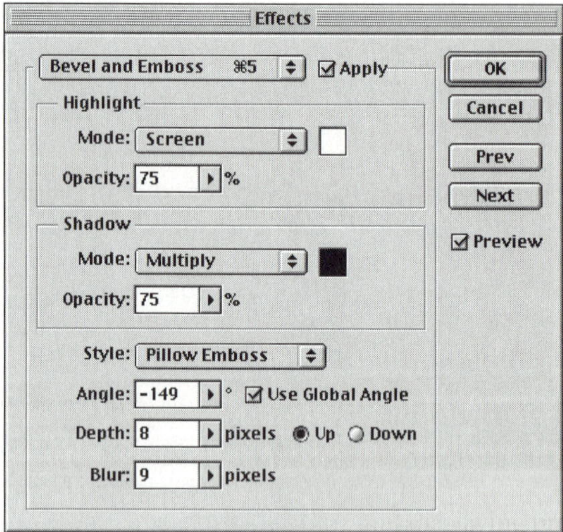

Your image should look something like this:

Finishing Touches

1. Make the Background layer active. Create the following foreground and background colors for the gradient.

Foreground	Background
Red: 41	Red: 242
Green: 43	Green: 202
Blue: 92	Blue: 133

   Command/Control-A to select all of the background layer. Select the Linear Gradient tool. Be sure that it is set Foreground to Background. Holding the Shift key, drag a straight line from the bottom of the image to the top. Deselect.

2. Press "D" for default colors then Press "X" so that white is the foreground color. Choose the regular Type tool and click in the lower left corner. Use Flamingo Bold 24 point, 28 point leading, flush left, Anti-Aliased. Enter the following text:

   "Tours forming NOW!
   Call 1-800-987-6789"

   Select all the text and set Tracking back to 25. Position the type with the Move tool so that it clears the other graphics and looks like this:

3. One more touch. With that type layer active, choose Layer>Effects>Bevel and Emboss. Use a Pillow Emboss and the settings below. Change the Highlight and Shadow color each to match the foreground and the background used respectively in step one above.

File>Save a copy... allows you to flatten layers and save in several file formats with one step. It's a good idea to also save a Photoshop version of the file with layers intact for further editing.

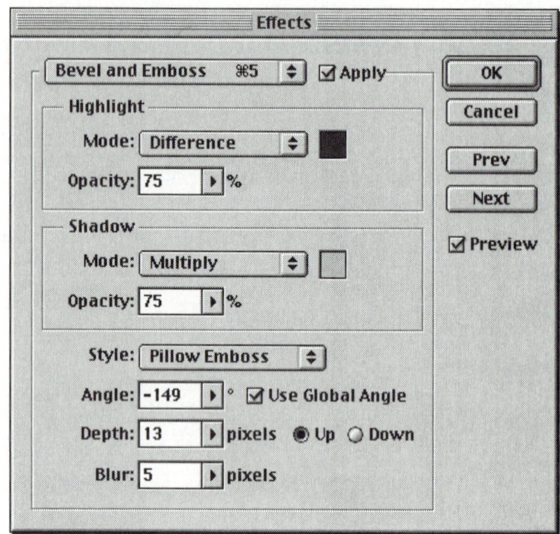

4. Save and name the file as "Maui.PSD" into your **Work in Progress** folder.

Preparing Files for the Web

1. Merge all visible layers.
2. Select File>Save As...>JPEG. Name the file "MauiRGB.JPG".
3. Select an appropriate compression level. Greater compression (the lower the number) discards more data. Less compression results in a better-looking photo, but it loads much slower.
4. Leave the file open for the next operation.

Preparing Files for Traditional Litho

1. Select Image>Mode>CMYK.
2. Select File>Save As...>TIFF. Name the file "MauiCMY.TIF".
3. Close the file.

Project D: Rough Riders Ad

Ads are put to a variety of uses: they may be used in magazines, in newspapers, and on a company's web page. The Rough Riders ad will be put to all these uses.

Composite Images

1. Open the image **Couple on a Rock.TIF** from the **SF-Intro Photoshop** folder.
2. Double-click the background layer and rename the layer "Couple."
3. Select the Rectangular Marquee tool. Double-click it to display the Options palette.
4. Change Style in the Options palette to Fixed Size. Change Width to 550 and height to 400.

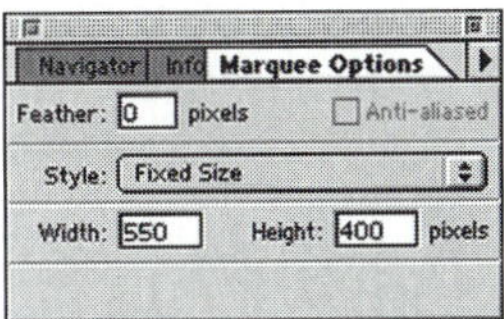

5. Click the image with the Marquee tool and center the marquee on the couple as shown below:

6. Choose Select>Modify>Expand and enter a value of 10 pixels.

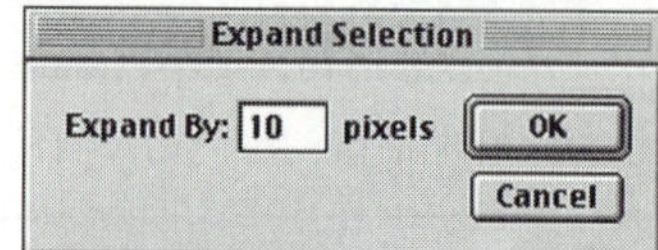

7. Choose Select>Feather and enter 5 pixels in the dialog box.

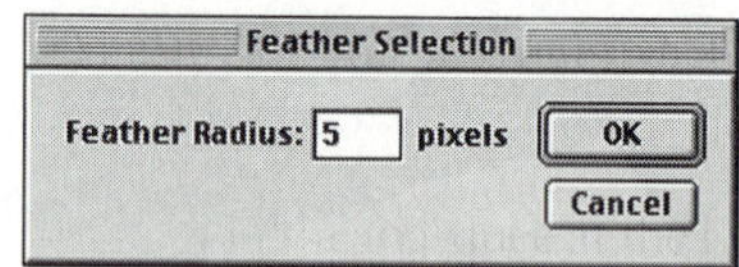

Press "M" to toggle between the Rectangular and Elliptical Marquee tools.

8. On the Channels palette, click the second icon at the bottom of the palette, the Save Selection icon.
9. Open the image **Shoe.TIF** located in the **SF-Intro Photoshop** folder.
10. Press Command/Control-A to select all and Copy the image to the clipboard.
11. Close the Shoe image. Switch to **Couple on a Rock.TIF**. Press Command/Control-V. On the Layers palette, name the layer "Shoe" and click OK. Make certain that the new layer is positioned above the Couple layer.
12. Select the Rectangular Marquee. In the Options palette, change Width to 250 and Height to 170.
13. Center the Marquee over the shoe. Position it so that the bottom of the selection box is level with the bottom of the shoe.

14. Choose Select>Modify>Expand and enter a value of 10 pixels, then choose Select>Feather and feather 5 pixels. Click the second icon on the Channels palette to save the selection.
15. Save the image into your **Work in Progress** folder as "Rough Riders Ad.PSD".

Create a Custom Image Border

1. Press Command/Control-D to deselect. Activate the Channels palette and click on Channel #4 (Alpha 1).
2. Select Filter>Pixelate>Crystallize and enter a value of 7 pixels. Note that the image will not appear in the Crystallize preview window.

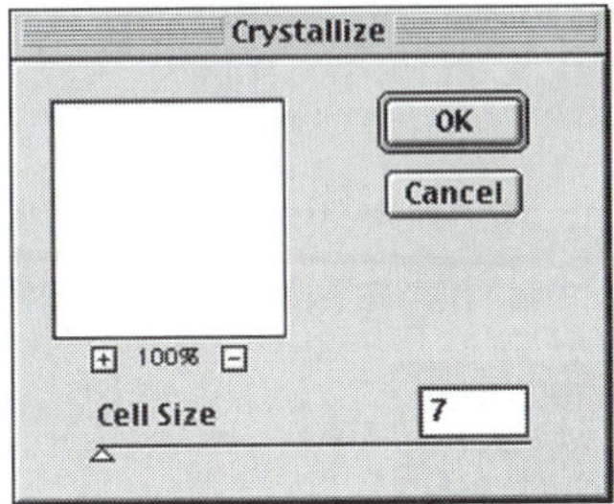

3. Select Image>Adjust>Threshold and enter a value of 245. The Threshold command turns all of the pixels in the image to black-and-white, depending on the value you select.

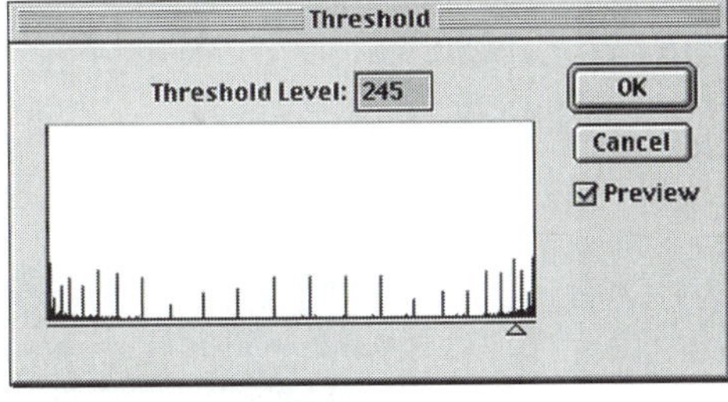

4. Select Filter>Blur>Gaussian Blur and enter a value of 0.3.
5. Select Channel #5. Choose Filter>Pixelate>Crystallize for 7 pixels; Image>Adjust>Threshold with a value of 245; and Filter>Blur>Gaussian Blur at 0.3 pixels.
6. Activate the Layers palette. Click on the Couple layer.
7. Choose Select>Load Selection. Load Alpha 1 and make certain that the Invert checkbox is checked.
8. Press the Delete or Backspace key to remove the outer portions of the image, leaving a ragged border.

Command/Control-F repeats the last applied filter with the same settings you used previously.

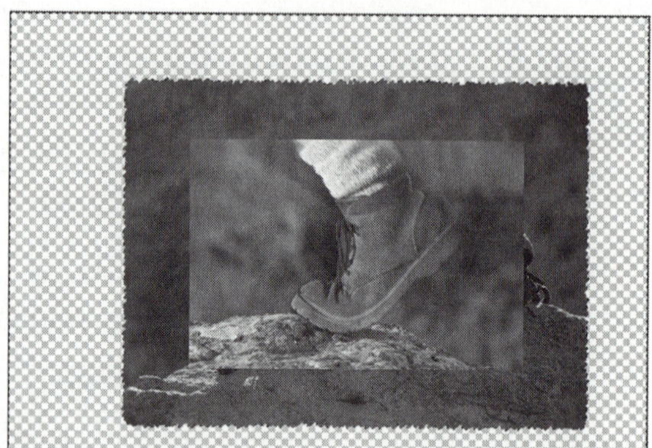

Command/Control-Shift-I is the same as choosing Select>Inverse.

9. Activate the Shoe layer. Choose Select>Load Selection and load Alpha 2. Make certain that the Invert checkbox is checked. Press the Delete key.
10. Press Command/Control-Shift-I to invert the selection. Press "D" to turn your background color to black.
11. Select Edit>Stroke and stroke the border with a 3-pixel line. Check the Center option.
12. Press Command/Control-D to deselect.
13. With the Move tool, move the shoe image to the upper left corner as shown below and Save the image.

Creating Drop Shadows

1. Select the *Couple* layer.
2. From the Layer menu, select Layer>Effects>Global Angle, set it to 120 degrees, and make certain that the Preview box is checked.
3. Select Layer>Effects>Drop Shadow. Make the settings Mode: Multiply; Opacity: 60%; Angle (check Use Global Angle); Distance: 6 pixels; Blur: 6 pixels; Intensity: 0%, and click OK.
4. Select the *Shoe* layer.

5. Select Layer>Effects>Drop Shadow. Make the settings Mode: Multiply; Opacity: 60%; Angle (check Use Global Angle); Distance: 4 pixels; Blur: 4 pixels; Intensity: 0%, and click OK.

6. Click the New Layer icon at the bottom of the Layers palette to add a new layer. Name the layer "White Background." Move it to the bottom of the Layers palette, either by dragging it, or by selecting Layer>Arrange>Send to Back (Command/Control-Shift-[).

7. Save the file.

8. Press "D," then "X" to change the foreground color to white. Press Option/Alt-Delete or Option/Alt-Backspace to fill the entire layer with white.

9. Select File>Place and place the image **Rough Rider Logo.EPS** from the **SF-Intro Photoshop** folder. Position in overlapping the edge of the image as shown below. Press Return. Note that a new layer is created named "Rough Rider Logo.EPS".

10. Move the layer to the top of the Layers palette.

11. Press Command/Control-I to invert the colors in the logo, changing black to white.

Option/Alt-clicking a layer "Eye" turns off all layers except that layer. Option/Alt-clicking it again turns on all layers.

Each time type is added, a new type layer will be created, named by the first few words you have typed. This makes for easy recognition, and ease of editing.

12. Change the Layer blending mode for this layer to Difference on the Layers palette.

13. Activate the Shoe layer.
14. Activate the Move tool. With the arrow keys, nudge the shoe and shadow until they are even at the top with the Rough Rider logo.
15. Save the image.

Adding Type and Logos

1. Press "D" to change the foreground color to black.
2. Select the Type tool. Click in the lower left corner of the image. Select the typeface ATC Tequila. Set the Size to 42 pixels and the Leading to 36. Align the type flush left. Make certain that the tracking box is empty.
3. In the Type box enter the following type without quote marks:

   "ACTION
   SHOE
   COMPANY"

4. Position the bottom of the type level with the bottom of the couple image as shown below. Rename the layer "Type" and position it at the top of the Layers palette.

5. Activate the Shoe layer and select the Move tool. Use the Arrow keys to nudge the shoe left or right to line up with the type, if necessary.
6. Select File>Place to place the image **Footprint Logo.EPS** from the **SF-Intro Photoshop** folder. Press Return or Enter.

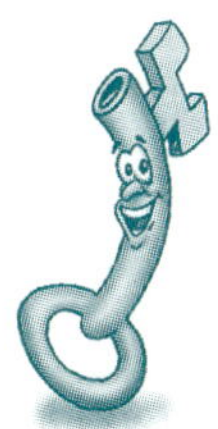

If layers are linked, Numeric Transform will alter all linked layers at the same time.

7. Move the **Footprint Logo.EPS** layer to the top of the Layers palette.

8. Open the Numeric Transform dialog box from Edit>Transform>Numeric. Scale the image to 40%; make certain that Constrain Proportions is checked. Enter "–50" in the Angle box in the Rotate section, then press Return or Enter.

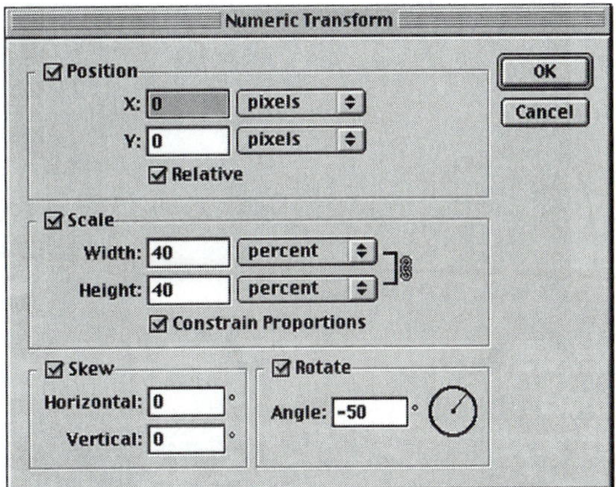

9. Position the footprint above the ACTION SHOE COMPANY type and overlapping the image, as shown below.

10. Change the foreground color to white.

11. Select the Type tool and click in the bottom center of the Couple image.

12. Change the Font to ATC Sands. Set Size at 33 pixels, and Delete any value in the Leading box. Alignment should be set to Center. In the Type box, enter "Not for the faint at heart."

13. Position the type with its baseline about a half inch from the bottom of the Couple image.

14. Link the Couple layer and the "Not for…" type layer. First select the Couple layer to make it the base layer, then click on the type layer.

15. Select Layer>Align Linked>Horizontal Center. The type will center itself from side to side on the Couple layer.

16. With the Cropping tool, crop the image, leaving equal white space all the way around.

17. Select Image>Canvas Size. Make the canvas 7.5 inches wide by 5 inches high. Set the placement grid to centered.
18. Select the *White Background* layer. Set the foreground color to white. Press Option/Alt-Delete to fill the layer.

19. Save, but leave the file open.

Preparing Files for the Web

1. Merge all visible layers.
2. Select File>Save As…>JPEG. Name the file "RoughRiderRGB.JPG".
3. Select an appropriate compression level. Greater compression (the lower the number) discards more data. Less compression results in a better-looking photo, but it loads much slower.
4. Leave the file open for the next operation.

Preparing Files for Traditional Litho

1. Select Image>Mode>CMYK.
2. Select File>Save As…>TIFF. Name the file "RoughRiderCMY.TIF".
3. Leave the file open for the next operation.

Preparing Files for the Newspaper

1. Select Image>Mode>Grayscale.
2. Save the file as TIFF with the name "RoughRiderG.TIF". The "G" lets you know that it is a grayscale image.
3. Close the file.

Notes:

Project E: Gulls Poster

In this project, you'll create an image for display. This type of poster would be produced in small quantities, so we'll assume that it will be printed to an RGB-savvy device.

Prepare the Image

1. Open the file labeled **Gull.TIF** from the **SF-Intro Photoshop** folder.
2. Select the Magic Wand tool from the Toolbar (type W), and press the Return key to display the options box for the Magic Wand tool. Use the tool at its default setting, Tolerance 32, Anti-Alias box checked, and Use All Layers unchecked.

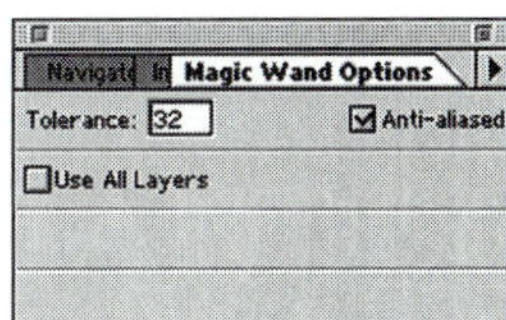

3. Click once on the sky a little above the gull. All the blue pixels that make up the sky are quickly selected. Go to Select>Inverse, or press Command/Control-Shift-I to change the selection from the sky to the gull.

   As you can see, this photograph is tailor-made for the Magic Wand as the sky is very close to the same color blue all over. The wand's Anti-Alias option helps to smooth the transition from the edge of the gull to the blue of the sky. A feather of 1–1.5 pixels would help to eliminate a slight blue edge surrounding the gull, but it would also eliminate the selection of a fine area of the feathers. Because you will be working against a blue background, feathering will be unnecessary.
4. Copy and Paste the gull back into the image. Doing so creates a new layer. This allows the artist complete freedom to move, size down, and rotate the layer independently of the background layer. Name this layer "Gull 2".
5. Rename the background layer "Gull". This step is necessary because there are some things that can't be done to a layer named background.
6. After renaming the layer, select Edit>Transform>Flip Horizontal. This will result in 2 gulls facing each other.
7. Select the Move tool and activate the Gull 2 layer. Position the copied gull, below and slightly to the left of the original.

Add to the Composition

1. Go to Image>Canvas Size. Enter a value of 7 for the width and 5 for the height. Click OK or press the Enter key. The dialog box allows the original image to be positioned in any of 9 areas before adding to the canvas size, which allows freedom of composition. Accept the default position (the center box).

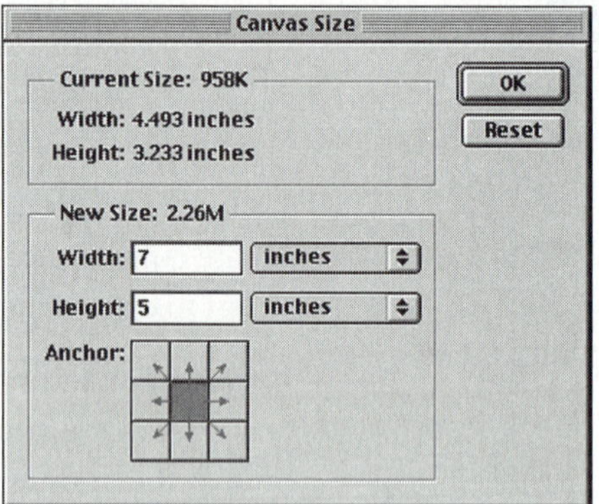

2. Next add a new layer (click the new layer icon at the bottom of the layer stack). Move the new layer to the bottom of the stack.

3. Use the Eyedropper tool to sample some color from the blue sky and fill the new layer (Edit>Fill>Foreground Color).

4. Add Noise from Filter>Noise>Add Noise with an Amount of 12 with a Distribution of Gaussian.

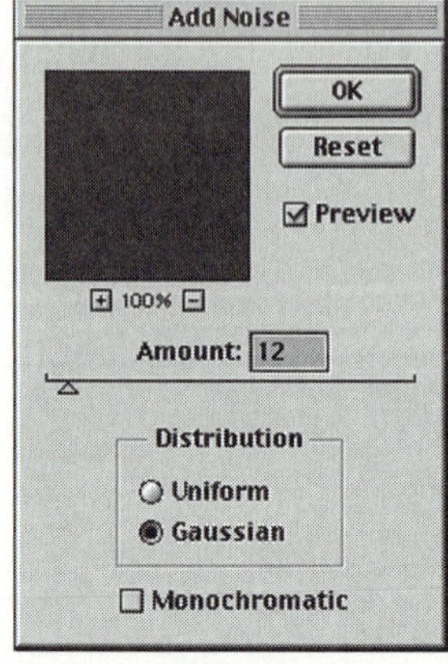

5. Apply a texture from Filter>Texture>Texturizer>Sandstone. Adjust the controls until you get a texture you like, press enter or click OK. (We used a Scaling of 120% and a Relief of 6.)

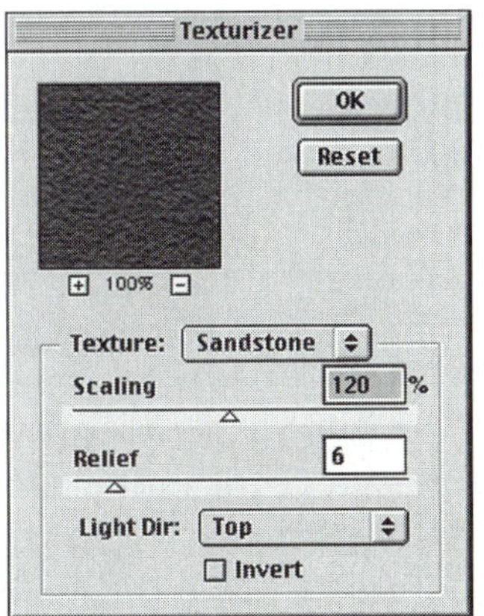

Adding Accent

Photoshop allows for quick and easy selection of pixels on a layer by holding down the Command/Control key and clicking on the layer that contains what you want to select. In this case you need to select the original image of the gull against the blue sky so that you can add the white accent line around it.

1. Type "D" to set the foreground and background colors to their defaults (black & white) and type "X" to switch white to the foreground.
2. Command/Control-click on the Gull layer. Go to Edit>Stroke, set the value to 9 pixels and choose centered for the placement of your stroke, then press Enter.

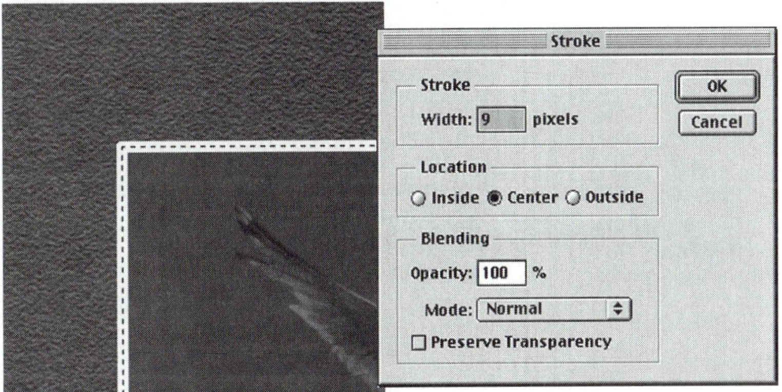

3. Deselect, then use the Move tool to position the image down and slightly to the right of the original gull layer.
4. Select the Gull 2 layer. Command/Control-click to quickly select the gull. Move the copied gull into its final position using the Move tool. Let the tip of the wing extend beyond the accent line.

5. Add a new layer and position it just below the copied gull. Name this layer Gull Shadow. A selection is active on the active layer even if the pixels originally selected are not there. This allows us to fill this gull shaped selection on this new layer with a color. Do that now with black (Edit>Fill>Background Color). Press Command/Control-D to deselect.
6. Go to Filter>Blur>Gaussian and enter a value of around 9 –15 to soften the edge of what will be the shadow. Be certain to Preserve Transparency is unchecked for the layer.
7. Use the Move tool to move the shadow down and slightly left.
8. Finally move the Gull Shadow layer below the Gull layer so that only the wing tip extending beyond the white accent line casts a shadow.

There you have it — an image worthy of framing and displaying proudly on your wall as a testament to your growing skill with this powerful software. By this point you should be mentally sorting through your own images looking for others to prepare for display.

Preparing Files for RGB-Savvy Printing

1. Merge all visible layers.
2. Select File>Save As…>TIFF. Name the file "Gulls.TIF".
3. Close the file.

Project F: Concert Poster

Concert posters are often produced in smaller quantities, from RGB-savvy printers and color copiers. This poster would likely be reproduced from such a device, and might also be used as a newspaper ad.

Creating Background

1. Create a New RGB document 4.25 inches wide by 5.75 inches high, at 100 ppi, with White Contents. Note that if we were creating an actual poster for output, the dimensions would be much larger and would require a lot more RAM.
2. Click the foreground color swatch to bring up the Color Picker. Locate the area near the bottom that lists R:, G:, and B: (for the Red, Green, Blue colorspace). Click the "R" radio button and enter "50" in the box. Press the Tab key to progress to the next box; set Green at 65, and Blue at 135. Click OK.

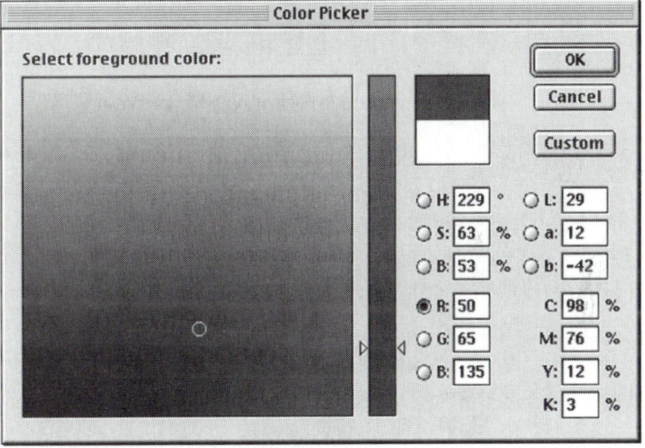

3. Press Option/Alt-Delete to fill the *Background* layer with the blue you've just created.
4. Click the New Layer icon at the bottom of the Layers palette to add a new layer. Call it "Star Field".
5. Press "D" to return to the default colors, then press Option/Alt-Delete to fill the new layer with black.
6. Select Filter>Noise>Add Noise. Change the Amount to 100 and make the noise Gaussian and Monochromatic. Click OK.

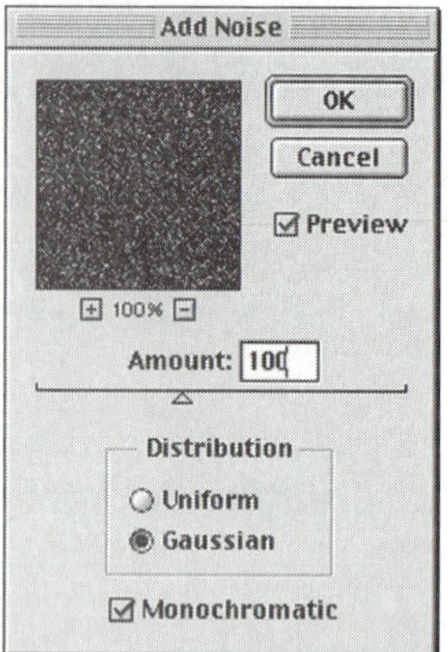

7. Select Filter>Stylize>Diffuse. Click on the Darken Only button. Click OK.

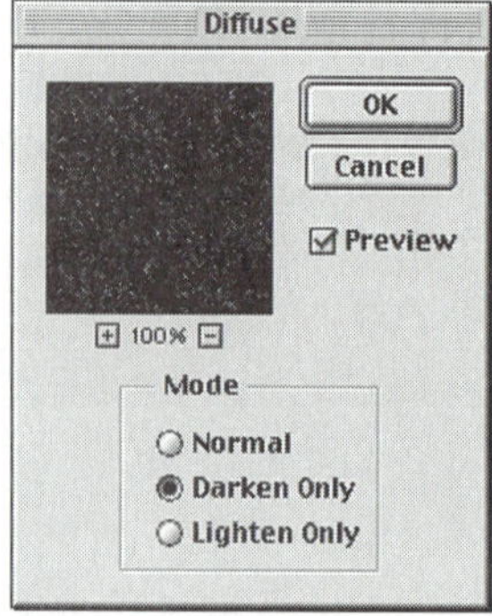

Command-Option-F or Control-Alt-F accesses the previously used filter, but allows you to change the filter settings.

8. Press Command/Control-F twice to run the Diffuse filter two more times.

9. Press Command/Control-L to display the Levels menu. Move the white slider to about 125 so the stars become visible on the screen.

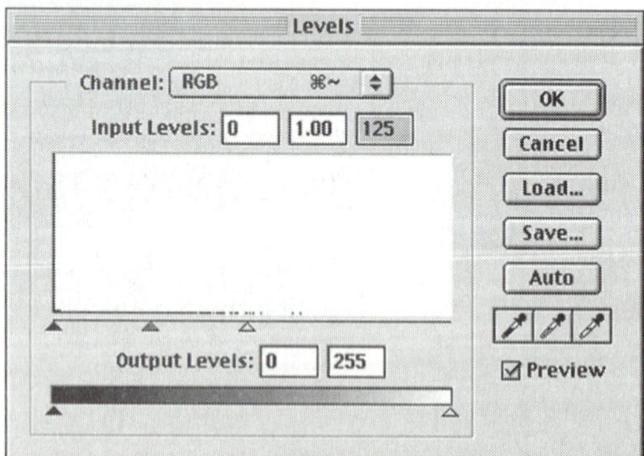

10. Set the layer blending mode for the star field to Lighten. The sky will turn blue.

11. Add a new layer. Name it "Gradient". Place it above the Star Field layer in the Layers palette.
12. Double-click the Linear Gradient tool. Set the Gradient to Foreground to Transparent, and click the Reverse box.
13. Click on the foreground color swatch. Set Red 140, Green 0, Blue 100. Click OK.
14. Hold down the Shift key and start a gradient about one-fifth of the way down the image. Bring it all the way down to the bottom of the image. If you wish, activate the Rulers from View>Show Rulers (or type Command/Control-R).

Holding the Shift key while drawing a gradient, using most other tools, or moving an item constrains movement horizontally or vertically.

15. Save the document as a Photoshop document named "Concert Poster.PSD" within your **Work in Progress** folder.

Creating Water Texture

1. Create a new layer called "Water". Position the layer above the *Gradient* layer in the Layers palette.
2. Press "D" then "X" to change the foreground color to white.
3. Select the Rectangular Marquee. In the Options palette, change the Style to Fixed Size. Change the Width to 425 pixels and the Height to 135 pixels.
4. Click on the image and position the marquee at the bottom of the image.

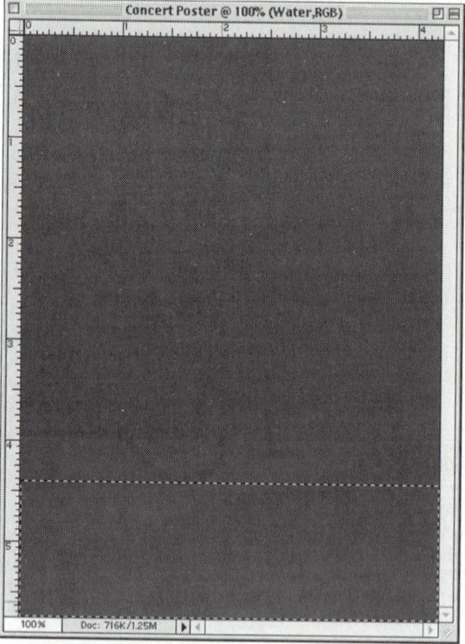

5. Fill the section with white.
6. Select Filter>Noise>Add Noise. Set Amount to 500 and make the noise Gaussian and Monochromatic.
7. Select Filter>Blur>Motion Blur. Set the Angle to 0 and the Distance to 40 pixels.

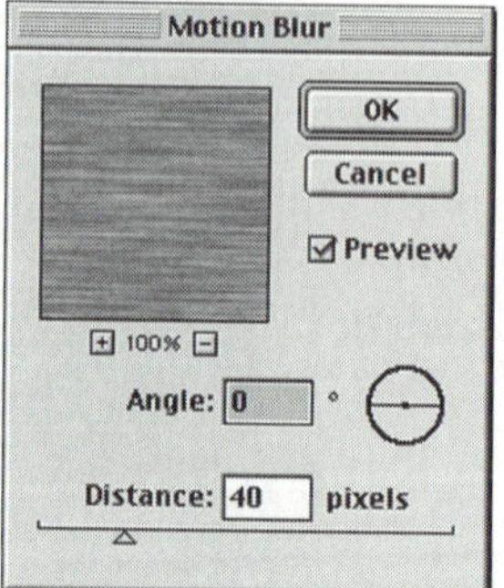

8. Select Image>Adjust>Autolevels to allow Photoshop to automatically adjust the highlight, shadow, and midtone areas. Then choose Image>Adjust>Hue and Saturation.

The Hue and Saturation dialog box may be accessed through Command/Control-U.

9. Click the Colorize checkbox. Change Hue to 240, Saturation to 50, and Lightness to –45. Click OK.

10. Deselect. Notice that the water looks a little strange on the left and right edges. Choose Image>Canvas Size. Set the Width to 375 pixels, the Height to 525 pixels; leave the placement grid in the center. Click OK.

11. Click Proceed when the clipping warning dialog box appears.

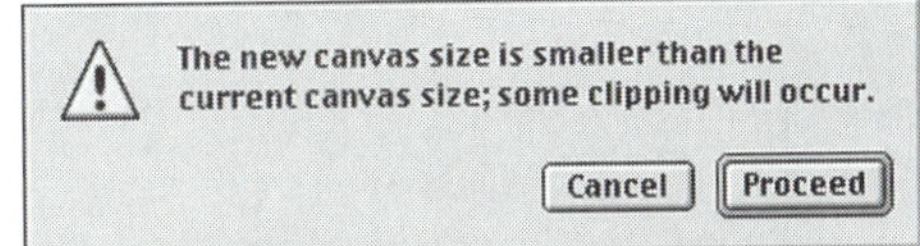

12. Save the image.

Adding Artwork

1. Open the file **Palm Silhouette.TIF** located in the **SF-Intro Photoshop** folder.

2. Press Command/Control-A to select all of the image, then Copy the image to the clipboard. Close the file.

3. Paste the palm tree image into the concert poster. Name the new layer "Palm Tree".

4. Reposition the tree within the layer using the Move tool, as shown below. Line it up on the right side of the image, with no space showing at the top or right. Keep as much of the trunk as possible.

5. Make certain that the Palm Tree layer is above the Water layer in the Layers palette. Change the blending mode for the layer to Multiply.

6. Select Edit>Purge>Clipboard to free up RAM.

7. Save the image.

Creating Sailboat Silhouette

1. Open the image **Sailboat.TIF** located in the **SF-Intro Photoshop** folder.
2. Using the Lasso tool, trace the outline the sailboat. Exclude the people on the deck and the ropes as shown below.

Don't worry about outlining fine details since we're going to turn this image into a silhouette.

3. Open the Paths palette and click the third button from the left to make the path into a selection.
4. Choose Select>Save Selection then deselect the image (Command/Control-D).
5. Turn off Paths. On the Channels palette, activate Channel #4 (Alpha 1).

Command/Control-I Inverts (makes a negative of) your image.

Your Info palette is one of your best friends. Whenever you're making adjustments to documents, you'll want to keep it visible.

6. Press Command/Control-I to invert the colors in the image, creating a black boat on a white background. Select All.
7. Copy the image to the clipboard, and Close the Sailboat image without saving. With the Concert Poster active, Press Command/Control-V to paste it into a new layer. Name the new layer "Sailboat". Press Return.
8. If it isn't there already, move the layer to the top of the Layers palette (Command/Control-Shift-Bracket). Change the blending mode for the Sailboat layer to Multiply.
9. Make certain that the Info palette is visible and the Move tool is active. Select Edit>Transform>Scale. Scale the image to about 50% while holding the Shift key. Watch the Info palette to gauge percentage while scaling. Double-click the image.
10. Select Edit>Transform>Rotate. Rotate the image about 5 degrees, until the bottom of the boat is aligned horizontally. Press Return to finish the scaling and rotation.
11. Select the sailboat with the Move tool and reposition it as shown below.

12. Change the foreground color to black. Double-click the Line tool and set the line width to 3 pixels.
13. Draw a line from the top of the sail to the tip of the bow of the sailboat, as shown.

14. Save the image.

Creating Reflections

1. Add a new layer to the image. Call it "Land".
2. Position this layer just above the *Water* layer.
3. Use the Lasso tool to draw a rough land shape on the right horizon, sloping into the water. Don't worry about the shape overlapping the water, because we'll be deleting the overlapping image area.

4. Fill the layer with black.

5. Command/Control-click the Water layer to load the layer's transparency, press Delete or Backspace to remove the unwanted part of land. Deselect.

6. Duplicate the Sailboat layer by dragging the layer onto the New Layer icon at the bottom of the Layers palette. Double-click the layer and rename it "Sailboat Reflection".
7. Place the layer below the Sailboat layer in the palette.
8. Select Edit>Transform>Flip Vertical.
9. Select the Move tool. Hold down the Shift key and reposition the image below the sailboat as shown in the illustration.

10. Change the layer Opacity to 50%.
11. Duplicate the *Land* layer and rename it "Land Reflection".
12. Select Edit>Transform>Flip Vertical.
13. With the Move tool, hold down the Shift key and reposition the image as shown:

If you know what layer opacity will be used, you may set the opacity at the same time as you name the layer.

14. Make certain that the Info palette is visible. Choose Edit>Transform>Scale.
15. Grab the bottom right handle — don't press the Shift key — and move the handle up until the Info palette reads about 100% in width and about 80% in height. Press Return/Enter.
16. Change the layer Opacity to 50%. Deselect all.
17. Save the image.

Simplifying the Image

1. The file has so many layers that it is getting rather large. We need to simplify the image a little. Select the *Background* layer.
2. Turn off all layers except the *Background* layer, the *Gradient* layer, and the *Star Field* layer. Click on Background.
3. Press Command/Control-Shift-E to merge all visible layers. This will merge these layers into the Background layer; its name remains Background.
4. Turn on all layers except the *Background* and *Water* layers.

5. Click the Sailboat layer, and merge visible layers. This merges all the visible layers into the Sailboat layer.
6. Double-click the Sailboat layer and rename it "Artwork".
7. Turn on all layers. Make certain that the blending mode for the Artwork layer is set to Multiply. Save a Copy… as "Concert Poster Final". This way, if you need to, you may return to the multilayered original image.

Adding Type

1. Select the Artwork layer.
2. Change the foreground color to white.
3. Click the Type tool near the trunk of the palm tree.
4. Set the Font to ATC Kiwi, Size 42 pixels, Leading 39, and select the Align right button.
5. In the Type box, without quotation marks, type:

   "HANDEL'S
   WATER
   MUSIC"

   Click OK.
6. Use the Move tool to reposition the type as shown below.

If letters fit together poorly (such as the "AT" combination here), place the cursor between the letter pair and adjust the kerning.

7. Click the Type tool in the water at the bottom of the image, near the palm tree.

8. Set Font to ATC Rum Runner Script. Change the Size to 24 pixels. Set the Leading to 30, and the Alignment to Flush right.

9. In the Type box enter the following text:

   "Music on the Bay
   Outdoor Concert
   July 17, 1999
   8:00pm – 11:00pm"

   Click OK.

10. Use the Move tool to reposition the type. Line the type up on the right side with the "Handel's Water Music" type.

11. Save the document.

Finishing Touches

1. Create a new layer named "Moon" and position it below the Artwork layer.

2. Select the Elliptical Marquee tool. Constrain the tool to draw a circle over the palm tree as shown. Make certain that Anti-Aliased is checked in the Marquee Options palette and that the blending mode is Normal.

3. Fill the moon with white. Deselect and reposition if necessary.
4. Create a new layer named "Right Light". Place it below the Artwork layer.
5. Use the Polygon Lasso to draw the selection as shown below, from the center of the palm tree to the left edge of the image. Close the selection by double-clicking or by single-clicking when the cursor shows an "O" next to the tool when the tool matches the starting point.

6. From the Swatches palette pick a pale yellow.
7. Fill the selection with yellow. Deselect, then press the "4" key to change the layer Opacity to 40%.
8. Create a new layer named "Left Light". Position it below the Artwork layer on the Layers palette.
9. Use the Polygon Lasso to draw the selection as shown below. Close the selection by double-clicking.

10. Fill the selection with yellow; deselect and change the layer Opacity to 40%.
11. Deselect, then sit back and admire your work.

12. Save the file.

Prepare Files for Output

Now that you have a Photoshop file, you need to prepare a file for the printer and for the newspaper.

Preparing Files for RGB-savvy Printers

1. Merge all visible layers.
2. Select File>Save As…>TIFF. Name the file "Concert.TIF".
3. Leave the file open for the next operation.

Preparing Files for the Newspaper

4. Select Image>Mode>Grayscale.
5. Save the file as TIFF with the name "ConcertG.TIF". The "G" lets you know that it is a grayscale image.
6. Close the file.

Notes:

Project G: Banana Boat Table Tent

This project could be used as a print ad or on a web page. We'll construct it with those possibilities in mind.

Coloring a Logo

1. Open the file **Banana Boat BW.EPS**, located in the **SF-Intro Photoshop** folder. This file was created in Illustrator, and therefore is a vector image. Photoshop must rasterize the file before you can edit it.

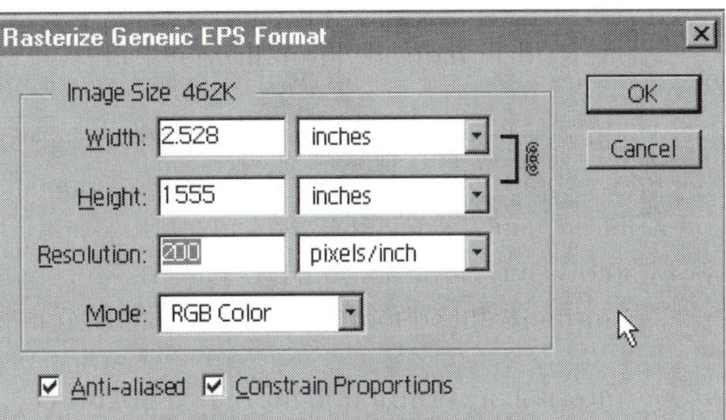

2. The Rasterize dialog box allows you to set the size, resolution, and color mode of the image. Leave the Height and Width at their defaults but be certain that the height and width units are set to inches. Change Resolution to 200 pixels/inch and Mode to RGB Color. Make certain that with this, and any Illustrator import, the Anti-Aliased checkbox is checked. Click OK.

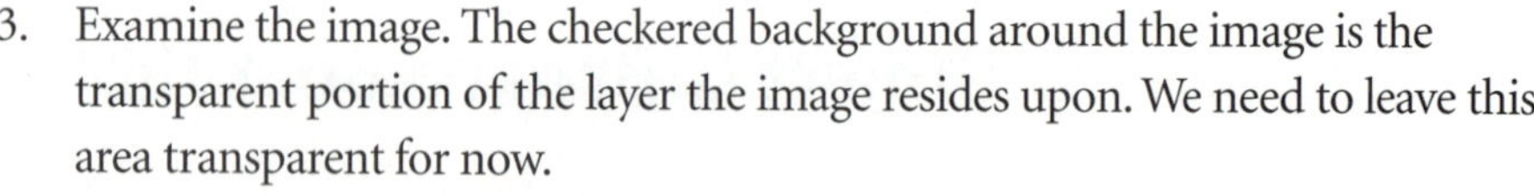

3. Examine the image. The checkered background around the image is the transparent portion of the layer the image resides upon. We need to leave this area transparent for now.
4. Zoom in on an "A" in "BANANA."
5. Select the Paint Bucket and change the foreground color to yellow.
6. On the Options palette, set Tolerance to 200. Click inside the letter. Notice that the edges are abrupt. Depending on the letter you selected, the bottom of the letter may overfill, joining the serifs in the "A" together.

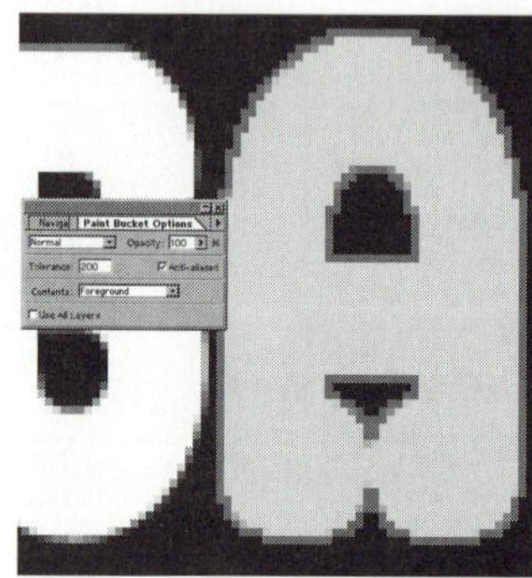

Press the "K" key to activate the Paint tool. Don't ask us why it's K; it just is.

7. Press Command/Control-Z to undo the fill, change the Tolerance to 150, and click inside the letter again. Notice that the serifs look much better, but much of the Anti-Aliasing is still lost, making the letter appear jagged. Undo again.

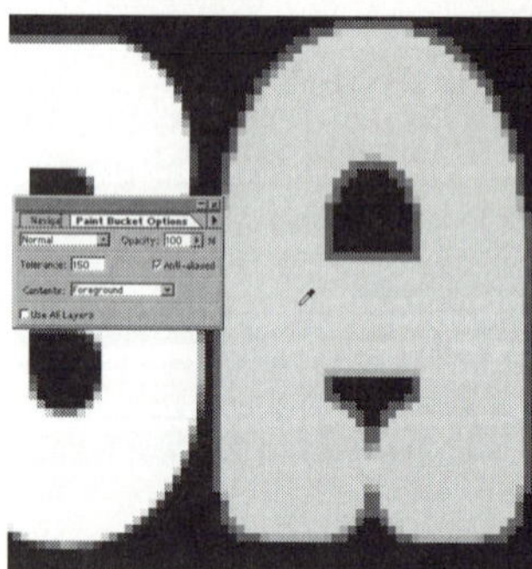

8. Set Tolerance to 15 and try again. The yellow blends smoothly into the black.

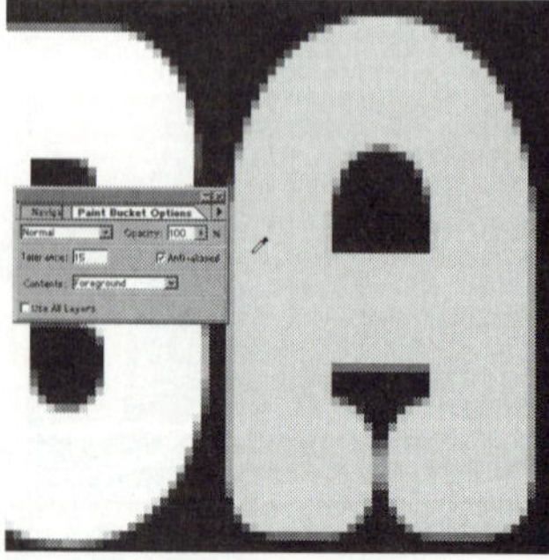

9. Double-click the Hand tool to make the image fill the window. Using the Paint Bucket tool, fill all of the letters and the boat with yellow. Leave the sail white.

We usually work with the Clone tool set to aligned, because it's more exact and easier to copy elements such as folds and highlights. We use both methods, often swapping back and forth between the two styles. By experimenting with different opacity settings and using a soft brush, you can usually avoid creating artifacts during the cloning and retouching process.

10. Save and name the image "Banana Boat Colored.PSD" in your **Work in Progress** folder before closing.

Removing a Logo

1. Open the image **Coffee AlFresco.TIF** from the **SF-Intro Photoshop** folder. We're going to remove the logo and the word COFFEE from the umbrella.
2. With the rectangular Marquee tool, select an area at the lower right side of the flap to use as a pattern (Edit>Define Pattern).

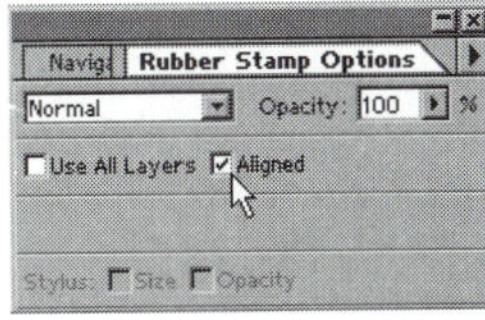

3. Select a medium-small, soft brush. Double-click the Pattern Stamp tool and make sure the Aligned button is unchecked. Set the Opacity to 70%.

4. Begin painting over the text. To avoid repetitions, which reduce the realism of this technique, after every few strokes you should redefine the pattern to change

the area you are copying from. Work on a small area at a time, and use several short strokes rather than a few long ones.

5. If you've accidentally copied the wrong part of the image, don't worry about it. We'll take care of that in a minute. For now, just make sure all of the type is obscured. Since opacity is set to 70%, it will take some extra strokes to cover the text, but it will yield a more natural result.

6. Check to see if there are areas that are painted incorrectly. Click on the History palette, History Options, and check Allow Non-Linear History. Revert to the history state which includes the error, delete it, and carefully paint the areas that you need to revert.

When retouching, it's important to pay attention to the lightness or darkness of a region you're copying from. Be certain to select a cloning area that has similar lightness or density values so that your work isn't obvious. You don't want to use a dark area to retouch a lighter one — the results will be visible.

7. Now let's remove the logo. Select the Rubber Stamp tool. Option/Alt-click the clear area at the lower left of the logo.

8. Select a medium-sized soft brush, and paint the logo with the blank area. Remember to change the area you are copying from periodically to avoid repetitions. It's best when cloning with texture to select areas near the area you're cloning, to preserve the highlights and shadows. When removing the left half of the logo, clone from the area to the left of the logo; when removing the right or bottom of the logo, clone from the area to the right of, or below, the logo.

Press the "S" key to select the Rubber Stamp tool.

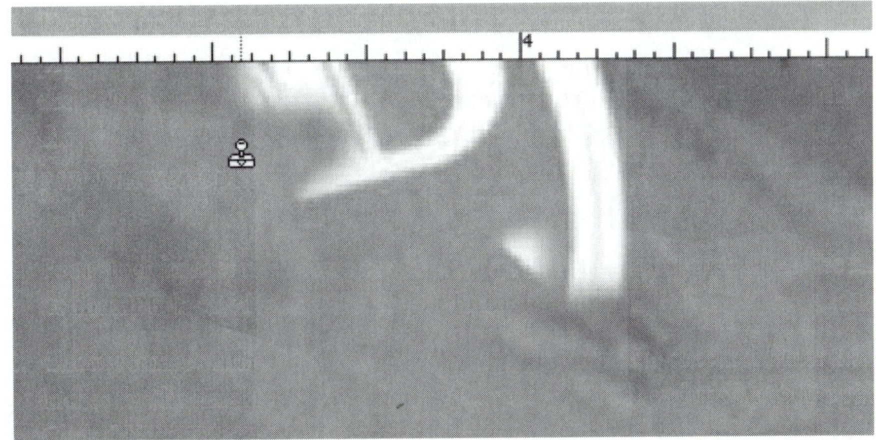

9. Continue painting and reverting to a history state, if necessary, until the image looks perfect to you.

10. Save the image as "Banana Boat Table Tent.PSD" into your **Work in Progress** folder.

Filling with Hue

1. We did a great job removing the logo when learning to use the Rubber Stamp. Unfortunately, the client hates red and his corporate color is PMS 273. Using the Lasso tool and the selection techniques you've learned, select the red umbrella. Make your selection as clean as possible.

2. Click on the foreground color swatch to bring up the Color Picker, then click Custom.

3. Make sure Book is set to Pantone Coated. Quickly type "273" to advance to our PMS color in the Color Picker. Remember, Photoshop will *not* produce an actual PMS color; instead, it creates the closest color it can find using process colors. Click OK.

4. Choose Fill from the Edit menu.

5. Change the blending mode to Hue; make certain that Opacity is set to 100% and Use is set to Foreground Color. Click OK.

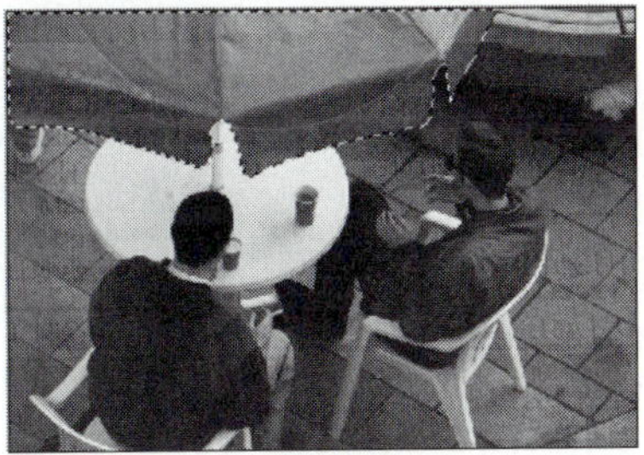

6. Deselect and Save the image as a Photoshop document, "Coffee Alfresco.PSD" into your **Work in Progress** folder and keep it open.

Adding the Logo

1. Open **Banana Boat Colored.PSD** from your **Work in Progress** folder.
2.. Press Command/Control-A to select the entire image. Press Command/Control-C to copy the image to the clipboard, then Close the file.
3. Press Command/Control-V to paste the logo into the coffee image. The logo will be pasted into a new layer.
4. Select Edit>Transform>Scale. An eight-handled box appears around the logo. Drag the corner handles to Scale; don't forget to press and hold the Shift key *before* dragging to make certain that the height and width remain proportional while scaling. Reduce the image so that it is about two-thirds the width of a single umbrella segment.
5. Press Return or Enter to finish scaling.
6. Select All. Press Command/Control-C to copy the scaled version to the clipboard. We'll be using the scaled logo twice, and copying the scaled version will ensure that they are the same size.
7. Select Edit>Transform>Rotate and rotate the image to the left by dragging the corner handles so that it is at the same angle as the middle umbrella segment.
8. Press Return to finish the rotation. Use the Move tool to reposition the logo on top of the umbrella.

9. Press Command/Control-V to paste the scaled copy of the logo into the image.

While we're scaling and rotating in two steps, you can choose Edit>Free Transform and do them both at the same time. You should always think about the most efficient way to use a process before you start working.

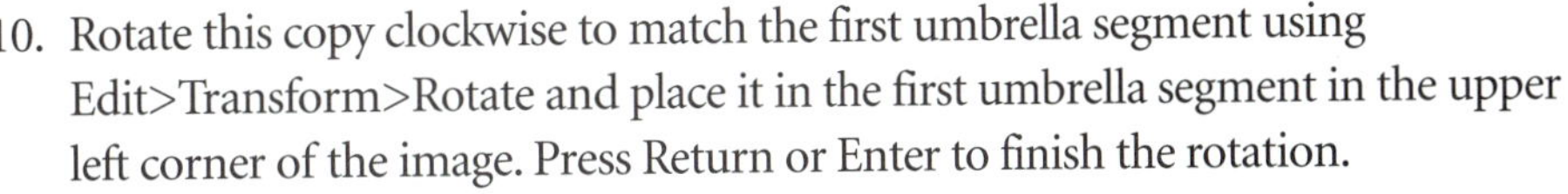

10. Rotate this copy clockwise to match the first umbrella segment using Edit>Transform>Rotate and place it in the first umbrella segment in the upper left corner of the image. Press Return or Enter to finish the rotation.

11. Press Command/Control-E to Merge Down the two logo layers permanently. Save the file.

Cleaning Up the Image

1. Use the Rubber Stamp tool to clean up the spots on the sidewalk in the lower right corner of the image.
2. Zoom in on the small stain on the table to the left of the umbrella pole.
3. Use the Eyedropper tool to set the foreground color to match the table by selecting a clean white area near the spot.

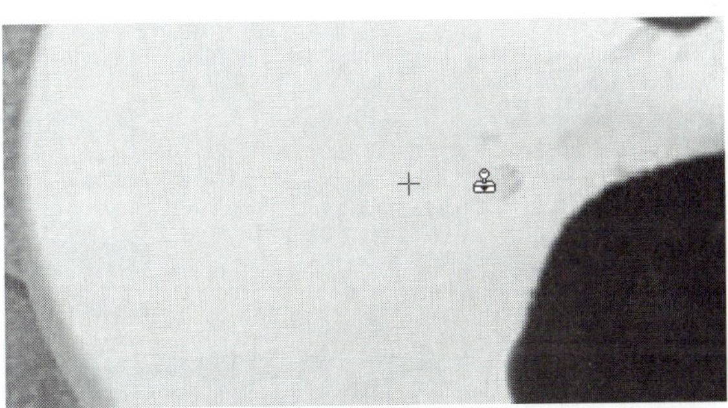

4. Select the Paintbrush tool; set Opacity to 50%. Choose a fairly small, hard-edged brush and use short strokes to remove the spot from the table.
5. There is a pile of snow in the upper right corner of the image, surrounded by a near-black pool of water. Use the Eyedropper to select the black water as foreground color.

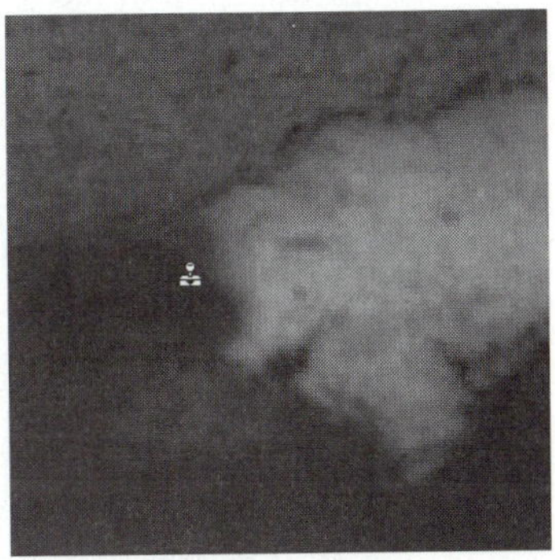

6. Select the Airbrush tool and the 65-pixel soft brush. Set Pressure to 50%. Carefully cover the snow with black to make it resemble deep shadows. Blend it softly into the stone planter at top right.
7. Save the file.

Finishing Touches

1. In the Swatches palette, click on bright yellow to change the foreground color to yellow.

2. Select the Type tool (not Type Mask tool). Click in the upper right corner.

3. Change the Font to ATC Coral Reef. Change the Size to 24 points with 24 leading, -100 Tracking, and Center Alignment. (You can change the tracking later if you don't like it.) Make certain that you've checked Anti-Aliased if it's not already turned on.

4. In the type box, enter the following text. Click OK when you're done.

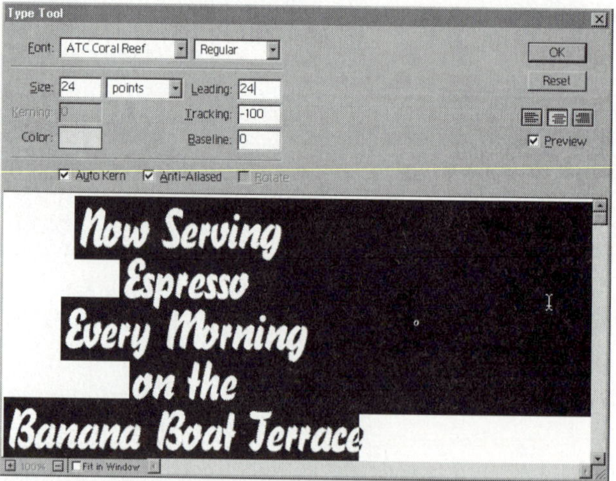

5. With the Move tool, reposition the type, if necessary, to match the image:

6. Open the image **Banana Boat Colored.PSD**. Press Command/Control-A to select all of the image. Press Command/Control-C to copy the image to the clipboard, then Close the file.

7. Make certain that the Info palette is open; if it is not, select Window>Show Info. Press Command/Control-V to paste the image onto the coffee image.

Press the "I" key to select the Eyedropper. You can change any painting tool into the Eyedropper temporarily by pressing the Option key (Macintosh) or the ALT key (Windows). When you let go, the painting tool will reappear.

8. Select Edit>Transform>Numeric to display the Numeric Transform dialog box. Make sure Scale and Constrain Proportions are checked. Enter 75% for either Height or Width. Click OK.

9. Center the logo at the bottom of the image. Hold down the Shift key to constrain its movement as you drag it downward.

10. Use the Marquee tool to select the line of type "A Drinking Establishment" at the bottom of the image, invert the colors (Command/Control-I), changing the black to white.

11. Save the image before closing.

Press the "A" key to access the Airbrush.

Preparing Files for the Web

1. Merge all visible layers.

2. Select File>Save As…>JPEG. Name the file "RoughRiderRGB.JPG".

3. Select an appropriate compression level. Greater compression (the lower the number) discards more data. Less compression results in a better-looking photo, but it loads much slower.

4. Leave the file open for the next operation.

You might notice that we don't flatten our images before we save them. If you do, making changes later can be difficult. You can always Save a Copy of an image with flattened layers (it's an option when you choose Save a Copy) for use in other applications.

Preparing Files for Traditional Litho

1. Select Image>Mode>CMYK.
2. Select File>Save As...>TIFF. Name the file "RoughRiderCMY.TIF".
3. Leave the file open for the next operation.

Preparing Files for the Newspaper

1. Select Image>Mode>Grayscale.
2. Save the file as TIFF with the name "RoughRiderG.TIF". The "G" lets you know that it is a grayscale image.
3. Close the file.

Project H: Salute to Veterans Poster

Posters are often produced in smaller quantities, from RGB-savvy printers and color copiers. This poster would likely be reproduced from such a device, in a larger size, and could also be produced as flyers on a traditional printing press. It could also be used as a newspaper ad. Of course, if we were creating an actual poster for output, the dimensions would be larger.

Create the Base Document

1. Create a New RGB document with a width of 4.25 inches, a height of 5.5 inches, a resolution of 150 ppi, and white content.
2. Activate the rulers (View>Show Rulers, or Command/Control-R), and pull guides from them. Position the guides at .25 inches in from each edge. If we were printing a letter-size page, we'd need a proportional amount of space to allow for the photocopier's nonprinting area. Use the Info palette to see the position of the guides while dragging from the ruler.
3. Be certain that the colors are set to default (press "D"). Click on the background swatch and create a new background color 5C, 10M, 50Y, and 0K.
4. Double-click on the Linear Gradient tool to display the corresponding Options palette. Set the gradient to Foreground to Background. Beginning at about the two inch mark horizontally and half inch mark vertically, draw a linear gradient to a point approximately 2.5 inches horizontal and 5 inches. Using the Info palette, it will read X: 2.0, Y: 0.5 at the start and X: 2.5, Y: 5.0 when you've finished defining your tint.

When documents are printed without having been placed in a page layout program, adequate room must be left around the edges for the press or copier to function effectively.

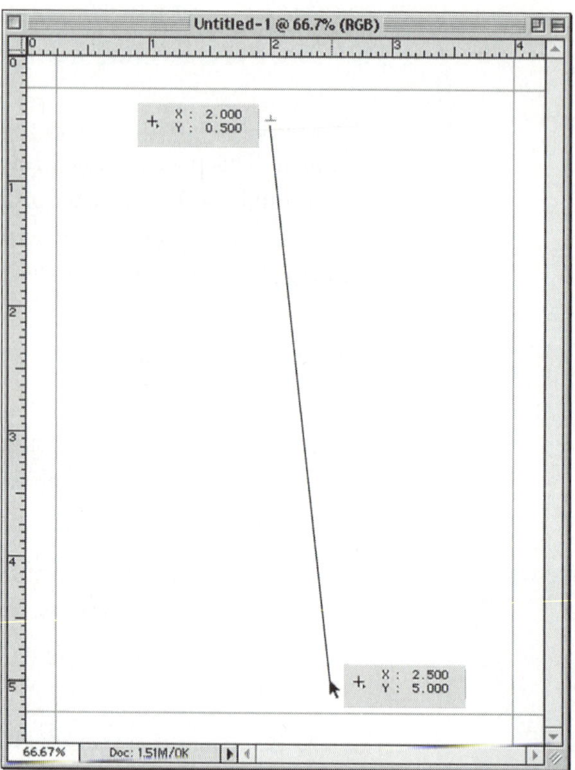

5. From the Filter>Blur menu, apply a Gaussian Blur with a radius of one pixel.

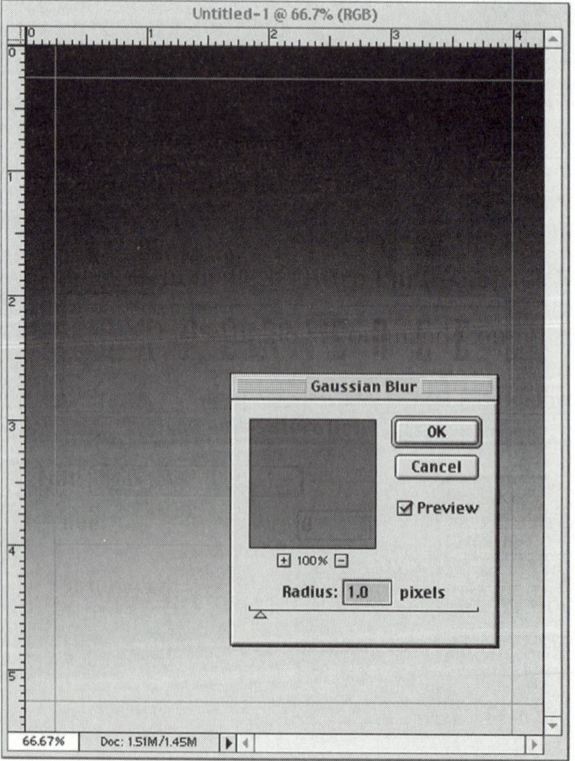

Add Silhouetted Images

1. From the **SF-Intro Photoshop** folder, open the **Flag.PSD** image. Crop the image tight, and silhouette the flag, using the Magic Wand and Lasso tools. (The flagpole should be removed, too.)
2. Copy the silhouetted flag to the clipboard and Paste it into the new document. Name the layer "Flag". Close the **Flag.PSD** file.

Rulers and guides will allow you to move around your document and place elements much more easily. They can be toggled on and off using Command/ Control-R and Command/ Control-;.

3. Holding down the Shift key to constrain the movement to vertical, drag it to the bottom of the document. Save the document as "Salute.PSD" into your **Work in Progress** folder.
4. From the **SF-Intro Photoshop** folder, open the file **Iwo Jima.PSD**. Silhouette the soldiers and flag with the Magic Wand and Lasso tools. Don't forget to remove the background in the midst of the image. When the image is silhouetted, tighten up your work by using Select>Modify>Contract by 1 pixel.
5. Copy the silhouetted image to the clipboard and Paste it into the Salute document. Position the image you've copied at 3/16″ from the left and the base at 3.75″ from the top. (You can pull in a couple of guides and the image will snap to these points.) Close the Iwo Jima image. Remove any new guides you used to place the image.

It's easy to forget that areas in the midst of an image may need to be removed. One trick that often works is to create a square of a truly obnoxious color and place it behind the image. If you can't see any of it, you probably don't have the image correctly silhouetted.

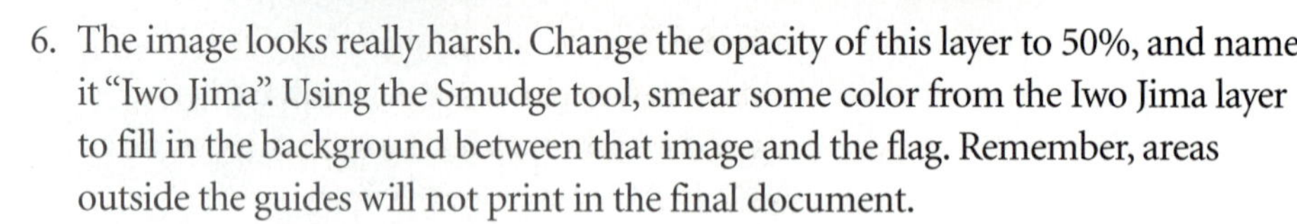

6. The image looks really harsh. Change the opacity of this layer to 50%, and name it "Iwo Jima". Using the Smudge tool, smear some color from the Iwo Jima layer to fill in the background between that image and the flag. Remember, areas outside the guides will not print in the final document.
7. This Veteran's Day Salute will feature, in addition to its variety show, dancing to music of the era. We're going to suggest that with a Big Band picture. From the **SF-Intro Photoshop** folder, open **Big Band.PSD.**
8. Carefully silhouette the trumpeter, again remembering to cut out the background inside image area (between his arms and inside the trumpet itself).
9. Copy the trumpeter to the clipboard and Paste it into the Salute document. Position it on the right-hand side, just above the star, and about 1/16″ outside your guide.

10. Name the layer "Big Band", and move it below the *Flag* layer. Close the **Big Band.PSD** file.

11. Let's apply an appropriate shadow to this layer. Duplicate the Big Band layer, and move it to the top level. Rename it "Big Band Shadow".

12. From Image>Adjust>Hue/Saturation, set Saturation to -100.

13. From Edit>Transform, flip the image vertical.

14. From Edit>Transform, rotate the image so that the bell of the trumpet is just under the second star on the second row up and move it so that it mirrors the visible part of the trumpeter.

15. From the Levels menu, drag the Output Levels lightness pointer all the way to the left so there is no highlight at all. Output Levels should read 0/0.

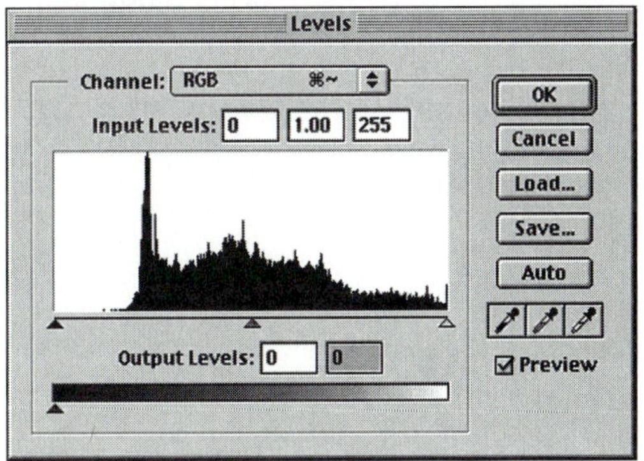

16. Change the opacity to 25%. Apply a Gaussian Blur with a pixel width of 3.

17. Remove the excess shadow by selecting the area while the layer is active, and Save the file.

18. The bugle means many things to veterans — from the hated Reveille to haunting Taps. It will also be prominent in the variety show's performance of "Boogie Woogie Bugle Boy." From your **SF-Intro Photoshop** folder, open **Bugle.PSD**.

19. Silhouette the bugle. Don't leave any shadow, since we'll be adding our own.

20. When you're done creating the silhouette, feather the image (Select>Feather…) 0.5 pixels to soften the edges. Cut to the clipboard, and Paste it into the **Salute.PSD** document.

21. Move the layer to the top (Command/Control-Shift-]) and name it "Bugle". Close the **Bugle.PSD** file without saving.

22. The bugle is disproportionately large. Be certain that the Info palette is open so that you can refer to it. To resize it, go to Edit>Transform>Scale. Hold down the Shift key and resize to 85%. Double-click on the image.

23. Position the bugle in the blue field of the flag, about 1/16″ in from the right side guide, with the bell of the horn just into the first white stripe.

24. Create a drop shadow using Layer>Effects>Drop Shadow. Set the Opacity to 50%; the Global Angle will be used by default; Set Distance 10 pixels; Blur: 20 pixels; Intensity: 20%. Click OK.

25. Move the layer below the *Big Band shadow layer*.

26. Save the file.

Add and Colorize an EPS Image

1. No Veteran's Day salute would be complete without Uncle Sam. Open the **Uncle Sam.PSD** file from the **SF-Intro Photoshop** folder. Although the image is black-and-white, it is already saved as an RGB document. However, we'll want to colorize it for our poster.

2. Select All, and Copy the image to the clipboard. Paste it into the Salute document, name the layer "Uncle Sam", and close **Uncle Sam.PSD**.

3. Before we resize, let's add some color. With the Eyedropper tool, select a red from one of the stripes of the flag. This will load it as the foreground color. With the Magic Wand tool, select the black stripes in Uncle Sam's hat. Fill them with red.

4. Select a blue from the field of the flag, and load that as the foreground color. With the Magic Wand tool, select the hatband. Fill it with color. Now select the jacket. You'll note that some areas other than the jacket are selected. Don't worry about that. With the Paintbrush tool and a medium brush, paint the collar areas. Change to a large brush to paint the rest of the coat. Leave accents for the hands, head, and shirt in black. Deselect.

5. From the Edit menu, select Transform>Numeric and Scale the layer to 50% (be certain that the Constrain box is checked). Move it to a position 1/16″ from the bottom left guides.

Colorizing a black-and-white image can be relatively easy as we've seen here, or the image may need to be colored pixel-by-pixel.

6. Apply the same drop shadow you used for the bugle layer — Opacity, 50%; Global Angle; Distance, 10 pixels; Blur, 20 pixels; Intensity, 20%. Click OK.

Adding Type

1. Press "D" to set the default colors, then exchange white to the foreground color. Type "Veteran's Day" in 18-point ATC Cabana Bold; on the following line, type "SALUTE" in 78-point ATC Flamingo Extra Bold. Highlight both lines and set the leading at 72 point. Kern or track to taste. (The apostrophe ['] is Option-Shift-] on the Macintosh and Alt-0146 on the numeric keypad for Windows.)

2. Position the type 3/16″ inside the upper left guides.
3. Move the type layer just below the Big Band layer.

4. Using the Magic Wand tool, select the U, T, and E.
5. Create a new layer called "Type Fade". Give it an opacity of 50%. Fill the selected areas with white. Move the Type Fade layer to the top level and deselect.
6. With the Type tool selected, type, in 14-point Cabana Bold, with 18 point leading (without the quotes):

   "7:00p.m. – Midnight
   April 11, 1999
   Central Square Meetinghouse"
7. Position the type on the uppermost layer, 3/16″ (.44″) from the left and 2.25″ from the top.
8. With the Eyedropper tool, select a light gold tone from the bell of the bugle.
9. Type, in 16-point Cabana Bold Italic, with 18-point leading (without the quotes):

   "I want YOU to join
   US for a SWINGing
   evening of fun."
10. Position the type at 1 7/8″ (1.875″) from the left and 4.5″ from the top.

11. From the Layer>Effects menu, add a Drop Shadow with 75% opacity, a distance and blur of 5 pixels.
12. Create a new layer and move it to the top. Name it "Nonprint Area".
13. Using the Rectangular Marquee, select the live area of the image (the area bounded by the guides). Select Inverse (Command/Control-Shift-I). Fill the area with white.
14. Re-select the live area of the image (Select>Inverse). Select>Modify>Border>4 pixels, to create a border.
15. Create a new Border layer, and move it to the top. Name the layer Border.
16. Select the Paint Bucket tool, and make sure that the Anti-Aliaseds option is unchecked. Fill the border with the black.
17. To see how the image will look, deselect, then select View>Hide Guides.

18. Save the document.

Prepare Files for Output

Now that you have a Photoshop file, you need to prepare a file for the printer and for the newspaper.

Preparing Files for RGB-savvy Printers

1. Merge all visible layers.
2. Select File>Save As…>TIFF. Name the file "SalutRGB.TIF".
3. Leave the file open for the next operation.

Preparing Files for Traditional Litho

4. Select Image>Mode>CMYK.
5. Select File>Save As…>TIFF. Name the file "SalutCMY.TIF".
6. Leave the file open for the next operation.

Preparing Files for the Newspaper

7. Select Image>Mode>Grayscale.
8. Save the file as TIFF with the name "SalutG.TIF". The "G" lets you know that it is a grayscale image.
9. Close the file.

Notes:

Glossary

Achromatic

By definition, having no color; therefore, completely black or white or some shade of gray.

Acrobat

This program by Adobe Systems, Inc. allows the conversion (using Acrobat Distiller) of any document from any Macintosh or Windows application to PDF format, which retains the page layout, graphics, color, and typography of the original document. It is widely used for distributing documents online because it is independent of computer hardware. The only software needed is a copy of Acrobat Reader, which can be downloaded free.

Adaptive Palette

A sampling of colors taken from an image, and used in a special compression process usually used to prepare images for the world wide web.

Additive Color Process

The additive color process is the process of mixing red, green, and blue light to achieve a wide range of colors, as on a color television screen. See Subtractive Color.

Adjacent Color

The eye will respond to a strong adjacent color in such a way as to affect the perception of the particular color in question. That is, a color having different adjacent colors may look different than it does in isolation. Also referred to as metamarism.

Adobe Systems Incorporated

A major software developer responsible for the creation of the PostScript page description language (see PostScript), used in almost all graphic arts environments. PostScript resides in a printer or Raster Image Processor (see Raster Image Processor) and is used to convert graphics from the screen to high-resolution output. Adobe also develops the highly popular Photoshop, Illustrator, PageMaker, and Premiere graphics and video applications, in addition to a range of others.

Algorithm

A specific sequence of mathematical steps to process data. A portion of a computer program that calculates a specific result.

All signature folding dummy

A folding dummy in which all of the signatures that make up the job are used to determine the page arrangement for each signature. Also known as a Job Worksheet.

Alpha Channel

An 8-bit channel of data that provides additional graphic information, such as colors or masking. Alpha channels are found in some illustration or graphics programs, and are used in video production.

Anti-Aliasing

A graphics software feature that eliminates or softens the jaggedness of low-resolution curved edges.

Archival storage

The process of storing data in a totally secure and safe manner. Archiving differs from backup in that it's meant to be used to restore entire systems or networks, rather than providing quick and easy access to specific files or folders.

Art

Illustrations and photographs in general; that is, all matter other than text that appears in a mechanical.

Artifact

By definition, something that is artificial, or not meant to be there. An artifact can be a blemish or dust spot on a piece of film, or unsightly pixels in a digital image.

Ascender

Parts of a lower-case letter that exceed the height of the letter "x". The letters b, d, f, h, k, l, and t have ascenders.

ASCII

The American Standard Code for Information Interchange, which defines each character, symbol, or special code as a number from 0 to 255 (8 bits in binary). An ASCII text file can be read by any computer, and is the basic mode of data transmission on the Internet.

ATM (Adobe Type Manager)

A utility program which causes fonts to appear smooth on screen at any point size. It's also used to manage font libraries.

Backing Up

The process of making copies of current work or work-in-progress as a safety measure against file corruption, drive or system failure, or accidental deletion. Backing up work-in-progress differs from creating an archive (see Archiving) for long-term storage or system restoration.

Banding

A visible stair-stepping of shades in a gradient.

Banner

A large headline or title extending across the full page width, or across a double-page spread.

Baseline

The implied reference line on which the bases of capital letters sit.

Bézier Curves

Curves that are defined mathematically (vectors), in contrast to those drawn as a collection of dots or pixels (raster). The advantage of these curves is that they can be scaled without the "jaggies" inherent in enlarging bitmapped fonts or graphics.

Bindery marks

Marks that appear on a press sheet to indicate how the sheet should be cropped, folded, collated, or bound.

Binding

In general, the various methods used to secure signatures or leaves in a book. Examples include saddle-stitching (the use of staples in a folded spine), and perfect-bound (multiple sets of folded pages sewn or glued into a flat spine).

Bit (Binary Digit)

A computer's smallest unit of information. Bits can have only two values: 0 or 1. This can represent the black and white (1-bit) pixel values in a line art image. Or in combination with other bits, it can represent 16 tones or colors (4-bit), 256 tones or colors (8-bit), 16.8 million colors (24-bit), or a billion colors (30-bit). These numbers derive from counting all the possible combinations (permutations) of 0 or 1 settings of each bit: 2 x 2 x 2 x 2 = 16 colors; 2 x 2 x 2 x 2 x 2 x 2 x 2 x 2 = 256 colors; 2 x 2 x 2 x 2 x 2 x 2 x 2 x 2 x 2 x 2 x 2 x 2 x 2 x 2 x 2 x 2 x 2 x 2 x 2 x 2 x 2 x 2 x 2 x 2= 16.8 million colors.

Bitmap image

An image constructed from individual dots or pixels set to a grid-like mosaic. Each pixel can be represented by more than one bit. A 1-bit image is black and white because each bit can have only two values (for example, 0 for white and 1 for black). For 256 colors, each pixel needs eight bits (2 8). A 24-bit image refers to an image with 24 bits per pixel (2 24), so it may contain as many as 16,777,216 colors. Because the file must contain information about the color and position of each pixel, the disk space needed for bitmap images is usually quite significant. Most digital photographs and screen captures are bitmap images.

Bitmapped

Forming an image by a grid of pixels whose curved edges have discrete steps because of the approximation of the curve by a finite number of pixels.

Black

The absence of color; an ink that absorbs all wavelengths of light.

Blanket

The blanket, a fabric coated with natural or synthetic rubber wrapped around the cylinder of an offset press, transfers the inked image from the plate to the paper.

Bleed

Page data that extends beyond the trim marks on a page. Illustrations that spread to the edge of the paper without margins are referred to as "bled off."

Blend

See Graduated fill.

Blind Emboss

A raised impression in paper made by a die, but without being inked. It is visible only by its relief characteristic.

Blow up

An enlargement, usually of a graphic element such as a photograph.

Body Copy

The text portion of the copy on a page, as distinguished from headlines.

Border

A continuous line that extends around text; or a rectangular, oval, or irregularly-shaped visual in an ad.

Bounding Box

The imaginary rectangle that encloses all sides of a graphic, necessary for a page layout specification.

Brightness

1. A measure of the amount of light reflected from a surface. 2. A paper property, defined as the percentage reflection of 457-nanometer (nm) radiation. 3. The intensity of a light source. 4. The overall percentage of lightness in an image.

Bullet

A marker preceding text, usually a solid dot, used to add emphasis; generally indicates that the text is part of a list.

Burn

1. To expose an image onto a plate. 2. To make copies of ROM chips or CD-ROMs. 3. To darken a specific portion of an image through photographic exposure.

Byte

A unit of measure equal to eight bits (decimal 256) of digital information, sufficient to represent one text character. It is the standard unit measure of file size. (See also Megabyte, Kilobyte, and Gigabyte).

Cab

See Flat.

Calibration

Making adjustments to a color monitor and other hardware and software to make the monitor represent as closely as possible the colors of the final printed piece.

Calibration Bars

A strip of reference blocks of color or tonal values on film, proofs, and press sheets, used to check the accuracy of color registration, quality, density, and ink coverage during a print run.

Callout

A descriptive label referenced to a visual element, such as several words connected to the element by an arrow.

Camera Ready

A completely finished mechanical, ready to be photographed to produce a negative from which a printing plate will be made.

Cap Line

The theoretical line to which the tops of capital letters are aligned.

Caps

An abbreviation for capital letters.

Caps and Small Caps

A style of typesetting in which capital letters are used in the normal way, while the type that would normally be in lower case has been changed to capital letters of a smaller point size. A true small-caps typeface does not contain any lower-case letters.

Caption

The line or lines of text that identify a picture or illustration, usually placed beneath it or otherwise in close proximity.

CD-ROM

A device used to store approximately 600MB of data. Files are permanently stored on the device and can be copied to a disk but not altered directly. ROM stands for Read-Only Memory. Equipment is now available on the consumer market for copying computer files to blank CD-ROMs.

Center marks

Press marks that appear on the center of all sides of a press sheet to aid in positioning the print area on the paper.

Character Count

The number of characters (letters, figures, signs or spaces) in a selected block of copy. Once used to calculate the amount of text that would fit on a given line or region when physically setting type.

Choke

See Trapping

Chooser

A part of the Macintosh operating system that permits selection of a printer or other peripheral device. Chooser is also used to access resources on a network.

Chroma

The degree of saturation of a surface color in the Munsell color space model.

Cromalin

A single-sheet color proofing system introduced by DuPont in 1971 and still quite popular in the industry. It uses a series of overlaid colorants and varnish to simulate the results of a press run.

Chromaticity Diagram

A graphical representation of two of the three dimensions of color. Intended for plotting light sources rather than surface colors. Often called the CIE diagram.

Cicero/Didot Point

The cicero is a unit of horizontal distance slightly larger than the pica, used widely in continental Europe. A cicero equals 0.178 inches, or 12 Didot points.

Clipboard

The portion of computer memory that holds data that has been cut or copied. The next item cut or copied replaces the data already in the clipboard.

Cloning

Duplication of pixels from one part of an image to another.

CMS

See Color Management System

CMYK

Acronym for cyan, magenta, yellow, and black, the four process color inks which, when properly overprinted, can simulate a subset of the visible spectrum. See also color separation. Also refers to digital artwork that contains information necessary for creating color separations.

CMYK (Cyan, Magenta, Yellow, Black)

Acronym for the process colors cyan, magenta, yellow, and black (subtractive primaries) used in color printing. The letter K stands for "Key," although it is commonly used to refer to the Black ink that is added to the three colors when necessary. When printing black text as part of a four-color process, only the black ink is used. A normal four-color separation will have a plate for each of the four colors. When combined on the printed piece, the half-tone dots of each color give the impression of the desired color to the eye.

Coated

Printing papers having a surface coating (of clay or other material) to provide a smoother, more even finish with greater opacity.

Cold type

Type produced by photographic or digital methods, as opposed to the use of molten metal as in the old Linotype machine.

Collate

To gather separate sections or leaves of a publication together in the correct order for binding.

Collate and cut

Multiple signatures that are stacked then cut to be later placed in sequential order, drilled, and placed in three-ring binders.

Color Balance

The combination of yellow, magenta, and cyan needed to produce a neutral gray. Determined through a gray balance analysis.

Color Cast

The modification of a hue by the addition of a trace of another hue, such as yellowish green, pinkish blue, etc. Normally, an unwanted effect that can be corrected.

Color Chart

A printed chart of various combinations of CMYK colors used as an aid for the selection of "legal" colors during the design phase of a project.

Color Control Strip

A printed strip of various reference colors used to control printing quality. This strip is normally placed outside the "trim" area of a project, as a guide and visual aid for the pressman.

Color Conversion

Changing the color "mode" of an image. Converting an image from RGB to CMYK for purposes of preparing the image for conventional printing.

Color Correction

The process of removing casts or unwanted tints in a scanned image, in an effort to improve the appearance of the scan or to correct obvious deficiencies, such as green skies or yellowish skin tones.

Color Gamut

The range of colors that can be formed by all possible combinations of the colorants of a given reproduction system (printing press) on a given type of paper.

Color Key

An overlay color proof of acetate sheets, one for each of the four primary printing inks. The method was developed by 3M Corporation and remains a copyrighted term.

Color Management System

A process or utility that attempts to manage color of input and output devices in such a way that the monitor will match the output of any CMS-managed printer.

Color Model

A system for describing color, such as RGB, HLS, CIELAB, or CMYK.

Color overlay

A sheet of film or paper whose text and art correspond to one spot color or process color. Each color overlay becomes the basis for a single printing plate that will apply that color to paper.

Color Picker

A function within a graphics application that assists in selecting a color.

Color Proof

A printed or simulated printed image of the color separations intended to produce a close visual representation of the final reproduction for approval purposes and as a guide to the press operator.

Color Separation

The process of transforming color artwork into four components corresponding to the four process colors. If spot colors are used, additional components may be created containing only those items that will appear in the corresponding spot color layer. Each component is imaged to film or paper in preparation for making printing plates that correspond to each ink.

Color Sequence

The color order of printing the cyan, magenta, yellow, and black inks on a printing press. Sometimes called rotation or color rotation.

Color Space

Because a color must be represented by three basic characteristics depending on the color model, the color space is a three-dimensional coordinate system in which any color can be represented as a point.

Color Temperature

The temperature, in degrees Kelvin, to which a blackbody would have to be heated to produce a certain color radiation. (A "blackbody" is an ideal body or surface that completely absorbs or radiates energy.) The graphic arts viewing standard is 5,000 K. The degree symbol is not used in the Kelvin scale. The higher the color temperature, the bluer the light.

Color Transparency

A positive color photographic image on a clear film base that must be viewed by transmitted light. It is preferred for original photographic art because it has higher resolution than a color print. Transparency sizes range from 35mm color slides up to 8x10in. (203x254mm).

Colorimeter

An optical measuring instrument designed to measure and quantify color. They are often used to match digital image values to those of cloth and other physical samples.

Column rule

A thin vertical rule used to separate columns of type.

Combination signatures

Signatures of different sizes inserted at any position in a layout.

Comp

Comprehensive artwork used to present the general color and layout of a page.

Compose

To set copy into type, or lay out a page.

Composite proof

A version of an illustration or page in which the process colors appear together to represent full color. When produced on a monochrome output device, colors are represented as shades of gray.

Compression

A digital technique used to reduce the size of a file by analyzing occurrences of similar data. Compressed files occupy less physical space, and their use improves digital transmission speeds. Compression can sometimes result in a loss of image quality and/or resolution.

Condensed Type

A typeface in which the width of the letters has been reduced. Condensed type can be a specific font, or the result of applying a percentage of normal width by a formatting command.

Continuous Tone

An image such as an original photograph in which the subject has continuous shades of color or gray tones through the use of an emulsion process. Continuous tone images must be screened to create halftone images in order to be printed.

Contrast

The relationship between the dark and light areas of an image.

Copyright

Ownership of a work by the originator, such as an author, publisher, artist, or photographer. The right of copyright permits the originator of material to prevent its use without express permission or acknowledgment of the originator. Copyright may be sold, transferred, or given up contractually.

CorelDRAW

A popular drawing program originally designed for the Windows environment, but now available as a Macintosh program. CorelDRAW is known to create files that can cause printing and/or output problems in many prepress environments.

Creep

The progressive extension of interior pages of the folded signature beyond the image area of the outside pages. Shingling is applied to correct for creep.

Crop Marks

Printed short, fine lines used as guides for final trimming of the pages within a press sheet.

Cropping

The elimination of parts of a photograph or other original that are not required to be printed.

Crossover

An element in a book (text, line art, or other graphic)that appears on both pages of a reader spread crossing over the gutter.

Custom printer description file

A file containing information specific to a type of output device; used in conjunction with a standard PPD file to customize the printing process.

DCS (Desktop Color Separation)

Acronym for Desktop Color Separation, a version of the EPS file format. DCS 1.0 files are composed of five PostScript files for each color image: cyan, magenta, yellow, and black file, plus a separate low-resolution FPO image to place in a digital file. In contrast, DCS 2.0 files have one file that stores process color and spot color information.

Default

A specification for a mode of computer operation that operates if no other is selected. The default font size might be 12 point, or a default color for an object might be white with a black border.

Densitometer

An electronic instrument used to measure optical density. Reflective (for paper) and transmissive (for film).

Descender

The part of a lower-case letter that extends below the baseline (lower edge of the x-height) of the letter. The letters y, p, g, and j contain descenders.

Desktop

1. The area on a monitor screen on which the icons appear, before an application is launched. 2. A reference to the size of computer equipment (system unit, monitor, printer) that can fit on a normal desk; thus, desktop publishing.

Desktop Publishing (DTP)

Use of a personal computer, software applications, and a high-quality printer to produce fully composed printed documents. DTP is, in reality, an incorrect term these days. In the early days of Macintosh and PostScript technology, the term Desktop Publishing inferred that the materials produced from these systems was somehow inferior (as opposed to

professional publishing). Now, the overwhelming majority of all printed materials - regardless of the quality - are produced on these systems, up to and including nationally famous magazines, catalogs, posters, and newspapers

Die line

In a digital file, the outline used to mark where cutting, stamping, or embossing the finished printed piece will occur. Uses to create a particular shape, such as a rolodex card.

Digital

The use of a series of discrete electronic pulses to represent data. In digital imaging systems, 256 steps (8 bits, or 1 byte) are normally used to characterize the gray scale or the properties of one color. For text, see ASCII.

Digital Camera

A camera which produces images directly into an electronic file format for transfer to a computer.

Digital Proofs

Digital proofs are representations of what a specific mechanical will look like when output and reproduced on a specific type of printing press. The difference with a digital proof is that it is created without the use of conventional film processes and output directly from computer files.

Dingbat

A font character that displays a picture instead of a letter, number or punctuation mark. There are entire font families of pictographic dingbats; the most commonly used dingbat font is Zapf Dingbats. There are dingbats for everything from the little airplanes used to represent airports on a map, to telephones, swashes, fish, stars, balloons - just about anything.

Direct-to-plate

Producing printing plates directly from computer output without going through the film process.

Disk Operating System (DOS)

Software for computer systems that supervises and controls the running of programs. The operating system is loaded into memory from disk by a small program which permanently resides in the firmware within the computer. The major operating systems in use today are Windows95 and WindowsNT from Microsoft, the Macintosh OS from Apple Computer, and a wide range of UNIX systems, such as those from Silicon Graphics, SUN Microsystems, and other vendors.

Dithering

A technique used in images wherein a color is represented using dots of two different colors displayed or printed very close together. Dithering is often used to compress digital images, in special screening algorithms (see Stochastic Screening) and to produce higher quality output on low-end color printers.

Document

The general term for a computer file containing text and/or graphics.

Dongle

A security device that usually plugs into your keyboard or printer port, that allows copy-protected software to run on your system. Such protected software will only run on systems with the dongle present. This prevents a single copy of software from running on any but one machine at a time.

Dot Gain

The growth of a halftone dot that occurs whenever ink soaks into paper. This growth can vary from being very small (on a high-speed press with fast-drying ink and very non-porous paper) to quite dramatic, as is the case in newspaper printing, where a dot can expand 30% from its size on the film to the size at which it dries. Failure to compensate for this gain in the generation of digital images can result in very poor results on press. Generally speaking, the finer the screen (and therefore, the smaller the dot) the more noticeable dot gain will be.

Double-page Spread

A design that spans the two pages visible to the reader at any open spot in a magazine, periodical, or book.

Downloadable Fonts

Typefaces that can be stored on disk and then downloaded to the printer when required for printing.

DPI (Dots Per Inch)

The measurement of resolution for page printers, phototypesetting machines and graphics screens. Currently graphics screens use resolutions of 60 to 100 dpi, standard desktop laser printers work at 600 dpi, and imagesetters operate at more than 1,500 dpi.

Drop Shadow

A duplicate of a graphic element or type placed behind and slightly offset from it, giving the effect of a shadow.

Drum Scanner

A color scanner on which the original is wrapped around a rotary scanning drum. See Scanner.

DSC

Acronym for the Adobe Document Structure Conventions, designed to provide a standard order and format for information so applications that process PostScript, such as PressWise, can easily find information about a document's structure and imaging requirements. These conventions allow specially formatted PostScript comments to be added to the page description; applications can search for these comments, but PostScript interpreters usually ignore them. TrapWise requires that the PostScript in incoming files is formatted using conventional DSC comments, so certain functions may not work properly if the file is not DSC-conforming.

Duotone

The separation of a black-and-white photograph into black and a second color having different tonal values and screen angles. Duotones are used to enhance photographic reproduction in two-three-or sometimes four-color work. Often the second, third, and fourth colors are not standard CMYK inks.

Dye

A soluble coloring material, normally used as the colorant in color photographs.

Dye Transfer

A photographic color print using special coated papers to produce a full color image. Can serve as an inexpensive proof.

Electrostatic

The method by which dry toner is transferred to paper in a copier or laser printer, and liquid toners are bonded to paper on some large-format color plotters.

Element

The smallest unit of a graphic, or a component of a page layout or design. Any object, text block, or graphic might be referred to as an element of the design.

Elliptical Dot Screen

A halftone screen having an elliptical dot structure.

Embedding

1. Placing control codes in the body of a document. 2. Including a complete copy of a text file or image within a desktop publishing document, with or without a link (see Linking).

Emulsion

The coating of light-sensitive material (silver halide) on a piece of film or photographic paper.

En Dash

A dash - often used in hyphenated word pairs - that is usually half the width of an em dash.

En Space

A space that is usually equal to half the width of an em space.

EPS

Acronym for encapsulated PostScript, a single-page PostScript file that contains grayscale or color information and can be imported into many electronic layout and design applications.

EPS (Encapsulated PostScript)

Acronym for file format used to transfer PostScript data within compatible applications. An EPS file normally contains a small preview image that displays in position within a mechanical or used by another program. EPS files can contain text, vector artwork, and images.

Expanded Type

Also called extended, a widened version of a typeface design. Type may be extended artificially within a DTP application, or designed as such by the typeface designer. See also Condensed Type.

Export

To save a file generated in one application in a format that is readable in another application.

Extension

A modular software program that extends or expands the functions of a larger program. A folder of Extensions is found in the Macintosh System Folder.

Fill

To add a tone or color to the area inside a closed object in a graphic illustration program.

Film

Non-paper output of an imagesetter or phototypesetter.

Film assembly

See Stripping.

Filter

In image editing applications, a small program that creates a special effect or performs some other function within an image.

First signature folding dummy

A folding dummy that determines the page arrangement for a single signature layout template. This template can then be applied to a job that requires multiple signatures, and PressWise will correctly impose all the pages based on the numbering sequence and binding method specified by the first signature.

Flat

Individual film assembled onto a carrier readied for contacting or platemaking. Referred to as a cab in gravure printing.

Flat Color

Color that lacks contrast or tonal variation. Also, flat tint.

Flatbed Scanner

A scanner on which the original is mounted on a flat scanning glass. See Scanner.

Flexographic printing

A rotary letterpress process printing on a press using a rubber plate that stretches around a cylinder making it necessary to compensate by distorting the plate image. Flexography is used most often in label printing, often on metal or other non-paper material.

Floating Accent

A separate accent mark that can be placed under or over another character. Complex accented characters such as in foreign languages are usually available in a font as a single character.

Flood

A user-defined screened or solid box that prints on and completely covers a PressWise blank page. Can be used to print a flat tint on the page, or to produce a mask for manual stripping in existing film-based pages.

Flop

To make a mirror image of visuals such as photographs or clip art.

Folder

1. The digital equivalent of a paper file folder, used to organize files in the Macintosh and Windows operating systems. The icon of a folder looks like a paper file folder. Double-clicking it opens it to reveal the files stored inside. 2. A mechanical device which folds preprinted pages into various formats, such as a tri-fold brochure.

Folding dummy

A template used for determining the page arrangement on a form to meet folding and binding requirements. See also All signature folding dummy and First signature folding dummy.

Font

A font is the complete collection of all the characters (numbers, uppercase and lowercase letters and, in some cases, small caps and symbols) of a given typeface in a specific style; for example, Helvetica Bold.

Force Justify

A type alignment command which causes the space between letters and words in a line of type to expand to fit within a line. Often used in headlines, and sometimes used to force the last line of a justified paragraph, which is normally set flush left, to justify.

Form

In PressWise, the front or back of a signature.

Four-color Process

See Process Colors

FPO

Acronym for For Position Only, a term applied to low-quality art reproductions or simple shapes used to indicate placement and scaling of an art element on mechanicals or camera-ready artwork. In digital publishing, an FPO can be low-resolution TIFF files that are later replaced with high-resolution versions. An FPO is not intended for reproduction but only as a guide and placeholder for the prepress service provider.

Frame

In desktop publishing, (1.) an area or block into which text or graphics can be placed; (2.) a border on .

FreeHand

A popular vector-based illustration program available from Macromedia.

Full Measure

A line set to the entire line length.

G (Gigabyte)

One billion (1,073,741,824) bytes (230) or 1,048,576 kilobytes.

Galley Proof

Proofs, usually of type, taken before the type is made up into pages. Before desktop publishing, galley proofs were hand-assembled into pages.

Gamma

A measure of the contrast, or range of tonal variation, of the midtones in a photographic image

Gamma Correction

1. Adjusting the contrast of the midtones in an image. 2. Calibrating a monitor so that midtones are correctly displayed on screen.

Gamut

See Color Gamut

GASP

Acronym for Graphic Arts Service Provider, a firm that provides a range of services somewhere on the continuum from design to fulfillment.

GCR (Gray component replacement)

A technique for adding detail by reducing the amount of cyan, magenta, and yellow in chromatic or colored areas, replacing them with black.

GIF - Graphics Interface File

A CompuServe graphics file format that is used widely for graphic elements in Web pages.

Global Preferences

Preference settings which affect all newly created files within an application.

Gradient fill

See Graduated fill.

Graduated fill

An area in which two colors (or shades of gray or the same color) are blended to create a gradual change from one to the other. Graduated fills are also known as blends, gradations, gradient fills, and vignettes.

Grain

Silver salts clumped together in differing amounts in different types of photographic emulsions. Generally speaking, faster emulsions have larger grain sizes.

Graininess

Visual impression of the irregularly distributed silver grain clumps in a photographic image, or the ink film in a printed image.

Gray Balance

The values for the yellow, magenta, and cyan inks that are needed to produce a neutral gray when printed at a normal density.

Gray Component Replacement

See GCR

Grayscale

1.An image composed in grays ranging from black to white, usually using 256 different tones of gray. 2. A tint ramp used to measure and control the accuracy of screen percentages on press. 3. An accessory used to define neutral density in a photographic image.

Greeking

1. A software technique by which areas of gray are used to simulate lines of text below a certain point size. 2. Nonsense text use to define a layout before copy is available.

Grid

A division of a page by horizontal and vertical guides into areas into which text or graphics may be placed accurately.

Grind-off

The roughing up at the back (or spine) of a folded signature, or of two or more gathered signatures, in preparation for perfect binding.

Gripper edge

The leading edge of a sheet of paper, which the grippers on the press grab to carry the paper through a press.

Group

To collect graphic elements together so that an operation may be applied to all of them simultaneously.

GUI

Acronym for Graphical User Interface, the basis of the Macintosh and Windows operating systems.

Gutter

Extra space between pages in a layout. Sometimes used interchangeably with Alley to describe the space between columns on a page. Gutters can appear either between the top and bottom of two adjacent pages or between two sides of adjacent pages. Gutters are often used because of the binding or layout requirements of a job — for example, to add space at the top or bottom of each page or to allow for the grind-off taken when a book is perfect bound.

Hairline Rule

The thinnest rule that can be printed on a given device. A hairline rule on a 1200 dpi imagesetter is 1/1200 of an inch; on a 300 dpi laser printer, the same rule would print at 1/300 of an inch.

Halftone

An image generated for use in printing in which a range of continuous tones is simulated by an array of dots that create the illusion of continuous tone when seen at a distance.

Halftone Tint

An area covered with a uniform halftone dot size to produce an even tone or color. Also called flat tint or screen tint.

Hard Drive

A rigid disk sealed inside an airtight transport mechanism that is the basic storage mechanism in a computer. Information stored may be accessed more rapidly than on floppy disks and far greater amounts of data may be stored.

High Key

A photographic or printed image in which the main interest area lies in the highlight end of the scale.

High Resolution File

An image file that typically contains four pixels for every dot in the printed reproduction. High-resolution files are often linked to a page layout file, but not actually embedded in it, due to their large size.

Highlights

The lightest areas in a photograph or illustration.

HLS

Color model based on three coordinates: hue, lightness (or luminance), and saturation.

HSV

A color model based on three coordinates: hue, saturation and value (or luminance).

HTML (HyperText Markup Language)

The language, written in plain (ASCII) text using simple tags, that is used to create Web pages, and which Web browsers are designed to read and display. HTML focuses more on the logical structure of a page than its appearance.

Hue

The wavelength of light of a color in its purest state (without adding white or black).

Hyperlink

An HTML tag directs the computer to a different Anchor or URL (Uniform Resource Locator). The linked data may be on the same page, or on a computer anywhere in the world.

Hyphenation Zone

The space at the end of a line of text in which the hyphenation function will examine the word to determine whether or not it should be hyphenated and wrapped to the next line.

Icon

A small graphic symbol used on the screen to indicate files or folders, activated by clicking with the mouse or pointing device.

Illustrator

A vector editing application owned by Adobe Systems, Inc.

Imaging

The process of producing a film or paper copy of a digital file from an output device.

Imagesetter

A raster-based device used to output a computer page-layout file or composition at high resolution (usually 1000 - 3000 dpi) onto photographic paper or film, from which to make printing plates.

Import

To bring a file generated within one application into another application.

Imposition

The arrangement of pages on a printed sheet, which, when the sheet is finally printed, folded and trimmed, will place the pages in their correct order.

Indexed Color Image

An image which uses a limited, predetermined number of colors; often used in Web images. See also GIF.

Indexing

In DTP, marking certain words within a document with hidden codes so that an index may be automatically generated.

Initial Caps

Text in which the first letter of each word (except articles, etc.) is capitalized.

Inline Graphic

A graphic that is inserted within a body of text, and may be formatted using normal text commands for justification and leading; inline graphics will move with the body of text in which they are placed.

Intensity

Synonym for degree of color saturation.

International Paper Sizes

The International Standards Organization (ISO) system of paper sizes is based on a series of three sizes A, B and C. Series A is used for general printing and stationery, Series B for posters, and Series C for envelopes. Each size has the same proportion of length to width as the others. The nearest ISO paper size to conventional 8-1/2 x 11 paper is A4.

ISO

The International Standards Organization.

Jaggies

Visible steps in the curved edge of a graphic or text character that results from enlarging a bitmapped image.

Job state

The state of working in PressWise while one or more jobs are open. Opposite of no-job state.

JPG or JPEG

A compression algorithm that reduces the file size of bitmapped images, named for the Joint Photographic Experts Group, an industry organization that created the standard; JPEG is a "lossy" compression method, and image quality will be reduced in direct proportion to the amount of compression.

Justification

The alignment of text along a margin or both margins..

Kelvin (K)

Unit of temperature measurement based on Celsius degrees, starting from absolute zero, which is equivalent to -273 Celsius (centigrade); used to indicate the color temperature of a light source.

Kerning

Moving a pair of letters closer together or farther apart, to achieve a better fit or appearance.

Key (Black Plate)

In early four-color printing, the black plate was printed first and the other three colors were aligned (or registered) to it. Thus, the black plate was the "key" to the result.

Keyline

A thin, often black border around a picture or a box indicating where to place pictures. In digital files, the keylines are often vector objects while photographs are usually bitmap images.

Kilobyte (K, KB)

1,024 (210) bytes, the nearest binary equivalent to decimal 1,000 bytes. Abbreviated and referred to as K.

Knockout

A printing technique that represents overlapping objects without mixing inks. The ink for the underlying element does not print (knocks out) in the area where the objects overlap. Opposite of overprinting.

L*a*b

The lightness, red-green attribute, and yellow-blue attribute in the CIE Color Space, a three-dimensional color mapping system.

Landscape

Printing from the left to right across the wider side of the page. A landscape orientation treats a page as 11 inches wide and 8.5 inches long.

Laser printer

A high quality image printing system using a laser beam to produce an image on a photosensitive drum. The image is transferred to paper by a conventional xerographic printing process. Current laser printers used for desktop publishing have a resolution of 600 dpi. Imagesetters are also laser printers, but with higher resolution and tight mechanical controls to produce final film separations for commercial printing.

Layer

A function of graphics applications in which elements may be isolated from each other, so that a group of elements may be hidden from view, locked, reordered or otherwise manipulated as a unit, without affecting other elements on the page.

Layout

The arrangement of text and graphics on a page, usually produced in the preliminary design stage.

Leaders

A line of periods or other symbols connecting the end of a group of words with another element separated by some space. For example, a table of contents may consist of a series of phrases on separate lines, each associated with a page number. Promotes readability in long lists of tabular text.

Leading ("ledding")

Space added between lines of type. Usually measured in points or fractions of points. Named after the strips of lead which used to be inserted between lines of metal type. In specifying type, lines of 12-pt. type separated by a 14-pt. space is abbreviated "12/14," or "twelve over fourteen."

Letterspacing

The insertion or addition of white space between the letters of words.

Library

In the computer world, a collection of files having a similar purpose or function.

Ligature

Letters that are joined together as a single unit of type such as oe and fi.

Lightness

The property that distinguishes white from gray or black, and light from dark color tones on a surface.

Line Art

A drawing or piece of black and white artwork, with no screens. Line art can be represented by a graphic file having only one-bit resolution.

Line Screen

The number of lines per inch used when converting a photograph to a halftone. Typical values range from 85 for newspaper work to 150 or higher for high-quality reproduction on smooth or coated paper.

Linking

An association through software of a graphic or text file on disk with its location in a document. That location may be represented by a "placeholder" rectangle, or a low-resolution copy of the graphic.

Linotype-Hell

The manufacturer of imagesetters such as the Linotronic that process PostScript data through an external Raster Image Processor (RIP) to produce high resolution film for printing.

Lithography

A mechanical printing process used for centuries based on the principle of the natural aversion of water (in this case, ink) to grease. In modern offset lithography, the image on a photosensitive plate is first transferred to the blanket of a rotating drum, and then to the paper.

Lossy

A data compression method characterized by the loss of some data.

Loupe

A small free-standing magnifier used to see fine detail on a page. See Linen Tester.

LPI

Lines per inch. See Line Screen.

Luminosity

The amount of light, or brightness, in an image. Part of the HLS color model.

LZW

The acronym for the Lempel-Ziv-Welch lossless data- and image-compression algorithm.

M, MB (Megabyte)

One million (1,048,576) bytes (220) or 1,024 Kilobytes.

Macro

A set of keystrokes that is saved as a named computer file. When accessed, the keystrokes will be performed. Macros are used to perform repetitive tasks.

Margins

The non-printing areas of page, or the line at which text starts or stops.

Mask

To conform the shape of a photograph or illustration to another shape such as a circle or polygon.

Masking

A technique that blocks an area of an image from reproduction by superimposing an opaque object of any shape.

Match Print
A color proofing system used for the final quality check.

Mechanical
A pasted-up page of camera-ready art that is to be photographed to produce a plate for the press.

Mechanical Dot Gain
See Dot Gain

Medium
A physical carrier of data such as a CD-ROM, video cassette, or floppy disk, or a carrier of electronic data such as fiber optic cable or electric wires.

Megabyte (MB)
A unit of measure of stored data equaling 1,024 kilobytes, or 1,048,576 bytes (1020).

Megahertz
An analog signal frequency of one million cycles per second, or a data rate of one million bits per second. Used in specifying computer CPU speed.

Menu
A list of choices of functions, or of items such as fonts. In contemporary software design, there is often a fixed menu of basic functions at the top of the page that have pull-down menus associated with each of the fixed choices.

Metafile
A class of graphics that combines the characteristics of raster and vector graphics formats; not recommended for high-quality output.

Metallic Ink
Printing inks which produce an effect of gold, silver, bronze, or metallic colors.

Midtones or Middletones
The tonal range between highlights and shadows.

Misregistration
The unwanted result of incorrectly aligned process inks and spot colors on a finished printed piece. Misregistration can be caused by many factors, including paper stretch and improper plate alignment. Trapping can compensate for misregistration.

Modem
An electronic device for converting digital data into analog audio signals and back again (Modulator-DEModulator.) Primarily used for transmitting data between computers over analog (audio frequency) telephone lines.

Moiré
An interference pattern caused by the out-of-register overlap of two or more regular patterns such as dots or lines. In process-color printing, screen angles are selected to minimize this pattern.

Monochrome
An image or computer monitor in which all information is represented in black and white, or with a range of grays.

Monospace
A font in which all characters occupy the same amount of horizontal width regardless of the character. See also Proportional Spacing.

Montage
A single image formed by assembling or compositing several images.

Mottle
Uneven color or tone.

Multimedia
The combination of sound, video images, and text to create a "moving" presentation.

Nested signatures
Multiple signatures that are folded, gathered, and placed one inside another, and then saddle-stitched at the spine.

Network
Two or more computers that are linked to exchange data or share resources. The Internet is a network of networks.

Neutral
Any color that has no hue, such as white, gray, or black.

Neutral density
A measurement of the lightness or darkness of a color. A neutral density of zero (0.00) is the lightest value possible and is equivalent to pure white; 3.294 is roughly equivalent to 100% of each of the CMYK components.

Noise
Unwanted signals or data that may reduce the quality of the output.

Non-breaking Space
A typographic command that connects two words with a space, but prevents the words from being broken apart if the space occurs within the hyphenation zone. See Hyphenation Zone.

Non-reproducible Colors
Colors in an original scene or photograph that are impossible to reproduce using process inks. Also called out-of-gamut colors.

Normal Key
A description of an image in which the main interest area is in the middle range of the tone scale or distributed throughout the entire tonal range.

Nudge
To move a graphic or text element in small, preset increments, usually with the arrow keys.

Object-oriented art
Vector-based artwork composed of separate elements or shapes described mathematically rather than by specifying the color and position of every point. This contrasts to bitmap images, which are composed of individual pixels.

Oblique
A slanted character (sometimes backwards, or to the left), often used when referring to italic versions of sans-serif typefaces.

Offset
In graphics manipulation, to move a copy or clone of an image slightly to the side and/or back; used for a drop-shadow effect.

Offset Lithography
A printing method whereby the image is transferred from a plate onto a rubber covered cylinder from which the printing takes place (see Lithography).

Opacity
1. The degree to which paper will show print through it. 2. Settings in certain graphics applications that allow images or text below the object whose opacity has been adjusted, to show through.

OPI

1. Acronym for Open Prepress Interface. 1. A set of PostScript language comments originally developed by Aldus Corporation for defining and specifying the placement of high-resolution images in PostScript files on an electronic page layout. 2. Incorporation of a low resolution preview image within a graphic file format (TIF, EPS, DCS) that is intended for display only. 3. Software device that is an extension to PostScript that replaces low-resolution placeholder images in a document with their high-resolution sources for printing.

Optical Disks

Video disks that store large amounts of data used primarily for reference works such as dictionaries and encyclopedias.

Output device

Any hardware equipment, such as a monitor, laser printer, or imagesetter, that depicts text or graphics created on a computer.

Overlay

A transparent sheet used in the preparation of multicolor mechanical artwork showing the color breakdown.

Overprint

A printing technique that lays down one ink on top of another ink. The overprinted inks can combine to make a new color. The opposite of knock-out.

Overprint Color

A color made by overprinting any two or more of the primary yellow, magenta, and cyan process colors.

Overprinting

Allowing an element to print over the top of underlying elements, rather than knocking them out (see Knockout). Often used with black type.

Page Description Language (PDL)

A special form of programming language that describes both text and graphics (object or bit-image) in mathematical form. The main benefit of a PDL is that makes the application software independent of the physical printing device. PostScript is a PDL, for example.

Page Layout Software

Desktop publishing software such as PageMaker or QuarkXPress used to combine various source documents and images into a high quality publication.

Page Proofs

Proofs of the actual pages of a document, usually produced just before printing, for a final quality check.

PageMaker

A popular page-layout application produced by Adobe Systems.

Palette

1. As derived from the term in the traditional art world, a collection of selectable colors. 2. Another name for a dialog box or menu of choices.

Panose

A typeface matching system for font substitution based on a numeric classification of fonts according to visual characteristics.

Pantone Matching System

A system for specifying colors by number for both coated and uncoated paper; used by print services and in color desktop publishing to assure uniform color matching.

Parallel fold

A folding method in which folds of a signature are parallel.

Pasteboard

In a page layout program, the desktop area outside of the printing page area, on which elements can be placed for later positioning on any page.

PCX

Bitmap image format produced by paint programs.

PDF (Portable Document Format)

Developed by Adobe Systems, Inc. (and read by Adobe Acrobat Reader), this format has become a de facto standard for document transfer across plat-forms.

Perfect binding

A binding method in which signatures are "ground off" at the spine of the book and then bound with adhesive, so each page is glued individually to the spine.

Perspective

The effect of distance in an image achieved by aligning the edges of elements with imaginary lines directed toward one to three "vanishing points" on the horizon.

Photoshop

The Adobe Systems image editing program commonly used for color correction and special effects on both the Macintosh and PC platforms.

Pi Fonts

A collection of special characters such as timetable symbols and mathematical signs. Examples are Zapf Dingbats and Symbol. See also Dingbats.

Pica

A traditional typographic measure-ment of 12 points, or approximately 1/ 6 of an inch. Most DTP applications specify a pica as exactly 1/6 of an inch.

PICT/PICT2

A common format for defining bitmapped images on the Macintosh. The more recent PICT2 format supports 24-bit color.

Pixel

Abbreviation for picture element, one of the tiny rectangular areas or dots generated by a computer or output device to constitute images.

PMS

See Pantone Matching System

PMT

Photo Mechanical Transfer - positive prints of text or images used for paste-up to mechanicals.

Point

A unit of measurement used to specify type size and rule weight, equal to (approximately, in traditional typeset-ting) 1/72 inch.

Polygon

A geometric figure consisting of three or more straight lines enclosing an area. The triangle, square, rectangle, and star are all polygons.

Portrait

Printing from left to right across the narrow side of the page. Portrait orientation on a letter-size page uses a standard 8.5-inch width and 11-inch length.

Positive

A true photographic image of the original made on paper or film.

Posterize, Posterization

The deliberate constraint of a gradient or image into visible steps as a special effect; or the unintentional creation of steps in an image due to a high LPI value used with a low printer DPI.

Postprocessing Applications

Applications, such as trapping programs or imposition software, that perform their functions after the image has been printed to a file, rather than in the originating application.

PostScript

1. A page description language developed by Adobe Systems, Inc. that describes type and/or images and their positional relationships upon the page. 2. An interpreter or RIP (see Raster Image Processor) that can process the PostScript page description into a format for laser printer or imagesetter output. 3. A computer programming language.

PostScript Printer Description file

See PPD.

PPD

Acronym for PostScript Printer Description, a file format developed by Adobe Systems, Inc., that contains device-specific information enabling software to produce the best results possible for each type of designated printer.

PPI

Pixels per inch; used to denote the resolution of an image.

Preferences

A set of defaults for an application program that may be modified.

Prepress

All work done between writing and printing, such as typesetting, scanning, layout, and imposition.

Prepress Proof

A color proof made directly from electronic data or film images.

Press sheet

In sheet-fed printing, the paper stock of common sizes that is used in commercial printing.

Primary Colors

Colors that can be used to generate secondary colors. For the additive system (i.e., a computer monitor), these colors are red, green, and blue. For the subtractive system (i.e., the printing process), these colors are yellow, magenta, and cyan.

Printer Command Language

PCL — a language, that has graphics capability, developed by Hewlett Packard for use with its own range of printers.

Printer fonts

The image outlines for type in PostScript that are sent to the printer.

Process colors

The four transparent inks (cyan, magenta, yellow, and black) used in four-color process printing. See also Color separation; CMYK.

Profile

A file containing data representing the color reproduction characteristics of a device determined by a calibration of some sort.

Proof

A representation of the printed job that is made from plates (press proof), film, or electronic data (prepress proofs). It is generally used for customer inspection and approval before mass production begins.

Proportional Spacing

A method of spacing whereby each character is spaced to accommodate the varying widths of letters or figures, thus increasing readability. Books and magazines are set proportionally spaced, and most fonts in desktop publishing are proportional. With proportionally spaced fonts, each character is given a horizontal space proportional to its size. For example, a proportionally spaced "m" is wider than an "i."

Pt.

Abbreviation for point.

QuarkXPress

A popular page-layout application.

Queue

A set of files input to the printer, printed in the order received unless otherwise instructed.

QuickDraw

Graphic routines in the Macintosh used for outputting text and images to printers not compatible with PostScript.

RAM

Random Access Memory, the "working" memory of a computer that holds files in process. Files in RAM are lost when the computer is turned off, whereas files stored on the hard drive or floppy disks remain available.

Raster

A bitmapped representation of graphic data.

Raster Graphics

A class of graphics created and organized in a rectangular array of bitmaps. Often created by paint software, fax machines, or scanners for display and printing.

Raster Image Processor (RIP)

That part of a PostScript printer or imagesetting device that converts the page information from the PostScript Page Description Language into the bitmap pattern that is applied to the film or paper output.

Rasterize

The process of converting digital information into pixels at the resolution of the output device. For example, the process used by an imagesetter to translate PostScript files before they are imaged to film or paper. See also RIP.

Reflective Art

Artwork that is opaque, as opposed to transparent, that can be scanned for input to a computer.

Registration

Aligning plates on a multicolor printing press so that the images will superimpose properly to produce the required composite output.

Registration Color

A default color selection that can be applied to design elements so that they will print on every separation from a PostScript printer. "Registration" is often used to print identification text that will appear outside the page area on a set of separations.

Registration marks

Figures (often crossed lines and a circle) placed outside the trim page boundaries on all color separation overlays to provide a common element for proper alignment.

Resolution

The density of graphic information expressed in dots per inch (dpi) or pixels per inch (ppi).

Retouching

Making selective manual or electronic corrections to images.

Reverse Out

To reproduce an object as white, or paper, within a solid background, such as white letters in a black rectangle.

RGB

Acronym for red, green, blue, the colors of projected light from a computer monitor that, when combined, simulate a subset of the visual spectrum. When a color image is scanned, RGB data is collected by the scanner and then converted to CMYK data at some later step in the process. Also refers to the color model of most digital artwork. See also CMYK.

Rich Black

A process color consisting of sold black with one or more layers of cyan, magenta, or yellow.

Right Reading

A positive or negative image that is readable from top to bottom and from left to right.

Right-angle fold

A folding method in which any successive fold of a signature is at right angles to the previous fold.

RIP

See Raster Image Processor

ROM

Read Only Memory, a semiconductor chip in the computer that retains startup information for use the next time the computer is turned on.

Rosette

The pattern created when color halftone screens are printed at traditional screen angles.

Rotation

Turning an object at some angle to its original axis.

RTF

Rich Text Format, a text format that retains formatting information lost in pure ASCII text.

Rubylith

A two-layer acetate film having a red or amber emulsion on a clear base used in non-computer stripping and separation operations.

Saddle-stitching

A binding method in which each signature is folded and stapled at the spine.

Sans Serif

Sans Serif fonts are fonts that do not have the tiny lines that appear at the top of and bottom of letters.

Saturation

The intensity or purity of a particular color; a color with no saturation is gray.

Scaling

The means within a program to reduce or enlarge the amount of space an image will occupy by multiplying the data by a scale factor. Scaling can be proportional, or in one dimension only.

Scanner

A device that electronically digitizes images point by point through circuits that can correct color, manipulate tones, and enhance detail. Color scanners will usually produce a minimum of 24 bits for each pixel, with 8 bits each for red, green, and blue.

Screen

To create a halftone of a continuous tone image (See Halftone).

Screen Angle

The angle at which the rulings of a halftone screen are set when making screened images for halftone process-color printing. The equivalent effect can be obtained electronically through selection of the desired angle from a menu.

Screen Frequency

The number of lines per inch in a halftone screen, which may vary from 85 to 300.

Screen Printing

A technique for printing on practically any surface using a fine mesh (originally of silk) on which the image has been placed photographically. Preparation of art for screen printing requires consideration of the resolution of the screen printing process.

Screen Shot

A printed output or saved file that represents data from a computer monitor.

Screen Tint

A halftone screen pattern of all the same dot size that creates an even tone at some percentage of solid color.

SCSI

Small Computer Systems Interface, a standard software protocol for connecting peripheral devices to a computer for fast data transfer.

Selection

The act of placing the cursor on an object and clicking the mouse button to make the object active.

Self-Cover

A cover for a document in which the cover is of the same paper stock as the rest of the piece.

SEP

A PostScript file format created from PageMaker that can contain multiple pages as well as links in the form of OPI comments to high-resolution images, in color or in black and white.

Separation

See Color separation.

Serif

A line or curve projecting from the end of a letter form. Typefaces designed with such projections are called serif faces.

Service Bureau

A business that specializes in producing film for printing on a high-resolution imagesetter.

SGML

Standard Generalized Markup Language, a set of semantics and syntax that describes the structure of a document (the nature, content, or function of the data) as opposed to visual appearance. HTML is a subset of SGML (see HTML).

Sharpness

The subjective impression of the density difference between two tones at their boundary, interpreted as fineness of detail.

Shortcut

1. A quick method for accessing a menu item or command, usually through a series of keystrokes. 2. The icon that can be created in Windows95 to open an application without having to penetrate layers of various folders. The equivalent in the Macintosh is the "alias."

Silhouette

To remove part of the background of a photograph or illustration, leaving only the desired portion.

Skew

A transformation command that slants an object at an angle to the side from its initial fixed base.

Small caps

A type style in which lowercase letters are replaced by uppercase letters set in a smaller point size.

Smart Quotes

The curly quotation marks used by typographers, as opposed to the straight marks on the typewriter. Use of smart quotes is usually a setup option in a word processing program or page layout application

Snap-to (guides or rulers)

An optional feature in page layout programs that drives objects to line up with guides or margins if they are within a pixel range that can be set. This eliminates the need for very precise, manual placement of an object with the mouse.

Soft or Discretionary Hyphen

A hyphen coded for display and printing only when formatting of the text puts the hyphenated word at the end of a line.

Soft Return

A return command that ends a line but does not apply a paragraph mark that would end the continuity of the style for that paragraph.

Spectrophotometer

An instrument for measuring the relative intensity of radiation reflected or transmitted by a sample over the spectrum.

Specular Highlight

The lightest highlight area that does not carry any detail, such as reflections from glass or polished metal. Normally, these areas are reproduced as unprinted white paper.

Spine

The binding edge at the back of a book that contains title information and joins the front and back covers.

Spot Color

Any pre-mixed ink that is not one of or a combination of the four process color inks, often specified by a Pantone swatch number.

Spread

Two facing pages that can be worked on as a unit, and will be viewed side by side in the final publication.

Stacking Order

The order of the elements on a PostScript page, wherein the topmost item may obscure the items beneath it if they overlap.

Standard Viewing Conditions

A prescribed set of conditions under which the viewing of originals and reproductions are to take place, defining both the geometry of the illumination and the spectral power distribution of the light source.

Step-and-repeat

A layout in which two or more copies of the same piece are placed on a single plate. This is useful for printing several copies of a small layout, such as a business card, on a single sheet. Also called a multiple-up layout.

Stet

Used in proof correction work to cancel a previous correction. From the Latin; "let it stand."

Stochastic Screening

A method of creating halftones in which the size of the dots remains constant but their density is varied; also known as frequency-modulated (or FM) screening.

Stripping

The act of manually assembling individual film negatives into flats for printing. Also referred to as film assembly.

Stroke, Stroking

Manipulating the width or color of a line.

Stuffit

A file compression utility used in the Macintosh environment.

Style

A set of formatting instructions for font, paragraphing, tabs, and other properties of text.

Style Sheet

A file containing all of the tags and instructions for formatting all parts of a document; style sheets create consistency between similar documents.

Subhead

A second-level heading used to organize body text by topic.

Subscript

Small-size characters set below the normal letters or figures, usually to convey technical information.

Substitution

Using an existing font to simulate one that is not available to the printer.

Subtractive Color

Color which is observed when light strikes pigments or dyes, which absorb certain wavelengths of light; the light that is reflected back is perceived as a color. See CMYK and Process Color.

Superscript

Small characters set above the normal letters or figures, such as numbers referring to footnotes.

System Folder

The location of the operating system files on a Macintosh.

Tabloid

Paper 11 inches wide x 17 inches long.

Tagged Image File Format (TIFF)

A common format for used for scanned or computer-generated bitmapped images.

Tags

The various formats in a style sheet that indicate paragraph settings, margins and columns, page layouts, hyphenation and justification, widow and orphan control and other parameters.

Template
A document file containing layout and styles by which a series of documents can maintain the same look and feel.

Text
The characters and words that form the main body of a publication.

Text Attribute
A characteristic applied directly to a letter or letters in text, such as bold, italic, or underline.

Text wrap
See Wrap

Texture
1. A property of the surface of the substrate, such as the smoothness of paper. 2. Graphically, variation in tonal values to form image detail. 3. A class of fills in a graphics application that give various appearances, such as bricks, grass, etc.

Thin Space
A fixed space, equal to half an en space or the width of a period in most fonts.

Thumbnails
1. The preliminary sketches of a design. 2. Small images used to indicate the content of a computer file.

TIFF
See Tagged Image File Format

Tile
1. A type of repeating fill pattern. 2. Reproduce a number of pages of a document on one sheet. 3. Printing a large document overlapping on several smaller sheets of paper.

Tint
1. A halftone area that contains dots of uniform size; that is, no modeling or texture. 2. The mixture of a color with white.

Tip In
The separate insertion of a single page into a book either during or after binding by pasting one edge.

Toggle
A command that switches between either of two states at each application. Switching between Hide and Show is a toggle.

Tracking
Adjusting the spacing of letters in a line of text to achieve proper justification or general appearance.

Transfer Curve
A curve depicting the adjustment to be made to a particular printing plate when an image is printed.

Transparency
A full color photographically produced image on transparent film.

Transparent Ink
An ink that allows light to be transmitted through it.

Trapping
The process of creating an overlap between abutting inks to compensate for imprecise registration in the printing process.

Trim
After printing, mechanically cutting the publication to the correct final dimensions. The trim size is normally indicated by marks on the printing plate outside the page area.

Trim page size
Area of the finished page after the job is printed, folded, bound, and cut.

TrueType
An outline font format used in both Macintosh and Windows systems that can be used both on the screen and on a printer.

Type 1 Fonts
PostScript fonts based on Bézier curves encrypted for compactness that are compatible with Adobe Type Manager.

Type Family
A set of typefaces created from the same basic design but in different weights, such as bold, light, italic, book, and heavy.

Typesetting
The arrangement of individual characters of text into words, sentences, and paragraphs.

Typo
An abbreviation for typographical error. A keystroke error in the typeset copy.

UCR (undercolor removal)
A technique for reducing the amount of magenta, cyan, and yellow inks in neutral or shadow areas and replacing them with black.

Undertone
Color of ink printed in a thin film.

Unsharp Masking
A digital technique (based on a traditional photographic technique) performed after scanning that locates the edge between sections of differing lightness and alters the values of the adjoining pixels to exaggerate the difference across the edge, thereby increasing edge contrast.

Uppercase
The capital letters of a typeface as opposed to the lowercase, or small, letters. When type was hand composited, the capital letters resided in the upper part of the type case.

Utility
Software that performs ancillary tasks such as counting words, defragmenting a hard drive, or restoring a deleted file.

Varnish Plate
The plate on a printing press that applies varnish after the other colors have been applied.

Varnishing
A finishing process whereby a transparent varnish is applied over the printed sheet to produce a glossy or protective coating, either on the entire sheet or on selected areas.

Vector Graphics
Graphics defined using coordinate points, and mathematically drawn lines and curves, which may be freely scaled and rotated without image degradation in the final output. Fonts (such as PostScript and TrueType), and illustrations from drawing applications are common examples of vector objects. Two commonly used vector drawing programs are Illustrator and FreeHand. A class of graphics that overcomes the resolution limitation of bitmapped graphics.

Velox
Strictly, a Kodak chloride printing paper, but used to describe a high-quality black & white print of a halftone or line drawing.

Vertical Justification

The ability to automatically adjust the interline spacing (leading) to make columns and pages end at the same point on a page.

Vignette

An illustration in which the background gradually fades into the paper; that is, without a definite edge or border.

Visible Spectrum

The wavelengths of light between about 380 nm (violet) and 700 nm (red) that are visible to the human eye.

Watermark

An impression incorporated in paper during manufacturing showing the name of the paper and/or the company logo. A "watermark" can be applied digitally to printed output as a very light screened image.

Web Press

An offset printing press that prints from a roll of paper rather than single sheets.

White Light

Light containing all wavelengths of the visible spectrum.

White Space

Areas on the page which contain no images or type. Proper use of white space is critical to a well-balanced design.

Window Shade

A type of text block used in certain applications, such as PageMaker. Windowshades have handles at the top and bottom which, when dragged with the mouse, will reveal or conceal text.

Wizard

A utility attached to an application or operating system that aids you in setting up a piece of hardware, software, or document.

WYSIWYG

An acronym for "What You See Is What You Get," (pronounced "wizzywig") meaning that what you see on your computer screen bears a strong resemblance to what the job will look like when it is printed.

X-height

The height of the letter "x" in a given typeface, which represents the basic size of the bodies of all of the lowercase letters (excluding ascenders and descenders).

Xerography

A photocopying/printing process in which the image is formed using the electrostatic charge principle. The toner replaces ink and can be dry or liquid. Once formed, the image is sealed by heat. Most page printers currently use this method of printing.

Zero Point

The mathematical "origin" of the coordinates of the two-dimensional page. The zero point may be moved to any location on the page, and the ruler dimensions change accordingly.

Zip

1. To compress a file on a Windows-based system using a popular compression utility (PKZIP). 2. A removable disk made by Iomega (a Zip disk) or the device that reads and writes such disks (a Zip drive).

Zooming

The process of electronically enlarging or reducing an image on a monitor to facilitate detailed design or editing and navigation.

Index

NOTES

Notes

Notes